CONTENTS

S0-BWI-900

FROMMER'S

COMPREHENSIVE TRAVEL GUIDE

LAS VEGAS '93-'94

by Rena Bulkin

PRENTICE HALL TRAVEL

NEW YORK • LONDON • TORONTO • SYDNEY • TOKYO • SINGAPORE

FROMMER BOOKS

Published by Prentice Hall General Reference
A division of Simon & Schuster Inc.
15 Columbus Circle
New York, NY 10023

ISBN: 0-671-84683-3
ISSN: 0899-3262

Design by Robert Bull Design
Maps by Ortelius Design

FROMMER'S EDITORIAL STAFF
Vice President/Editorial Director: Marilyn Wood
Senior Editor/Editorial Manager: Alice Fellows
Senior Editor: Lisa Renaud
Editors: Charlotte Allstrom, Thomas F. Hirsch, Peter Katucki, Sara Hinsey
Raveret, Theodore Stavrou
Assistant Editors: Margaret Bowen, Lee Gray, Chris Hollander, Ian Wilker
Editorial Assistant: Gretchen Henderson
Managing Editor: Leanne Coupe

Manufactured in the United States of America

LIST OF MAPS

INVITATION TO THE READERS

In researching this book, I have come across many wonderful establishments, the best of which I have included here. I'm sure that many of you will also come across appealing hotels, inns, restaurants, guesthouses, shops, and attractions. Please don't keep them to yourself. Share your experiences, especially if you want to comment on places that have been included in this edition that have changed for the worse. You can address your letters to:

Rena Bulkin
Frommer's Las Vegas '93–'94
c/o Prentice Hall Travel
15 Columbus Circle
New York, NY 10023

A DISCLAIMER

Readers are advised that prices fluctuate in the course of time and travel information changes under the impact of the varied and volatile factors that affect the travel industry. Neither the author nor the publisher can be held responsible for the experiences of readers while traveling. Readers are invited to write to the publisher with ideas, comments, and suggestions for future editions.

SAFETY ADVISORY

Whenever you're traveling in an unfamiliar city or country, stay alert. Be aware of your immediate surroundings. Wear a moneybelt and keep a close eye on your possessions. Be particularly careful with cameras, purses, and wallets, all favorite targets of thieves and pickpockets.

INTRODUCING LAS VEGAS

Las Vegas is a city designed for overindulgence—an anything-goes kind of place where you're encouraged to eat too much (at low-priced lavish buffets), drink too much (liquor is gratis at gaming tables), spend too much, and sleep too little. Leave your real life back home. In this 24-hour, neon-lit playground you can leer at sexy showgirls prancing around in topless costumes, hoot and holler at the craps tables, and watch a volcano erupting while you're walking down the street. Everyone's always let it all hang out in Las Vegas. Jimmy Durante—the first performer at the Flamingo—demolished a $1,600 piano on opening night just for kicks. Which was nothing compared to the high jinks of Flamingo owner Bugsy Siegel and his cohorts.

More than Chicago, it's Sinatra's kind of town, offering more superstar entertainment every night of the week than any other city in the world. It seems that every performer ends up in Las Vegas at some time. Even such unlikely people as Noel Coward, Woody Allen, Bob Dylan, Buster Keaton, the Beatles, Pavarotti, and Orson Welles have played the Strip's showrooms. And Las Vegas audiences have witnessed many great moments in entertainment history. For instance:

In 1962 former President Harry Truman, in town to address the American Legion, joined Jimmy Durante in a piano duet at the Sands.

Elvis and Liberace once appeared together at the Riviera (Elvis played piano, Liberace guitar, and they donned each other's flamboyant costumes for the occasion).

Paul Anka and Wayne Newton surprised pal Tony Orlando by joining him onstage during his opening night at the Riviera in 1977 and belting out his trademark song, "Tie a Yellow Ribbon," for an ecstatic audience.

A year after Gracie Allen retired, Jack Benny—in full drag—performed in her stead one night with George Burns at the Sahara Congo Room.

And it was only years later that audiences realized they had witnessed entertainment history in the making when Judy Garland brought her 9-year-old daughter Liza onstage at the Flamingo in 1957.

Major sporting events take place on a regular basis—from

WHAT'S SPECIAL ABOUT LAS VEGAS

Hotels that Are Sightseeing Attractions

☐ The Mirage, gleaming white and gold on the Strip, with its erupting volcano, white tigers, dolphin habitat, and coral reef aquarium.

☐ Caesars Palace, reflecting the decadent grandeur of ancient Rome, with lavish statuary (some of it animated), spectacular fountains, on-premises centurions, Omnimax movies, and other thrills both ancient and modern.

☐ Circus Circus, for circus acts and carnival games on its mezzanine level.

☐ Excalibur, a turreted medieval castle on the Strip with many attractions for children.

Nearby Sightseeing Highlights

☐ The engineering marvel of Hoover Dam and Lake Mead National Recreation Area, offering all water sports, desert hiking, and other activities in a spectacular setting.

☐ Red Rock Canyon, for additional magnificent canyon vistas.

☐ Valley of Fire, more awe-inspiring canyon scenery, with incredible sandstone formations.

After Dark

☐ The incomparable Siegfried & Roy, illusionists par excellence, at the Mirage. Best show in town.

☐ *Enter the Night,* at the Stardust, a top-of-the-line Las Vegas spectacular with unbelievable laser and lighting effects.

☐ *Splash,* at the Riviera—a lively aquacade revue.

☐ Your favorite headliners, wherever they might be appearing.

Buffets

☐ Bally's lavish Sterling Sunday Brunch—opulent fare in opulent surroundings.

☐ Ditto the Sunday Champagne Brunch at the Golden Nugget.

Sports

☐ Major boxing matches at Bally's, Caesars Palace, Las Vegas Hilton, the Mirage, and Riviera hotels.

---

championship boxing matches to championship poker playoffs, not to mention bizarre daredevil feats such as Evel Knievel's near-fatal motorcycle jump over the fountains fronting Caesars Palace.

And then there's gambling. Fortunes are won and lost (usually lost) on a roll of the dice. But we all secretly believe we'll beat the odds and sail out of town with big bucks (preferably in a limo)—like the young bride on her honeymoon who hit the jackpot to the tune of $1 million after playing the slots at Caesars for just three minutes! Such stories abound, and even sober folks can contract gambling

IMPRESSIONS

It is highwayman and whore on the desert road, a
city . . . dedicated to waste and excess, heartless . . . a town
where probably nothing good or worthwhile has ever happened,
nor ever will . . .
—TREVOR FISHLOCK, *AMERICANS AND NOTHING ELSE*

In some ways Las Vegas is still the wild West. For me, that's part
of the attraction. This town is the closest thing to an unstructured
society . . . anywhere in the world.
—STEVE WYNN

fever upon hearing them . . . not to mention watching the electronic
billboards on the Strip displaying ever-increasing multimillion-dollar
progressive slot jackpots. A little over a decade ago $1 slot machines
caused a sensation in the casinos. Today—in sumptuous high-roller
precincts—you can bet $1,500 on a single pull! On the other hand,
there are still penny slots in some downtown casinos.

But even if you don't want to gamble, you can have a great
vacation here. Plush hotels charge about half what their counterparts
in other cities do, and offer numerous resort facilities—immense
pools, tennis, health clubs, and more. Shows are reasonably priced.
Food is cheap (a full prime-rib dinner can be had for $5). And many
great attractions are within easy driving distance—magnificent desert
canyon vistas at Red Rock and Valley of Fire, pine-forested Mount
Charleston, Hoover Dam (an awe-inspiring engineering feat even in
today's high-tech world), and the recreational pleasures of Lake
Mead among them. Or you can just stroll the Strip at night and enjoy
the world's most spectacular sound and light show.

It's amazing to think that just a hundred years ago all you would
have found here was a desert wilderness.

1. CULTURE, HISTORY & BACKGROUND

GEOGRAPHY

Las Vegas is located in the southeastern corner of Nevada, 290 miles
from Los Angeles, California, and the Pacific Ocean; about 450 miles
from the Reno/Lake Tahoe area; 300 miles from Phoenix; and 450
miles from Salt Lake City, Utah. It sits in an isolated valley in the
middle of the Mojave Desert, and is one of the hottest and driest
urban areas in the United States.

The site of Las Vegas and most of Nevada was for eons covered by
a shallow inland sea; massive sand dunes left as the sea retreated
petrified into sandstone, which has been sculpted by wind, water, and

massive fault action into the almost lunar promontories you'll see for hundreds of miles around the city in all directions. What little flora and fauna there is atop the region's vivid reddish earth is highly adapted to life in the harsh, arid climate—drought-resistant shrubs and trees such as creosote, yucca, sagebrush, and joshua trees, and hardy animals such as desert bighorn sheep and an abundance of jackrabbits and other rodents.

During centuries past, visitors must have found the oasis at Las Vegas that rose out of this inhospitable desert just as unlikely a sight as all that glittering neon can seem to people approaching the city today. The underground artesian pressure that fed the oasis has been taxed by the city's burgeoning population, but the water provided by such man-made reservoirs as Lake Mead has assured that the city can continue to grow. And just as engineering and technology allows Las Vegas to expand, so it also allows the visitor to experience in relative comfort the unique and peaceful beauty of the desert that surrounds the bustling city.

DATELINE

- **Prehistory** Archaeological studies show humans occupying Las Vegas region from 3000 B.C. Hunter-gatherers called the Anasazi ("the ancient ones") live here from the first century A.D.
- **1150 A.D.** Anasazi leave the area. Nomadic Paiutes become the dominant group.
- **1829** Expedition of Mexican traders camped 100 miles from the present site of Las Vegas send scout Rafael Rivera to explore the surrounding desert. He discovers a verdant oasis—Las Vegas Springs.
- **1831–1848** Artesian spring waters of Las Vegas serve as a watering place on the Old

(continues)

HISTORY

For many centuries the land that would become Nevada was inhabited only by various Native American tribes—the Paiute, Shoshone, and Washoe. It wasn't until 1826 that white men stepped foot in the future state, and not until 1829 that Rafael Rivera, a scout for Mexican traders, entered a verdant valley nurtured by desert springs and called it Las Vegas ("the meadows"). From 1831 to 1848 these springs served as a watering place on the Old Spanish Trail for trading caravans plying the route between Santa Fe and the California coast. Explorer, soldier, and pathfinder Col. John C. Frémont (for whom downtown's main thoroughfare is named) rested near the headwaters of Las Vegas Springs on an overland expedition in 1844. A decade later Congress established a monthly mail route through Las Vegas Springs. And in 1855 Mormon leader Brigham Young sent 30 missionaries to Las Vegas to help spread the flow of Mormonism between Salt Lake City and southern California. Just north of what is today downtown (what would they think if they could see it now?) the Mormon colony built an adobe fort and dwellings. They grew crops, baptized Paiutes, and mined lead in the nearby mountains. However, none of these ventures proved successful, and the ill-fated settlement was abandoned after just three years.

The next influx into the area was a result of mining fever in the early 1860s, but this too soon subsided. However, gold prospector Octavius Decatur Gass stayed behind and, in 1865, built the 640-acre Las Vegas Ranch using structures left by the Mormons as his base. As owner of all the valley's water, Gass finally found "gold" offering services to travelers passing through. He planted crops and fruit orchards, started vineyards, raised cattle, established cordial relations with the Paiutes (he even learned their language), and served as a legislator. His was the first significant settlement in the area. By 1900 the Las Vegas valley had a population of 30.

A TENT CITY IN THE WILDERNESS

The city of Las Vegas was officially born in 1905 when the Union Pacific Railroad connecting Los Angeles and Salt Lake City decided to route its trains through this rugged frontier outpost, selected for its ready supply of water and the availability of timber in the surrounding mountains. On a sweltering day in May, 1,200 townsite lots were auctioned off to an assemblage of eager pioneers and real estate speculators who came from all over the country. The railroad depot was at the head of Fremont Street (site of today's Amtrak station). Championing the location was Montana senator William Clark, who had paid the astronomical sum (for those times) of $55,000 for the nearby Las Vegas Ranch and springs. The coming of a railroad more or less ensured the growth of the town. As construction began, tent settlements, saloons, ramshackle restaurants, boardinghouses, and shops developed apace. The early tent hotels charged a dollar to share a double bed with a stranger for eight hours! Early businesses thrived serving railroad men and prospectors from nearby mining operations.

By present-day standards, the new town was not a pleasant place to live. Prospectors' burros roamed the streets braying loudly, generally creating havoc and attracting swarms of flies. There were no screens, no air conditioners, no modern showers or baths (the town's bathhouse had but one tub) to ameliorate the fierce summer heat.

DATELINE

Spanish Trail, a Mexican trade route between Santa Fe and Los Angeles.

- **1855** Mormon colony of 30 missionaries establishes settlement just north of today's downtown and builds a 150-square-foot adobe fort, a portion of which still remains. Unsuccessful in its aims, it is disbanded in 1858.
- **1861** President James Buchanan authorizes formation of the territory of Nevada.
- **1864** President Lincoln proclaims Nevada 36th state of the Union. Las Vegas, however, is still part of the Territory of Arizona.
- **1865** Gold prospector Octavius D. Gass builds Las Vegas Ranch—first permanent settlement in Las Vegas—on site of the old Mormon fort.
- **1867** Arizona cedes 12,225 square miles to Nevada, which assumes its present shape. Las Vegas is now in Nevada.
- **1880s** Due to mining fever, the population of Nevada soars to over 60,000 in 1880. The white man's incursion into Nevada

(continues)

DATELINE

devastates the Pai-
utes, who are forced
onto reservations.

- **1895** San Francis-
can inventor Charles
Fey creates a three-
reel gambling
device—the first
slot machine.
- **1905** Railroad
connecting Salt Lake
City and Los Ange-
les routes its trains
through Las Vegas
and auctions off
1,200 lots in the offi-
cial townsite.
- **1907** Fremont
Street—the future
"Glitter Gulch"—
gets electric lights.
- **1909** Gambling is
made illegal in Ne-
vada, but Las Vegas
pays little heed.
- **1911** William
Howard Taft, first
American president
to pass through Las
Vegas, waves at
residents from his
train.
- **1928** Congress
authorizes Hoover
Dam 30 miles away,
bringing thousands
of workers to the
area. Later, Las
Vegas will capitalize
on hundreds of thou-
sands who come to
see the engineering
marvel.
- **1931** Gambling is
legalized once again.
- **1932** The 100-
room Apache Hotel
opens downtown.
- **1933** Prohibition
is repealed. Las
(continues)

Streets were rutted with dust pockets up to a foot deep that rose in great gusts as stage-coaches, supply wagons, and 20-animal mule teams careened over them. It was a true pioneer town, complete with saloon brawls and shootouts. Discomforts notwith-standing, gaming establishments, hotels, and nightclubs—some of them seedy dives, oth-ers rather luxurious—sprang up and pros-pered in the Nevada wilderness. A red-light district grew up on Second Street between Ogden and Stewart avenues. And gambling, which was legal until 1909, flourished.

THE EIGHTH WONDER OF THE WORLD
For many years after its creation, Las Vegas was a mere whistlestop town. That all changed in 1928 when Congress authorized the building of nearby Boulder Dam (later renamed Hoover Dam), bringing thousands of workers to the area. Gambling had once more been legalized in Nevada in 1931, and Fremont Street's gaming empori-ums and speakeasies drew workers from the dam. Upon the dam's completion, the Las Vegas Chamber of Commerce worked hard to lure the hordes of tourists who came to see the engineering marvel (it was called "the eighth wonder of the world") to its casinos. Las Vegas was about to make the transition from a sleepy desert town to "a town that never sleeps." But it wasn't until the early years of World War II that visionary entrepreneurs began to glimpse its glittering future.

LAS VEGAS GOES SOUTH
Contrary to a popular conception, Bugsy Siegel didn't actually stake a claim in the middle of nowhere—he just built a few blocks south of already extant properties. Development a few miles south of downtown on Highway 91 (the future Strip) was already underway in the 1930s, with establishments like the Pair-O-Dice Club (later to become the 91 Club) and the Last Frontier (today simply the Frontier). And in 1941 El Rancho Vegas, ultraluxurious for its time, went up on the same remote stretch of highway (across the street from where the Sahara now stands). According to legend, Los Angeles hotelier Thomas E. Hull had been driving by the site when his car broke down. Noticing the

extent of passing traffic, he decided to build there. Hull invited scores of Hollywood glitterati to his grand opening, and El Rancho Vegas soon became the hostelry of choice for visiting film stars. Beginning a trend that is still going on today, each new property tried to outdo previous hotels in luxurious amenities and thematic splendor. In 1943 the Last Frontier (the Strip's second hotel) created an authentic western setting by scouring the Southwest in search of authentic pioneer furnishings for its rooms, hiring Zuni craftsmen to create baskets and hangings, and picking up guests at the airport in a horse-drawn stagecoach. The Last Frontier also presaged a new era when it brought stage and screen star Sophie Tucker to its showroom for a 2-week engagement in 1944 with much attendant hoopla. Tucker's train was met with a parade, and "the last of the red-hot mammas" was conveyed to the hotel in a fire truck. Las Vegas was on its way to becoming the entertainment capital of the world.

Las Vegas promoted itself in the 1940s as a town combining Wild West frontier friendliness with glamour and excitement. As Chamber of Commerce President Maxwell Kelch aptly put it in a 1947 speech, "Las Vegas has the impact of a Wild West show, the friendliness of a country store, and the sophistication of Monte Carlo." Throughout the decade, the city was largely a regional resort—Hollywood's celebrity playground. Clara Bow and Rex Bell (he was a star of westerns) bought a ranch in Las Vegas and there entertained luminaries like the Barrymores, Norma Shearer, Clark Gable, and Errol Flynn. The Hollywood connection gave the town glamour in the public's mind. So did the mob connection (something Las Vegas has spent decades trying to live down), which manifested early on when notorious underworld gangster Benjamin "Bugsy" Siegel (with partners Lucky Luciano and Meyer Lansky) built the fabulous Flamingo, a tropical paradise and "a real class joint." Hollywood people found the gangsters glamorous and vice versa—and the public was entranced by both. In 1947, the Club Bingo opened across the street from El Rancho Vegas, bringing a new game to town. The Thunder-

DATELINE

Vegas's numerous speakeasies become legit.

● **1934** The city's first neon sign goes up over the Boulder Club downtown.

● **1941** The luxurious El Rancho Las Vegas is the first hotel on the Strip. Downtown, the El Cortez opens.

● **1944** Major star Sophie Tucker plays the Last Frontier, which had opened the previous year.

● **1946** Benjamin "Bugsy" Siegel's Flamingo extends boundaries of the Strip. Sammy Davis, Jr., debuts at the Last Frontier. Downtown is dubbed "Glitter Gulch" and gets two new hotels—the Golden Nugget and the Eldorado.

● **1947** United Airlines inaugurates service to Las Vegas.

● **1948** The Thunderbird becomes the fourth hotel on the Strip.

● **1950** The Desert Inn adds country club panache to the Strip.

● **1951** First of many atom bombs tested in the desert just 65 miles from Las Vegas. An explosion of another sort takes place

(continues)

DATELINE

when Sinatra debuts at the Desert Inn.

• **1952** The Club Bingo (opened in 1947) becomes the desert-themed Sahara. The Sands' Copa Room enhances the city's image as an entertainment capital.

• **1954** The Showboat pioneers buffet meals and bowling alleys in a new area of downtown.

• **1955** The Strip gets its first high-rise hotel—the nine-story Riviera—which pays Liberace the unprecedented sum of $50,000 to open its showroom. The Riviera is the ninth hotel on the Strip. A month later, the Dunes is the tenth.

• **1956** The Fremont opens downtown, and the Hacienda becomes the southernmost hotel on the Strip.

• **1957** The Dunes introduces bare-breasted showgirls in its *Minsky Goes to Paris* revue. The most luxurious hotel to date, the Tropicana, opens on the Strip.

• **1958** The 1,065-room Stardust opens as world's largest resort complex with a spectacular production show from *(continues)*

bird, the fourth hotel on the Strip, opened in 1948.

A steady stream of name entertainers followed Sophie Tucker into Las Vegas, adding to the city's tourist appeal. In 1947 Jimmy Durante opened the showroom at the Flamingo. Other headliners of the 1940s included Dean Martin and Jerry Lewis, comedian Jack Carter, tap-dancing legend Bill "Bojangles" Robinson, the Mills Brothers (who first recorded "Bye-Bye Blackbird"), skater Sonja Henie, Frankie Laine, Vic Damone, and Joe E. Lewis. Future Las Vegas legend Sammy Davis, Jr., debuted at El Rancho Vegas in 1945.

And while the Strip developed, downtown kept pace with new hotels like the El Cortez, the Nevada Biltmore, the Golden Nugget, and the Eldorado Club. By the end of the decade, Fremont Street was known as "Glitter Gulch," its profusion of neon signs proclaiming round-the-clock gaming and entertainment.

THE 1950s: BUILDING BOOMS AND A-BOMBS

Las Vegas entered the new decade as a city (no longer a frontier town) with a population of about 50,000, its future as a tourist mecca ensured by postwar affluence and improved highways. Photographs indicate that Las Vegas was more glamorous in the 1950s than it is today. Men donned suits and ties, women floor-length gowns, to attend shows and even for casino gambling. Hotel growth was phenomenal. The Desert Inn, opening in 1950 with headliners Edgar Bergen and Charlie McCarthy, brought country club elegance (including an 18-hole golf course and tennis courts) to the Strip. In 1951 the Eldorado Club downtown became Benny Binion's Horseshoe Club, which would gain fame as the home of the annual World Series of Poker. A year later, the Club Bingo entered a new incarnation as the African desert-themed Sahara (with camels guarding its portals), and the Sands emerged to further brighten the star-studded Strip. One of the Sands' major backers was Copacabana nightclub owner Jack Entratter who, being very well connected in show biz, brought major talent and stunning showgirls to its Copa Room. In 1954 the Showboat sailed into a new area east of downtown.

People said it would never last in such a remote location. They were wrong. The Showboat innovated buffet meals and a bowling alley (106 lanes to date) and offered round-the-clock bingo. In 1955 the Last Frontier became the New Frontier and the Côte d'Azur–themed Riviera became the ninth big hotel to go up on the Strip. Breaking the ranch-style mode, it was, at nine stories, the Strip's first high-rise. Liberace, one of the hottest names in show business, was paid the unprecedented sum of $50,000 a week to dazzle audiences in the Riviera's posh Clover Room. The Dunes opened immediately after, topped by a 30-foot fiberglass sultan; the 15-story Fremont Hotel downtown became the highest building in Las Vegas; and the Hacienda extended the boundaries of the Strip by opening two miles south of the nearest resort. Elvis appeared at the New Frontier in 1956, but wasn't a huge success; his fans were too young to fit the Las Vegas tourist mold. In 1957 the Tropicana joined the Hacienda at the far end of Las Vegas Boulevard. Billing itself as "the Tiffany of the Strip," it offered 40 tropically lush acres and a musical extravaganza starring Eddie Fisher. In 1958 the $10 million, 1,065-room Stardust upped the spectacular stakes by importing the famed *Lido de Paris* from the French capital. It became one of the longest-running shows ever to play Las Vegas. The Stardust was also the first hotel to bring massive serious neon to the Strip in the form of a 216-foot sign emblazoned with over 7,000 feet of neon tubing and 11,000 lamps. The year after it opened it absorbed the Royal Nevada next door.

Throughout the 1950s most of the above-mentioned hotels competed for performers whose followers spent freely in the casinos. The advent of big-name Strip entertainment tolled a death knell for glamorous nightclubs in America; owners simply could not compete with the astronomical salaries paid to Las Vegas headliners. Major fifties stars of the Strip included Rosemary Clooney, Nat King Cole, Peggy Lee, Milton Berle, Judy Garland, Red Skelton, Ernie Kovacs, Abbott and Costello, Ray Bolger, Tommy and Jimmy Dorsey, Fred Astaire and Ginger Rogers, the Andrews Sisters, Zsa Zsa

DATELINE

France, the *Lido de Paris*.

● **1959** The Las Vegas Convention Center goes up, presaging the city's future as a major convention city. Another French production, the still-extant *Folies Bergère*, opens at the Trop.

● **1960** The Rat Pack, led by Chairman of the Board Frank Sinatra, holds 3-week "Summit Meeting" at the Sands. A championship boxing match— the first of many— takes place at the Convention Center. El Rancho Las Vegas, the Strip's first property, burns to the ground.

● **1963** McCarran International Airport opens. Casinos and showrooms are darkened for a day as Las Vegas mourns the death of President John F. Kennedy.

● **1965** The 26-story Mint alters the Fremont Street skyline. Muhammad Ali defeats Floyd Patterson at the Las Vegas Convention Center.

● **1966** The Aladdin becomes the first new hotel on the Strip in nine years, soon eclipsed by the unparalleled grandeur of Caesars Pal-
(continues)

Gabor, Marlene Dietrich, Billy Eckstine, and Gordon McRae. Two performers whose names have ever since instantly evoked Las Vegas—Frank Sinatra and Wayne Newton—made their debuts. Mae West not only performed in Las Vegas, she cleverly bought up a half mile of desolate Strip frontage between the Dunes and the Tropicana.

The same competition for the tourist dollar brought nationally televised sporting events such as the P.G.A.'s Tournament of Champions to the Desert Inn golf course (the winner got a wheelbarrow filled with silver dollars!). And it was in the 1950s that the wedding industry took hold and Las Vegas became one of the nation's most popular venues for "goin' to the chapel." It was and is easy. Nevada requires no blood test or waiting period. Celebrity weddings of the 1950s that sparked the trend included singer Dick Haymes and Rita Hayworth, Fernando Lamas and Arlene Dahl, Joan Crawford and Pepsi chairman Alfred Steele, Carol Channing and TV exec Charles Lowe, and Paul Newman and Joanne Woodward.

On a grimmer note, the fifties also heralded the atomic age in Nevada, with nuclear testing going on just 65 miles northwest of Las Vegas. A chilling 1951 photograph shows a mushroom-shaped cloud from an atomic bomb test visible over the Fremont Street horizon. Throughout the decade, about a bomb a month was detonated in the nearby desert.

THE 1960s: THE RAT PACK...

The very first month of the new decade made entertainment history when the Sands hosted a 3-week "Summit Meeting" in the Copa Room presided over by Chairman of the Board Frank Sinatra with Rat Pack cronies Dean Martin, Sammy Davis, Jr., Peter Lawford, and Joey Bishop. Eisenhower, Khrushchev, and Winston Churchill were all invited. They didn't attend, but showroom guests who witnessed their antics are probably still dining out on the stories. No other Las Vegas show tickets have ever been more coveted or difficult to obtain. One night Sinatra bodily picked up Sammy Davis, Jr., and said, "Ladies and gentleman, I want to thank you for giving me this valuable NAACP trophy." He then dropped him in the lap of a man in a ringside seat who happened to be Senator John F. Kennedy. Davis looked up and quipped, "It's perfectly all right with me, Senator, as long as I'm not being donated to George Wallace or James Eastland." The Rat Pack returned to the Copa stage in 1961 for an onstage birthday party for Dean Martin with a 5-foot-high cake in the shape of a whiskey bottle. Martin threw the first slice, and a food fight ensued. The riotous clan kept Las Vegas amused for most of the decade.

On November 25, 1963, Las Vegas mourned the death of President John F. Kennedy with the rest of the nation. Between 7am and midnight, all the neon lights went off, casinos stood empty, and showrooms were dark.

The building boom of the fifties took a brief respite. The Strip's first property, the El Rancho Vegas, burned down in 1960. And the first new hotel of the decade—the first to be built in nine years—was the exotic Aladdin in 1966. A year after it opened the Aladdin hosted the most celebrated Las Vegas wedding of all time when Elvis Presley married Priscilla Beaulieu. In 1966 Las Vegas also hailed Caesar—Caesars Palace that is—a Lucullan pleasure palace whose grand opening was a million-dollar, 3-day Roman orgy with 1,800 guests. Its Carrara marble reproductions of ancient temples, heroic arches, and classical statuary were a radical departure from the more ersatz glitz of earlier Strip hotels. In the same time frame, the Mint and the Four Queens altered the downtown skyline.

. . . AND A PACK RAT During the sixties negative attention focused—with good reason—on mob influence in Las Vegas. Of the 11 major casino hotels that had opened in the previous decade, 10 were believed to be financed with mob money. Attorney General Robert Kennedy ordered the Department of Justice to begin seriously scrutinizing Las Vegas gaming operations. Then, like a knight in shining armor, Howard Hughes rode into town. He was not, however, on a white horse. Ever eccentric, he

DATELINE

flood causes over $1 million in damages.
• **1976** Fittingly, pioneer aviator Howard Hughes dies aboard a plane en route to a Houston hospital. Martin and Lewis make up after a 20-year feud.
• **1978** Leon Spinks dethrones "the Greatest" (Muhammad Ali) at the Las Vegas Hilton. Crimesolver Dan Tanna (Robert Urich) makes the streets of "Vega$" safer—and better known.
• **1979** A new international arrivals building goes up to accommodate increased foreign traffic at McCarran International Airport.
• **1980** McCarran International Airport embarks on a 20-year, $785 million expansion program. Las Vegas celebrates its 75th birthday. A devastating fire destroys the MGM Grand and leaves 84 dead, 700 wounded. Bally's takes over the property.
• **1981** Siegfried & Roy begin a record-breaking run in their own show, *Beyond Belief,* at the Frontier.
• **1982** A Las Vegas street is *(continues)*

DATELINE

named Wayne New-
ton Boulevard.

• **1985** Another
child-oriented attrac-
tion, Wet 'n Wild,
opens on the Strip.

• **1989** Steve Wynn
makes headlines
with his spectacular
Mirage, fronted by
an erupting volcano.
He signs spellbind-
ers Siegfried & Roy
to a 5-year $57 mil-
lion showroom con-
tract (since
extended)!

• **The 1990s** The
medieval Arthurian
realm of Excalibur is
the new "world's-
largest-resort" title
holder with 4,032
rooms, a claim it will
relinquish when the
MGM Grand's new
5,000-plus-room
megaresort/theme
park opens in 1994.
Also in the works—
the Luxor, a 2,500-
room 30-story
Egyptian-themed
pyramid, and Steve
Wynn's new Treas-
ure Island, based on
the novel by Robert
Louis Stevenson.

arrived in town (for security rather than health reasons) in an ambulance. The reclusive billionaire moved into a Desert Inn penthouse on Thanksgiving Day in 1966 and never set foot outside the hotel for the next four years! He used it as headquarters for a $300 million hotel- and property-buying spree which included the D.I. itself (in 1967). He was as "bugsy" as Benjamin Siegel any day, but his pristine reputation helped bring respectability to the desert city and re verse its gangland stigma. It was widely felt that if the gaming business was really shady, Howard Hughes would not be in it. Hughes purchased the Sands along with half a dozen other hotels and casinos, the airport, an airline, and a local TV station. Topless showgirls and hookers were persona non grata at his properties, and showroom comedians were warned to "keep it clean." For decades he provided fodder for Strip performers. "You're wondering why I don't have a drink in my hand?" Frank Sinatra asked a Sands audience one night. "Howard Hughes bought it."

Las Vegas became a family destination in 1968 when Circus Circus burst on the scene with the world's largest permanent circus and a "junior casino" comprising dozens of carnival midway games on its mezzanine level. The Landmark and the dazzling International (today the Hilton) pioneered a new area of town on Paradise Road near the Convention Center in 1969. That same year Elvis made a triumphant return to Las Vegas at the International's showroom and went on to become one the city's all-time legendary performers. His fans had come of age. Even today, scores of Elvis imitators play the showroom circuit, and, who knows, maybe the King himself is looking on.

The Thunderbird Hotel, hoping to establish Las Vegas as "the Broadway of the West," presented Rodgers and Hammerstein's *Flower Drum Song*. It was a smash hit. Soon the Riviera picked up *Bye, Bye, Birdie,* and, as the decade progressed, *Mame* and *The Odd Couple* played at Caesars Palace. While Broadway played the Strip, production shows such as the Dunes' *Casino de Paris* became ever more lavish, expensive, and technically innovative. Some showroom stars of the 1960s were "Funny Girl" Barbara Streisand and funny ladies Phyllis Diller and Carol Burnett, Little Richard (billing himself as "the bronze Liberace"), Louis Armstrong, Bobby Darin, the Supremes, Steve Allen, Johnny Carson, Bob Newhart, the Smothers Brothers, and Aretha Franklin. Liza Minnelli filled her mother's shoes and Nancy Sinatra's boots were made for walking. And Tom Jones wowed 'em at the Flamingo.

THE 1970s: MERV, MIKE, MGM & MAGIC In 1971, the 500-room Union Plaza opened at the head of Fremont Street on the site of the old Union Pacific Station. It had what was, at the time, the world's largest casino, and its showroom specialized in Broadway shows. The same year talk show host Merv Griffin began taping at Caesars Palace, taking advantage of a ready supply of local headliner guests. He helped further popularize Las Vegas by bringing it into America's living rooms every afternoon. Rival Mike Douglas soon followed suit at the Las Vegas Hilton.

The year 1973 was eventful: The Holiday Inn (today Harrah's) built a Mississippi riverboat complete with towering smokestacks and foghorn whistle which was immediately dubbed "the ship on the Strip." Dean Martin headlined in the celebrity room of the magnificent new $100 million MGM Grand, named for the movie *Grand Hotel*. Over 800 tons of marble were imported from Italy just for the fountain at the front entrance, and sculptors in three Italian towns were kept busy for two years making columns and statues for the property. Facilities included everything from a jai alai fronton to the largest shopping mall in the state. And over at the Tropicana, illusionists extraordinaire Siegfried & Roy began turning ladies into tigers and themselves into legends in the *Folies Bergère*. Several years later they moved on to *Hallelujah, Hollywood* and the *Lido de Paris*. Whatever show they were in was the hottest ticket in town. And it still is.

Two major disasters hit Las Vegas in the 1970s. A flash flood devastated the Strip, causing over $1 million in damage. Hundreds of cars were swept away in the raging waters. And gambling was legalized in Atlantic City. Las Vegas's hotel business slumped as fickle tourists checked out the new East Coast gambling mecca.

On a happier note, audiences were moved when Frank Sinatra patched up a 20-year feud by introducing Dean Martin as a surprise guest on Jerry Lewis's 1976 Muscular Dystrophy Telethon at the Sahara. Martin and Lewis hugged and made up. Who would balk Sinatra?

As the decade drew to a close, Dan Tanna began investigating crime in glamorous "Vega$," an international arrivals building went up at McCarran International Airport, and dollar slot machines caused a sensation in the casinos. Hot performers of the seventies included José Feliciano, Ann Margaret, Tina Turner, Englebert Humperdinck, Ben Vereen, Bill Cosby, Sonny and Cher, Tony Bennett, the Neils (Diamond and Sedaka), Joel Grey, Mel Tormé, Bobby Darin, Johnny Carson, Gregory Hines (with his brother and dad), Donny and Marie, the Jackson 5, Gladys Knight and the Pips, and that "wild and crazy guy" Steve Martin. Debbie Reynolds introduced her daughter Carrie with a duet performance before a Desert Inn audience. Shirley MacLaine began an incarnation at the Riviera. And country was now cool; the names Johnny Cash, Bobby Gentry, Charlie Pride, and Roy Clark went up in marquee lights.

THE 1980s: THE CITY ERUPTS! Las Vegas was booming once again. McCarran Airport began a 20-year, $785 million expansion program. In 1980 a devastating fire swept through the MGM Grand, leaving 84 dead and 700 wounded. Shortly thereafter, Bally acquired the property and created a cheerful megaresort with so many facilities you need never leave. It billed itself as the "city within a city."

Siegfried & Roy were no longer just the star segment of various stage spectaculars. Their own show, *Beyond Belief,* ran for six years at the Frontier, playing a record-breaking 3,538 performances to sell-out audiences every night. It became the most successful attraction in the city's history.

In 1989, Steve Wynn made Las Vegas sit up and take notice. His gleaming white and gold Mirage was fronted by five-story waterfalls, lagoons, and lush tropical foliage—not to mention a 50-foot volcano that dramatically erupted spewing great gusts of fire another 50 feet into the air every 15 minutes after dark! Inside were dolphin and royal white tiger habitats, a rain forest under a 90-foot atrium dome, and a 20,000-gallon simulated coral reef aquarium whose residents included six sharks and 1,000 colorful tropical fish. Wynn gave world-renowned illusionists Siegfried & Roy carte blanche—and more than $30 million—to create the most spellbinding show Las Vegas had ever seen (don't miss it).

> ✪ **Illusionists Siegfried & Roy now stand alone as the most successful entertainers in Las Vegas history.**

Stars of the eighties included Eddie Murphy, Don Rickles, Roseanne Barr, Bob Newhart, Dionne Warwick, Paul Anka, the Captain and Tennille, Donna Summer, Rich Little, George Carlin, David Brenner, Barry Manilow, Bernadette Peters, Flip Wilson, and Diahann Carroll. Country continued to be cool, as evidenced by frequent headliners Willie Nelson, Kenny Rogers, Dolly Parton, Crystal Gale, Merle Haggard, Mickey Gilley, Kris Kristofferson, and Barbara Mandrell. Joan Rivers posed her famous question "Can we

---

IMPRESSIONS

Benny often found it necessary to arbitrate business differences with a .45 automatic.

—FROM AN ARTICLE IN *TEXAS MONTHLY* (OCT. 1991) ABOUT BENNY BINION, FOUNDER OF THE FAMED BINION'S HORSESHOE HOTEL AND CASINO

talk?" and bug-eyed comic Rodney Dangerfield complained he "got no respect."

THE 1990s: KING ARTHUR MEETS KING TUT   The decade began with a blare of trumpets heralding the rise of a turreted medieval castle fronted by a moated drawbridge and staffed by jousting knights and fair damsels. Excalibur, inspired by the romantic legend of King Arthur, was the largest resort in the world. Its interior had so many stone castle walls that a Strip comedian quipped "it looks like a prison for Snow White." Like Circus Circus (same owner), it abounds in family attractions—carnival games, puppet shows, jugglers, magicians, high-tech thrill cinemas, and a major show called *King Arthur's Tournament* that is geared to youngsters. Excalibur reflects the nineties marketing trend that promotes Las Vegas as a family destination.

Arthurian legend wasn't the only romantic thing going. More than 75,000 couples tied the knot here in 1991. The same year, some 20.3 million tourists, 2 million conventioneers among them, visited the city and contributed about $4.5 billion to casino coffers.

Las Vegas is on a roll. Even in these hard economic times (or perhaps because of them) tourists are flocking to its casino resorts in hopes of getting rich quick. Hotels are running close to 100% occupancy, and three major new Strip properties are in the works. MGM Grand is building a 5,000-plus room megaresort which will house the world's largest casino and a 33-acre theme park based on *The Wizard of Oz*. The folks who brought you Circus Circus and Excalibur have already broken ground for the Egyptian-themed Luxor, a gleaming 30-story reflective bronze pyramid on the Strip with 2,500 rooms and a full-size replica of King Tut's tomb. Its front entrance will evoke the Hanging Gardens of Babylon, and guests

○ **The scores of wedding chapels in town are one source of Las Vegas's air of round-the-clock celebration—more than 75,000 couples tied the knot here in 1991.**

will be transported to their rooms from the registration desk via boats on the "River Nile." And Steve Wynn's new Treasure Island, adjacent to the Mirage, will be fronted by a replica of the small bay village described in Stevenson's novel. Here, once every hour, a pirate ship and the HMS *The Sir Francis Drake* will engage in a full-scale cannon battle on the Strip.

As Las Vegas history continues to be written, one can only wonder, "What will they think of next?" Tune in next edition to find out.

2. FAMOUS LAS VEGANS

Benny Binion   (1904–89) This feisty Texan, who misspent his youth punching cattle, horse trading, running illegal craps games, and bootlegging, came to Las Vegas in 1947 with a suitcase full of money. He bought a casino, renamed it the Horseshoe, and made it famous for the highest limits in town and the annual World Series of Poker. When he died, Binion was a casino czar worth $100 million. His family are still major players in town.

Nicholas "Nick the Greek" Dandolos (1893–1966) America's most famous gambler, Nicholas Andrea Dandolos was a reckless high-stakes player who became a Las Vegas legend. At 18, Nick came to Montreal and—with some inside information—quickly accumulated half-a-million dollars at the racetrack. He blew it just as quickly in Chicago at cards and dice. He is said to have won and lost more than $500 million in his lifetime. He spurned offers of hotel partnerships that would have made him financially independent. Raking in house percentages, he claimed, would have robbed him of the thrill of betting. He died broke.

Jackie Gaughan (b. 1920) A Nebraska native who ran a bookie joint in an Omaha cigar store, Gaughan started out in Las Vegas by buying a 3% interest in the Boulder Club in 1946. In 1951 he bought a 3% interest in the Flamingo. He went on to run the city's only race and sports book, the Saratoga, until 1959. In 1963 he bought the El Cortez. He now owns six downtown Las Vegas properties, including the Gold Spike, the Plaza, Las Vegas Club, the Western Hotel & Bingo Parlor, and the Showboat. His son Michael owns the Barbary Coast and the Gold Coast.

Howard Hughes (1905–76) Howard Hughes was the man who gave Las Vegas respectability. The richest man in America, he arrived in town in 1966 at a time when the Justice Department had begun focusing on mob involvement in Nevada gaming operations. Eccentric though he was (he hated sunlight and had the windows of his Desert Inn accommodations blacked out), his casino- and hotel-buying spree was a public relations bonanza for Las Vegas. The gambling public trusted him, and they began to trust Las Vegas casinos. During his 4-year residency, he became Nevada's largest employer, putting 8,000 people on his payroll. At one time his seven casinos accounted for 17% of the state's gaming revenues.

Kirk Kerkorian (b. 1917) The self-made son of Armenian immigrants who fled a Turkish massacre by cattle boat, Kerkorian grew up in California, where he dropped out of school in the eighth

---

IMPRESSIONS

They printed a lot of crap about Ben. He just wanted to be somebody. He used to pal around with Clark Gable, Gary Cooper, Cary Grant, and a lot of other big stars. I used to copy a lot of Ben's mannerisms when I played gangsters. Ben and the other tough guys . . . they were like gods to me. Ben had class, he was a real gentleman, and a real pal.
—FORMER MOVIE STAR GEORGE RAFT ON HIS PAL BENJAMIN "BUGSY" SIEGEL

grade. He was a successful amateur boxer and a World War II army pilot. After the war, he started his own airline, beginning with one used C-47; when he sold the company in 1969 he walked off with $104 million. He built the International Hotel and bought the Flamingo, both of which he eventually sold to Hilton. He went on to build the MGM Grand in the 1970s (today Bally's). He is currently building a billion-dollar MGM Grand megaresort (the world's largest casino hotel) on the Strip, with an adjacent theme park based on *The Wizard of Oz*. Kerkorian is also Chrysler Corporation's largest single shareholder.

Thomas "Amarillo Slim" Preston   (birthdate unknown) In May 1972, Thomas Preston, a colorful Texas cattle rancher with a slow drawl, loped off with $60,000 at Binion's third World Series of Poker. Preston is a legendary gambler who has made—and won—many bizarre bets. He beat daredevil Evel Knievel at golf using a hammer instead of a club, outplayed Minnesota Fats at pool using a broom handle for a cue, and topped a Ping-Pong champ using a Coke bottle for a paddle.

Benjamin "Bugsy" Siegel   (1906–47) A nefarious underworld kingpin, Siegel opened his dream hotel—the mob-financed $6 million Flamingo—in December 1946. He was gunned down in Los Angeles six months later at the home of his girlfriend Virginia Hill. Though he was never convicted of any crime (witnesses tended to suffer mysterious deaths), Siegel once boasted to fellow casino owner Del Webb that he had killed 20 men. His suite in the Flamingo—with extra-thick walls, a secret trapdoor, and four exits—still exists, as does the rose garden he planted. Siegel was an enthusiastic gardener.

Steve Wynn   (b. 1942) Wynn, whose father owned a chain of East Coast bingo parlors, first got into Las Vegas real estate by purchasing a small parking lot next to Caesars. He later sold it back to Caesars and used the money to bankroll his purchase of the Golden Nugget in 1969. In 1989 Wynn's $620 million Mirage revolutionized the Strip with Disneyesque attractions such as dolphin and tiger habitats, an indoor rain forest, and an erupting volcano. To date the Mirage is the most successful property in the history of gaming, and Wynn is a major player in this town. He will soon open Treasure Island, another Strip extravaganza property with a swashbuckling pirate theme.

3. RECOMMENDED BOOKS & FILMS

In its short life span, Las Vegas has inspired hundreds of books, running the gamut from Hunter Thompson's description of a psychedelic lost weekend to an almost infinite number of gambling manuals. The following list is a good starting point for further reading. Almost all of the below-listed books are available from the

Gambler's Book Club, 630 S. 11th St., Las Vegas, NV 89101 (tel. 702/382-7555 or 800/634-6243 to order).

BOOKS

History/Nonfiction/Biographies/Memoirs

Alvarez, A., *The Biggest Game in Town* (Houghton Mifflin, 1983). The inside story of Binion's annual World Series of Poker. Alvarez penetrates the mindset of world-class poker players.

Demaris, Ovid, and Ed Reid, *Green Felt Jungle* (Trident Press, 1963). A fast-paced expose of Las Vegas mobsters and racketeers. May be difficult to find.

Graham, Jefferson, *Vegas: Live and in Person* (Abbeville Press, 1989). A pictorial history that captures the glitz and glitter of Las Vegas from the 1930s through the 1980s.

Holden, Tony, *Big Deal—Confessions of a Professional Poker Player* (Viking Penguin, 1992). Walter Matthau, a dedicated player, calls this the "best book about poker I've ever read."

Jennings, Dean, *We Only Kill Each Other* (Pocket Books, 1967). Everything you always wanted to know about "Bugsy" Siegel and Virginia Hill.

Knepp, Donn, *Las Vegas—the Entertainment Capital* (Lane Publishing Co., 1987). A fascinating anecdote-filled history enhanced by hundreds of photographs.

Maggio, Frank, *Las Vegas Calling* (TAD Publishing Ltd., 1975). A pictorial history.

Maguglin, Robert O., *Howard Hughes: His Achievements & Legacy* (Sunrise, 1992). The latest attempt to unveil the all-time enigmatic personality.

Paher, Stanley W., *Las Vegas as it Began—as it Grew* (Nevada Publications, 1971). An entertaining history of Las Vegas.

Solkey, Lee, *Dummy Up and Deal* (GBC Press, 1980). The lifestyle, training, problems, and perks of Las Vegas blackjack dealers.

Young, Jeannine, *Las Vegas Trivia* (self-published, 1988). Nostalgia, inside info, and interesting anecdotes about Las Vegas.

Fiction

Biggle, Lloyd, Jr., *A Hazard of Losers* (Council Oaks Books, 1991). A detective story focusing on a keno scam in a Las Vegas casino.

McCullough, Clint, *Nevada* (St. Martin's Press, 1986). This account of fictional Las Vegas dynasty builder Meade Slaughter is a roman à clef based on bigger-than-life characters in Las Vegas and other gambling locales.

Powers, Tim, *Last Call* (Charnel House, 1992). A spine-chilling novel about gambling, spiritualism, superstition, and wagering for your soul!

Puzo, Mario, *Fools Die* (G.P. Putnam's Sons, 1978). Set in Las Vegas, it's replete with mobsters, high rollers, hookers, hustlers, and other criminally minded characters.

Thompson, Hunter, *Fear and Loathing in Las Vegas: A Savage Journey to the Heart of the American Dream* (Fawcett Popular Library, 1971). A diary of Thompson's totally decadent Las Vegas "trip."

Gambling How-To

Andersen, Ian, *Turning the Tables on Las Vegas* (Vintage Books, 1976). Using a nom de plume, an experienced gambler tells you how to manipulate casinos for your own benefit.

Cardoza, Avery, *How to Win at Gambling* (Cardoza Publishing, 1991). A worthy wagerers manual.

Crevelt, Dwight and Louise, *Slot Machine Mania* (Gollehon Press, 1988). How slot machines work, strategies, how people try to cheat, myths, and superstitions.

Crevelt, Dwight and Louise, *Video Poker Mania* (Gollehon Press, 1991). Learn everything about video poker machines—the different types, how they operate, how to win.

Dickkerson, Kenneth, *How to Win Games of Chance* (Ballantine, 1992). Covers everything from slot machines to horse racing.

Frome, Lenny, *Expert Video Poker for Las Vegas* (Compu-Flyers, 1990). Video poker guru Frome tells you how to hit the big jackpots.

Percy, George, *Seven Card Stud* (self-published, 1979). Mandatory reading for serious players.

Renneisen, Robert, *How to be Treated Like a High Roller—Even Though You're Not One* (Carol Publishing Group, 1992). The title says it all.

Silberstang, Edwin, *The Winner's Guide to Casino Gambling* (Signet, 1985). How to play—and win—all casino games and other insider tips. An easy-to-read manual for neophytes.

Sklansky, David, *Hold'Em Poker* (self-published, 1976). Charts, tables, and sound advice on how to win the game.

Vinson, Barney, *Las Vegas Behind the Tables* (Gollehon Press, 1986). Learn what goes on behind the scenes in counting rooms, how games are supervised, what casino bosses really do, and more.

FILMS

Since its inception, hundreds of films have used the glittering excitement of Las Vegas as a setting. Some examples: *The Hazards of Helen* (1915), *Las Vegas Nights* (1940), *Heldorado* (1945), *The Las Vegas Story* (1952), *Meet Me in Las Vegas* (1956), *Viva Las Vegas* (1964), *The Only Game in Town* (1970), *The Godfather Part II* (1973), *Harry & Tonto* (1973), *Lost in America* (1985), *Things Change* (1988), *Sister Act* (1991), *Bugsy* (1991), *Honeymoon in Vegas* (1992), *Honey, I Blew Up the Kid* (1992).

CHAPTER 2

PLANNING A TRIP TO LAS VEGAS

Las Vegas isn't a destination that requires a great deal of advance planning. However, you might want to read through the sightseeing and excursions chapters (7 and 12) in order to figure out how you want to budget your time.

1. SOURCES OF INFORMATION

For advance information write or call the **Las Vegas Convention & Visitors Authority,** 3150 Paradise Rd., Las Vegas, NV 89109 (tel. 702/892-7575). They can send you a comprehensive packet of brochures, a map, show guide, events calendar, and attractions list; help you find a hotel that meets your specifications; and answer any questions.

Another good information source is the **Las Vegas Chamber of Commerce,** 2301 E. Sahara Ave., Las Vegas, NV 89104 (tel. 702/457-4664).

And for information on all of Nevada, including Las Vegas, contact the **Nevada Commission on Tourism,** Capitol Complex, Carson City, NV 89710 (tel. 800/638-2328).

WHAT THINGS COST IN LAS VEGAS	U.S. $
Taxi from the airport to the Strip	7–10.00
Taxi from the airport to downtown	12–15.00
Minibus from the airport to the Strip	3.25
Minibus from the airport to downtown	4.50
Double at the Desert Inn (expensive)	75–135.00
Double at Harrah's (moderate)	45–89.00
Double at Motel Six (budget)	33.99
Three-course dinner at Palace Court for one without tax and tip (very expensive)	70.00

	U.S. $
Three-course dinner at Chin's for one without tax and tip (expensive)	35.00
Three-course dinner at Tony Roma's for one without tax and tip (moderate)	22.00
Three-course dinner at Chili's for one without tax and tip (budget)	15.00
All-you-can-eat buffet dinner at Circus Circus	3.99
All-you-can-eat buffet dinner at Caesars Palace	10.95
Bottle of beer	2.25
Coca-Cola	1.50
Cup of coffee	1.25
Roll of ASA 100 Kodacolor film, 36 exposures	4.70
Show ticket for *Lance Burton: A Magical Journey* (drinks, tax, and gratuity extra)	19.95
Show ticket for *Enter the Night* (including two drinks, tax, and gratuity)	24.90
Show ticket for headliners at Caesars (including tax and gratuity, drinks extra)	40–66.00
Show ticket for Siegfried & Roy (including two drinks, tax, and gratuity)	73.00
Telephone call	.25

2. WHEN TO GO — CLIMATE & EVENTS

Since most of a Las Vegas vacation is usually spent indoors, you can have a good time here year round. The most pleasant seasons, as you'll see from the chart below, are spring and fall, especially if you want to take in some of the outdoor attractions described in chapters 7 and 12. On the other hand, off-season, hotel rates are slashed, buffet lines shorter, and show tickets easier to obtain. Weekdays are less crowded than weekends. Holidays are always a mob scene accompanied by high hotel prices. Hotel prices also skyrocket when big conventions and special events are taking place. Call the Las Vegas Convention & Visitors Authority (800/332-5333) to find out if a major convention is on when you're planning your trip; if so, you might want to change the date.

One thing you'll hear again and again is that even though Las Vegas gets very hot, the dry desert heat is not uncomfortable. This is true. Humidity averages a low 22%, and even on very hot days there's apt to be some breeze. Also, except on the hottest summer days, there's relief at night when temperatures often drop as much as 20°.

Las Vegas's Temperatures (in degrees Fahrenheit)

	Jan	Feb	Mar	Apr	May	June	July	Aug	Sept	Oct	Nov	Dec
Average	44	50	57	66	74	84	91	88	81	67	54	47
High	55	62	69	79	88	99	105	103	96	82	67	58
Low	33	39	44	53	60	68	76	74	65	53	41	36

LAS VEGAS CALENDAR OF EVENTS

You may be surprised to learn that Las Vegas does not offer as many annual events as most tourist cities. The reason: Las Vegas wants people in the casinos, not off at Renaissance fairs and parades. When in town, check the local paper and call the **Las Vegas Convention & Visitors Authority** (tel. 892-0711) or **Chamber of Commerce** (tel. 457-4664) to find out about other events going on during your visit.

JANUARY

☐ **The PBA Invitational.** The Showboat Hotel, 2800 Fremont St. (tel. 385-9123), hosts this major bowling tournament every January.

MARCH

☐ **The LPGA Invitational.** Top women golfers compete in this major tournament at the Desert Inn late March or early April. For details call 382-6616.

APRIL

☐ **The World Series of Poker.** This famed 22-day event takes place at Binion's Horseshoe Casino, 128 Fremont St. (tel. 382-1600), in April or May, with high-stakes gamblers and show-biz personalities (Gabe Kaplan and Telly Savalas in past years) competing for six-figure purses. To enter, players must put up $10,000. It costs nothing to go watch the action.
☐ **PGA Senior Golf Classic.** This 4-day event in late April or early May takes place at the Desert Inn. For details call 382-6616.

MAY

☐ **Cinco de Mayo.** The Hacienda Hotel, 3950 Las Vegas Blvd. S. (tel. 739-8911), hosts an annual Cinco de Mayo pool party on an evening early in the month. Guests enjoy a sumptuous Mexican buffet, free margaritas, and musical entertainment. Admission is $12.95 per person.

☐ **Helldorado.** This Elks-sponsored western heritage celebration takes place over a 4-day Thursday-to-Sunday weekend in late May or early June. There are western dress ("be seen in jeans") parades, carnival rides and midway games, and four major Professional Rodeo Cowboys Association (PRCA) rodeos at the Thomas & Mack Center of the University of Nevada at Las Vegas. For information call the Elks Lodge at 870-1221 or check the local papers.

JULY

☐ **July 4th.** The Mirage, 3400 Las Vegas Blvd. S. (tel. 791-7111), enhances its nightly volcano-eruption show with fireworks.

SEPTEMBER

☐ **Oktoberfest.** This boisterous autumn holiday is celebrated from mid-September through the end of October at the Mount Charleston Restaurant & Lounge (tel. 386-6899 or 800/955-1314) with music, folk dancers, sing-alongs around a roaring fire, special decorations, and Bavarian cookouts.

OCTOBER

☐ **U.S. Triathlon Series.** Competitors must complete an arduous course consisting of a bike ride, swimming, and a 10K run. For details call 731-2115.

☐ **PGA Invitational Golf Tournament.** This 5-day championship event is played on three courses. The purse is over $2 million and the event is televised. For details call 382-6616.

DECEMBER

✪ *NATIONAL FINALS RODEO This is the superbowl of rodeos, attended by close to 200,000 people each year. The top 15 male rodeo stars compete in six different disciplines: calf roping, bulldogging, Brahma bull riding, team roping, saddle bronc riding, and bareback bronc riding. And the top 15 women compete in barrel riding. An all-around "cowboy of the year" is chosen and receives a purse of over $2 million. In connection with this event, hotels book country stars in their showrooms, and there's a cowboy shopping spree—a trade show for western gear—at a hotel selected annually.*

*   **Where:** At the 18,000 seat Thomas & Mack Center of UNLV. **When:** The first 10 days of the month. **How:** Order*

tickets as far in advance as possible by calling Las Vegas Events at 731-2115.

☐ **The Las Vegas Football Bowl.** This championship football event in mid-December pits the winners of the Mid-American Conference against the winners of the Big West Conference. The action takes place at the 32,000-seat Silver Bowl. For ticket information call 731-2115.

☐ **New Year's Eve.** This is a biggie (reserve your hotel room early). Downtown, Fremont Street is closed to traffic between Third and Main streets, and there's a big block party with two dramatic countdowns to midnight (the first is at 9pm, midnight on the East Coast). There are fireworks. On the Strip, New Year's Eve is celebrated with a big gala at the Mirage.

There's also a big New Year's Eve gala at the Mount Charleston Restaurant & Lounge (tel. 702/386-6899 or 800/955-1314). Make dinner reservations early and book a hotel room at the nearby Mount Charleston Hotel (tel. 702/872-5500). Details in Chapter 5.

3. WHAT TO PACK

Most of the year, the weather's warm to sweltering and you'll want the lightest possible clothing for outdoors. However, since you'll be spending a lot of time in air-conditioned hotels, casinos, restaurants, and showrooms, do bring a jacket or sweater. Cool nights, even in summer, can also necessitate light outerwear. During the day, dress is generally casual. At night, most people (not all) dress up a bit for dinner and shows. Some of the more expensive restaurants require jackets and ties for men. I think most people will be more comfortable bringing at least one or two elegant outfits for evening wear. Downtown hotels are more casual than Strip hotels.

In winter pack a light coat and hat, but don't get carried away—this isn't Wisconsin.

If you're planning to visit rugged outdoor attractions such as the Valley of Fire or Red Rock Canyon take comfortable shoes and clothing for hiking. And don't forget your bathing suit.

A few extras: I always like to pack a 75- or 100-watt light bulb, since bedside lamps seldom provide adequate wattage for reading. And Las Vegas is one of the few cities in America where hotels—especially budget hotels—don't routinely supply hair dryers and irons. And even those hotels that supply them tend to have inconvenient rules (for example, they must be returned in one hour).

4. TIPS FOR SPECIAL TRAVELERS

FOR THE DISABLED Write or call **The Independent Living Program,** Nevada Association for the Handicapped, 6200 W.

Oakey Blvd., Las Vegas, NV 89102 (tel. 702/870-7050). They can recommend hotels and restaurants that meet your needs, help you find a personal attendant, advise about transportation, and answer all questions.

In addition, the **Nevada Commission on Tourism,** Capitol Complex, Carson City, NV 89701 (tel. 800/638-2328), offers a free accommodations guide to Las Vegas hotels that includes access information.

Some nationwide resources include the following: For accessibility information contact the **Travel Information Service,** Moss Rehabilitation Hospital, 1200 W. Tabor Rd., Philadelphia, PA 19141 (tel. 215/456-9602), which charges nominally for mailing materials.

Evergreen Travel Service/Wings on Wheels Tours, 4114 198th Ave. SW, Suite 13, Lynwood, WA 98036 (tel. 206/776-1184 or 800/435-2288), offer tours designed for the blind, the visually impaired, the hearing impaired, the elderly, and the physically or mentally disabled.

Recommended books: *Access to the World: A Travel Guide for the Handicapped* by Louise Weiss offers tips for the disabled on travel and accessibility (H. Holt & Co.). You can charge it by calling 800/488-5233. Price is $12.95, plus $2 for shipping. And a publisher called **Twin Peaks Press,** Box 129, Vancouver, WA 98666 (tel. 206/694-2462 or 800/637-2256 for orders only), specializes in books for the disabled. Write for their *Disability Bookshop Catalog,* enclosing $2.

Amtrak (tel. 800/USA-RAIL) provides redcap service, wheelchair assistance, and special seats with 72-hours notice. The disabled are also entitled to a 25% discount on one-way regular coach fares. Disabled children age 2 to 15 can also get the 25% discount on already discounted one-way fares. Documentation from a doctor or an ID card proving your disability is required. Amtrak also provides wheelchair-accessible sleeping accommodations on long-distance trains, and service dogs are permissible and travel free of charge. Write for a free booklet called *Amtrak's America* from Amtrak Distribution Center, P.O. Box 7717, Itasca, IL 60143, which has a chapter detailing services for passengers with disabilities.

Greyhound (tel. 800/752-4841) allows a disabled person to travel with a companion for a single fare and, if you call 48 hours in advance, they will arrange help along the way.

FOR SENIORS Always carry some form of photo ID so that you can take advantage of discounts wherever they're offered. And it never hurts to ask.

If you haven't already done so, consider joining the **American Association of Retired Persons** (AARP), 601 E St. NW, Washington, DC 20049 (tel. 202/434-2277). Annual membership costs $8 per person or per couple. You must be 50 to join. Membership entitles you to many discounts. Write to Purchase Privilege Program, AARP Fulfillment, 601 E St. NW, Washington, DC 20049, to receive AARP's *Purchase Privilege* brochure—a free list of hotels, motels, and car-rental firms nationwide that offer discounts to AARP members. **AARP Travel Experience from American Express,** 400 Pinnacle Way, Suite 450, Norcross GA

30071 (tel. 800/927-0111 for land tours, 800/745-4567 for cruises), arranges a wide array of discounted group tours for members. Nonmembers can travel with AARP members at the same discounted prices.

Elderhostel is a national organization that offers low-priced educational programs for people over 60 (your spouse can be of any age; nonspouse companions must be at least 50). Programs are generally a week long, and prices average about $300 per person, including room, board, and classes. For information on programs in Nevada call or write Elderhostel headquarters, 75 Federal St., Boston, MA 02110-1941 (tel. 617/426-7788), and ask for a free catalog.

Amtrak (tel. 800/USA-RAIL) offers a 15% discount off the lowest available coach fare (with certain travel restrictions) to people 62 or over.

Greyhound also offers discounted fares for senior citizens. Call your local Greyhound office for details.

FOR SINGLE TRAVELERS   The main problem for single travelers is meeting up with other people. In Las Vegas, that's not terribly difficult. In the casinos, you can easily strike up a conversation at a gaming table, and, of course, hotel bars are convivial. Outdoor group activities such as river rafting (see Chapter 7) are also good ways to meet people.

FOR STUDENTS   The key to securing discounts is valid student ID. Be sure to carry such and keep your eyes open for special student prices.

FOR FAMILIES   Las Vegas in the nineties is doing its utmost to promote itself as a family destination. Kids just adore the place. Everything for them is geared to having fun; nothing is educational. See numerous "Cool for Kids" suggestions in Chapter 7. A few general suggestions to make traveling with kids easier:

Get the Kids Involved   Let them, if they're old enough, write to the tourist offices for information and color brochures. If you're driving, give them a map on which they can outline the route. Let them help decide your sightseeing itinerary.

Packing   Although your home may be toddler-proof, hotel accommodations are not. Bring blank plugs to cover outlets and whatever else is necessary.

En Route   Carry a few simple games to relieve the tedium of traveling. A few snacks will also help and save money. If you're using public transportation (Amtrak, airlines, bus), always inquire about discounted fares for children.

Accommodations   Children under 12, and in many cases even older, stay free in their parents' rooms in most hotels. Look for establishments that have pools and other recreational facilities (see "Frommer's Cool for Kids: Hotels" in Chapter 5).

5. GETTING THERE

BY PLANE Las Vegas is served by **McCarran International Airport** (tel. 702/739-5743), just a few minutes drive from the southern end of the Strip. McCarran is rather unique among airports in that it includes a vast casino area of over 700 slot machines. Though these are reputed to offer lower paybacks than hotel casinos (the airport has a captive audience and doesn't need to draw repeat customers), I can never resist the lure of throwing in a few quarters on arrival.

Major carriers flying into McCarran include America West, Delta, Southwest, Continental, United, USAir, Northwest, and American.

Generally, the least expensive fares (except for specially promoted discount fares announced in newspaper travel sections) are advance-purchase fares that involve certain restrictions. For example, in addition to paying for your ticket 3 to 21 days in advance of your trip, you may have to leave or return on certain days, stay a maximum or minimum number of days, and so on. Also, advance-purchase fares are often nonrefundable. Nonetheless, the restrictions are usually within the framework of one's vacation plans. The further in advance you reserve, the better your options, since sometimes there are a limited number of seats sold at discounted rates.

Just what kind of savings are we talking about with advance-purchase fares? At this writing, if you flew on Delta, regular round-trip coach fares and lowest advance-purchase fares are as follows between Las Vegas's McCarran International Airport and these cities:

	Regular Fare	Advance Purchase
N.Y.–Las Vegas	$740	$260
Boston–Las Vegas	$780	$270
Chicago–Las Vegas	$620	$220
New Orleans–Las Vegas	$660	$230
Los Angeles–Las Vegas	$128	$ 40

By the time you read this, fares will no doubt have changed, but the vast savings for advance-purchase tickets will still hold.

When you make airline reservations on any carrier, also inquire about money-saving packages that include hotel accommodations, car rentals, tours, and so on, with your airfare. For instance, a **Delta Dream Vacation** package (tel. 800/872-7786), priced at about $325 to $510 per person based on double occupancy, includes round-trip coach transportation, hotel accommodations (tax in-

FROMMER'S SMART TRAVELER:
AIRFARES

1. Shop all the airlines that fly to Las Vegas.
2. Always ask for the lowest-priced fare, not just a discount.
3. A good travel agent should have all current fare information at his or her fingertips and can do the above steps for you; it doesn't cost anything to use a travel agent.
4. Ask about senior-citizen discounts (usually 10%).
5. Buy tickets in advance; fares are usually lower.
6. Check the Sunday travel section of major newspapers for discount fares.
7. Consider changing your travel dates by a day or two to obtain a lower fare.

cluded) for two nights, an economy rental car with unlimited mileage for the first 24 hours after arrival, and many bonuses such as two-for-one admissions to shows, complimentary gifts and museum admissions, discounts on tours, and fun books. Prices vary with the season, seat availability, and hotel choice.

BY TRAIN The Las Vegas **Amtrak** station (tel. 702/386-6896 or 800/USA-RAIL) is downtown at Main and Fremont streets, directly behind Jackie Gaughan's Plaza Hotel/Casino. Amtrak connects just about the entire country with Las Vegas, and, like the airlines, it offers discounted fares. A limited number of seats are set aside for these special fares, and many people reserve them months in advance. Therefore, the sooner you reserve, the greater your likelihood of success. Discounted coach fares are refundable, so you don't lose anything by reserving far in advance. There are some restrictions as to the dates you may travel, mostly around busy holiday times. And travel Monday through Thursday is usually cheaper than weekend travel. At this writing, regular round-trip coach fares and discount fares are as follows between Las Vegas and these cities:

	Regular Fare	Advance Purchase
N.Y.–Las Vegas	$478	$259
Boston–Las Vegas	$478	$259
Chicago–Las Vegas	$410	$212
New Orleans–Las Vegas	$646	$229
Los Angeles–Las Vegas	$132	$ 77

Do inquire (tel. 800/321-8684) about money-saving packages that include hotel accommodations with your train fare.

BY BUS **Greyhound** buses (tel. 702/384-9561) connect the entire country with Las Vegas. They pull into a downtown terminal at

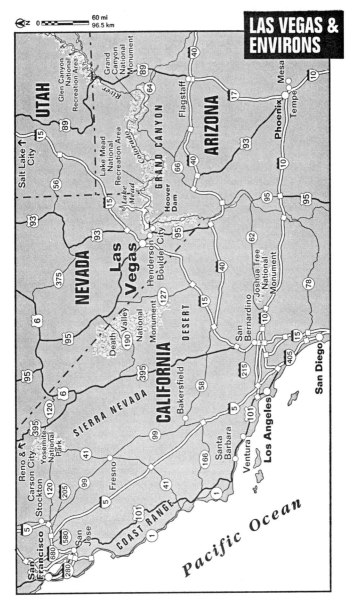

LAS VEGAS & ENVIRONS

Main and Carson streets, directly adjacent to the Amtrak station. Buses coming into town make three stops on the Strip—at the Tropicana, Harrah's, and the Riviera hotels. Fare structure on buses tends to be complex, but the good news is that when you call to make a reservation, the agent will always give you the lowest-fare options. Once again, advance-purchase fares, booked 3 to 21 days prior to travel, represent savings up to 50%.

BY CAR The principal highway connecting Las Vegas to the rest of the country is I-15, which links Montana, Idaho, and Utah with southern California. From the East Coast take I-70 or I-80 west to I-15 south. From the southeast take I-40 west to Kingman, Arizona, and U.S. 93 north to downtown Las Vegas (Fremont Street). From the south take I-10 west to Phoenix and U.S. 93 north to Las Vegas. From San Francisco, take I-80 east to Reno and U.S. 95 south to Las Vegas. Do note driving precautions listed under "Driving" in Chapter 4's "Fast Facts: Las Vegas" section.

CHAPTER 3

FOR FOREIGN VISITORS

Although American fads and fashions have spread across Europe and other parts of the world so that America may seem like familiar territory before your arrival, there are still many peculiarities and uniquely American situations that any foreign visitor will encounter.

1. PREPARING FOR YOUR TRIP

ENTRY REQUIREMENTS

DOCUMENTS   Canadian nationals need only proof of Canadian residence to visit the United States. Citizens of Great Britain and Japan need only a current passport. Citizens of other countries, including Australia and New Zealand, usually need two documents: a valid **passport** with an expiration date at least six months later than the scheduled end of their visit to the United States and a **tourist visa** available at no charge from a U.S. embassy or consulate.

To get a tourist or business visa to enter the United States, contact the nearest American embassy or consulate in your country; if there is none, you will have to apply in person in a country where there is a U.S. embassy or consulate. Present your passport, a passport-size photo of yourself, and a completed application, which is available through the embassy or consulate. You may be asked to provide information about how you plan to finance your trip or show a letter of invitation from a friend with whom you plan to stay. Those applying for a business visa may be asked to show evidence that they will not receive a salary in the United States. Be sure to check the length of stay on your visa; usually it is six months. If you want to stay longer, you may file for an extension with the Immigration and Naturalization Service once you are in the country. If permission to stay is granted, a new visa is not required unless you leave the United States and want to reenter.

MEDICAL REQUIREMENTS No inoculations are needed to enter the United States unless you are coming from, or have stopped over in, areas known to be suffering from epidemics, particularly cholera or yellow fever.

If you have a disease requiring treatment with medications containing narcotics or drugs requiring a syringe, carry a valid signed prescription from your physician to allay any suspicions that you are smuggling drugs.

CUSTOMS REQUIREMENTS Every adult visitor may bring in, free of duty: one liter of wine or hard liquor; 200 cigarettes or 100 cigars (but no cigars from Cuba) or three pounds of smoking tobacco; $100 worth of gifts. These exemptions are offered to travelers who spend at least 72 hours in the United States and who have not claimed them within the preceding six months. It is altogether forbidden to bring into the country foodstuffs (particularly cheese, fruit, cooked meats, and canned goods) and plants (vegetables, seeds, tropical plants, and so on). Foreign tourists may bring in or take out up to $10,000 in U.S. or foreign currency with no formalities; larger sums must be declared to Customs on entering or leaving.

INSURANCE

There is no national health system in the United States. Because the cost of medical care is extremely high, we strongly advise every traveler to secure health coverage before setting out.

You may want to take out a comprehensive travel policy that covers (for a relatively low premium) sickness or injury costs (medical, surgical, and hospital); loss of, or theft of your baggage; trip-cancellation costs; guarantee of bail in case you are arrested; costs of accident, repatriation, or death. Such packages (for example, "Europe Assistance" in Europe) are sold by automobile clubs at attractive rates, as well as by insurance companies and travel agencies.

2. GETTING TO THE U.S.

Travelers from overseas can take advantage of the **APEX (Advance Purchase Excursion) fares** offered by all the major U.S. and European carriers. Aside from these, attractive values are offered by **Icelandair** on flights from Luxembourg to New York and by **Virgin Atlantic Airways** from London to New York/Newark.

Some large American airlines (for example, TWA, American Airlines, Northwest, United, and Delta) offer travelers—on their transatlantic or transpacific flights—special discount tickets under the name **Visit USA**, allowing travel between any U.S. destinations at minimum rates. They are not on sale in the United States, and must, therefore, be purchased before you leave your foreign point of departure. This system is the best, easiest, and fastest way to see the United States at low cost. You should obtain information well in advance from your travel agent or the office of the airline concerned, since the conditions attached to these discount tickets can be changed without advance notice.

The visitor arriving by air, no matter what the port of entry, should cultivate patience and resignation before setting foot on U.S. soil. Getting through immigration control may take as long as two hours on some days, especially summer weekends. Add the time it takes to clear Customs and you will see that you should make very generous allowance for delay in planning connections between international and domestic flights—an average of two to three hours at least.

In contrast, travelers arriving by car or by rail from Canada will find border-crossing formalities streamlined to the vanishing point. And air travelers from Canada, Bermuda, and some places in the Caribbean can sometimes go through Customs and Immigration at the point of departure, which is much quicker and less painful.

For further information about travel to and arriving in New York see "Getting There" in Chapter 2 and "Arriving" in Chapter 4, Section 1.

FAST *FOR THE FOREIGN TRAVELER*

Automobile Organizations Auto clubs will supply maps, suggested routes, guidebooks, accident and bail-bond insurance, and emergency road service. The major auto club in the United States, with 955 offices nationwide, is the **American Automobile Association (AAA).** To join in Las Vegas call 702/870-9171 or toll free 800/336-4357. Membership costs $55 for the first year, $35 for each consecutive year. The AAA can provide you with an **International Driving Permit** validating your foreign driving license. Members of some foreign auto clubs have reciprocal arrangements with AAA and enjoy its services at no charge. If you belong to an auto club, inquire about AAA reciprocity before you leave home.

Automobile Rentals To rent a car you need a major credit card, or you'll have to leave a sizable cash deposit ($100 or more for each day). A valid driver's license is required, and you usually need to be at least 21 (sometimes older). Some companies do rent to younger people but add a daily surcharge. Be sure to return your car with the same amount of gas you started out with; rental companies charge excessive prices for gasoline. All of the major car-rental companies are represented in Las Vegas. Budget Rent A Car offers a special 20% discount to readers of this book (see Chapter 4, Section 2 for details).

Business Hours **Banks** open weekdays from 9am to 3pm, although there's 24-hour access to the automatic tellers (ATMs) at most banks and other outlets. Generally, **offices** open weekdays from 9am to 5pm. **Stores** are open six days a week with many open on Sundays, too; department stores usually stay open until 9pm at least one day a week.

Climate See Chapter 2, Section 2.

Currency & Exchange   The U.S. monetary system has a decimal base: one American **dollar** ($1) = 100 **cents** (100¢).

Dollar **bills** commonly come in $1 ("a buck"), $5, $10, $20, $50, and $100 denominations (the last two are not welcome when paying for small purchases and are not accepted in taxis or at subway ticket booths).

There are five **coin** denominations: 1¢ (one cent or "penny"); 5¢ (five cents or "nickel"); 10¢ (ten cents or "dime"); 25¢ (twenty-five cents or "quarter"); and 50¢ (fifty cents or "half dollar").

Traveler's checks denominated in dollars are accepted without demur at most hotels, motels, restaurants, and large stores. But as any experienced traveler knows, the best place to change traveler's checks is at a bank.

Credit cards are the method of payment most widely used: VISA (BarclayCard in Britain), MasterCard (EuroCard in Europe, Access in Britain, Diamond in Japan), American Express, Diners Club, Carte Blanche, and Discover. You can save yourself trouble by using "plastic" rather than cash or traveler's checks in 95% of all hotels, motels, restaurants, and retail stores. A credit card can also serve as a deposit for renting a car, as proof of identity (often carrying more weight than a passport), or as a "cash card," enabling you to draw money from banks that accept them.

Currency Exchange   The very reliable **Thomas Cook Currency Services, Inc.,** in business since 1841, offers a wide variety of services. They handle about 130 currencies; sell commission-free foreign and U.S. traveler's checks, drafts, and wire transfers; and do check collections (including Eurochecks). Rates are competitive and service excellent. Always inquire at Thomas Cook about the optimum way to exchange your money on entering and leaving the United States or any country. They maintain an office at the JFK Airport International Arrivals Building in New York (tel. 718/656-8444 or 800/582-4496). At this writing new offices are in the works both at La Guardia Airport in New York (in the Delta terminal) and at McCarran International Airport in Las Vegas. Call the above toll-free number for information.

Las Vegas casinos also exchange foreign currency, usually at a good rate.

Note: The "foreign-exchange bureaus" so common in Europe are rare even at airports in the United States and nonexistent outside major cities. Try to avoid having to change foreign money, or travelers checks denominated other than in U.S. dollars, at small-town banks, or even at branches in a big city; in fact, leave any currency other than U.S. dollars at home—it may prove more nuisance to you than it's worth.

Drinking Laws   See "Fast Facts: Las Vegas" in Chapter 4.

Electric Current   The United States uses 110 to 120 volts, 60 cycles, compared to 220 to 240 volts, 50 cycles, as in most of Europe. In addition to a 100-volt converter, small appliances of non-American manufacture, such as hair dryers or shavers, will require a plug adapter, with two flat, parallel pins.

Embassies & Consulates   All embassies are located in the national capital, Washington, D.C.; some consulates are located in major cities, and most nations have a mission to the United Nations in New York City. Foreign visitors can obtain telephone numbers for their embassies and consulates by calling "Information" in Washington, D.C. (tel. 202/555-1212).

Emergencies   Call 911 to report a fire, call the police, or get an ambulance. If you encounter traveler's problems call the **Traveler's Aid Society,** a nationwide, nonprofit, social-service organization geared to helping travelers in difficult straits. Their services might include reuniting families separated while traveling, providing food and/or shelter to people stranded without cash, or even emotional counseling. If you're in trouble, seek them out. In Las Vegas there are Traveler's Aid offices at McCarran International Airport (702/261-5234) and at 953 E. Sahara Ave., at Maryland Parkway in the Commercial Center at the northeast corner (tel. 702/369-4357). Both locations are open Monday to Friday 8am to 4pm.

Gasoline [Petrol]   One U.S. gallon equals 3.75 liters, while 1.2 U.S. gallons equals one imperial gallon. You'll notice there are several grades (and price levels) of gasoline available at most gas stations. And you'll also notice that their names change from company to company. The unleaded ones with the highest octane are the most expensive (most rental cars take the least expensive "regular" unleaded) and leaded gas is the least expensive, but only older cars can take this any more, so check if you're not sure.

Holidays   On the following legal national holidays, banks, government offices, post offices, and many stores, restaurants, and museums are closed:

January 1 (New Year's Day)
Third Monday in January (Martin Luther King Day)
Third Monday in February (Presidents Day, Washington's Birthday)
Last Monday in May (Memorial Day)
July 4 (Independence Day)
First Monday in September (Labor Day)
Second Monday in October (Columbus Day)
November 11 (Veteran's Day/Armistice Day)
Last Thursday in November (Thanksgiving Day)
December 25 (Christmas)

Also celebrated in some cities and states are the following:

February 12 (in the North) (Lincoln's Birthday)
March 17 (St. Patrick's Day)
April 19 (Patriot's Day)

Finally, the Tuesday following the first Monday in November is Election Day, and is a legal holiday in presidential-election years.

Languages   Major Las Vegas hotels usually have multilingual employees. Unless your language is very obscure, they can usually supply a translator on request.

Legal Aid   The foreign tourist, unless positively identified as a member of the Mafia or of a drug ring, will probably never become involved with the American legal system. If you are pulled up for a minor infraction (for example, of the highway code, such as speeding), never attempt to pay the fine directly to a police officer; you may wind up arrested on the much more serious charge of attempted bribery. Pay fines by mail, or directly into the hands of the clerk of the court. If accused of a more serious offense, it is wise to say and do nothing before consulting a lawyer. Under U.S. law, an arrested person is allowed one telephone call to a party of his or her choice. Call your embassy or consulate.

Mail   If you want your mail to follow you on your vacation, you need only fill out a change-of-address card at any post office. The post office will also hold your mail for up to one month. If you aren't sure of your address, your mail can be sent to you, in your name, **c/o General Delivery** at the main post office of the city or region where you expect to be. The addressee must pick it up in person and produce proof of identity (driver's license, credit card, passport, etc.).

Generally to be found at intersections, mailboxes are blue with a red-and-white stripe and carry the inscription "U.S. MAIL." If your mail is addressed to a U.S. destination, don't forget to add the five-figure postal code, or ZIP (Zone Improvement Plan) Code, after the two-letter abbreviation of the state to which the mail is addressed (CA for California, MA for Massachusetts, NY for New York, and so on).

The main post office in Las Vegas is immediately behind the Circus Circus Hotel at 1001 Circus Circus Dr. (tel. 702/735-2525). It's open Monday to Friday 9am to 5pm. You can also always mail letters and packages at your hotel.

Newspapers/Magazines   National newspapers include the *New York Times, USA Today,* and the *Wall Street Journal.* National news weeklies include *Newsweek, Time,* and *U.S. News & World Report.* There are two Las Vegas dailies—the *Las Vegas Review Journal* and the *Las Vegas Sun.* And at every hotel desk, you'll find dozens of local magazines, such as *Vegas Visitor, What's On in Las Vegas, Showbiz Weekly,* and *Where To in Las Vegas,* that are chock-full of helpful information.

Radio & Television   Audiovisual media, with three coast-to-coast networks—ABC, CBS, and NBC—joined in recent years by the Public Broadcasting System (PBS) and the cable network CNN, play a major part in American life. In big cities, televiewers have a choice of about a dozen channels (including the UHF channels), most of them transmitting 24 hours a day, without counting the pay-TV channels showing recent movies or sports events. All options are usually indicated on your hotel TV set. You'll also find a wide choice of local radio stations, each broadcasting particular kinds of talk shows and/or music—classical, country, jazz, pop, gospel—punctuated by news braodcasts and frequent commercials.

Safety   Whenever you're traveling in an unfamiliar city, stay alert. Be aware of your immediate surroundings. Wear a money belt—or better yet, check valuables in a safety-deposit box at your hotel. Keep a close eye on your possessions and be sure to keep them in sight when you're seated in a restaurant, theater, or other public place. Don't leave valuables in your car—even in the trunk. In casinos, be especially aware of where your purse or wallet is at all times. Every city has its criminals. It's your responsibility to be aware and be alert even in the most heavily touristed areas.

Taxes In the United States there is no VAT (Value-Added Tax), or other indirect tax at a national level. Every state, and each city in it, has the right to levy its own local tax on all purchases, including hotel and restaurant checks, airline tickets, and so on. In Las Vegas, sales tax is 7%, hotel room tax 8%.

Telephone, Telegraph, Telex **Pay phones** are an integral part of the American landscape. You will find them everywhere: at street corners; in bars, restaurants, public buildings, stores, service stations; along highways; and so on. Outside the metropolitan areas public telephones are more difficult to find. Stores and gas stations are your best bet.

Unlike the mail and the railroads, the telephone is not a public-service system. It is run by private corporations, which perhaps explains its high standard of service. In Las Vegas local calls cost 25¢.

For **long-distance** or **international calls,** stock up with a supply of quarters; the pay phone will instruct you when, and in what quantity, you should put them into the slot. For direct overseas calls, first dial 011, followed by the country code (Australia, 61; New Zealand, 64; United Kingdom, 44; and so on), and then by the city code and the number of the person you wish to call. For Canada and long-distance calls in the United States, dial 1 followed by the area code and number you want.

Before calling from a hotel room, always ask the hotel phone operator if there are any telephone surcharges. These are best avoided by using a public phone, calling collect, or using a telephone charge card.

For **reversed-charge or collect calls,** and for **person-to-person calls,** dial 0 (zero, *not* the letter "O") followed by the area code and number you want; an operator will then come on the line, and you should specify that you are calling collect, or person-to-person, or both. If your operator-assisted call is international, ask for the overseas operator.

For local **directory assistance** ("information"), dial 411; for **long-distance information,** dial 1, then the appropriate area code and 555-1212.

Like the telephone system, **telegraph** and **telex** services are provided by private corporations like ITT, MCI, and above all, Western Union, the most important. You can bring your telegram in to the nearest Western Union office (there are hundreds across the country), or dictate it over the phone (a toll-free call, 800/325-6000). You can also telegraph money, or have it telegraphed to you, very quickly over the Western Union system.

Telephone Directory See "Yellow Pages," below.

Time The United States is divided into four **time zones** (six, if Alaska and Hawaii are included). From east to west, these are: eastern standard time (EST), central standard time (CST), mountain standard time (MST), Pacific standard time (PST), Alaska standard time (AST), and Hawaii standard time (HST). Always keep changing time zones in mind if you are traveling (or even telephoning) long distances in the United States. For example, noon in New York City (EST) is 11am in Chicago (CST), 10am in Denver (MST), 9am in Los Angeles (PST), 8am in Anchorage (AST), and 7am in Honolulu (HST). Las Vegas is PST.

Daylight saving time is in effect from the last Sunday in April through the last Saturday in October (actually, the change is made at 2am on Sunday) except in Arizona, Hawaii, part of Indiana, and Puerto Rico. Daylight saving time moves the clock one hour ahead of standard time.

Tipping This is part of the American way of life, on the principle that you must expect to pay for any service you get. Here are some rules of thumb:

Bartenders: 10% to 15%.
Bellhops: at least 50¢ per piece; $2 to $3 for a lot of baggage.
Blackjack dealers: it's customary to tip a few dollars if you've had a big win.
Cab drivers: 15% of the fare.
Cafeterias, fast-food restaurants: no tip.
Casino barmaids: drinks are free, tip $1.
Chambermaids: $1 a day.
Checkroom attendants (restaurants, theaters): $1 per garment.
Cinemas, movies, theaters: no tip.
Doormen (hotels or restaurants): not obligatory.
Gas-station attendants: no tip.
Hairdressers: 15% to 20%.
Keno runners: it's customary to tip a few dollars if you've had a big win.
Redcaps (airport and railroad station): at least 50¢ per piece, $2 to $3 for a lot of baggage.
Restaurants, nightclubs: 15% to 20% of the check.
Sleeping-car porters: $2 to $3 per night to your attendant.
Valet parking attendants: $1.

Toilets Foreign visitors often complain that public toilets are hard to find in most U.S. cities. True, there are none on the streets, but the visitor can usually find one in a bar, restaurant, hotel, museum, department store, or service station—and it will probably be clean (although the last-mentioned sometimes leaves much to be desired). Note, however, a growing practice in some restaurants and bars of displaying a notice that "toilets are for the use of patrons only." You can ignore this sign, or better yet, avoid arguments by paying for a cup of coffee or soft drink, which will qualify you as a patron. The cleanliness of toilets at railroad stations and bus depots may be more open to question, and some public places are equipped with pay toilets, which require you to insert one or two 10¢ coins (dimes) into a slot on the door before it will open.

Yellow Pages There are two kinds of telephone directories available to you. The general directory is the so-called **White Pages,** in which private and business subscribers are listed in alphabetical order. The inside front cover lists the emergency number for police, fire, and ambulance, and other vital numbers (like the Coast Guard, poison-control center, crime-victims hotline, and so on). The first few pages are devoted to community-service numbers, including a guide to long-distance and international calling, complete with country codes and area codes.

The second directory, printed on yellow paper (hence its name, **Yellow Pages**), lists all local services, businesses, and industries by type of activity, with an index at the back. The listings cover not only such obvious items as automobile repairs by make of car, or drugstores (pharmacies), often by geographical location, but also restaurants by type of cuisine and geographical location, bookstores by special subject and/or language, places of worship by religious denomination, and other information that the tourist might otherwise not readily find. The *Yellow Pages* also include city plans or detailed area maps, often showing postal ZIP codes and public transportation routes.

THE AMERICAN SYSTEM OF MEASUREMENTS

LENGTH

1 inch (in.)	=	2.54cm					
1 foot (ft.)	=	12 in.	=	30.48cm	=	.305m	
1 yard	=	3 ft.	=	.915m			
1 mile (mi.)	=	5,280 ft.	=	1.609km			

To convert miles to kilometers, multiply the number of miles by 1.61 (for example, 50 mi. × 1.61 = 80.5km). Note that this conversion can be used to convert speeds from miles per hour (m.p.h.) to kilometers per hour (km/h).

To convert kilometers to miles, multiply the number of kilometers by .62 (for example, 25km × .62 = 15.5 mi.). Note that this same conversion can be used to convert speeds from kilometers per hour to miles per hour.

CAPACITY

1 fluid ounce (fl. oz.)	=	.03 liter		
1 pint	=	16 fl. oz.	=	.47 liter
1 quart	=	2 pints	=	.94 liter
1 gallon (gal.)	=	4 quarts	=	3.79 liter
	=	.83 Imperial gal.		

To convert U.S. gallons to liters, multiply the number of gallons by 3.79 (example, 12 gal. × 3.79 = 45.58 liters.)

To convert U.S. gallons to Imperial gallons, multiply the number of U.S. gallons by .83 (example, 12 U.S. gal. × .83 = 9.95 Imperial gal.).

To convert liters to U.S. gallons, multiply the number of liters by .26 (example, 50 liters × .26 = 13 U.S. gal.).

To convert Imperial gallons to U.S. gallons, multiply the number of Imperial gallons by 1.2 (example, 8 Imperial gal. × 1.2 = 9.6 U.S. gal.).

WEIGHT

1 ounce (oz.)	=	28.35 grams		
1 pound (lb.)	=	16 oz.	=	453.6 grams
	=	.45 kilograms		
1 ton	=	2,000 lb.	=	907 kilograms
	=	.91 metric ton		

To convert pounds to kilograms, multiply the number of pounds by .45 (example, 90 lb. × .45 = 40.5kg).

To convert kilograms to pounds, multiply the number of kilos by 2.2 (example, 75kg × 2.2 = 165 lb.).

AREA

1 acre	=	.41 hectare		
1 square mile (sq. mi.)	=	640 acres	=	2.59 hectares
	=	2.6km		

To convert acres to hectares, multiply the number of acres by .41 (example, 40 acres × .41 = 16.4ha).

To convert square miles to square kilometers, multiply the number of square miles by 2.6 (example, 80 sq. mi. × 2.6 = 208km).

To convert hectares to acres, multiply the number of hectares by 2.47 (example, 20ha × 2.47 = 49.4 acres).

To convert square kilometers to square miles, multiply the number of square kilometers by .39 (example, 150km × .39 = 58.5 sq. mi.).

TEMPERATURE

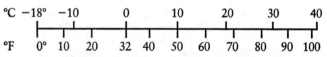

To convert degrees Fahrenheit to degrees Celsius, subtract 32 from °F, multiply by 5, then divide by 9 (example, 85F − 32 × 5/9 = 29.4C).

To convert degrees Celsius to degrees Fahrenheit, multiply °C by 9, divide by 5, and add 32 (example, 20°C × 9/5 + 32 = 68°F).

CHAPTER 4

GETTING TO KNOW LAS VEGAS

1. ORIENTATION
2. GETTING AROUND
• FAST FACTS: LAS VEGAS

Located in the southernmost precincts of a wide, pancake-flat valley, Las Vegas is the biggest city in the state of Nevada. Treeless mountains form a scenic backdrop to hotels awash in neon glitter. For tourism purposes, the city is very compact.

1. ORIENTATION

ARRIVING

BY PLANE   McCarran International Airport is just a few minutes drive from the southern end of the Strip. It's a big, modern airport, with a vast bank of slot machines that let you get into the spirit of Las Vegas immediately upon deplaning. Getting to your hotel from the airport is a cinch.

   Bell Transportation Corporation (tel. 702/739-7990) runs 20-passenger **minibuses** daily between the airport and all major Las Vegas hotels and motels almost around the clock (4:30am to 2am). Buses from the airport depart every 8 to 10 minutes. For departure from your hotel, call at least two hours in advance. Cost is $3.25 per person each way to Strip and Convention Center hotels, $4.50 to downtown properties.

   A **taxi** between the airport and a Strip or Convention Center hotel will run you about $7 to $10, $12 to $14 for downtown hotels. *Note:* There's a $1.20 surcharge added to the meter rate when you're coming from the airport.

BY TRAIN   If you come into town on **Amtrak** (tel. 702/386-6896 or 800/USA-RAIL), you'll arrive at a depot in the heart of downtown at Main and Fremont streets. From there, you can a take a taxi to your hotel or board a bus at Fremont and Third streets (three blocks away) to any Strip hotel. A taxi to the Strip will cost about $10. Bus fare is $1.25.

BY BUS   **Greyhound buses** (tel. 702/384-9561) pull into a downtown terminal at Main and Carson streets, directly adjacent to the Amtrak station. En route, buses coming into town make three stops on the Strip—at the Tropicana, Harrah's, and the Riviera hotels. Once again, you can take a taxi or catch the bus at Fremont and Third streets to any Strip hotel.

TOURIST INFORMATION

All major Las Vegas hotels provide comprehensive tourist information at reception desks and/or sightseeing and show desks. Other good information sources are: the **Las Vegas Convention & Visitors Authority,** 3150 Paradise Rd., Las Vegas, NV 89109 (tel. 702/892-7550 or 800/332-5333); the **Las Vegas Chamber of Commerce,** 2301 E. Sahara Ave., Las Vegas, NV 89104 (tel. 702/457-4664); and, for information on all of Nevada, including Las Vegas, the **Nevada Commission on Tourism,** Capitol Complex, Carson City, NV 89710 (tel. 800/638-2328).

FOR TROUBLED TRAVELERS The **Traveler's Aid Society** is a nationwide, nonprofit, social-service organization geared to helping travelers in difficult straits. Their services might include reuniting families separated while traveling, providing food and/or shelter to people stranded without cash, or even emotional counseling. If you're in trouble, seek them out. In Las Vegas there are Traveler's Aid offices at McCarran International Airport (702/261-5234) and at 953 E. Sahara Ave., at Maryland Parkway in the Commercial Center at the northeast corner (tel. 702/369-4357). Both locations are open Monday to Friday 8am to 4pm.

CITY LAYOUT

Nothing could be simpler than the layout of Las Vegas—especially the three areas of interest to tourists.

THE STRIP The Strip is probably the most famous 3½-mile stretch of highway in the nation. Officially Las Vegas Boulevard South, it contains most of the top hotels in town and offers almost all of the major showroom entertainment. It extends from just below Tropicana Avenue at the southernmost end—where you'll find the Hacienda, Excalibur, and Tropicana hotels—to Sahara Avenue, where the Sahara hotel anchors the northern boundary.

CONVENTION CENTER This is a sort of eastern addendum to the Strip that has grown up around the Las Vegas Convention Center. Las Vegas is one of the nation's top convention cities, attracting about 2 million conventioneers each year. The major hotel in this section is the Las Vegas Hilton, but in recent years Marriott has built Residence Inn and Courtyard properties here, and many excellent smaller hotels and motels are arrayed southward along Paradise Road. All of these offer close proximity to the Strip.

DOWNTOWN Also known as "Glitter Gulch," downtown Las Vegas (centered on Fremont Street between Main and Ninth streets) was the first section of the city to develop hotels and casinos. For the

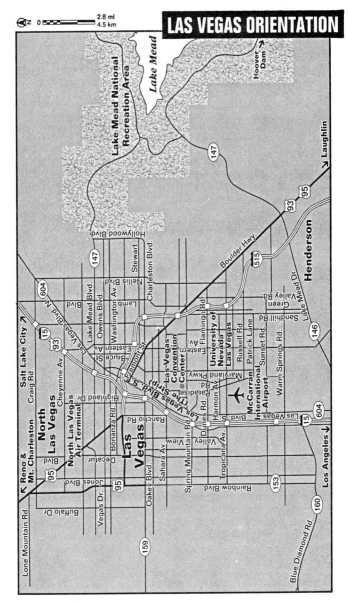

LAS VEGAS ORIENTATION

2.8 mi
0 ___ 4.5 km

Lake Mead

Lake Mead National Recreation Area

Hoover Dam →

→ Laughlin

Lake Mead Blvd.

Hollywood Blvd.

Stewart

Charleston Blvd.

Nellis Blvd.

Boulder Hwy.

Green Valley Rd.

Lake Mead Dr.

Sandhill Rd.

Henderson

147

515

93

95

146

604

← Salt Lake City

15

93

95

Craig Rd.

Cheyenne Av.

Lake Mead Blvd.

Owens Blvd.

Washington Av.

Bonanza Rd.

Lamb Blvd.

Bruce St.

Eastern Av.

Fremont St.

Las Vegas Convention Center

Flamingo Rd.

University of Nevada Las Vegas

Russell Rd.

Patrick Lane

Sunset Rd.

Warm Springs Rd.

North Las Vegas Air Terminal

Highland Dr.

Rancho Rd.

Paradise Rd.

Harmon Av.

McCarran International Airport

Las Vegas Blvd.

← Reno & Mt. Charleston

North Las Vegas

Las Vegas

Decatur Blvd.

Jones Blvd.

Vegas Dr.

Oakey Blvd.

Sahara Av.

Spring Mountain Rd.

Valley View

Maryland Pkwy.

Dunes Rd.

Tropicana Av.

Rainbow Blvd.

153

Buffalo Dr.

Lone Mountain Rd.

159

160

Blue Diamond Rd.

15

604

Los Angeles →

most part, it's more casual than the Strip—a "just-folks" kind of place—and room rates are generally lower. There are exceptions, however, most notably the gleaming white, palm-fringed Golden Nugget, which looks like it belongs in Monte Carlo. And, conversely, there are also some very inexpensive properties on and adjacent to the Strip. It is easier to find casinos offering low minimum bets downtown. Also, should you want to go casino hopping, this area is more compact and the hotels closer together. Las Vegas Boulevard runs all the way into Fremont Street downtown (about a 5-minute drive). The area between the Strip and downtown is a seedy stretch dotted with tacky wedding chapels, bail-bond operations, pawnshops, and cheap motels.

2. GETTING AROUND

I can't think of any tourist destination easier to navigate than Las Vegas. The hotels are the major attractions and they're grouped in two large clumps on and around the Strip/Convention Center area and downtown. Even first-time visitors will feel like old hands after a day or two.

BY PUBLIC TRANSPORTATION Buses operated by Gray Line ply a route from the Hacienda Hotel at the southernmost end of the Strip to Ogden Avenue and Fourth Street (via Casino Center Boulevard) downtown, stopping at all major hotels on the way. You can pick up a bus back to the Strip at the corner of Fremont and Third streets. Bus fares are a uniform $1.25, and exact change is required. If you plan on using the bus a lot, purchase a 10-ride commuter card from the driver for $8. Buses run every 15 minutes from 6am to 12:45am and every half hour from 12:45am to 6am. For further transit information, phone 384-3540.

Or you can hop aboard a classic streetcar replica run by **Las Vegas Strip Trolley** (tel. 382-1404). These old-fashioned dark-green trolley cars have interior oak paneling and are comfortably air conditioned. Like the buses, they run northward from the Hacienda, making stops at all major hotels between it and the Sahara, looping back via the Las Vegas Hilton. They do not, however, go downtown. Trolleys run every 20 to 30 minutes daily between 9:30am and 2am. The fare is $1, and exact change is required.

BY CAR Though it is possible to get around without a car in Las Vegas, I love to have one at my disposal. Parking is a pleasure, since all casino hotels offer valet service. That means that for a mere $1 tip you can park right at the door. And in sweltering summer heat, the valet will bring back your car with the air conditioning already turned on. In addition, though bus tours are available to nearby attractions, a car lets you explore at your own pace rather than according to a tour schedule.

All of the major car-rental companies are represented in Las Vegas. **Budget** (tel. 800/527-0700), by far the lowest-priced of the major rental agencies, has six locations in town, including one on the Strip (directly across from the Mirage at 3235 Las Vegas Blvd. S.) and one at the airport. They rent economy cars (with unlimited mileage) at $16 to $36 a day, intermediate cars at $18 to $38, and full-size cars at $20 to $40. Weekly rates begin at $89. And if you show this book, any of Budget's Las Vegas locations will give you a **20% discount off regular rental rates.** Budget also offers the largest fleet of luxury cars in town and rents vans, trucks, and pickups. Do inquire about the company's nationwide frequent-rental program, which allows you to obtain credit with each rental towards car upgrades and even free rental days.

BY TAXI   Since cabs line up in front of all major hotels, the easiest way to get around town is by taxi. Cabs charge $2.20 for the first one-seventh of a mile and 20¢ for each additional one-seventh of a mile (that translates to $1.40 for each additional mile). A taxi from the airport to the Strip will run you $7 to $9, from the airport to downtown $12 to $14, and between the Strip and downtown about $10. You can often save money by sharing a cab with someone going to the same destination (up to five people can ride for the same fare).

If you want to call a taxi, any of the following companies can provide one: **Desert Cab Company** (tel. 376-2687 or -2688), **Whittlesea Blue Cab** (tel. 384-6111), and **Yellow/Checker Cab Company** (tel. 873-2000 or 873-2227).

FAST   LAS VEGAS
FACTS

Airport   Las Vegas is served by **McCarran International Airport,** 5757 Wayne Newton Blvd. (tel. 702/739-5743), just a few minutes' drive from the southern end of the Strip. Immediately upon deplaning you'll hear the jingle of slot machines.

You can take a **minibus** (tel. 739-7990) between the airport and all major hotels and motels. Cost is $3.25 per person up to the Sahara Hotel (the last on the Strip), $4.50 between the airport and downtown properties. A **taxi** from the airport to Strip hotels is about $7 to $10, $12 to $15 to downtown hotels.

Ambulances   See "Emergencies" below.

Area Code   702.

Babysitters   Most hotels offer child-care services. If yours does not, contact **Around the Clock Child Care** (tel. 365-1040). In business since 1985, this reputable company clears its sitters with the Health Department, the sheriff, and the FBI and carefully screens references. Charges are $30 for four hours for one or two children, $5.50 for each additional hour, with surcharges for additional children and on holidays. Sitters are on call seven days a week, 24 hours a day, and they come to your hotel. Call at least two hours in advance. See also the **Las Vegas Hilton** listing in Chapter 5.

Banks   Banks are generally open 9 or 10am to 3pm, and most have Saturday hours. See also "Cash and Credit" below.

Car Rentals   See "Getting Around" in this chapter.

Cash & Credit   It's extremely easy—too easy—to obtain cash in Las Vegas. Most casino cashiers will cash personal checks and can exchange foreign currency, and just about every casino has a machine that will provide cash on a wide variety of credit cards.

Climate   See "When to Go—Climate & Events" in Chapter 2.

Crime   See "Safety" below.

Dentists & Doctors   Hotels usually have lists of dentists and doctors should you need one. In addition, they are listed in the **Centel Yellow Pages.**

For dentist referrals you can also call the **Clark County Dental Society** (tel. 435-7767), weekdays 9am to noon and 1 to 5pm; when the office is closed a recording tells you who to call for emergency service.

You can see a doctor at the **Desert Springs Hospital,** 4231 S. Nellis Blvd., at Boulder Highway (tel. 733-6875). Open Monday to Friday 8am to 5pm. No appointment is necessary.

Driving   Since driving in the outskirts of Las Vegas—for example, from California—involves desert driving, you must take certain precautions. It's a good idea to check your tires, water, and oil before leaving. Take at least five gallons of water in a clean container that can be used for either drinking or the radiator. Pay attention to those road signs suggesting when to turn off your car's air conditioner. And don't push your luck with gas—it may be 35 miles, or more, between stations. If your car overheats, do not remove the radiator cap until the engine has cooled, and then remove it only very slowly. Add water to within an inch of the top of the radiator.

Drugstores   During the day, there are numerous pharmacies in the area of the Strip, and nonprescription drugstore items can usually be purchased at your hotel gift shop. For late-night emergencies, there are several 24-hour pharmacies in town, including **White Cross Drugs,** 1700 Las Vegas Blvd. S. at Oakey Boulevard (tel. 382-1733, 384-8075 for prescriptions); and **Sav-on Drugs,** 1360 E. Flamingo Rd., at Maryland Parkway in the Mission Center (tel. 737-0595, 731-5373 for prescriptions).

Emergencies   Dial 911 to contact the police or fire departments or to call an ambulance. See also "Hospital Emergency Wards" below.

Eyeglasses   A company whose name is its phone number, **732-EYES,** has several branches in Las Vegas, the most convenient one at 3507 S. Maryland Pkwy., across the street from the Boulevard Mall. The above phone number is operative 24 hours a day. During store hours, Monday to Saturday 9am to 6pm, call the store direct at 732-3758. They offer same or next-day service. An examination for glasses is $25, for contacts $79. Walk-ins are welcome, and they have thousands of frames to choose from, including many designer frames.

Hairdressers   There are hair salons for men and women in just about every major hotel.

Highway Conditions   For recorded information call 486-3116.

Holidays   Holidays are the most popular times to visit Las Vegas, and in that regard they are also the worst times to visit. Hotels run close to 100% occupancy, room rates skyrocket, show tickets are more difficult to obtain, buffet lines longer, and so on. The same situation can occur when vast conventions are in town, such as COMDEX, which brings about 100,000 conventioneers early in November. Call the Convention and Visitors Authority (see below) to find out if major conventions will be in town when you plan to travel.

Hospital Emergency Wards   A 24-hour emergency service with outpatient and trauma-care facilities is available at the **University Medical Center of Southern Nevada Memorial Hospital,** 1800 W. Charleston Blvd., at Shadow Lane (tel. 383-2000; the emergency-room entrance is on the corner of Hastings and

Rose streets). **Humana Hospital Sunrise,** 3186 Maryland Pkwy., between Desert Inn Road and Sahara Avenue (tel. 731-8080), the largest proprietary hospital west of the Mississippi, also has emergency facilities.

Hot Lines Rape Crisis Center (tel. 366-1640), **Suicide Prevention** (tel. 731-2990).

Information The primary tourist information center is the **Las Vegas Convention & Visitors Authority,** 3150 Paradise Rd., Las Vegas, NV 89109 (tel. 702/892-7550 or 800/332-5333); open Monday to Friday 7am to 6pm, Saturday and Sunday 8am to 5pm. They make room reservations, provide show information, supply maps and brochures, and can answer all inquiries.

An additional source for brochures, maps, and information on accommodations is the **Las Vegas Chamber of Commerce.** 2301 E. Sahara Ave., Las Vegas, NV 89104 (tel. 702/457-4664).

For maps, events calendars, brochures, and other information on all of Nevada, including Las Vegas, contact the **Nevada Commission on Tourism,** Capitol Complex, Carson City, NV 89710 (tel. 800/638-2328).

Libraries The largest in town is the **Clark County Library** branch at 1401 Flamingo Rd., at Maryland Parkway (southeast corner, tel. 733-7810). Hours are Monday to Thursday 9am to 9pm, Friday and Saturday 9am to 5pm, Sunday 1 to 5pm.

Liquor & Gambling Laws You must be 21 to drink or gamble. There are no closing hours in Las Vegas for the sale or consumption of liquor, even on Sunday.

Newspapers/Periodicals There are two Las Vegas dailies—the *Las Vegas Review Journal* and the *Las Vegas Sun.* The Review Journal's Friday edition has a helpful "Weekend" section with a comprehensive guide to shows and buffets. And at every hotel desk, you'll find dozens of local magazines, such as *Vegas Visitor, What's On in Las Vegas, Showbiz Weekly,* and *Where To in Las Vegas,* that are chock-full of helpful information.

Parking Valet parking is one of the great pleasures of Las Vegas. When you visit another hotel for its casino, restaurants, or show, you can pull right up to the door and have the valet take your car. It's well worth the dollar tip (given when the car is returned) to save walking a city block from the far reaches of hotel parking lots, particularly in summer when the temperature is often over 100. Another summer plus: the valet will turn on your air conditioning, so you don't have to get into an oven on wheels.

Poison Humana Hospital Sunrise (listed above) has a 24-hour **Poison Information Center.** Call 732-4989.

Police For emergencies call 911. For nonemergency matters call 795-3111.

Population 298,637.

Post Office The main post office is immediately behind the Circus Circus Hotel at 1001 Circus Circus Dr. (tel. 735-2525). It's open Monday to Friday 9am to 5pm. You can also always mail letters and packages at your hotel.

Religious Services Las Vegas has more houses of worship on a per capita basis than any other metropolitan area in the country, and we all know what everybody is praying for. The houses of worship listed below are on or near the Strip. Consult the Centel Yellow Pages under "Churches" for other locations and denominations, or inquire at your hotel desk.

Baptist: First Baptist Church, 300 S. Ninth St., at Bridger Ave., downtown (tel. 382-6177). **Episcopal:** Christ Church, 200 S. Maryland Pkwy. at St. Louis Ave. (tel. 735-7655). **Jewish (conservative):** Temple Beth Shalom, 1600 E. Oakey Blvd., near the Strip (tel. 384-5070). **Jewish (reformed):** Temple Beth Am, 501 S. Ninth St., at Clark Ave., downtown (tel. 385-5366). **Lutheran:** Reformation Lutheran, 580 E. St. Louis Ave., near the Strip (tel. 732-2052). **Methodist:** First United Methodist, 231 S. Third St., at Bridger Avenue, downtown (tel. 382-9939). **Presbyterian, United:** First Presbyterian, 1515 W. Charleston Blvd., a block west of I-15 (tel. 384-4554). **Roman Catholic:** Guardian Angel Cathedral, 302 E. Desert Inn Rd., at the Strip (tel. 735-5241). **Southern Baptist:** First Southern Baptist, 700 E. St. Louis Ave., at Sixth St. (tel. 732-3100).

Safety   In Las Vegas vast amounts of money are always on display, and criminals find many easy marks. Don't be one of them. At gaming tables, men should keep wallets well concealed and out of the reach of pickpockets, and women should keep handbags in plain sight (on laps). Unless your hotel room has an in-room safe, check valuables in a safety-deposit box at the front desk.

Show Tickets   See Chapter 11 for details on obtaining show tickets.

Taxes   Clark County hotel room tax is 8%, sales tax 7%.

Taxis   See "Getting Around" above in this chapter.

Time & Temperature   Dial 118.

Weather   Call 734-2010.

Weddings   Las Vegas is one of the easiest places in the world to tie the knot. There's no blood test, no waiting period, the ceremony and license are inexpensive, chapels are open around-the-clock, and your honeymoon destination is right at hand. Over 75,000 marriages are performed here each year. Get a license downtown at the **Clark County Marriage License Bureau,** 200 S. Third St., at Bridger Avenue (tel. 702/455-3156). Open 8am to midnight Monday to Thursday and 8am Friday through midnight Sunday. On legal holidays they're open 24 hours. The cost of a marriage license is $35, cost of the ceremony $25 to $30, and use of a chapel about $50. Flowers, photographers, video recordings, limos, and other extras are readily available.

Among the many famous folk who've married here: Roger Vadim (to both Brigitte Bardot and Jane Fonda), Elvis and Priscilla Presley, Frank and Mia Sinatra, Mickey Rooney (several times), and—a few couples who are still together at this writing—Paul Newman and Joanne Woodward, Bruce Willis and Demi Moore, and Steve Lawrence and Eydie Gorme.

Wedding chapels abound, and there's something for every taste and pocketbook. Most romantic settings are at Mount Charleston or on a boat on Lake Mead (see Chapter 7). One of the most popular is the historic **Candlelight Wedding Chapel,** 2855 Las Vegas Blvd. S. (tel. 702/735-4179 or 800/962-1818). The Candlelight, along with most other wedding chapels in town, can meet any requests (given advance notice) to stage your wedding in a limousine, a hot-air balloon, in one of the nearby canyons, any eccentric setting you might think of. A service called **Las Vegas Wedding and Rooms** (tel. 800/322-VOWS) can give you a full rundown on all options.

CHAPTER 5

LAS VEGAS ACCOMMODATIONS

1. VERY EXPENSIVE
- FROMMER'S SMART TRAVELER: HOTELS
2. EXPENSIVE
- FROMMER'S COOL FOR KIDS: HOTELS
3. MODERATE
4. INEXPENSIVE
5. HOSTELS

Las Vegas has over 77,000 hotel and motel rooms, with another 11,000 scheduled for completion by mid-1994. Why the building boom? Though Las Vegas already has many more rooms than other big cities, its annual occupancy rate (close to 85%) is also considerably higher than the national average. As one of America's top 10 convention cities, it frequently fills existing hotels to the bursting point. Booking well in advance is recommended.

The city's accommodations profile is rather unique. Here the hotel norm is a 24-hour megaresort (the world's 10 largest hotels are located in Las Vegas) with 6 to 10 restaurants, lavish entertainment showrooms and lounges, shopping arcades, fully equipped health clubs, swimming pools, and, most important, vast casinos. And these megaresorts charge considerably less for rooms than equivalent properties in other major cities. The price of a room in a deluxe Las Vegas hotel would get you accommodations at a moderate hotel in any other tourist mecca. The reason: The casino is the raison d'être for most properties here. Inexpensive hotel rooms are one of many lures.

Note, too, that while many cities offer reduced rates on weekends, in Las Vegas room rates are lower Sunday to Thursday, go up on Friday and Saturday, and soar during holidays and when large conventions are in town. If you have some flexibility in planning the dates of your vacation, you can save quite a bit. Off-season (December to February and July to August) rates are the lowest, unless there are big conventions in town.

GETTING THE MOST FOR YOUR HOTEL DOLLAR When the town is full up, top rates are charged, and there's little you can do about it. However, when business isn't quite so brisk, you can cut deals. Using toll-free numbers, call around town and ask reservations clerks if they can undercut the first rates quoted. Often, they will. A hotel makes zero dollars per night on an empty room. Hence, though they don't bruit it about (for obvious reasons), most hotels would rather reduce rates than leave a room unoccupied. Whatever rate you settle on, ask for a confirmation number (written confirmation if possible), and check the rate again when you register at the hotel. Also, always inquire about reduced-price packages when you reserve.

If you're willing to chance it, an especially advantageous time to secure reduced rates is late in the afternoon or early evening on the day of your arrival when a hotel's likelihood of filling up with full-price bookings is remote.

RESERVATIONS SERVICES If you get harried when you have to haggle, use a free service offered by **City-Wide Reservations,** 1321 S. Maryland Pkwy., Las Vegas, NV 89104 (tel. 702/388-7044 or 800/733-6644). They'll find you a hotel room in the price bracket you desire that meets your specific requirements. Because they book rooms in volume, they are able to get discounted rates. Not only can they book rooms, they can arrange packages (including meals, transportation, show tickets, car rentals, and other features) and group rates.

The **Las Vegas Convention and Visitors Authority** also runs a room reservations hot line (tel. 800/332-5333) which can be helpful.

WHERE TO STAY There are basically two areas of town—**the Strip/Convention Center** and **downtown.** Since it's only a 5-minute ride by car or bus between downtown and Strip hotels, there's really no such thing as a bad location. Personally, I like to stay on the Strip, but there are people who prefer the more casual downtown ambience. If you've never been to Las Vegas before, I'd suggest staying on the Strip and checking out downtown for possible future visits.

Another factor in your choice is whether to stay at a casino or noncasino hotel. A casino hotel, especially a major one, is a kind of multifacility city within a city that offers nonstop gaming, shows, and excitement. It can be great if you're the kind of person who thrives in the heart of the action. If you'd rather visit the action but retire to more tranquil surroundings at night, choose a noncasino hotel. The hotel that gives you the best of both worlds is the Desert Inn—a refined casino hotel with a country-club atmosphere.

HOW TO READ THE LISTINGS The hotels and motels listed in this chapter are divided first by location, then alphabetically by price category with different types of lodging (for example, casino or noncasino hotels) separated. My personal favorites in all categories are starred, and those that offer especially good value are marked with $ signs.

1. VERY EXPENSIVE

The category "very expensive" is a bit misleading. These are the top hotels in town, most of them offering vast casinos, a wide array of restaurants, glamorous showrooms, and many other facilities. But the rates they charge would be considered "high moderate" in other major cities. Even if you're staying elsewhere, read through these listings; some of the hotels described below are sightseeing attractions in their own right. You don't have to stay at these high-toned places to avail yourself of their posh restaurants, casinos, and showrooms.

ON THE STRIP/CASINO HOTELS

CAESARS PALACE, 3570 Las Vegas Blvd. S., just north of Flamingo Rd., Las Vegas, NV 89109. Tel. 702/731-7110 or toll free 800/634-6661. Fax 702/731-6636. 1150 rms, 350 suites. A/C TV TEL

$ Rates: $95–$160 single, $110–$175 double, $475–$7,500 suite. Extra person $20. Children under 12 free in parents' room. AE, DISC, JCB, MC, V. **Parking:** Free (self and valet).

Designed to reflect the decadent grandeur of ancient Rome, Caesars has been a major player on the Strip since its opening in 1966. This world-class resort is a Roman pleasure palace where guests are greeted by gladiators and centurions, classical marble statuary graces public areas, and cocktail waitresses are costumed as goddesses. Its several entrances are graced by 18 spectacular fountains (Evel Knievel once attempted to jump over them on a motorcycle), Roman temples, heroic arches, golden charioteers, and elegant driveways lined by 50-foot Italian cypresses. Caesars pioneered the "People Mover" concept, using moving walkways to convey visitors from the Strip into the hotel. Today there are three of these conveyances, leading to the casino, the Omni Theater, and the Forum shops—a Rodeo Drive–style shopping complex. Caesars has not only kept up with the competition over three decades, it's continually upped the ante, setting new standards for glamour and excitement.

Accommodations occupy four towers, and rooms are looking great following a $90 million-plus renovation in 1991. There are too many decorator schemes to describe here, but you will likely enjoy lavish bath facilities with marble flooring, European fixtures, oversized marble tubs (about half are Jacuzzis), and spacious showers. Art in the rooms keeps to the Greco-Roman theme (some rooms have classical sculptures in niches), furnishings tend to neoclassic styles, and design elements such as Roman columns, pilasters, and pediments are common. Many rooms have four-poster beds with a mirrored ceilings. I particularly like the Centurion Tower junior suites ($175 double) with plush living room areas. All rooms are equipped with AM/FM alarm-clock radios, three phones (bedside, bath, and desk), and remote-control color cable TVs with free HBO, gaming instructions, and hotel information stations. Most rooms have private safes.

Dining Caesars has a well-deserved reputation for superior in-house restaurants. There are nine in the hotel, plus dining facilities in the new Forum shopping area. All are highly recommended.

The hotel's premier restaurant, the exquisite **Palace Court,** holds its own with prestigious gourmet dining rooms anywhere in the country. Details in Chapter 6.

A second gourmet room, **Bacchanal,** recreates a multicourse

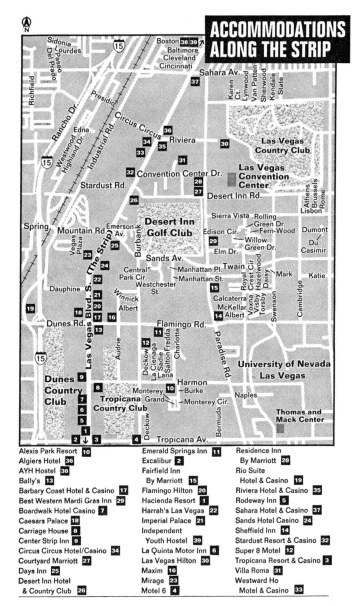

ACCOMMODATIONS ALONG THE STRIP

Roman feast in fittingly sumptuous surroundings, complete with scantily clad "wine goddesses." It's quite an experience. Details in Chapter 6.

Neros, specializing in prime aged steaks and fresh seafood (dozens of varieties of fresh fish are flown in daily), also features duck, chicken, veal, and lamb dishes. An extensive wine list complements the menu. The restaurant's octagonal design is a contemporary interpretation of the Spanish Madejar style, with an eight-pointed star radiating from the ceiling. Tiered copper walls form a gleaming inverse pyramid, a modernistic crystalline chandelier is suspended over a vast floral centerpiece, and white-linened tables are romantically lit by hurricane lamps. Dinner only; entrées $18.50–$40.

Just off the casino is Caesars' elegant Japanese restaurant, **Ah'So,** fronted by an oak-floored terrace lit by paper lanterns. Inside, seating areas under pine and cherry trees are divided by arched bridges spanning flower-bordered streams, and a waterfall cascades over faux lava rock. Japanese music complements the sound of splashing waters. Prix-fixe multicourse teppanyaki dinners ($45 per person) are featured.

The pretty crystal-chandeliered **Primavera,** with pink-clothed tables, bamboo fan-back chairs, and ficus trees in big terra-cotta pots, has a wall of Palladian windows overlooking the pool. A jade carpet accents pink cotton draperies with green trimmed swag valances, while complementing a pistachio and white lattice wall covering. Al fresco terrace seating under white canvas umbrellas is especially lovely at night when poolside trees are lit by tiny lights. Open breakfast, lunch, and dinner. You can start the day here with egg-battered Italian coffee cake griddled to a golden brown or poached eggs and grilled pancetta. The menu features homemade pasta and specialties from all regions of Italy. Lunch entrées are $9.50–$16.50, dinner entrées $11.50–$29.50.

Empress Court, fronted by a two-story double-balustraded staircase encircling a koi pond, is aquatically themed from its coral reef aquarium to its etched-glass fish-motif room dividers. Seating is in black lacquer chinoiserie chairs at elegantly appointed tables, and Chinese dulcimer music enhances the ambience. Opened in 1988, Empress Court's dedication ceremony included a traditional lion dance to ward off evil spirits. The menu offers first-rate Cantonese cuisine and specializes in fresh seafood. Dinner only; most entrées $12–$20; multicourse prix-fixe dinners $35 and $50 per person.

In **Cafe Roma,** Caesars' 24-hour coffee shop, murals of pastoral Roman landscapes behind arches create a scenic window effect. This is a very comfortable restaurant with a wide-ranging menu that runs the gamut from filet mignon to seafood enchiladas, from kung pao chicken to burgers, salads, and sandwiches.

La Piazza Food Court is a great choice for families. See Chapter 11 for details.

And finally, Caesars contains the lavish **Pallatium Buffet,** described in detail in Chapter 6.

The new Forum shops will be opening several restaurants shortly after this book goes to press. Important additions to the Las Vegas dining scene will include **Spago** (Wolfgang Puck's famed L.A. celebrity haunt), a branch of New York's **Carnegie Deli,** and the **Palm.**

There are several casino lounges, among them the **Discus Bar** in the Forum Casino, the **Galleria Lounge** near the baccarat area, and the **Olympic** casino lounge. The **Neptune** pool bar is open seasonally. And the **Post-Time** snack bar near the Olympiad Race and Sports Book serves sandwiches, snacks, and drinks.

Services Car-rental desk, 24-hour room service, 24-hour concierge, shoeshine, complimentary gaming lessons.

Facilities   Casino, four outdoor tennis courts and pro shop, photography shop, two extensive shopping arcades (see Chapter 10), state-of-the-art video game arcade, American Express office, full-service unisex salon (including waxing, facials, and body treatments), barbershop, tour and show desks.

Caesars' magnificent Olympic-size swimming pool, focal point of the exquisitely landscaped "Garden of the Gods," was inspired by the Pompeii Baths of Rome. Shaped like a Roman shield and surrounded by classical statuary, it is tiled with Carrara marble and dramatically lit by a colonnade of stately lamps. A 28-foot diameter whirlpool spa centered by a water nymph adjoins. A second pool with three large fountains and "lounging islands" is located on the upper level of the garden. The Roman Tower health spa is an extensive facility offering Universal equipment, treadmills, stair machines, Lifecycles, racquetball/basketball courts, steam, sauna, whirlpool, tanning beds, massage, aroma therapy, facials, refreshments, and a sun deck.

DESERT INN HOTEL & COUNTRY CLUB, 3145 Las Vegas Blvd. S., between Desert Inn Rd. and Sands Ave., Las Vegas, NV 89109. Tel. 702/733-4444 or toll free **800/ 634-6906. Fax 702/733-4774. 726 rms, 95 suites. A/C TV TEL**

$ Rates: $75–$135 single or double, $105–$175 minisuite $150– $1,500 suite. Extra person $15. Children under 12 free in parents' room. Inquire about golf, spa, and other packages. AE, CB, DC, DISC, JCB, MC, V. **Parking:** Free (self and valet).

Many people consider the Desert Inn the most prestigious address on the Strip. Country-club elegance is the keynote here: The emphasis is on first-rate service, fine restaurants, and extensive resort facilities. The property occupies 200 exquisitely landscaped acres of rock gardens, flower beds, duck ponds, waterfalls, and tree-shaded lawns. Strolling the grounds is almost like visiting a botanical garden or arboretum. The hotel opened in 1950, with Edgar Bergen and Charlie McCarthy premiering in the showroom. Howard Hughes (and later his estate) owned the D.I. from 1967 to 1988 and lived here in the late 1960s. It is my favorite Las Vegas hotel.

Stunning rooms—named for famous golf courses and tennis stadiums—offer substantial comfort. The most luxurious accommodations, in the nine-story St. Andrews Tower, are decorated in shades of mauve, with furnishings in traditional styles and beautiful floral-print bedspreads and pillow shams. They have big velvet-upholstered sofas strewn with throw pillows, oversized closets with full-length mirrors, and baths with whirlpool tubs and showers. The less expensive rooms in the 14-story August Tower are also lovely; they're done in shades of blue with bleached oak furnishings and polished pink granite accents. In the same price category are Forest Hills rooms in a two-story building. Pebble Beach accommodations are all minisuites with sitting room areas. Decorated in southwestern color schemes (apricot/teal/taupe), they offer wet bars and small refrigerators, dressing areas, oversized tubs, and canvas-shaded brick patios or balconies overlooking whirlpool spas. Headliners, high rollers, and other well-heeled citizens stay in the Wimbledon Building's duplex suites, with private pools or 4000-square-foot penthouses. All D.I.

rooms offer AM/FM alarm-clock radios, superior bath toiletries, and remote-control color cable TVs with Spectravision movie options, a hotel-information channel narrated by Rich Little, and a gaming-instruction channel featuring Suzanne Somers.

Dining The opulent **Monte Carlo Room** has been one of the city's most highly regarded dining rooms for several decades. See Chapter 6 for details.

HoWan offers specialties from many regions of China. At the entrance is a beautiful reef aquarium filled with tropical fish, candlelit white-linened tables are adorned with fresh flowers, and silk-shaded chandeliers and sconces provide soft lighting. Ornate wood carvings and china dishes are displayed, and Chinese paintings are set in silk and brocade wall inserts. Notable entrées include lobster tail in ginger and green onion, almond pressed duck, and barbecued lamb on a bed of mustard greens. Dinner only; entrées $9.75–$26.

Portofino—with oak and marble floors, potted palms, and large Carrara marble room dividers—overlooks the casino. Its spacious semicircular booths are upholstered in rich purple velvet. Northern Italian cuisine is featured. A meal here might consist of an appetizer of baked oysters topped with pepper and bacon sauce, an entrée of sautéed fresh sea bass in lemon/mustard/butter sauce with a side dish of spaghetti alla carbonara, and a dessert of fresh fruit with zabaglione. Dinner only; entrées $18–$30, pasta dishes $11–$14.

La Promenade, a delightful plant-filled 24-hour coffee shop with a 30-foot windowed wall overlooking the pool, offers seating in comfortable velvet-upholstered booths and armchairs under immense fringed gold-silk umbrellas. You can get anything here from a grilled cheese sandwich to broiled lobster in drawn butter, including many Jewish deli specialties like gefilte fish, creamed herring, and bagels with Nova lox.

The stone-walled **Champions Deli,** on the golf course, also serves deli fare—pastrami and corned beef sandwiches and the like. A lavish Sunday brunch is served in the showroom (see Chapter 6). The **Starlight Theatre,** a plush casino lounge, offers name entertainment at night, sporting events (on a large-screen TV) during the day. It's one of two casino bars.

Services 24-hour room service, concierge, shoeshine.

Facilities Casino, tour and show desks, car-rental desk, beauty salon/barbershop, shops (men's and women's clothing, gifts and sundries, jewelry, logo items), golf and tennis pro shops.

The verdant, palm-studded 18-hole Desert Inn Golf Course (*Golf Digest* calls it one of America's top resort courses) is the home of

---

IMPRESSIONS

There was a magic in this place. It was like stepping back into the frontier. Casino owners were king. They owned the town. They were glamorous. They had beautiful women and lots of money.
—HOTEL/CASINO MAGNATE STEVE WYNN, RECALLING HIS FIRST
IMPRESSIONS OF LAS VEGAS WHEN HE VISITED AS A BOY

three prestigious annual PGA professional tournaments (more about this challenging course in Chapter 7).

But even if it had no casino or golf course, the D.I. could function as a luxury spa retreat, offering water-therapy programs (there are hot, warm, and cool tubs), private whirlpools with recliner seats, salt rubs, loofah scrubs, herbal wraps, massages, eucalyptus facials, paraffin treatments, tanning beds, steam, and sauna. It's not all pampering. The cardiovascular fitness center has treadmills, Lifecycles, Stairmasters, free weights, a small pool and sun deck, aerobics classes, a full line of Kaiser workout machines, and a jogging parcourse with exercise stations. You can relax, postworkout, in a TV lounge. The hotel has a large swimming pool in a garden setting with adjoining whirlpool, poolside snack/cocktail bar, and pool sundries shop. The D.I.'s tennis complex comprises 10 tournament-class courts, five of them lit for night play; expert instruction and practice ball machines are available. And, finally, there are two shuffleboard courts.

MIRAGE, 3400 Las Vegas Blvd. S., between Flamingo Rd. and Sands Ave., Las Vegas, NV 89109. Tel. 702/791-7111 or toll free 800/627-6667. Fax 702/791-7446. 3,044 rms, 279 suites. A/C TV TEL

$ Rates: Single or double $79–$109 Sun–Thurs, $99–$179 Fri–Sat and holidays; suites $250–$3,000. Extra person $15. Children 12 and under free in parents' room. AE, CB, DC, DISC, MC, V. **Parking:** Free (self and valet).

Steve Wynn's gleaming white and gold Mirage redefines spectacular in a town where spectacular is a way of life. Occupying 102 acres, it's fronted by more than a city block of cascading waterfalls and tropical foliage centering on a very active "volcano": after dark, it erupts every 15 minutes, spewing fire 100 feet above the lagoons below! Step inside the hotel and you're in a verdant rain forest—a 90-foot domed atrium where paths meander through palms, banana trees, waterfalls, and serene pools. Every morning you can see gardeners planting dozens of new orchids and other tropical blooms here. And behind the front desk is a 53-foot, 20,000-gallon simulated coral reef aquarium stocked with over 1,000 colorful tropical fish, including six sharks.

In addition, the hotel contains a habitat for rare white tigers belonging to performers Siegfried & Roy, and another for six Atlantic bottlenose dolphins, a site of fascinating educational tours. The Mirage corporation has been active in protesting fishing practices harmful to dolphins and serves only "dolphin-safe" tuna in its restaurants. And no fur is sold in Mirage boutiques.

Rooms are decorated in prints and color palettes taken from exotic flowers, birds, and undersea life in the tropics. Bamboo/rattan furnishings and brightly colored whimsical artworks enhance the South Seas theme. In-room amenities include remote-control color cable TVs with in-house information stations, phones with FAX and computer jacks, and AM/FM alarm-clock radios. Tower deluxe rooms have a more sophisticated look—they're done in black and white with mauve and teal accents and offer upgraded bath amenities.

Further up the price scale are gorgeous executive kings done in garden/resort motifs and offering large whirlpool tubs. Accommodations are housed in three 30-story towers.

Dining **Kokomo's,** situated in the tropical rain forest atrium, offers seating under bamboo-thatched roofing and trellised bougainvillea vines. Comfortable upholstered rattan furnishings and candlelit white-linened tables—some overlooking lagoons and waterfalls—are set amid lofty palms and giant ferns. The menu features steaks, chops, prime rib, and seafood, supplemented by burgers and tropical salads at lunch. Dinner entrées $14.50–$38.

Mikado, under a starlit sky at night, offers diners a candlelit setting with a sunken tropical rock garden, lotus pond, and sheltering pines. Teppanyaki cooking is featured along with à la carte Japanese specialties and a sushi bar. Dinner only; entrées $11–$20.

At **Moongate,** also under a starlit sky, seating is in an open courtyard defined by classical Chinese architectural facades and tiled rooflines. White doves perch on cherry tree branches, and intricately hand-carved walls frame a moon-gate tableau. The menu offers Cantonese and Szechuan specialties. Dinner only; most entrées $14–$17.

A cobblestone passage evoking a European village street leads to **Restaurant Riva,** a very pretty dining room predominantly decorated in peach tones, with raw silk wall coverings and upholstery. Candlelit at night, its walls are hung with gilt-framed still-life paintings, windows with swagged draperies. Sophisticated northern Italian fare is served. Dinner only; entrées $11.50–$27.

Off the same quaint street is the **Bistro,** a charming belle-époque setting with rich mahogany paneling, art nouveau designs on mirrored walls, Toulouse-Lautrec–style murals, and pink-clothed tables lit by shaded brass oil lamps. Fare is French/continental, ranging from escargots in brioche to rack of lamb in mustard/honey glaze encrusted with chopped pecans and served with avocado/lemon butter sauce. Dinner only; entrées $16–$30.

The circular **California Pizza Kitchen,** under a thatch-roofed dome, is in the center of the casino overlooking the race and sports book. A bank of video monitors lets you follow the action while dining on oak-fired pizzas with toppings ranging from duck sausage to goat cheese. Calzones, salads, and pasta dishes are served here, too. Open 11am–11pm Sun–Thurs, till 2am Fri–Sat; all entrées under $10.

The **Caribe Café** is the Mirage's festive 24-hour coffee shop, and it keeps to the tropical theme with bamboo furnishings upholstered in bright tropical colors, murals of jungle foliage, and planters of birds of paradise. It's designed to evoke an open-air Caribbean village. Even the entranceway is lined with faux banana palms and mango trees.

Additional food and beverage facilities include **Coconuts,** an attractive ice-cream parlor; the **Paradise Café,** an al fresco terrace with umbrella tables overlooking the pool (drinks and light fare are served); the **Lagoon Saloon** in the rain forest, specializing in tropical drinks (the bartop is a glass-covered beach strewn with seashells) and offering live music; the **Baccarat Bar,** where a pianist

IMPRESSIONS

Supercalafragilisticexpialadocious!
—GOVERNOR BOB MILLER'S REACTION UPON
FIRST VISITING THE MIRAGE.

---

entertains nightly; the poolside **Dolphin Bar;** and the **Sports Bar** in the casino. See also **"Buffets"** in Chapter 6.

Services 24-hour room service, 24-hour concierge, overnight shoeshine on request, morning newspaper delivery.

Facilities Casino, car-rental desk, shops (designer boutiques for men and women, logo/Siegfried & Roy merchandise, costume jewelry, gifts, activewear), unisex hairdresser and salon offering all beauty services (waxing, body treatments, facials, and much more), state-of-the-art video game arcade, business-services center.

The Mirage health club is the most extensive hotel facility in town, offering a large selection of Nautilus, Universal, Cybex, and Keiser equipment, treadmills, stair machines, Gravitron, free weights, sauna, steam, whirlpool, and massage.

Waterfalls cascade into the hotel's immense swimming pool (it has a quarter-mile shoreline) in a lush tropical setting where lagoons link palm-lined islands. Kids will enjoy big pool slides. Free swimming lessons and water aerobics classes take place daily. Private poolside cabanas equipped with phones, free drinks, refrigerators, misting systems, rafts, and radios can be rented for $75 a day.

CONVENTION CENTER AREA/ A CASINO HOTEL

LAS VEGAS HILTON, 3000 Paradise Rd. at Riviera Blvd.,

 FROMMER'S SMART TRAVELER: HOTELS

1. Try to avoid visiting Las Vegas during busy holiday weekends and when major conventions are in town. To find out the latter call the **Las Vegas Convention and Visitors Authority** (tel. 800/332-5333).
2. Travel during the week if possible; rates are lowest Sunday through Thursday.
3. Bargain with the reservations clerk. An unoccupied room nets a hotel zero dollars, and whatever you pay is better than that.
4. Use reservations services such as **City-Wide Reservations** (tel. 800/733-6644); they obtain lower rates by booking rooms in volume.
5. Ask about special discounts for students, corporate employees, senior citizens, or military personnel.

Las Vegas, NV 89109. Tel. 702/732-5111 or toll free 800/732-7117. Fax 702/732-5249. 2900 rms, 274 suites. A/C TV TEL

$ Rates: Single or double $85–$175, suites $250–$750. Extra person $20. Children of any age free in parents' room. Off-season rates may be lower, subject to availability. Inquire about attractively priced packages. AE, CB, DC, DISC, ER, JCB, MC, V. **Parking:** Free (self and valet).

Its 375-foot tower dominating the desert horizon, this dazzling megahotel occupies 80 acres overlooking the blue lakes and manicured lawns of an adjacent 18-hole golf course. Barbra Streisand and Cary Grant presided at the hotel's 1969 opening, and Elvis Presley made a dramatic return to live performances at the Hilton Showroom the same year. The Hilton is simply magnificent—from its lobby and casino glittering with massive Austrian crystal chandeliers, to its comprehensive resort facilities, plush superstar showroom, and corps of distinguished restaurants—not to mention the largest convention and meeting facilities in the world. You will be impressed.

Rooms are fittingly attractive, decorated in southwestern colors (muted shades of turquoise, mauve, and peach) with verdigris accents and bleached oak furnishings. Paintings of cacti enhance this motif. Some rooms have sofas and/or dressing rooms; most contain in-room safes. All offer phones with computer jacks and voice mail messaging, AM/FM alarm-clock radios, and remote-control color cable TVs (cached in handsome armoires) with free HBO, Spectravision movie options, an in-house information channel, and video checkout capability.

Dining **Le Montrachet,** the Hilton's premier haute-cuisine French restaurant, is detailed in Chapter 6.

Also meriting a listing in Chapter 6 is **Paco's,** a very authentic Mexican restaurant.

Most dramatic of the Hilton's restaurants is **Benihana Village,** a spectacular pagoda-roofed Oriental fantasyland with meandering streams spanned by arched wooden bridges, cascading waterfalls, and lush plantings. It's the scene of an ongoing Disneyesque show nightly, with dancing waters bathed in colored lights, animated musical birds, a talking tree in a rock garden, claps of thunder and flashes of lightning, and electronic fireworks displays. Teppanyaki, hibachi, and robata (Japanese barbecue) dinners are featured. Dinner only; entrées (including soup, salad, rice, green tea, and several side dishes) mostly $12.75–$24.50; combination dinners $26.75–$35.50.

The adjoining **Garden of the Dragon,** presided over by a fiery-eyed dragon atop a pagoda, has seating in chinoiserie chairs amid lush tropical greenery and bamboo groves. From here, you can view the above-mentioned show at Benihana. The menu offers regional Chinese specialties. You might begin with panfried pot stickers (dumplings) served with chili sauce and vinegar and follow up with an entrée of spicy Szechuan kung pao chicken, whole Peking duck, Mongolian beef, or Cantonese steamed fish in ginger soy sauce; Thai fried noodles are yet another option. Dinner only; entrées $12.50–$36 (less for rice, noodle, and vegetable dishes).

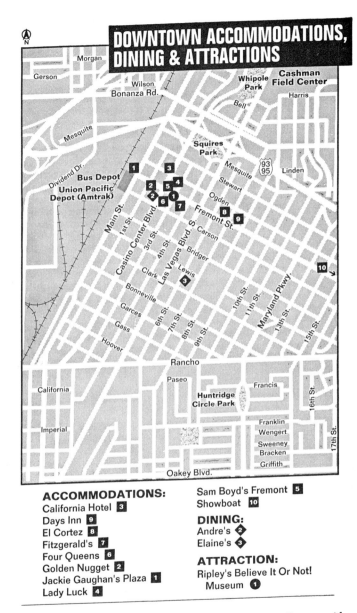

DOWNTOWN ACCOMMODATIONS, DINING & ATTRACTIONS

ACCOMMODATIONS:
California Hotel **3**
Days Inn **9**
El Cortez **8**
Fitzgerald's **7**
Four Queens **6**
Golden Nugget **2**
Jackie Gaughan's Plaza **1**
Lady Luck **4**

Sam Boyd's Fremont **5**
Showboat **10**

DINING:
Andre's **2**
Elaine's **3**

ATTRACTION:
Ripley's Believe It Or Not!
Museum **1**

Andiamo, a charming Italian *ristorante,* seats diners amid planters of ficus trees and weathered columns. Decorated in soft hues (peach, beige, muted gray-greens), its cream walls are hung with scenic paintings of Italy. A gleaming copper cappuccino machine sits atop a marble table, and above the brass- and copper-accented exhibition kitchen is a colorful display of Italian food products. All pasta served here is made fresh on the premises. Northern Italian specialties range from pan-sautéed New York steak with a rosemary-garlic Barolo red wine sauce to bow-tie pasta tossed with roasted duck meat, wild mushrooms, white beans, and parmesan cheese in a white wine sauce. Order tiramisù for dessert. Dinner only; entrées $12–$23.75.

The **Hilton Steakhouse** specializes in mahogany-broiled prime cut, corn-fed beef—served with parsleyed lemon-garlic butter—and fresh seafood. Steaks, chops, chicken, and pork ribs are served with salad, cheese-topped sourdough bread, and fresh corn on the cob or baked potato. Seafood dishes, such as lobster tails or grilled Norwegian salmon in cilantro-lime butter, come with the same accompaniments but substitute Navajo rice (studded with red peppers and pine nuts) for corn and potato options. Traditional desserts include hot apple pie topped with Häagen-Dazs ice cream. The rustic interior, under a simulated starlit sky, has pine-paneled walls hung with cowboy/ranch artifacts and portraits of legendary westerners Louis L'Amour, William Boyd, Wild Bill Hickock, Zane Grey, and Frederic Remington. Tables are lit by big brass candle lamps.

Another beef eatery is the **Barronshire Room,** where an English club ambience derives from high-backed burgundy leather booths, crystal chandeliers and sconces, and walls hung with gilt-framed landscape and still-life paintings. The restaurant is patterned after the renowned Barronshire Inn in southern England. Savory prime rib, carved tableside from silver carts, is served with Yorkshire pudding, mashed potatoes, creamed horseradish, and salad. Other options are grilled salmon and chicken in Dijon mustard cream sauce, both served with salad and rice pilaf. For dessert, the chocolate soufflé is *de rigueur.*

The southwest-themed **Socorro Springs Café** is one of my favorite round-the-clock hotel coffee shops. Though seating 400, it divides into intimate, softly lit dining areas. Carpeted in Aztec motif, with rough-hewn beams overhead, its cream stucco walls are hung with historic photographs of Mexico, Native American rugs, and buffalo shields. Baskets and pottery are on display. You can get anything from light fare to a full-course dinner here.

There are nine bar/lounges at the Hilton. In addition the **Garden Snack Bar** serves the pool deck, the **Paddock Snack Bar** in the race and sports book features pizza, sandwiches, and other light fare items (not oats), and the **Casino Lounge** offers nightly entertainment. See also buffet listings in Chapter 6. *Note:* Children 12 and under dine in any Hilton restaurant for half the listed menu prices.

Services 24-hour room service (when you order breakfast it comes with a complimentary morning paper), shoeshine for men.

Facilities Casino, car-rental desk, tour and show desks, travel agency, shops (see Chapter 10 for details), two video game arcades (a large one in the North Tower and a smaller pool area facility), beauty salon/barbershop.

The third-floor roof comprises a beautifully landscaped 8-acre recreation deck with a vast swimming pool, a 24-seat whirlpool spa, six Har-Tru tennis courts lit for night play, a pro shop, Ping-Pong, and a nine-hole putting green. Also on this level is a luxurious, 17,000-square-foot, state-of-the-art health club offering Nautilus and Universal equipment, Lifecycles, treadmills, rowing machines, three whirlpool spas, steam, sauna, massage, and tanning beds. Guests are totally pampered: all workout clothing and toiletries are provided; there are comfortable TV lounges stocked with magazines; complimentary soft drinks and juices are served in the canteen; and beauty services include manicures, pedicures, salt and soap rubs, facials, and oxygen pep-up.

A unique Hilton facility is its Youth Hotel in the North Tower, designed for children 3 to 18. It even has overnight accommodation for 24 youngsters. Activities for teens include Ping-Pong and pool tables, air hockey, shuffleboard, and foosball. Suitable arts and crafts materials are supplied for all age groups, and preschoolers enjoy a playground, blocks, toys, and puzzles. Kids can also get involved in planning and staging magic or variety shows. The Youth Hotel is staffed by fully accredited childcare professionals. Complete food service is available. Hours are 9am–10pm Sun–Thurs, till midnight Fri–Sat. For details call 702/732-5706.

2. EXPENSIVE

This category includes mostly multifacility megahotels that are very similar to the above-listed properties. They're just a tad less spectacular. Also in this category are some exclusive noncasino properties.

ON THE STRIP/CASINO HOTELS

BALLY'S, 3645 Las Vegas Blvd. S., at Flamingo Rd., Las Vegas, NV 89109. Tel. 702/739-4111 or toll free 800/634-3434. Fax 702/794-2413. 2,563 rms, 265 suites. A/C TV TEL
$ Rates: $84–$109 single or double; concierge floor $129–$165 single or double with breakfast; suites $175–$1,500. Extra person $10. Children 18 and under free in parents' room. AE, CB, DC, JCB, MC, V. **Parking:** Free (self and valet).

You'll notice that Bally's is one of the most cheerful hotels on the Strip the minute you step from its glittering porte-cochere entranceway into the festival-themed casino. Light and airy, it has colorful confetti-motif carpeting and bunches of helium balloons tied to the gaming tables. A virtual "city within a city," as self-contained as the Biosphere, Bally's offers a vast array of casino games, superb restaurants, entertainment options, shops, and services. You need never step outside.

Since this used to be the MGM Grand, hallways are still lined with photographs of studio movie greats, and there are gold stars on room doors. Every guest is a star. Accommodations are large and attractively decorated in three color schemes—black and white, shades of mauve, or earth tones—with brass lamps and accents and handsome mahogany furnishings. All have sofas. Marble baths offer a full complement of bath amenities. Remote-control color TVs offer pay-movie options, video checkout, and even credit-card cash-advance capability. And there are candy, soda, and ice machines on every floor. Guests on the 22nd floor (Club Concierge) have the use of a plush private lounge where gratis continental breakfast and afternoon hors d'oeuvres are served. They also enjoy added amenities such as nightly turn down and morning newspaper delivery.

Dining **Gigi,** designed after a grand salon at Versailles, offers an ornate setting of crystal chandeliers, gilded plasterwork and trellising, and elegantly draped private alcoves backed by gilt-framed mirrors. Beautifully appointed tables are lit by shaded candle lamps. A harpist plays during dinner, and tableside flambé preparations add theatrical panache. Fare is classic French haute cuisine. You might begin with an appetizer of escargots bourguignon, followed by an entrée of tournedos de boeuf Rossini (with goose liver and truffles), and a dessert of crêpes Suzette. Dinner only; entrées $26–$34.

Barrymore's Steakhouse, named after the first family of American theater, evokes a posh private club. Gleaming brass chandeliers are suspended from a dark-stained oak and mahogany ceiling. Seating, at crisply white-linened tables, is in leopard skin-upholstered booths and black lacquer chairs. And walls are hung with large decorative copper medallions. A traditional steak and seafood menu is featured. Fare is first-rate, complemented by a very extensive wine list. Dinner only; entrées $17–$32.

Caruso's is yet another elegant precinct with crystal chandeliers and brass sconces, sienna velvet walls hung with gilt-framed mirrors, and seating in large, comfortable silk damask–upholstered chairs. Flowers grace every white-linened table. The fare is California-influenced Italian. Entrées run the gamut from grilled tuna steak with capers to bow-tie pasta tossed with chicken, porcini mushrooms, and sun-dried tomatoes in tomato cream sauce. Dinner only; entrées $11.25–$23. Caruso's is also the setting for Bally's famed Sterling Sunday brunch (see Chapter 6 for details).

Grapes is a pristine little eatery with bleached wood walls and marble floors. It's whimsically decorated with cute paintings of fish and Miró-like abstract designs. Light continental breakfast is served here, but primarily this is a wine and seafood bar serving raw oysters and the like. A goodly selection of wines and champagnes is available by the glass, or you might stop by for espresso or cappuccino and dessert. Excellent pizzas here, too. Also notable: a complete lunch for $5.95 and a full dinner for $9.95; the latter includes clam chowder or Caesar salad, an entrée such as roast prime rib with horseradish sauce, baked potato, vegetable, apple pie, and coffee. Open 7:30am–2pm and 4:30–11pm; all items under $10.

The Coffee Shop, bright and cheerful with red and blue upholstered chairs at bleached oak tables and murals of street scenes on the walls, is Bally's 24-hour facility. It offers all the expected Vegas coffee shop fare from snacks to full-course meals.

There's also a **Swensen's** on the premises, serving croissant and grilled sourdough sandwiches, salads, and, of course, malts, shakes, and sundaes. A good choice for people with kids. There are two casino bars; a poolside bar called **On the Rocks** specializes in tropical drinks; and the **Terrace Café,** a poolside eatery with umbrella tables under a striped awning offers light fare during the day. See also buffet listings in Chapter 6.

Services 24-hour room service, guest-services desk, shoeshine.

Facilities Casino, tour and show desks, car-rental desk, two video game arcades (a small one next to Swensen's and a state-of-the-art arcade called Aladdin's Castle), shopping arcade (details in Chapter 10), two wedding chapels, hairdresser/barber.

Bally's has a state-of-the-art health spa offering a full complement of Universal equipment, rowing machines, Lifecycles, treadmills, steam, sauna, whirlpool, massage, tanning bed, facials, salt rubs, and more (the facility is currently undergoing a $1.4 million renovation). There are 10 Har-Tru tennis courts, seven lit for night play, with a pro shop (lessons are available). A gorgeous palm-fringed sun deck surrounded by lush tropical plantings centers on an Olympic-size swimming pool and whirlpool. Weekends reggae bands entertain poolside. You can rent a private cabana with a stocked refrigerator (soft drinks and juices), newspapers, rafts, and a private phone for $65 a day.

FLAMINGO HILTON, 3555 Las Vegas Blvd. S., between Sands Ave. and Flamingo Rd., Las Vegas, NV 89109. Tel. 702/733-3111 or toll free **800/732-2111. Fax** 702/733-3353. 3,112 rms, 209 suites. A/C TV TEL

$ Rates: $59–$119 single or double, $200–$480 suite. Extra person $16. Children 18 and under free in parents' room. AE, CB, DC, DISC, ER, JCB, OPTIMA, MC, V. **Parking:** Free (self and valet).

The Flamingo has changed a great deal since Bugsy Siegel opened his 105-room oasis "in the middle of nowhere" in 1946. It was so luxurious for its time that even the janitors wore tuxedos. Jimmy Durante was the opening headliner, and the wealthy and famous flocked to the tropical paradise of swaying palms, lagoons, and waterfalls. Today the Flamingo is a senior citizen on the Strip with a colorful history but a fresh, new look. The grounds are still lush, and the original palms and sycamores are complemented by Russian and Chinese elms and olive trees, cobblestone pathways, fountains, and flower gardens. Siegel's dream of building "a real class joint" has been fulfilled.

Room decor in the over-3,000-room Tower varies considerably. Some rooms are decorated in shades of soft blue and peach for a resort look enhanced by pretty fabrics, light painted-wood furnishings, and lovely watercolors of tropical scenes. Other color schemes focus on soft earth tones, forest green, or coral. The hotel's original Oregon Building garden rooms have a kind of old-fashioned glitz. These, of course, include Bugsy's vast suite, into which he built trap door escape routes and tunnels, most of which are still extant. (Bugsy's suite is available at $400 per night.) Tower rooms offer panoramic views, garden rooms overlook the verdant grounds. Most accommodations have in-room safes, and all offer AM/FM alarm-clock radios and remote-control color TVs with pay-movie options, in-house information and gaming-instruction stations, a keno channel, video checkout, message retrieval, and account review.

Dining The Old West–themed **Beef Barron,** heralded by golden steer heads and a mural of a cattle roundup, is a "steak house forged in the spirit of our first great cattle ranchers." It has quality

IMPRESSIONS

*Wages are getting higher and hours are getting shorter. People
have got to have a place to spend their money.*
—CASINO MAGNATE KIRK KERKORIAN ON LAS VEGAS IN 1970

western art on the walls, steer-horn chandeliers, a mounted display of
antique guns, and potted cacti. The menu features sizzling steaks,
prime rib, barbecued chicken, roast duckling, fresh seafood, and rack
of lamb. Entrées come with "Texas caviar" (black-eyed peas vinaigrette), salad, vegetable, and ranch bread with jalapeño cheddar.
Flaming desserts (bananas Foster, cherries jubilee) are a specialty.
Dinner only; entrées $15.50–$23.

Fronted by a tiered terra-cotta fountain, **Alta Villa** is designed to
suggest an Italian village, with a vaulted ceiling, trellised grape arbors,
lots of plants, and grapevine-motif carpeting on flagstone floors. A
pretty ceramic-tiled exhibition kitchen is a focal point. Traditional
Italian entrées include scampi with pasta and fresh vegetables, pizzas,
and chicken piccata. Dinner only; entrées $8.75–$18.

A red ricksha sits outside the **Peking Market,** the interior of
which simulates an open marketplace in a bustling Chinese city.
Corrugated tin roofing, rough-hewn beams and columns, packing
crates, and shelves crammed with canned foodstuffs—not to mention a photomural of an actual Chinese market—enhance the
illusion. A central wood-burning brick oven casts a warm glow.
There's a wide choice of entrées including eagle's nest beef (shredded
beef stir-fried with Chinese vegetables and served in a nest), smoked
duck with Chinese plum sauce and ho gyn bread, and stir-fried
calamari with onions and peppers in a spicy black-bean sauce. Dinner
only; entrées mostly $8–$14.

The **Flamingo Room** is tropically themed—decorated in sea-
foam green and coral with potted ferns, pink neon tubing overhead,
and flamingo-motif chandeliers. A wall of windows overlooks the
pool, and big horseshoe-shaped booths make for comfortable
seating. It serves full breakfasts, and the dinner menu lists dozens of
gourmet items ranging from broiled Norwegian salmon béarnaise to
chicken Cordon Bleu. Dinner entrées include an extensive salad bar.
An early bird prime rib dinner served from 5–7pm is $7.65. Open
7am–noon, and 5–11pm; dinner entrées $15.95–$21.

Adjoining the above (separated by an etched-glass wall) is the
delightfully whimsical Food Fantasy, decorated with murals and
paintings of flamingos—wending their way through a Las Vegas
buffet line, gambling in a casino, and working out in a health club. It's
basically a fancy cafeteria open 6am–midnight.

Sushi Bar Hamada, a small facility in the lower shopping
arcade, serves Japanese breakfasts (egg, miso soup, fish, rice, and
seaweed), sushi, tempura, noodle dishes, and other specialties—
including Japanese beers—at lunch and dinner. Open 6:30am–
12:30am; Japanese breakfast $10, lunch entrées $8–$18, dinner
entrées $15–$26.50.

Lindy's Deli, a 24-hour coffee shop, is attractively decorated in southwestern colors (mauve, teal, and peach), with painted wood sculptures and pretty paintings. It offers the usual array of Las Vegas coffee shop fare, here including appetizing smoked fish platters (salmon, whitefish, sturgeon) with bagels and cream cheese.

See also buffet listings in Chapter 6. Off the casino is **Caravan Corner,** a casbahlike cocktail lounge with seating in tentlike curtained alcoves under minarets. The **Casino Lounge** offers live bands for dancing nightly. From the street-level **Promenade Bar** you can watch the bustling action on the Strip. And the **Terrace Café Snack Bar,** an adjunct of Lindy's, serves light fare, cocktails, and ice-cream sundaes poolside.

Services 24-hour room service, free gaming lessons, guest-services desk, multilingual services (interpreters available for over 35 languages, room-service menus and gaming guides available in six languages).

Facilities Casino, car-rental desk, tour and show desks, full-service beauty salon, travel agent, video game arcade, four all-weather championship tennis courts lit for night play (lessons and tennis clinics available), pro shop, shopping arcade (see Chapter 10 for details).

The Flamingo's vast fountain-centered swimming pool and palm-fringed sun deck take advantage of the hotel's gorgeous landscaping. A nice feature of the pool is its seating niches, where you can cool off without swimming—perhaps while reading a book or chatting with a friend. A large Jacuzzi spa adjoins. A smaller, but still nice-sized, second pool is the centerpiece of the two-story garden-room section.

There's a health club with treadmills, Lifecycles, Universal equipment, free weights, sauna, steam, a TV lounge, and hot and cold whirlpools. Exercise tapes are available, and spa services include massage, soap rub, salt glow, tanning beds, and oxygen pep-up.

RIVIERA HOTEL & CASINO, 2901 Las Vegas Blvd. S., at Riviera Blvd., Las Vegas, NV 89109. Tel. 702/734-5110 or toll free 800/634-6753. Fax 702/794-9451. 1,978 rms, 158 suites. A/C TV TEL

$ Rates: $59–$95 single or double, $125–$310 suite. Extra person $12. Children under 12 free in parents' room. Inquire about "Gambler's Spree" packages. AE, CB, DC, MC, V. **Parking:** Free (self and valet).

Opened in 1955 (Liberace cut the ribbon and Joan Crawford was official hostess of opening ceremonies), the Riviera is styled after the luxurious casino resorts of the Côte d'Azur. Its original nine stories made it the first "high-rise" on the Strip. Several towers later, the present-day Riviera is as elegant as ever.

Accommodations are richly decorated with handsome mahogany furnishings and burgundy or teal velvet bedspreads with matching gold-tasseled drapes. Half the rooms here offer pool views. Amenities include in-room safes and remote-control color cable TVs with pay-movie options and an in-house information station.

Dining **Kristofer's,** a candlelit steak and seafood restaurant overlooking the pool, has a tropical look with rattan chairs at copper-topped bamboo tables, overhead fans, and potted ferns. An exhibition kitchen adds excitement. Prix-fixe dinners ($19.95) include a glass of wine, a crock of cheese spread with crackers, salad, potato or rice, freshly baked bread and butter, and an entrée such as prime rib, steak (New York sirloin, porterhouse, or filet mignon), lamb chops, or broiled lobster. The adjoining lounge serves poolside fare. Open for dinner and Sunday brunch buffets.

Ristorante Italiano, under a simulated starlit sky, has a windowed wall backed by murals of Venice. Decorated in burgundy and mauve, it's a romantic setting with framed Italian art reproductions adorning brick walls and seating in roomy tapestry-upholstered booths. Classic Italian specialties are featured, among them fried calamari in spicy pizzaiola sauce, chicken cacciatore, and fettuccine Alfredo. Dinner only; most entrées $10.95 to $23.50 (veal and lobster dishes are pricier).

Kady's Brasserie is the Riveria's very cheerful 24-hour restaurant, with white tile walls, marble-topped tables, and seating in bright leather-upholstered red, blue, and yellow booths. A wall of windows overlooks the pool. Along with the usual coffee shop fare, Kady's menu offers Jewish deli specialties such as pastrami and corned beef sandwiches, bagels with Nova lox and cream cheese, chopped liver, herring in cream sauce, and matzoh ball soup.

Rik' Shaw (don't ask me what the punctuation means) features Chinese fare in an elegant candlelit room with crystal chandeliers and mirrored columns. Mauve velvet walls are hung with gilt-framed Chinese paintings. The fan-shaped menu offers traditional Cantonese specialties—lo mein, shrimp with lobster sauce, moo shu pork, beef with oyster sauce, and more. Dinner only; entrées $9.50–$22.95 (most are under $15).

An excellent choice for families is the **Mardi Gras Food Court,** which unlike most of its genre is extremely attractive. White canvas umbrella tables, Toulouse-Lautrec–style murals, and etched-glass dividers combine to create a comfortable French café ambience. Your food choices include a Burger King, pizza, tacos, rotisserie chicken, Chinese fare, deli sandwiches, gyros and falafel, Baskin-Robbins's 31 ice cream flavors and frozen yogurts, and La Patisserie's fresh-baked pastries. The Food Court is adjacent to the video game arcade, so you can relax over espresso while the kids run off and play. Open daily 10:30am–midnight.

See also buffet listings in Chapter 6. There are two casino bars, **Delmonico's** and the **Bistro Lounge;** the latter offers nightly live entertainment (details in Chapter 11).

Services 24-hour room service, shoeshine.

Facilities Casino (one of the world's largest), large arcade with carnival and video games, well-equipped health club (Lifecycles, stair machines, full complement of Universal and Paramount machines, free weights, steam, sauna, tanning, facials, salt/soap rubs, massage), Olympic-size swimming pool and sun deck, wedding chapel, beauty salon/barbershop, comprehensive business-services center, America West airlines desk, tour and show desks, car-rental desk, shops (see Chapter 10 for details), two Har-Tru tennis courts lit for night play.

A unique facility is Par T Golf—video simulations of seven world-class championship golf courses projected on a large screen. You might choose simulated play, for instance, at Pebble Beach in

California or St. Mellion in England. You swing and see your ball racing down the fairway; a computer tells you how far—and how far off to the left or right—you hit the ball. Equally unique here: a wine-tasting booth operated by Lakeside Cellars, a northern California winery.

SANDS HOTEL CASINO, 3355 Las Vegas Blvd. S., just south of Sands Ave., Las Vegas, NV 89109. Tel. 702/733-5000 or toll free 800/634-6901. Fax 702/732-1047. 675 rms, 40 suites. A/C TV TEL

$ Rates: $59–$109 single or double, $150–$250 suite. Extra person $4. Children under 12 free in parents' room. AE, CB, DC, DISC, MC, V. **Parking:** Free (self and valet).

The Sands, opened in 1952, with new wings added here and there, is a familiar Las Vegas landmark. New York show producer and Copacabana nightclub owner Jack Entratter was one of its original backers, and he used his show-biz contacts to bring superstar entertainment and gorgeous showgirls to the Copa Room stage. Jimmy Durante, Red Skelton, Debbie Reynolds, Jerry Lewis, and the famed "Rat Pack" (Frank Sinatra, Sammy Davis, Jr., Joey Bishop, and Dean Martin) were among those who made regular appearances. Entratter's efforts not only put the Sands on the map but helped establish Las Vegas as America's entertainment capital.

From the streets you'll see only a scalloped 18-story white circular tower. Not obvious are 10 smaller units named after famous racetracks—Hollywood Park, Aqueduct, Triple Crown, and others—which are grouped over a wide expanse of palm-fringed gardens. A major renovation is underway at this writing; by the time you read this, all of these garden rooms—most with patios—will be newly redecorated. Tower rooms have silk-look wall coverings and French provincial oak furnishings. Though the tower is circular, rooms are sizable (not little wedges), with large mirrors behind the beds further enhancing the feeling of spaciousness. All are equipped with enormous armoires, AM/FM alarm-clock radios, and remote-control color cable TVs with Spectravision movie and hotel information channels, video account review, and video checkout. Rooms on the top four floors have balconies.

Dining The richly oak-paneled and chandeliered Regency Room, with black tufted-leather booths and white-linened tables, is adorned by classical statuary depicting Greek goddesses Venus and Athena. The restaurant serves a daily Italian luncheon buffet (see Chapter 6 for details) and traditional à la carte haute-cuisine dinners. It's the kind of place where you begin with appetizers like pâté de foie gras and crab-stuffed artichoke hearts; entrées include filet mignon Wellington, Long Island duckling à l'orange, and roast rack of lamb bouquetière. Tableside flambé preparations are a specialty, so you can proceed to a dramatic finale with cherries jubilee or crêpes Suzette. Lunch $6.95, most dinner entrées $15.50–$24.50.

House of Szechwan, entered via imposing brass doors, is a most elegant setting for Chinese meals. Diners are ensconced in black lacquer chinoiserie chairs or forest-green velvet booths at pink-clothed tables lit by candles in pagoda-shaped holders. Soft lighting emanates from tassled lanterns and fan-shaped sconces, and brass-trimmed archways create intimate dining areas. The menu features both Cantonese and Szechuan specialties. Among the former are moo shu pork served with Chinese pancakes and hoisin sauce and "double happiness"—a combination of shrimp and scallops with fresh vegetables in wine sauce. The latter include jumbo king pao shrimp (with peanuts in hot chili sauce) and diced curried chicken with vegetables. Dinner only; most entrées $11.75–$15.25. A full early bird meal served weekdays 4–6pm is $6.95.

The Garden Terrace, the 24-hour coffee shop, is large and pleasant with big planters of greenery and a windowed wall overlooking the pool and flower beds. A wide-ranging menu offers such diverse choices as blackened Cajun chicken, Greek salad, Mexican fajitas, and steamed Maine lobster with drawn butter. A full prime rib dinner served 11am–2am is just $4.95.

The **Ice Cream Parlor & Deli,** an informal cafeteria serving light fare (salads, pizza, deli sandwiches, sundaes), adjoins the Garden Terrace, there's a seafood bar in the casino, and the **Winners Circle Lounge** offers live nightly entertainment.

Services 24-hour room service.

Facilities Casino, tour and show desks, video game arcade, shops (gift shop, men's and women's clothing, logo items), beauty salon, nine-hole putting green.

There's a V-shaped pool with a tropically landscaped sun deck and a poolside bar. A smallish men's and women's health club (men have slightly more facilities, among them a Universal 21-station unit and a stair machine) offers treadmills, Lifecycles, rowing machines, and cross-country ski machines. Both sections also feature whirlpools, sauna, steam, and massage.

TROPICANA RESORT & CASINO, 3801 Las Vegas Blvd. S., at Tropicana Ave., Las Vegas, NV 89109. Tel. 702/739-2222 or toll free 800/634-4000. Fax 702/739-2469. 1,788 rms, 120 suites (casino use only). A/C TV TEL

$ Rates: $65–$95 single or double. Extra person $10. Children under 18 free in parents' room. AE, CB, DC, MC, V. **Parking:** Free (self and valet).

Billing itself as "the island of Las Vegas," the Tropicana is a South Seas resort right on the Strip. Heralded by 35-foot Easter Island heads, a 25-foot waterfall, outrigger canoes, and flaming torchiers, it comprises a lush tropical landscape of manicured lawns, towering palms, oleanders, weeping willows, and crepe myrtles. There are dozens of waterfalls, thousands of exotic flowers, lagoons, aquariums, and koi ponds. Flamingos, swans, macaws, toucans, and Brazilian parrots live on "the island," their effect enhanced by in-ground speakers emitting jungle sounds and calypso music.

Rooms in the Paradise Tower are traditional-looking with French provincial furnishings and turn-of-the-century-look wallpapers. The newer Island Tower rooms have a more tropical resort feel. They're decorated in pastel colors like pale pink and sea-foam green, with splashy tropical-print bedspreads and bamboo furnishings; some have beds with mirrored walls and ceilings. All Trop rooms offer couches, in-room safes, AM/FM alarm-clock radios, and remote-control color TVs with Spectravision movies, account review, video checkout, and channels for in-house information and gaming instruction.

Dining Rhapsody is the Trop's crystal-chandeliered and candlelit gourmet room, with big velvet-upholstered burgundy booths and comfortable teal velvet armchairs complemented by leaf-motif carpeting in the same hues. A wall of windows overlooks the pool area's waterfalls and tropical plantings. A pianist entertains while you dine. The French/continental menu features items like beef Wellington and roast duckling in black raspberry liqueur. Dinner Fri–Mon; entrées $17.95–$29.95. A lavish Sunday brunch here with unlimited champagne is $17.95, $10.95 for children 10 and under.

Massive stone lions flank the entrance to **Mizuno's,** an attractive Japanese restaurant featuring teppanyaki dining. A meandering glass "stream" lit by Tivoli lights suggests running water, and sprigs of cherry blossom, Japanese lanterns, and an ancient temple bell complete the appropriately Eastern setting. Most of the food (shrimp, lobster, steak, vegetables) is prepared at your table grill by chefs who wield cooking knives with the panache of samurai warriors. The show is part of the fun. Western desserts like strawberry cheesecake and Häagen-Dazs ice cream are an option. Dinner only; most entrées $12–$24.

El Gaucho is elegantly rustic, with an Argentinian steak-house ambience comprised of rough-hewn beams overhead, burgundy leather booths, candlelit ceramic-tile tables, and pecky pine walls hung with cowhides, serapes, branding irons, and gaucho gear. Steak, prime rib, and seafood come with traditional accompaniments. Dinner only; entrées $17.95–$29.95.

Di Martino's, a cozy little Italian eatery, has white stucco walls, forest-green carpeting and upholstery, and lace-curtained windows overlooking a waterfall. Traditional Italian fare—pasta dishes, scampi, chicken parmigiana—is served. Dinner only; entrées $12.95–$21.95.

Winners, the Trop's 24-hour aqua and coral coffee shop, is underwater themed with murals of tropical fish, an actual reef aquarium, and reef-motif carpeting. The casino-themed menu offers "jungle jackpot" salads, "dice pit" sandwiches, and "sweet deal" desserts. A 10-ounce prime rib dinner is $11.95.

Another casual eatery is the three-tiered **Tropics,** with fountains, streams, and waterfalls running under, through, and around it and windows overlooking the tropical water park. Seating is in bamboo fan-backed chairs at umbrella tables, and the bar is under thatched roofing. Tropics' coffee shop menu lists sandwiches, salads, burgers, and a few hot entrées. On the island note, there's a macadamia-nut sundae for dessert. Breakfast and lunch only.

Down a level from the casino, in the Atrium Shopping area, is a **Baskin-Robbins** ice cream and frozen-yogurt parlor and **Antonio's Pizza Deli,** purveying hot dogs, pizza, deli sandwiches, and other light fare. The Trop's buffet room is discussed in Chapter 6. There's karaoke (your chance at pop fame) in the **Tropics Lounge** on Tuesday nights. The **Coconut Grove Bar** serves the pool area.

Services 24-hour room service, shoeshine.

Facilities Casino, health club (Universal equipment, stair machines, treadmills, exercise bikes, steam, sauna, Jacuzzi, massage, and tanning room), video game arcade, tour and show desks, wedding chapel, car-rental desk, beauty salon and barbershop, travel agent, shops (jewelry, chocolates, florist, women's footwear, logo items, women's fashions, sports clothing, gifts, newsstand).

Three swimming pools (one Olympic size) and three whirlpool spas are located in a 5-acre water park with 30 splashing waterfalls, lagoons, and lush tropical plantings. One pool has a 110-foot waterslide, another a swim-up bar/blackjack table.

CONVENTION CENTER AREA/ A NONCASINO HOTEL

RESIDENCE INN BY MARRIOTT, 3225 Paradise Rd., between Desert Inn Rd. and Convention Center Dr., Las Vegas, NV 89109. Tel. 702/796-9300 or toll free 800/ 331-3131. 144 studios, 48 penthouses. A/C TV TEL

$ Rates (including continental breakfast): $90–$125 studios (for up to two people), $99–$175 penthouses (for up to four people). Extra person $10. Children of any age free in parents' room. AE, CB, DC, DISC, MC, V. **Parking:** Free (self).

 Marriott's excellent Residence Inns are designed to offer travelers the ultimate in homeyness and hospitality. Staying here is like having your own apartment in Las Vegas. The property occupies seven acres of perfectly manicured lawns, tropical foliage, and neat flower beds. It's a great choice for families and business travelers.

F FROMMER'S COOL FOR KIDS:
HOTELS

Circus Circus (see p. 96) This is my first choice if you're traveling with the family. The location is right in the center of the Strip, and the mezzanine level offers ongoing circus acts daily from 11am to midnight, dozens of carnival games, and a state-of-the-art arcade with over 300 video and pinball games. There are also child-oriented eateries (such as McDonald's) and two swimming pools.

Excalibur (see p. 98) Under the same ownership as the above, Excalibur features a whole floor of midway games, a large video game arcade, crafts demonstrations, free shows for kids (puppets, jugglers, magicians), and thrill cinemas. It, too, has child-oriented eateries and two swimming pools, not to mention *King Arthur's Tournament* (details in Chapter 11).

Las Vegas Hilton (see p. 59) The Hilton has a Youth Hotel for youngsters 3 to 18 which can even provide overnight lodging. A vast swimming pool is also on the premises.

Accommodations are in 24 condolike, two-story wood and stucco buildings, fronted by little gardens. They're decorated in mauve and gray with peach or teal carpeting and bleached wood furnishings, and most have working fireplaces. Studios have adjoining sitting rooms with sofas and armchairs, dressing areas, and fully equipped eat-in kitchens complete with dishwashers. Every guest gets a welcome basket of microwave popcorn, coffee, and a soft drink on check-in. In-room amenities include AM/FM alarm-clock radios and remote-control color TVs with visitor-information channels and VCRs (you can rent movies nearby), and all rooms have balconies or patios. Duplex penthouses, some with cathedral ceilings, add an upstairs bedroom (with its own bath, phone, TV, and radio) and a full dining room.

Dining A big continental buffet breakfast (fresh fruits, yogurts, cereals, muffins, bagels, pastries) is served each morning in a delightful cathedral-ceilinged lobby lounge with a working fireplace. There's comfortable seating amid planters of greenery. Daily papers are set out here each morning, there's a large-screen TV and a stereo for guest use, and a selection of toys, games, and books is available for children. Weekdays, the lounge serves up complimentary afternoon buffets with beverages (beer, wine, coffee, soda), fresh popcorn, and daily varying fare (soup/salad/sandwiches, tacos, Chinese, barbecue, spaghetti, and so on). Both breakfast and lunch afford opportunities to socialize with other guests—a nice feature if you're traveling alone.

Services Local restaurants deliver food, and there's also a complimentary food-shopping service. Maids wash your dishes.

Facilities Car-rental desk, barbecue grills, coin-op washers and dryers, sports court (paddle tennis, volleyball, basketball). There's a good-sized swimming pool and whirlpool with a sun deck partially shaded by a canvas tent top. Guests can use the health club next door at Marriott Courtyard (details below), as well as those of the nearby Las Vegas Athletic Club, a state-of-the-art facility.

NEAR THE STRIP/A CASINO HOTEL

RIO SUITE HOTEL & CASINO, 3770 W. Flamingo Rd., at I-15, Las Vegas, NV 89114. Tel. 702/252-7777 or toll free 800/888-1818. Fax 702/253-6090. 430 suites. A/C TV TEL

$ Rates: Single or double Sun–Thurs $83, Fri–Sat and holidays $99–$139. Extra person $10. Children under 12 free in parents' room. AE, CB, DC, MC, V. **Parking:** Free (self and valet).

The Rio's gorgeous palm-fringed facade heralds a luxurious tropical resort—an ongoing "carnivale," enhanced by turquoise and pink neon lighting within and Brazilian music emanating from the Ipanema Bar. Its sandy beach—the only one in Las Vegas—is the scene of festive Tuesday night beach parties featuring live bands, volleyball, limbo contests, and a vast outdoor buffet. Though you're a few minutes from the Strip, you won't miss it at this lively casino hotel.

The spacious suites (each one is 600 square feet) are, unequivocally, the most gorgeous rooms in town. Decorated in resort hues (peach, mauve, turquoise, coral) with splash-of-color accents, they feature bamboo furnishings, half-canopy beds, paintings of parrots and toucans in jungle settings, and beautiful tropical floral-print bedspreads and drapes. Each suite has a wraparound sofa and coffee table and an upholstered chaise longue. Your remote-control TV, perched on an ornate plaster pedestal, has pay-movie options. Large dressing rooms offer lots of closet space, full-length mirrors, and makeup lighting. Other pluses: two phones (table and bedside), an in-room safe, stunning bath, marble-topped refrigerator, and coffee maker. And you'll enjoy great views of the Strip from a windowed wall.

Dining The elegant marble-floored and scagliola-columned **Antonio's** centers on a magnificent marble display table under a crystal chandelier. Overhead, a recessed ceiling is painted to look like sky. Beautiful tropical murals and still-life paintings adorn pale green walls, seating is in comfortable peach velvet-upholstered armchairs, and candlelit tables are exquisitely appointed with Villeroy & Boch china. An exhibition kitchen adds a theatrical note to the proceedings. Classic Italian cuisine is featured, with many pasta selections and entrées ranging from cioppino to chicken marsala. Dinner only; entrées $10.50–$17.95.

The **Beach Café,** overlooking the swimming pool and sandy beach, is the Rio's 24-hour facility. Tropically festive, it has walls decorated with colorful jungle birds and animals and booths upholstered in bright floral prints. There's additional seating at canvas umbrella tables on an awninged terra-cotta patio. In addition to the expected coffee shop fare, the Café features Mexican and Polynesian/Chinese specialties. Homemade desserts are a plus.

The **All American Bar & Grille** steak house is as American as baseball and apple pie. It's warmly inviting, with oak plank flooring and a massive brick fireplace (ablaze in winter). TV monitors over the bar broadcast sporting events, and walls are hung with sporting paraphernalia and posters. The 50 state flags hang over the bar, while oversized American flags fly from rafters 20 feet above. All beers made in the United States are served here. The menu, featuring a 10-ounce pork ribs dinner for $9.95, proffers mesquite-grilled steaks and seafood at dinner, burgers, salads, and sandwiches at lunch. Lunch items $4.50–$11.25, dinner entrées $8.95–$15.95.

Sonny's Deli, off the casino, not only looks like a New York delicatessen but serves up a credible pastrami or corned beef on rye. Good pizza here, too. It's open from 10am to the wee hours daily.

The **Ipenama Bar** in the casino specializes in rum-based tropical drinks like the Copa banana—banana liqueur, blackberry brandy, dark rum, and grenadine. Tropical drinks are also served at the awninged **poolside bar.** See also buffet listings in Chapter 6.

Services 24-hour room service, guest-services desk, shoeshine, complimentary shuttle to/from Harrahs on the Strip.

Facilities Casino, car-rental desk, tour and show desks, unisex hair salon (all beauty services, including massage and facials), small video game arcade, small fitness room (stair machine, rowing machine, Lifecycle, four-station exercise machine), shops (gifts, clothing for the entire family, logo merchandise). The Rio's shell-shaped pool—complete with waterfall—is famous for its adjoining sand beach. Beautifully landscaped, the pool area also offers a whirlpool and volleyball setup.

NEAR THE STRIP/NONCASINO HOTELS

ALEXIS PARK RESORT, 375 E. Harmon Ave., between Koval Lane and Paradise Rd., Las Vegas, NV 89109. Tel. 702/796-3300 or toll free **800/582-2228.** Fax 702/796-4334. 500 suites. A/C MINIBAR TV TEL

$ Rates: $95–$150 single or double one-bedroom suite, $150–$375 one-bedroom loft suite, $235–$1,100 larger suite. Extra person $15. Children 18 and under free in parents' room. AE, CB, DC, DISC, JCB, MC, V. **Parking:** Free (self and valet).

A low-key atmosphere, luxurious digs, and superb service combine to make Alexis Park the hotel choice of many showroom headliners and visiting celebrities. Alan Alda, Alec Baldwin, Jerry Lewis, Whitney Houston, Robert de Niro, Tony Orlando, Dolly Parton, and Shirley MacLaine are just a few of the superstars who've chosen this resort's discreet elegance over the more seemingly glamorous Strip casino/hotels. It's the kind of place where you can get a phone at your restaurant table or your suit pressed at 3am.

You'll sense the difference the moment you approach the palm-fringed entranceway, fronted by lovingly tended flower beds and a rock waterfall. The elegant peach lobby, with Saltillo tile flooring, has comfortable sofas amid immense terra-cotta pots of ferns, cacti, and calla lilies. And there's notably fine artwork throughout the public areas.

Spacious suites (the smallest units here are 450 square feet) are decorated in light resort colors with taupe lacquer furnishings. Loft suites have high cathedral ceilings. All are equipped with refrigerators, wet bars, coffee makers, AM/FM alarm-clock radios, two-line phones (one in each room of your suite) with computer jacks and voice mail, and remote-control color cable TVs (also one in each room) with free HBO and pay-movie options. Over a third of the suites have working fireplaces and/or Jacuzzi tubs.

Dining Pegasus, an exquisite award-winning gourmet dining room, is detailed in Chapter 6.

The Market Place is a light and airy restaurant with a lofty ceiling, peach walls, teal carpeting, and furnishings upholstered in a whimsical tropical-motif chintz. White-linened tables are elegantly appointed with royal blue napkins wound in drinking glasses, and planters of greenery and canvas awnings make for a gardenlike ambience. It's open from 6am–3pm and 6–11pm. The menu offers homemade pasta dishes and fresh fish and seafood. At lunch there are hearty croissant sandwiches.

The fish-themed **Pisces Lounge,** under a 30-foot shallow-domed ceiling with planters of greenery cascading from tiers overhead, provides live entertainment Tues–Sun night (see Chapter 11) and serves drinks, liqueur-laced coffees, pasta snacks, and desserts—both inside and on a patio overlooking the pool.

Services 24-hour room service, concierge on duty 8am–

midnight, morning newspapers (*Wall Street Journal* and *USA Today*) delivered to your door each morning, gratis shuttle to "four corners" (intersection of the Strip and Flamingo Rd. and site of many top hotels) and to/from airport.

Facilities Gift shop, unisex hair salon, two Har-Tru tennis courts lit for night play (tennis instruction and clinics available).

Behind the hotel are beautifully landscaped grounds with palm trees and pines, streams and ponds spanned by quaint bridges, gazebos, rock gardens, flower beds, and oleanders. Here you'll find a large fountain-centered swimming pool, two smaller pools, cabana bars, a whirlpool spa, umbrella tables, table tennis, and a nine-hole putting green. Every Sunday from 3:30–10pm there's a "Sunsplash" poolside party and barbecue buffet with a steel drum band ($12 per person); it's open to the public.

An on-premises health club features a six-station Paramount workout machine, Stairmasters, Lifecycles, treadmills, whirlpool, massage, steam, and sauna.

SHEFFIELD INN, 3970 Paradise Rd., between Twain Ave. and Flamingo Rd., Las Vegas, NV 89109. Tel. 702/796-9000 or toll free 800/777-1700. Fax 702/796-9000, ext. 410. 228 rms, 51 suites. A/C TV TEL

$ Rates (including continental breakfast): $98 per room for executive and double queens, $120 for one-bedroom suites, $200 for two-bedroom suites. AE, CB, DC, DISC, ER, MC, V. **Parking:** Free (self).

Its four mission-style terra-cotta roofed stucco buildings forming a "U" around a large courtyard, the Sheffield Inn offers a tranquil alternative to the razzle-dazzle of Strip hotels. Though you're just a minute (and a gratis shuttle ride) from major casinos, you'll feel like you're staying in a countryside retreat. Lovely grounds, with manicured lawns, lovingly tended flower beds, and a charming stone fountain, offer rustic benches, lawn games (croquet, badminton, volleyball), barbecue grills, and picnic tables. All this, along with suite accommodations (most with kitchens) and a stock of children's movies and games at the front desk, makes the Sheffield a good choice for families.

Accommodations are attractively decorated with forest-green carpeting, pale-peach stucco walls, oak or maple furnishings, and pretty floral-print bedspreads and drapes. Executive rooms have one queen-sized bed, a small refrigerator, wet bar, and microwave oven. Double queens are larger, but have no kitchen facilities. Spacious one- and two-bedroom suites offer large living rooms with sofa beds, dining areas, full kitchens (refrigerator, microwave, stove, and sink; cutlery, dishes, and cookware supplied), and phones and TVs in every room. Most accommodations have patios or balconies, and all feature baths with oversized whirlpool tubs, remote-control satellite TVs with free Showtime movies, and VCRs (movies can be rented in the lobby).

Dining Continental breakfast (juice, cereals, toast and muffins, fresh fruit, beverages) is served daily in a comfortably furnished lounge with a working fireplace and large-screen TV tuned to a morning news show. Gratis newspapers are provided as well. Vending machines on the premises sell snack fare and frozen meals, a shopping center where you can buy food adjoins, and many restaurants are within easy walking distance.

Services Room service 10am–10pm from a nearby Italian restaurant, one of several offering free food delivery.

Facilities Car-rental desk, tours (arranged at front desk), coin-op washers and dryers, medium-sized swimming pool and adjoining whirlpool. Guests can use extensive facilities at two nearby health clubs. A free 24-hour shuttle offers pick up and return to/from the airport, major hotels (Stardust, Mirage, Aladdin, Excalibur, Las Vegas Hilton), and the Fashion Show Mall (during mall hours) and Las Vegas Convention Center.

DOWNTOWN/A CASINO HOTEL

GOLDEN NUGGET, 129 E. Fremont St., at Casino Center Blvd., Las Vegas, NV 89101. Tel. 702/385-7111 or toll free 800/634-3454. Fax 702/386-8362. 1,803 rms, 104 suites. A/C TV TEL

$ Rates: Single or double Sun–Thurs $58–$98, Fri–Sat $120–$140; suites $210–$750. Extra person $12. Children under 12 free in parents' room. AE, CB, DC, DISC, MC, V. **Parking:** Free (self and valet).

Gleaming white and gold in the Las Vegas sun, its surrounding streets lined with tall swaying palms, the Golden Nugget looks more like a luxurious Côte d'Azur resort than a downtown hotel. And it is. Opened in 1946, it was the first building in Las Vegas constructed specifically for casino gambling. When Steve Wynn acquired the property in 1972, it had a plush Old West/Victorian decor. In the next decade Wynn took down all the neon signs, western art, and turn-of-the-century furnishings and created a magnificent first-class European-style resort with a stunning chandeliered white-marble lobby (no casino games in view), mirrored ceiling, gleaming brass accents, and lavish floral arrangements gracing public areas. The Nugget's sun-dappled interior spaces are a welcome change from the Las Vegas tradition of dim lighting.

Resort-style rooms are fittingly charming—light and airy, with valanced beds, delightful floral-print bedspreads and draperies, and furnishings in rattan, bamboo, and light woods. They're equipped with remote-control color cable TVs and AM/FM alarm-clock radios.

Dining **Elaine's,** named for Steve Wynn's wife, is a gem. Details on this haute-cuisine restaurant in Chapter 6.

Stefano's, off a gorgeous marble-floored courtyard, offers a festive setting for northern Italian cuisine, complete with singing waiters. Seating is in red-white-and-green-striped satin-upholstered chairs at candlelit white-linened tables. Murals of Venice behind trellised "windows" are designed to look like scenery, Venetian glass chandeliers are suspended from a coffered ceiling, and baroque elaboration includes cupids, ornate columns, and gilt-framed mirrors. Your meal here might begin with panfried oysters in a garlic mayonnaise sauce, followed by salmon sautéed with arugula and radicchio on a spicy pesto sauce (perhaps with a side of pasta), or sautéed sirloin with black olives, onions, mushrooms, garlic, oregano, and pepperoncini. For dessert, perhaps fresh strawberries with zabaglione. Dinner only; entrées $9.95–$27.25.

California Pizza Kitchen, part of an upscale chain of pizza restaurants, is a plush precinct with a stained-glass dome, black marble tables, a black-and-white marble checkerboard floor, and an exhibition kitchen where white-hatted chefs tend a glowing oak-burning oven. In addition to pizzas with trendy toppings ranging from duck sausage to Thai chicken, the menu offers calzones (you can get one stuffed with moo shu chicken here), salads, homemade pasta dishes, and grilled entrées such as herb-marinated chicken in white wine sauce. Desserts run the gamut from tiramisù to hot-fudge sundaes. Open 11am–3pm and 6–10pm; all entrées under $10.

Carson Street Café, the Nugget's 24-hour restaurant, evokes the elegant street cafés of the Champs-Elysées—albeit one overlooking a hotel lobby instead of a Paris street. The jewel-toned interior—under a white-fringed green awning, with upholstered bamboo furnishings, murals of park scenes, potted orange trees, and flower-bedecked tables—couldn't be lovelier. And the food is notably excellent. There are terrific salads, overstuffed deli sandwiches, unique breakfast items (such as eggs with Portuguese sausage and rice), and attractively priced specials (a full prime rib dinner for $7.95).

The Golden Nugget has one of the best buffets/Sunday brunches in Las Vegas (details in Chapter 6). In addition, a 24-hour snack bar in the casino offers deli sandwiches, pizza, and light fare, and there are four casino bars including the elegant **Claude's** and the **38 Different Kind of Beer Bar.**

Services   24-hour room service, shoeshine, concierge.

Facilities   Casino, car-rental desk, full-service unisex hair salon, shops (gifts, jewelry, designer fashions, sportswear, logo items), video game arcade.

The Nugget's top-rated health club offers a full line of Universal equipment, Lifecycles, Stairmasters, treadmills, rowing machines, gravitron, free weights, steam, sauna, tanning beds, and massage. Fresh fruit is available in elegant TV lounges (one for men, one for women), and a full array of complimentary toiletries is supplied. Salon treatments include everything from leg waxing to seaweed-mask facials. The spa's opulent Palladian-mirrored foyer is modeled after a salon in New York's Frick Museum.

The entrance to the hotel's immense swimming pool and outdoor whirlpool spa is graced by elegant marble swans and bronze fish sculptures. Fountains, palm trees, and verdant landscaping create a tropical setting, and a poolside bar serves the sun deck.

3. MODERATE

Most of my Las Vegas listings fall into this category, and, once again, the hotels quoted here are much cheaper than moderately priced listings in guidebooks to other tourist meccas.

ON THE STRIP/CASINO HOTELS

BARBARY COAST HOTEL & CASINO, 3595 Las Vegas Blvd. S., at Flamingo Rd., Las Vegas, NV 89109. Tel. 702/737-7111 or toll free 800/634-6755. Fax 702/737-6304. 184 rms, 12 suites. A/C TV TEL

$ Rates: Single or double Sun–Thurs $50–$75, Fri–Sat and holidays $75–$150; suite $150–$350. Extra person $5. Children under 12 free in parents' room. AE, CB, DC, DISC, JCB, MC, V.

Parking: Free (self and valet).

Evoking the romantic image of turn-of-the-century San Francisco—in the days when Chinatown opium dens, saloons, and gambling halls flourished—the Barbary Coast enjoys a terrific "four corners" Strip location. Everything keeps to the Old West theme, from the casino adorned with $2 million worth of magnificent stained-glass skylights and signage to the extremely charming Victorian-style rooms. The latter, decorated in shades of rose and gray, have half-canopied brass beds, gaslight-style lamps, oak moldings, period-look wallpapers, lace-curtained windows, and pretty floral carpets. All accommodations include little sitting parlors with entrances framed by floral chintz curtains. Walls are hung with watercolors of old San Francisco scenes.

Dining Michael's, the Barbary Coast's premier restaurant, is flamboyantly Victorian—an intimate dining room entered via frosted etched-glass doors, with white marble floors, red satin damask wall coverings, plush red velvet booths, and a gorgeous stained-glass dome overhead. A red rose graces every elegantly appointed table. The menu highlights charcoal-broiled steaks, chops, prime rib, and seafood. A meal here might comprise an appetizer of smoked Scotch salmon, followed by an entrée of fresh Dover sole meunière or prime sirloin steak au poivre in cognac cream sauce. Flambé tableside preparations and desserts are featured. Dinner only; entrées $28–$45.

The **Victorian Room,** a 24-hour coffee shop, is another attractive turn-of-the-century venue, with multipaned beveled mirror walls, stained-glass windows and skylights, and seating in red tufted-leather booths. In addition to an extensive coffee shop menu that runs the gamut from burgers to broiled Australian lobster tails, it offers Chinese entrées (almond chicken, Mongolian beef, sweet-and-sour pork) at lunch and dinner.

There's also a **McDonald's** on the premises—rather a nice one with an oak-beamed ceiling, beveled mirrors, and a stained-glass sign—open almost round the clock. And two bars serve the casino.

Services 24-hour room service, shoeshine.

Facilities Casino, Western Union office, tour and show desks, gift shop.

BOARDWALK HOTEL CASINO, 3750 Las Vegas Blvd. S., between Harmon and Tropicana Aves., Las Vegas, NV 89101. Tel. 702/735-1167 or toll free 800/635-4581. Fax 702/739-8152. 201 rms. A/C TV TEL

$ Rates: Single or double $38–$78 Sun–Fri, $48–$90 Sat. Extra person $6. Pets $10. Children 12 and under free in parents' room.

AE, CB, DC, DISC, ER, JCB, MC, V. **Parking:** Free at your room door.

In a previous incarnation (the 1970s) this was a Holiday Inn, and it still offers the traditional "no-surprises" kind of rooms for which that chain is famous. They're standard motel accommodations in tan and rust color schemes with oak furnishings. Amenities include AM/FM alarm-clock radios and cable TVs with pay-movie options and hotel-information channels. In-room coffee makers are available on request. And though this is a casino hotel, it has a real hotel lobby. One unexpected feature: a 150-foot bungee jump setup over the swimming pool!

Dining The **Porterhouse Room** has a wall of trellised windows hung with planters of philodendrons and red-clothed candlelit tables. It's casual—not fancy—with a steak-and-seafood menu that allows for many dining moods. You might drop in for a cheddar burger or a ham-and-cheese sandwich on sourdough bread. Or—for just $6.95—order a hearty 16-ounce porterhouse steak served with soup or salad, baked potato, and pinto beans. Another good choice is a $5.95 platter of deep-fried shrimp, fish, scallops, and oysters served with french fries and coleslaw. Dinner only; entrées $3.50–$8.50.

The 24-hour **Boardwalk Coffee Shop** is a turn-of-the-century setting. Walls covered with red flocked wallpaper are hung with old movie stills and posters. A specialty here is Bud's hobo stew served in a hollowed-out loaf of bread. An all-you-can-eat meal of codfish or catfish, fries, and coleslaw is $4.25, and a prime rib dinner is just $3.49 every Wednesday. Otherwise, the menu offers a good selection of coffee shop fare and everything is under $5.

A casino snack bar proffers deli sandwiches, homemade dough-nuts, and half-pound hot dogs with beverage for 99¢. And a casino lounge features live entertainment Thurs–Sat nights.

Services Room service 5–10pm.

Facilities Casino, two swimming pools, gift shop, RV and truck parking, coin-op washer and dryer, small video game arcade, tour and show desks. Guests can use health club facilities at an adjoining hotel.

HACIENDA RESORT, 3950 Las Vegas Blvd. S., between Tropicana Ave. and Russell Rd., Las Vegas, NV 89119. Tel. 702/739-8911 or toll free 800/634-6713. Fax 702/798-8289. 1,090 rms, 50 suites. A/C TV TEL

$ Rates: Garden rooms $28–$68 single or double, tower rooms $38–$78 single or double, $125–$350 suite. Holiday and convention rates may be higher. Extra person $8. Children 12 and under free in parents' room. AE, CB, DC, DISC, MC, V. **Parking:** Free (self and valet).

This south-of-the-border-themed hotel at the southern border of the Strip offers warm hospitality and pleasant surroundings. Unlike most Las Vegas hotels, its entrance does not lead directly into a casino but into a charming terra-cotta-floored lobby where white stucco archways are colorfully embellished with paintings of tropical birds, flowers, and fruit. To your right is a 20-foot waterfall with live palms and tropical plantings under a skylight. And when you do enter the casino, it's an attractive, low-key facility decorated with garland friezes rather than neon.

Rooms in the North Tower are decorated in rust or gray-blue color schemes with brass-accented walnut furnishings and quilted paisley bedspreads. Rooms in the newer South and Central towers have sturdy oak furnishings, but colors, artworks, and Aztec-print bedspreads and drapes combine to create a southwestern feel. A flagstone passageway lined with tropical plants, bamboo, and cactus meanders through the garden-room area; these rooms, in six low buildings grouped around the pool, also keep to a southwest theme. All Hacienda accommodations offer remote-control color cable TVs with pay-movie options, video checkout, and an in-house information channel. Garden-room guests can request refrigerators.

Dining The **Charcoal Room** is an intimate steak-and-seafood restaurant with semicircular black tufted-leather booths, candlelit white-linened tables, and Mexican-themed gilt-framed oil paintings on wide-plank pine walls. Amber lighting emanates from wrought-iron lamps. Flambé specialties, prepared tableside, add excitement. Entrées—such as filet mignon, prime rib, lobster tail in drawn butter, and chicken piccata—are served with a relish tray, cheeses and crackers, soup or salad, potato du jour, and a complimentary petit four. Dinner only; entrées $12.95–$21.95.

The southwestern-motif **Cactus Room,** a 24-hour restaurant, has peach adobe walls, with Mexican artifacts and terra-cotta pots of cactus set in arched stucco niches. Many Mexican entrées—fajitas, tacos, tamales, enchiladas—are offered in addition to the requisite coffee shop fare, and from 4pm–2am there are low-priced specials featuring a choice of prime rib, crab legs, or fried chicken.

El Grande Buffet, served in a "Mexican courtyard" with wrought-iron railings, ficus trees, and ceramic-tiled food stations, offers all-you-can-eat meals at breakfast, lunch, dinner, and Sunday brunch. Selections include hand-carved prime rib and baked ham, pizzas, fresh pastas tossed to order in a variety of sauces, and flaming desserts.

A new restaurant, the **New York Pasta Company,** will be opening shortly after this book goes to press; it will offer homemade pasta dishes and other Italian specialties. A pizza shop, deli, and frozen yogurt vendor are in the shopping arcade. There are two casino bars—the **Bolero Lounge,** featuring live entertainment and free margarita parties weekdays from 3–6pm, and the 24-hour **Island Cantina,** offering 64-ounce "megaritas."

Services Room service 6:30am–1:30pm and 4:30–11pm, guest-services desk (also functions as tour, show, and car-rental desk).

Facilities Casino, shops (men's and women's clothing, jewelry, gifts, liquor, logowear), video game arcade, beauty salon, night-lit tennis court, clover-shaped swimming pool and sun deck in a lush garden setting.

Camperland, a nicely landscaped 20-acre RV park on the premises, has spaces for 363 vehicles. In addition to complete hookups, it has a nearby convenience store, playground, swimming pool, rest rooms, showers, picnic tables/barbecue grills, and coin-op laundry facilities. Rate is $8.95 per night, including full hookup. For details call 702/739-8911.

HARRAH'S LAS VEGAS, 3475 Las Vegas Blvd. S., between Flamingo and Spring Mountain Rds., Las Vegas, NV 89109. Tel. 702/369-5000 or toll free **800/634-6765.** Fax 702/369-5008. 1,699 rms, 26 suites. A/C TV TEL

$ Rates: Single or double $45–$89 standard room, $55–$99 king, $71–$115 minisuite. Extra person $10. Children 12 and under free in parents' room. AE, CB, DC, DISC, ER, MC, V. **Parking:** Free (self and valet).

Harrah's glittering Mississippi riverboat facade—complete with 185-foot smokestacks and a foghorn that sounds at frequent intervals—has been a Las Vegas landmark since 1973. The centrally located "ship on the Strip" is docked at Jackson Square, a French Quarter–themed shopping area. In keeping with the property's New Orleans leitmotif, a costumed southern belle and riverboat gambler roam the casino greeting guests, and sometimes a Dixieland band plays outside the front door. And since Bill Harrah owns the world's largest antique car collection, a 1930 Model H Stutz Bearcat and a 1911 Maxwell are displayed in the lobby.

Rooms, off pleasant hallways hung with prints by Renoir, Van Gogh, and Degas, are very attractive. I like the resortlike accommodations in the 35-story Captain's Tower, decorated in peach and teal with bleached oak furnishings and verdigris accents. Spacious minisuites in the section, offering large sofas and comfortable armchairs, are especially desirable. In the 23-story Riverboat Tower, the color scheme is teal and mauve with dark-wood furnishings and grasspaper wall coverings. All rooms offer AM/FM alarm-clock radios and remote-control color cable TVs with hotel-information and keno channels, pay-movie options, and free Showtime movies.

Dining The plush **Claudine's** seats diners in roomy floral-tapestried booths at candlelit tables. There are gorgeous brass candelabra chandeliers overhead, peach watered-silk walls are hung with Renoir-like paintings, and intimate seating areas are created by cut-glass and brass dividers. It all adds up to a romantic turn-of-the-century setting for continental/steak-and-seafood meals, with entrées ranging from steak Diane to lightly poached salmon in sauce mousseline. After you dine relax over drinks in the adjoining piano bar lounge. Dinner only; entrées $14.95–$18.95.

The verdant garden-themed **Veranda,** Harrah's 24-hour coffee shop, is one of the prettiest on the Strip, with trellised archways serving as room dividers, pretty floral carpeting, and upholstered bamboo chairs. An extensive menu gives you a wide choice of light fare items and lists low-priced nightly entrées. For instance, grilled trout, roast turkey with sage dressing, or pot roast and vegetables are just $9.95, that price including a baked potato, soup, and unlimited trips to the salad bar.

An "old salt" mannequin guards the entrance to **Joe's Bayou,** a Creole/seafood restaurant. Nautically themed, with amber ship's lanterns suspended over candlelit tables, its walls are hung with riverboat paintings, fishnets, and racks of oars. Blackened red snapper is a specialty, served with salad, corn on the cob, hush puppies, and corn bread. And if you're not in the mood for seafood, a 16-ounce T-bone steak is an option. Dinner only; entrées *$9.95–$14.95.*

All That Jazz simulates a French Quarter street. Its walls are shuttered New Orleans house facades with wrought-iron balconies and window boxes; trees and streetlamps further the illusion. New Orleans jazz emanates from a player piano at night. Breakfast entrées include a gratis fruit and pastry bar; dinner entrées such as prime rib, battered shrimp, spicy chicken, or a pound of crablegs (*$6.95–$9.95*) include soup, salad bar, and dessert bar.

Similar in decor is the **Court of Two Gators,** a bar/lounge off the casino with ivied walls and a lofty skylight ceiling. Its dance floor is popular at night when live bands play jazz and oldies. Other lounges here include **Churchill Downs** in the race and sports book area (a snack bar called the **Derby Deli** adjoins), three casino bars, and the **Atrium Lounge** featuring live nighttime entertainment. See also buffet listings in Chapter 6.

Services   24-hour room service, including a special pizza and pasta menu, complimentary gaming lessons.

Facilities   Casino, car-rental desk, tour and show desks, nice-sized video game arcade, coin-op laundry, shops (see Chapter 10 for details), unisex hair salon. Harrah's has a beautiful Olympic-size swimming pool and sun deck area with a whirlpool, kids wading pool, cocktail and snack bar, and poolside shop selling T-shirts and sundries. The hotel's health club is one of the best facilities on the Strip, offering Lifecycles, treadmills, stair machines, rowing machines, lots of Universal equipment, free weights, whirlpool, steam, sauna, and massage; there are two TVs and a VCR for which aerobic exercise tapes are available.

IMPERIAL PALACE, 3535 Las Vegas Blvd. S., between Sands Ave. and Flamingo Rd., Las Vegas, NV 89109. Tel. 702/731-3311 or toll free 800/634-6441. Fax 702/735-8578. 2,412 rms, 225 suites. A/C TV TEL

$ Rates: $45–$100 single or double, $75–$150 "luv tub" suite, $150–$500 other suites. Extra person $12. Inquire about packages. AE, DC, DISC, MC, V. **Parking:** Free (self and valet).

The blue pagoda-topped Imperial Palace, its shoji-screenlike facade patterned after Japanese temple architecture, is the seventh-largest hotel in the world. Inside, the hotel keeps to its Asian theme with a dragon-motif ceiling and giant wind chime chandeliers in the casino. A unique feature on the fifth floor is the Imperial Palace Auto Collection of over 750 antique, classic, and special-interest vehicles spanning a century of automotive history (details in Chapter 7).

Rooms, decorated in tones of beige and tan, have bamboo-motif beds and furnishings perked up by bright tropical-look curtains and paintings. Remote-control color TVs offer in-house information channels. If you so desire, you can rent a "luv tub" suite with an enormous faux-marble bath (ample for two) and a canopied bed with a mirrored ceiling.

Dining   Embers, the I.P.'s gourmet room, is a plush venue with oak-framed mirrors adorning burgundy silk-covered walls, spacious candlelit booths, and a smoked-mirror ceiling with recessed pink neon tubing. The menu features many steak-and-seafood entrées—from tournedos au poivre in cognac cream sauce to fresh salmon trout amandine. Or you might opt for roast Long Island duck with lingonberries and wild rice. Dinner only; entrées mostly $10.95–$18.95.

The **Ming Terrace,** fronted by a valuable antique cloisonné incense burner from the People's Republic of China and a bamboo rickshaw, derives further ambience from Chinese screens and painted fans. Candles in fluted-glass holders provide soft lighting. The menu features Mandarin, Cantonese, and Szechuan specialties ranging from the prosaic (sweet-and-sour pork, chow mein, shrimp fried rice) to the exotic (sliced abalone with sautéed Chinese black mushrooms, spicy Mongolian beef, Peking or roast duck). Dinner only; most entrées $8.75–$20.95.

The **Rib House** is a rustic setting with exposed brick walls, wood-bladed fan chandeliers overhead, and heavy oak dividers defining seating areas. Light from frosted-glass sconces, candlelit tables, and a working fireplace casts a warm, cozy glow. Barbecued baby back ribs, chicken, and Texas-style beef ribs are the specialties, all served with salad, corn on the cob, and steak fries or a baked potato. Dinner only; entrées $9.95–$16.95.

The Seahouse, a casual nautically themed restaurant under a beamed ceiling, seats diners in captain's chairs. Low lighting emanates from brass ship's lanterns and candlelit tables. Fresh seafood entrées such as orange roughy sautéed with macadamia nuts and fettuccine Alfredo tossed with scallops are featured, but if you're not a fish fancier you can order filet mignon béarnaise or charbroiled lemon chicken. Dinner only; entrées mostly $11.95–$16.95.

The 24-hour **Teahouse** has pagoda eaves overhead, bamboo furnishings, and booths separated by shoji-screen dividers. It offers, in addition to the usual burgers, salads, sandwiches, and full entrées, buffet brunches ($5.95) weekdays and champagne Sunday brunches ($7.95) from 8am–3pm. A great buy here is a prime rib and champagne dinner featured nightly from 5–10pm for $7.95.

Pizza Palace—a cheerful eatery with wine-barrel facades adorning cream stucco and exposed-brick walls, red-and-white checkered tablecloths, big tufted-leather booths, and stained-glass lighting fixtures—serves regular and deep-dish pizzas, Italian sandwiches, and pasta dishes. An antipasto salad bar is a plus. Open 11am–midnight; entrées $3.75–$10.30, the latter for a large pizza with three toppings.

The **Emperor's Buffet,** on the third floor, has a South Seas decor comprised of thatched roofing, bamboo and rattan paneling, Polynesian carvings and totems, and seating in sea-green leather booths. Breakfast is served 7–11am ($3.99); lunch 11am–4pm ($4.49); dinner, featuring a carving station for ham and roast beef, 5–10pm ($4.99).

Betty's Diner, in the shopping arcade, serves sandwiches, pizza, nachos, hot dogs, malts and ice cream sundaes. **Burger Palace,** a cafeteria adjacent to the race and sports book, is attractively decorated with sports-themed murals; it serves burgers, sandwiches, and light fare. Adjoining it is the **Sports Bar** where you can follow the races over cocktails. Altogether, there are 10 cocktail bars/

lounges in the hotel, including the **Mai Tai Lounge** on the main floor and the **Poolside Bar** (both specializing in exotic Polynesian drinks), and the **Ginza, Geisha, Sake,** and **Kanpai** bars serving the casino.

Services 24-hour room service, gratis gaming lessons, shoeshine in casino.

Facilities Casino, health club (treadmills, Lifecycles, Stairmaster, Universal and Nautilus equipment, free weights, sauna, steam, massage, tanning, television lounge), show and tour desks, car-rental desk, travel agency, unisex hairdresser, wedding chapel, video game arcade, shopping arcade (gifts, women's fashions, a western shop, logo items, souvenirs). A nice-sized swimming pool is backed by a rock garden and waterfalls, its palm-fringed sun deck area also containing a Jacuzzi.

SAHARA HOTEL & CASINO, 2535 Las Vegas Blvd. S., at E. Sahara Ave., Las Vegas, NV 89109. Tel. 702/737-2111 or toll free 800/634-6666. Fax 702/791-2027. 1,945 rms, 90 suites. A/C TV TEL

$ Rates: $55–$85 single or double, $200 suite. Extra person $10. Children under 14 free in parents' room. AE, CB, DC, MC, V. **Parking:** Free (self and valet).

Fronted by a 222-foot sign spelling out its name in letters 18 feet high and 10 feet wide, the Sahara's come a long way since it opened in 1952 on the site of the old Club Bingo. It's gone from 200 to 2,000-plus rooms with new towers, a major showroom, and an impressive array of restaurants, shops, and services. One thing hasn't changed: It was the northernmost major hotel on the Strip when it opened, and so it remains. For some reason, Las Vegas Boulevard South has never really developed between the Sahara and downtown. The hotel is famous as the home of Jerry Lewis's Muscular Distrophy Labor Day telethons.

Rooms in the Tunis and Tangiers Towers are decorated in earth tones (beige and rust) with jade accents and grasspaper-look wall coverings embellished by framed floral prints. The largest accommodations are in the Alexandria Tower, these decorated in shades of rust and burgundy. And the original garden rooms, in two-story buildings, are cream and mauve with dark-wood furnishings. All are of the basic hotel room genre. Some Tower rooms have balconies, and all accommodations offer remote-control color TVs with pay-movie and gaming-instruction channels.

Dining   The House of Lords is a plush continental restaurant with exposed brick walls and rich mahogany paneling. Seating is in semicircular tufted red leather booths at white-linened tables lit by shaded candle lamps. You'll dine on fancy fare—escargots bourguignon, beef Wellington, roast quail stuffed with pine nuts and wild rice in pecan bourbon sauce, flambé desserts like cherries jubilee—with sorbet served between courses and complimentary petit fours as a finale. Dinner only; entrées $19.50–$30.

La Terrazza is an intimate Italian dining room on the third floor—a bi-level cream stucco grotto with a wall of windows overlooking the pool and tables lit by silk-shaded candle lamps. Four pastas (fettuccine, capellini, linguine, and ravioli) are offered with a choice of four sauces (bolognese, romano, pesto, and marinara). Or you might opt for an entrée such as stir-fried fresh vegetables and seafood on a bed of tomato capellini. Dinner only; entrées $7.95–$9.95. Tues–Sat 5–6pm, five-course early bird dinners—soup, salad, entrée, pasta, and dessert—are $9.95–$12.95.

The **Caravan Coffee Shop,** a 24-hour facility off the casino with windows overlooking the pool, is fronted by a kneeling camel. A mural of an Arab market further carries out the desert theme. Its extensive menu offers all the requisite coffee shop fare.

The **Turf Club Deli,** next to the Race and Sports Center, features Jewish deli fare—homemade matzoh ball soup, lox and bagels, latkes, pickled herring, and pastrami, corned beef, and brisket on rye. Open 8am–4pm; everything on the menu is under $6.

There are two buffets, the **Oasis** and the **Pacific Rim Dinner Show** (details in Chapters 6 and 11, respectively). Bar/lounges include two 24-hour casino bars (the **Safari Bar** and the **Sports Book Bar**), plus the **Casbar Lounge** offering top-notch live entertainment nightly from 6pm–4am.

Services 24-hour room service.

Facilities Casino, beauty salon/barbershop, car-rental desk, tour and show desks, shops (see Chapter 10), video game arcade, Northwest Airlines Desk. The Sahara has a vast swimming pool and sun deck with a pool shop and poolside bar in nearby thatched-roof structures. A smaller pool shares the same courtyard setting.

STARDUST RESORT & CASINO, 3000 Las Vegas Blvd. S., at Convention Center Dr., Las Vegas, NV 89109. Tel. 702/732-6111 or toll free 800/634-6757. Fax 702/732-6257. 2,140 rms, 160 suites. A/C TV TEL

$ Rates: Single or double Tower rooms $38–$48 Sun–Thurs, $70–$75 Fri–Sat, $85–$100 holidays; Villa rooms $32 Sun–Thurs, $50 Fri–Sat, $70 holidays; Motor Inn rooms $24 Sun–Thurs, $40 Sat–Sun, $65 holidays; suites $150–$500. Extra person $10. Children 12 and under free in parents' room. AE, CB, DC, MC, V. **Parking:** Free (self and valet).

Opened in 1958, the Stardust is a longtime resident of the Strip, its 188-foot, starry sign one of America's most recognized landmarks. Today fronted by a fountained exterior plaza, the Stardust has kept pace with a growing city. It recently opened a new 1,500-room tower and a 35,000 square-foot state-of-the-art meeting and conference center, part of a comprehensive $300 million expansion and renovation project. In the 1990s, the Stardust remains a brightly shining star on the Strip.

The newest rooms, in the 32-story West Tower, feature a modern decor; they're decorated in rich earth tones with black accents and bedspreads and drapes in bold abstract prints. East Tower rooms (my favorites) are light, airy, and spacious with peach carpeting and attractive sea-foam green floral-print bedspreads, upholstered headboards, and draperies. You can rent an adjoining parlor room with a sofa bed, Jacuzzi tub, refrigerator, and wet bar—a good choice for families. Also quite nice are Villa rooms in two-story buildings surrounding a large swimming pool. Decorated in soft southwestern pastels (mauve, beige, aqua), they have grasspaper-covered walls hung with attractive artwork. Private shaded patios overlooking the pool are a plus here. Least expensive rooms are in the Stardust's Motor Inn—four two-story white buildings with shuttered windows set far back on the property. They've been cheerfully decorated in southwestern resort colors, and if you don't mind being a block from the casino, they represent a good value. Motor Inn guests can park at their doors. All Stardust accommodations offer in-room safes and color cable TVs with Spectravision movie options and in-house information channels.

Dining   William B's, an elegant steak-and-seafood restaurant, is a clubby crystal-chandeliered precinct with dark oak-paneled walls, candlelit white-linened tables, and seating in comfortable upholstered armchairs. It's fronted by a handsome bar/lounge. The menu offers many tempting seafood appetizers such as steamed clams in herbed red-pepper cream sauce and shrimp scampi flamed in sherry. Entrées include choice aged beef and chops, a variety of veal and chicken dishes (marsala, piccata, parmigiana, and so on), and delicious seafood entrées ranging from Australian lobster tails in drawn butter to butter-sautéed orange roughy flambé in Grand Marnier cream sauce. Flambé desserts are a house specialty. Dinner only; entrees $14.95–$26.95.

Tres Lobos, designed to resemble the open courtyard of a Mexican hacienda, achieves its south-of-the-border ambience via colonnaded white stucco archways, beamed and vaulted ceilings, ceramic tile floors, murals of Mexico, indoor trees, fountains, statuary, and big planters of greenery. A plush adjoining lounge specializes in many-flavored margaritas (peach, banana, blue curaçao, piña colada, and so on). All the usual fajitas, burritos, enchiladas, and chimichangas are offered, along with less typical entrées such as garlic-sautéed shrimp in a delicate cream sauce with romano cheese, pine nuts, and artichoke hearts. Dinner only; entrées $5.95–$11.95.

Toucan Harry's Coffee Shop, the Stardust's 24-hour facility, is lushly tropical, with grass-green carpeting, abundant faux foliage, murals of tropical birds, overhead fans, bamboo-look chairs (most seating is in roomy booths), and a tented fabric ceiling. In addition to a vast array of sandwiches, salads, and full entrées (including many heart-smart low-fat, low-cholesterol items), Harry's features a full Chinese menu with over 50 dishes.

Ralph's Diner reflects America's current nostalgia craze. Fifties rock 'n' roll tunes (the Coasters, Drifters, Platters) emanate from an old-fashioned jukebox (there are also jukeboxes at each table), waitstaff is garbed in classic white diner uniforms, and the decor features a black-and-white checkerboard floor and chrome-plated Formica tables. All-American fare is served: stacks of buttermilk pancakes, burgers, hero sandwiches, chili, meat loaf, southern-fried chicken. An old-fashioned soda fountain turns out milk shakes, banana splits, and hot-fudge sundaes. And low-priced blue-plate specials are offered daily. Open 7am–10pm; everything is under $10, most items under $7.

Tony Roma's, which you may know from other locations, has a home at the Stardust; more about it—and the Stardust's **Warehouse Buffet**—in Chapter 6. **Short Stop,** a snack bar in the race and sports book area of the casino, serves sandwiches and light fare throughout the day. There are eight bars and cocktail lounges in the hotel, including the **Terrace Bar** in the casino with an al fresco seating area overlooking the pool and the **Starlight Lounge,** featuring live music nightly.

Services 24-hour room service, shoeshine.

Facilities Casino, beauty salon/barbershop, video game arcade, car-rental desk, tour and show desks, shops (gifts, candy, clothing, jewelry, logo items, liquor). There are two large swimming pools, one in the Villa section, the other between the East and West Towers. Both have attractively landscaped sun decks and poolside bars; the Towers pool area has three whirlpool spas. Guests can use the Las Vegas Sporting House directly behind the hotel, a state-of-the-art, 24-hour health club; its very extensive facilities are detailed in Chapter 7.

ON THE STRIP/NONCASINO HOTELS

LA QUINTA MOTOR INN, 3782 Las Vegas Blvd. S., between Tropicana and Harmon Aves., Las Vegas, NV 89109. Tel. 702/739-7457 or toll free 800/531-5900. Fax 702/736-1129. 114 rms. A/C TV TEL

$ Rates: Single or double $43–$53 Sun–Thurs, $55–$63 Fri–Sat. Extra person $5. Children 18 and under free in parents' room. AE, CB, DC, DISC, ER, JCB, MC, V. **Parking:** Free at your room door.

La Quinta is a San Antonio, Texas-based chain, and all of its properties are easily recognizable for their mission-style architecture—terra-cotta-roofed, cream stucco buildings with wrought-iron trim. Rooms are likewise southwestern in decor, utilizing a cream/rust color scheme with turquoise accents and Aztec-motif paintings and fabrics. Here, furnishings are oak, and in-room amenities include AM/FM alarm-clock radios and remote-control color cable TVs with pay-movie options.

There's a nice-sized pool and sun deck, and a big, comfortable 24-hour Carrows Restaurant adjoins. Carrows serves everything from breakfast burritos (one of many Mexican specialties) to USDA choice steaks, Italian pastas, and southern-fried chicken. Oven-fresh pies here, too. Coffee is served throughout the day in a pleasant lobby, and there's free transport to/from the airport. The Excalibur (see below), with its many restaurants and vast casino, is just a block away.

RODEWAY INN, 3786 Las Vegas Blvd. S., between Tropicana and Harmon Aves., Las Vegas, NV 89109. Tel. 702/736-1434 or toll free 800/350-1132. Fax 702/736-6058. 95 rms, 2 suites. A/C TV TEL

$ Rates: Single or double $45–$55 Sun–Thurs, $65–$85 Fri–Sat and holidays. Extra person $5. Pets $5. Children 18 and under free in parents' room. AE, CB, DC, DISC, ER, JCB, MC, V. **Parking:** Free at your room door.

Just next door to the above-mentioned La Quinta, the Rodeway is housed in a neat two-story cream brick building with shuttered windows. All of its rooms were recently renovated and given new light-wood furnishings, teal carpeting, and color-coordinated floral-print or paisley bedspreads. They're standard motel rooms, but nice ones, with big dressing room areas and in-room safes and coffee makers. You even get a remote-control color cable TV with free HBO.

Facilities include a Budget car-rental desk and a small swimming pool and sun deck. The front desk operates as a show and tour desk. Carrows 24-hour restaurant (see La Quinta above) is right next door, and, once again, Excalibur—with its many restaurants and enormous casino—is a block away. This is a clean, well-run property, with a manager who lives on the premises.

CONVENTION CENTER AREA/ A CASINO HOTEL

BEST WESTERN MARDI GRAS INN, 3500 Paradise Rd, between Sands Ave. and Desert Inn Rd., Las Vegas, NV 89109. Tel. 702/731-2020 or toll free 800/634-6501. Fax 702/733-6994. 315 minisuites. A/C TV TEL

$ Rates: Single or double Sun–Thurs $53–$63, Fri–Sat and holidays $59–$69. Extra person $6. Children 12 and under free in parents' room. AE, CB, DC, DISC, ER, JCB, MC, V. **Parking:** Free at your room door.

Opened in 1980, this well-run little casino hotel has a lot to offer. A block from the convention center and close to major hotels, its three-story building sits on nicely landscaped grounds with manicured lawns, trees, and shrubbery. There's a gazebo out back where guests can enjoy a picnic lunch.

Accommodations are all spacious queen-bedded minisuites with sofa-bedded living room areas and eat-in kitchens, the latter equipped with wet bars, refrigerators, and coffee makers. Rooms are attractively decorated in muted blues and earth tones, with rust/orange floral-print drapes and bedspreads. All offer AM/FM alarm-clock radios and color cable TVs with HBO and pay-movie options. Staying here is like having your own little Las Vegas apartment.

Dining A pleasant restaurant/bar off the lobby, with white-linened tables and fan chandeliers overhead, is open from 6:30am–11pm daily. It serves typical coffee shop fare, including an 8-ounce New York steak dinner for $7.50.

Services Free transport to/from airport and major Strip hotels.

Facilities Small casino (64 slots/video poker machines), small video game arcade, car-rental desk, tour and show desks, coin-op laundry, unisex hairdresser, gift shop, RV parking. The inn has a large swimming pool with a duplex sun deck and whirlpool.

CONVENTION CENTER AREA/NONCASINO HOTELS

COURTYARD MARRIOTT, 3275 Paradise Rd., between Convention Center Dr. and Desert Inn Rd., Las Vegas, NV 89109. Tel. 702/791-3600 or toll free 800/321-2211. Fax 702/796-7981. 137 rms, 12 suites. A/C TV TEL

$ Rates: Single or double $65 Sun–Thurs, $84 Fri–Sat; suites $92 Sun–Thurs, $112 Fri–Sat. Extra person $10. Children 16 and under free in parents' room. AE, CB, DC, DISC, MC, V. **Parking:** Free at your room door.

Housed in three-story terra-cotta-roofed stucco buildings, in an attractively landscaped setting of trees, shrubbery, and flower beds, the Courtyard is a welcome link in the Marriott chain. The concept for these limited-service lower-priced lodgings developed in the 1980s, and this particular property opened in 1989. Though services are limited, don't picture a no-frills atmosphere. This is a beautiful hotel, with a pleasant plant-filled lobby and very nice rooms indeed.

Like public areas, the rooms—most with king-size beds—still look spanking new. Attractively decorated in shades of gray and mauve, with sofas and handsome mahogany furnishings (including large desks), they offer AM/FM alarm-clock radios and remote-control color cable TVs with Spectravision movie options. All rooms have balconies or patios.

Dining   Off the lobby is a light and airy plant-filled restaurant with glossy oak paneling and tables. It serves buffet breakfasts, as well as à la carte lunches (mostly salads and sandwiches) and dinners (steak, seafood, pasta). It adjoins a comfortable lobby lounge with plush furnishings, a large-screen TV, and a working fireplace. Drinks are served here from 4–10:30pm. You can also have breakfast in this lounge and catch a morning TV news show.

Services   Room service 4–10pm, complimentary airport shuttle.

Facilities   Small exercise room (Lifecycles, a few pieces of Universal equipment, free weights), medium-sized swimming pool with adjoining whirlpool, picnic tables and barbecue grills, coin-op washers and dryers.

FAIRFIELD INN BY MARRIOTT, 3850 Paradise Rd., between Twain Ave. and Flamingo Rd., Las Vegas, NV 89109. Tel. 702/791-0899 or toll free **800/228-2800.** Fax 702/791-0899. 129 rms. A/C TV TEL

$ Rates (for up to five people): $35.95–$55.95 Sun–Thurs, $39.95–$59.95 Fri–Sat and holidays. AE, CB, DC, DISC, MC, V. **Parking:** Free (self).

Marriott developed the Fairfield Inn concept in the mid-1980s to offer a "new standard in economy lodging." This pristine property, opened in 1990, is a very pleasant place to stay. It has a comfortable lobby with sofas and armchairs—a simpatico setting in which to plan your day's activities over a cup of coffee (provided gratis all day).

Cheerful rooms are decorated in peach and teal, with mahogany furnishings and rather nice watercolors adorning ecru walls. King rooms have convertible sofas, and all accommodations offer well-lit work areas with desks, AM/FM alarm-clock radios, and remote-control color cable TVs with HBO. Local calls are free.

There are no dining facilities, but many restaurants are within easy walking distance. Facilities include a pool/whirlpool and sun deck with umbrella tables, car-rental and show desks, and a free shuttle to and from the airport. The front desk proffers warm hospitality.

NEAR THE STRIP/A CASINO HOTEL

MAXIM, 160 E. Flamingo Rd., between the Strip and Koval Lane, Las Vegas, NV 89109. Tel. 702/731-4300 or toll free 800/634-6987. Fax 702/735-3252. 754 rms, 46 suites. A/C TV TEL

$ Rates: Single or double $35–$45 Sun–Thurs, $49–$68 Fri–Sat; suites $125–$285. Extra person $5. Children under 12 free in parents' room. AE, DC, MC, V. **Parking:** Free (self and valet).

Just a short walk from the fabulous "four corners" configuration of luxury hotels (Bally's, Caesars, Flamingo Hilton, Dunes), the Maxim is a friendly property that has doubled in size since its 1977 opening. Rooms and public areas are currently undergoing a multimillion dollar renovation. Some accommodations already sport a new southwestern resort look. They're decorated in turquoise, mauve, and peach, with splashy floral-print bedspreads and drapes, bureaus topped by large oak-framed mirrors, attractive abstract paintings, and textured beige wallpapers. Older rooms, decorated in navy and earth tones, have sienna ultrasuede walls and photomurals of Las Vegas behind the beds. All offer remote-control cable TVs with pay-movie options and in-house information channels. If you like, you can rent a "players suite" with a whirlpool tub in the bedroom and a separate living room with wet bar.

Dining Da Vinci's, adorned with prints and a stained-glass rendering (on the front door) of Leonardo's works, is the Maxim's most elegant restaurant. Its pink-clothed tables are lit by brass candle lamps, and seating is in roomy velvet-upholstered chairs. A continental menu lists items like Dover sole meunière, broiled lamb chops with mint sauce, and steak Diane. Flambé table-side preparations are a specialty, including desserts such as cherries jubilee. Dinner only; pasta dishes $10–$12, most entrées $15–$25.

The Treehouse is the Maxim's 24-hour coffee shop, a very low-lit facility with planters of cloth greenery, oak tables, and a chrome ceiling with recessed red neon tubing. In addition to the requisite coffee shop fare, it features daily specials such as a USDA choice aged New York steak dinner served with soup or salad, rolls and butter, baked potato, and vegetables for $4.95.

JB's, a cheerful sidewalk café with a window wall and red-and-green-striped booths under an awning, is lit by globed street lamps. The booths are separated by planters of philodendrons. There's also a brick-floored ice-cream parlor–like interior room. Service is cafeteria style. The fare includes fresh-baked doughnuts, muffins, and pastries for breakfast. Later in the day you can order tacos, chili, burgers, homemade soups, pizzas, and ice-cream sundaes. Open 7am–11pm.

The **Grand Buffet,** served on the mezzanine level, is rather elegant, especially at dinner when candlelit tables are covered in white linen and a pianist entertains on a baby grand. Dinner ($4.95) is served nightly from 4–10pm, Sunday brunch ($6.95) 9am–3pm.

There are two casino cocktail lounges, the **Waterfall** and the **Cloud Nine.**

Services 24-hour room service, shoeshine.

Facilities Casino, car-rental desk, tour and show desks, small video game arcade, 24-hour gift shop that carries jewelry and logo items, beauty salon/barbershop, rooftop pool and sun deck with poolside bar.

NEAR THE STRIP/NONCASINO HOTELS

CARRIAGE HOUSE, 105 E. Harmon Ave., between Las Vegas Blvd. S. and Koval Lane, Las Vegas, NV 89109. Tel. 702/798-1020 or toll free 800/777-1700. Fax 702/798-1020, ext. 112. 150 suites. A/C TV TEL

$ Rates: $85 studio suites for one or two people, $95–$105 one-bedroom suites and condominiums for up to four people, $190 two-bedroom condominiums for up to six people. Inquire about low-priced packages. AE, CB, DC, DISC, ER, MC, V. **Parking:** Free (self).

Housed in nine-story white stucco building fronted by palm trees, this friendly, low-key resort hotel has a loyal repeat clientele. You enter into a large, comfortably furnished lobby where guests enjoy complimentary Monday afternoon wine-and-cheese parties. And the hotel caters to kids with welcome bags of cookies at check-in and gratis VCRs and movies on request; the front desk maintains a nice-sized movie library, and they'll even supply popcorn.

The very attractive suites, decorated in teal, peach, and mauve with brass-trimmed lacquer or bleached-oak furnishings, have small sitting areas and fully equipped kitchenettes with refrigerators, microwave ovens, coffee makers, toasters, and two- or four-burner ranges. Most have dishwashers as well. All units are equipped with AM/FM alarm-clock radios and remote-control color cable TVs with Showtime movie stations. One-bedroom units have full living rooms and dining areas, with phones, radios, and TVs in both rooms. Two-bedroom/two-bath condominiums have a king bed in each bedroom and a queen sofa in the living room. Both rooms and public areas are immaculate. Free local phone calls are a plus.

Dining Kiefers, an acclaimed rooftop restaurant-with-a-view is covered in detail in Chapter 6. Continental fare is featured. A pianist performs Tues–Sat nights in a plush adjoining lounge.

Services Complimentary transport 7am–11pm to/from airport and major Strip hotels.

Facilities Tour and show desks, coin-op laundry, Har-Tru tennis court lit for night play (no charge for play, balls, or racquets), swimming pool/sun deck, whirlpool.

DAYS INN, 3265 Las Vegas Blvd. S., just south of Sands Ave., Las Vegas, NV 89109. Tel. 702/735-5102 or toll free 800/325-2525. Fax 702/735-0168. 126 rms. A/C TV TEL

$ Rates: Single or double Sun–Thurs $42–$52, Fri–Sat $47–$57; king room $65 Sun–Thurs, $72 Fri–Sat. "Super Saver" rate ($39 single or double) if you reserve 30 days in advance via the above toll-free number. AE, CB, DC, DISC, MC, V. **Parking:** Free at your room door.

A central location just across the street from the Mirage, and clean basic motel rooms nicely decorated in shades of mauve and muted blue, make this Days Inn a viable choice. A third of the rooms have patios or balconies, and all offer remote-control color cable TVs with pay-movie options. King rooms have wet bars and refrigerators. A wide selection of complimentary bath amenities is available at the front desk, and free coffee is served in the lobby all day. There's a swimming pool but no restaurant.

EMERALD SPRINGS INN, 325 E. Flamingo Rd., between Koval Lane and Paradise Rd., Las Vegas, NV 89109. Tel. 702/732-9100 or toll free 800/732-7889. Fax 702/731-9784. 133 rms, 17 suites. A/C TV TEL

$ Rates: Single or double $65–$95 for studios, $95 suites, $100–$175 hospitality suites. Extra person $15. Children 18 and under free in parents' room. AE, CB, DC, DISC, MC, V. **Parking:** Free (self and valet).

Housed in three resortlike mauve-trimmed peach stucco buildings, Emerald Springs offers a friendly, low-key alternative to casino-hotel glitz and glitter. It's entered via a charming marble-floored lobby centered on a waterfall fountain and lush faux tropical plantings under a domed skylight. Off the lobby is a comfortably furnished lounge with a large-screen TV and working fireplace. Typical of the inn's hospitality is a bowl of apples for the taking at the front desk. However, though your surroundings here are serene, you're only two blocks from the heart of the Strip.

The property is still brand new (opened 1991), so public areas and rooms look especially clean and spiffy. Pristine hallways are hung with very nice abstract paintings and have small seating areas on every level. Rooms are beautifully decorated in teal and mauve with bleached-oak furnishings. Even the smallest accommodations (studios) offer small sofas, desks, and armchairs with hassocks. You also get two phones (desk and bedside), an in-room coffee maker, an AM/FM alarm-clock radio, a wet bar, a refrigerator, a remote-control color TV (concealed in an armoire) with HBO and pay-movie options; VCRs are available on request. There's a separate dressing room and a hair dryer in the bath. Suites add a living-room area with a large-screen TV to the above, an eat-in kitchenette with a microwave oven, a larger dressing room, and a Jacuzzi tub. Hospitality suites—the most spacious—have sitting room areas and dining tables, with TVs and phones in every room. A convenience here is parking at your room door.

Dining Just off the lobby (you can hear the splashing of the fountain and waterfall), the **Veranda Café** keeps to the hotel's mauve and teal color scheme. Potted ferns give it a bit of garden ambience, and you can dine al fresco on a covered patio overlooking the pool. A breakfast buffet is served, along with Mexican specialties, pizzas, sandwiches, salads, and a few full-course meals such as blackened prime rib with soup or salad and baked potato. During cocktail hour, hors d'oeuvres such as raw oysters, shrimp, and roast beef sandwiches are offered at cost in the adjoining bar/lounge.

Services Concierge, complimentary transport via limousine to/from airport and nearby casinos between 6:30am and 11pm, room service (dinner only), business services, gratis newspapers available at front desk.

Facilities Emerald Springs has a nice-sized pool/sun deck and whirlpool in an attractively landscaped setting. Guests can use the state-of-the-art nearby Las Vegas Athletic Club at no cost; an on-premises health club is in the works.

DOWNTOWN/CASINO HOTELS

DAYS INN, 707 E. Fremont St., at 7th St., Las Vegas, NV 89101. Tel. 702/388-1400 or toll free 800/325-2344 or 800/325-2525. Fax 702/388-9622. 140 rms, 7 suites. A/C TV TEL
$ **Rates** (for up to four people): $40–$60 for a one-bedded room, $45–$70 for a two-bedded room. Holiday rates can be considerably higher. "Super Saver" rate ($29 single or double) if you reserve 30 days in advance via the 800/325-2525 toll-free number (subject to availability). AE, CB, DC, DISC, JCB, MC, V. **Parking:** Free (self).

Opened in 1988, this Days Inn still looks quite new. Rooms, in a U-shaped three-story building, are cheerfully decorated in shades of mint and raspberry, with teal carpeting and oak-look furnishings. Brass-framed paintings of palm trees adorn the walls. There's a rooftop pool and sun deck, and the adjacent Franklin Bros. casino and 24-hour restaurant are nearing completion at this writing (24-hour room service will be offered).

JACKIE GAUGHAN'S PLAZA HOTEL/CASINO, 1 Main St., at Fremont St., Las Vegas, NV 89101. Tel. 702/386-2110 or toll free 800/634-6575. Fax 702/382-8281. 876 rms, 161 suites. A/C TV TEL
$ **Rates:** Sun–Thurs $40, Fri–Sat $50–$75; suites $60–$150. Extra person $8. Children under 12 free in parents' room. AE, CB, DC, DISC, MC, V. **Parking:** Free (self and valet).

Built in 1971 on the site of the old Union Pacific Railroad Depot, the Plaza, a double-towered, three-block-long property, permanently altered the Downtown skyline. Las Vegas's Amtrak station is right in the hotel, and the main Greyhound terminal adjoins it.

Rooms in both towers are large, standard hotel units—clean but not fancy. I prefer the newer South Tower accommodations, decorated in peach and muted green, with grasspaper wall coverings and oak furnishings in traditional styles.

Dining Center Stage Restaurant, under a domed skylight, is decorated in forest green with beige linen tablecloths and bamboo-motif brass chairs. Some seating offers spectacular views of Downtown and Strip nighttime neon glitter. The menu lists about a dozen entrées—prime rib, steaks, broiled pork chops, Alaskan crab legs with drawn butter, and others—all served with soup or salad, vegetables, potato or rice pilaf, and coffee. Dinner only; entrées $8.50–$11.95.

The **Plaza Coffee Shop,** a large, dimly lit 24-hour facility, keeps to the railroad theme with a mural of the Union Pacific depot on one wall. A specialty available throughout the day is a pound of Alaskan crab legs served with fettuccine Alfredo, garlic toast, soup or salad, and beverage for $6.95. Other evening-only full-meal specials feature baked stuffed chicken, panfried brook trout amandine, and roast sirloin. And a round-the-clock breakfast special gives you bacon and eggs with hash browns, toast, and coffee for just 99¢.

Kung Fu Plaza, like Center Stage, is done up in forest green. It's garden themed, with leaf-pattern wallpaper, white trellising looped with philodendrons, and seating in bamboo fan-back chairs. Chinese and Thai cuisines are featured. Cantonese dishes include roast duck, sweet-and-sour pork, ginger beef, and panfried jumbo shrimp sautéed in wine sauce. Thai fare ranges from spicy chicken curry with coconut milk to pad Thai—fresh bay shrimp sautéed with noodles, bean sprouts, peanuts, salted turnip, and egg. Open lunch and dinner; most entrées $5.95–$7.95.

Other food and beverage facilities include an ice-cream parlor (open 11am–11pm), a 24-hour casino snack bar, several casino cocktail bars, and the **Omaha Lounge** offering live entertainment in the casino almost around-the-clock.

Services   Guest-services desk (also handles shows and tours).

Facilities   Casino, car-rental desk, shops (gifts, liquor, jewelry), wedding chapel, beauty salon/barbershop. There's a sports deck with a nice-sized swimming pool, a ¼-mile outdoor jogging track, and four Har-Tru tennis courts lit for night play.

LADY LUCK CASINO HOTEL, 206 N. Third St., at Ogden Ave., Las Vegas, NV 89101. Tel. 702/477-3000 or toll free 800/523-9582. Fax 702/384-2832. 630 rms, 162 suites. A/C TV TEL

$ Rates: Single or double $43–$50 Sun–Thurs, $61–$83 Fri–Sat; junior suites $55–$66 Sun–Thurs, $83–$99 Fri–Sat. Extra person $8. AE, CB, DC, DISC, JCB, MC, V. **Parking:** Free (self and valet).

What is today Lady Luck opened in 1964 as Honest John's—a 2,000-square-foot casino with five employees, five pinball machines, and 17 slots. Today that casino occupies 30,000 square feet, and the hotel—including sleek 17- and 25-story towers—is a major downtown player taking up an entire city block. What it retains from earlier times is a friendly atmosphere—one that has kept customers coming back for decades. Eighty percent of Lady Luck's clientele is repeat business. I especially like the casino here, because windowed walls let daylight stream in—a rare phenomenon in this town.

Tower rooms are decorated in a variety of attractive color schemes, mostly utilizing muted southwestern hues (peach, mauve, beige, and teal) with handsome oak furnishings. All are equipped with small refrigerators, AM/FM alarm-clock radios, nice marble baths, and remote-control color cable TVs with Spectravision movie options. Junior suites in the West Tower have parlor areas with sofas and armchairs, separate dressing areas, and baths with whirlpool tubs. The original Garden Rooms are a little smaller and less spiffy looking in terms of decor; on the plus side, they're right by the pool and they're less expensive.

Dining   The **Burgundy Room** evokes Paris in the 1930s, with plush burgundy velvet-upholstered booths and period artworks on display, including lithographs and original prints by Erté,

Poucette, and Salvador Dalí and art deco sculptures by Max Le Verrier. Tables, set with pale pink linen cloths, are elegantly appointed and lit by Venetian hurricane lamps. The menu highlights steak, prime rib, pasta dishes, and fresh seafood, including live Maine lobster (you can choose your own from a tank). Tableside flambé preparations are a specialty. Hence, desserts include fresh berries flambé with a mixture of liqueurs served atop french vanilla ice cream. Dinner only; entrées $10.95–$19.95.

The **Emperor's Room** is also enhanced by museum-quality paintings, sculpture, and screens from the owner's collection, including an exact replica of a work called "Soldiers of Xian" dating from 2000 B.C. It's an elegant setting, with candlelit, white-linened tables and a Persian rug on the floor. A mural on one wall shows the route of Marco Polo's voyage to the Orient. Cantonese, Mandarin, and Szechuan entrées include moo shu pork with pancakes, spicy fried chicken in garlicky ginger sauce, and sautéed shrimps, scallops, and vegetables served in a crispy nest. Dinner only; most entrées $6.25–$11.25.

The **Brasserie,** a 24-hour coffee shop overlooking the casino action, is also Paris themed, its walls hung with French art nouveau posters. The extensive menu, however, is mostly American with a good selection of Mexican (quesadillas, burritos, chimichangas) and Chinese (kung pao chicken, Szechuan shrimp) specialties. Also noted are a number of heart-smart suggestions—not just the usual boring cottage cheese and fruit plate but original fare such as a Moroccan tabbouleh salad or broiled halibut in citrus sauce served with fresh fruit wedges and steamed vegetables.

In addition, there are daily buffets (details in Chapter 6), and ESPN sports are aired on three TV monitors in the **Casino Bar.**

Services 24-hour room service, multilingual front desk, free gaming lessons, complimentary airport shuttle.

Facilities Casino, tour and show desks, car-rental desk, gift shop, swimming pool and sun deck.

4. INEXPENSIVE

These are basically the lowest-priced hotels and motels in town. They include a few major Strip properties such as Circus Circus and Excalibur. Do keep in mind that off season you can sometimes get into hotels in the "Moderate" to "Very Expensive" categories at budget rates by bargaining with the reservations clerk.

ON THE STRIP/CASINO HOTELS

CIRCUS CIRCUS HOTEL/CASINO, 2880 Las Vegas Blvd. S., between Circus Circus Dr. and Convention Center Dr., Las Vegas, NV 89109. Tel. 702/734-0410 or toll free 800/634-3450 (800/634-6833 from AZ, CA, ID, OR, and UT). Fax 702/734-2268. 2,674 rms, 126 suites. A/C TV TEL

$ Rates: Sun–Thurs $21–$38 for up to four people, Fri–Sat $28–$49, holidays $48; suites Sun–Thurs $46, Fri–Sat $55,

two-bedroom parlor suite $129. AE, CB, DC, DISC, MC, V.
Parking: Free (self and valet).

Ⓢ A 123-foot clown (his name is Lucky) and a festive pink-and-white circus tent beckon visitors to Circus Circus, a hotel that revolutionized Las Vegas tourism by offering a wealth of entertainment for kids. The midway level features dozens of carnival games, a large state-of-the-art arcade (over 300 video and pinball games), trick mirrors, and ongoing circus acts under the big top from 11am to midnight daily. The world's largest permanent circus according to the *Guinness Book of World Records,* it features renowned trapeze artists, stunt cyclists, jugglers, performing pooches, magicians, acrobats, and high-wire daredevils. Spectators can view the action from much of the midway or get up close and comfy on benches in the performance arena. There's a "be-a-clown" booth where kids can be made up with washable clown makeup and red foam rubber noses. The carnival games comprise "a junior casino" (the winnings are stuffed animals). Kids can grab a bite to eat in McDonald's, also on this level. And the mezzanine overlooks the casino action, providing the security of looking down and waving to mom and dad. Circus clowns wander the midway creating balloon animals and cutting up in various ways. Sometimes they even work the front desk.

The thousands of rooms here occupy sufficient acreage to warrant a free Disney World–style monorail (another kid pleaser) and minibuses connecting its many components. Accommodations throughout are cheerful, decorated in bright red and blue color schemes. Some have ecru walls adorned with hot-air balloons, others feature striped wallpapers, and all utilize circus-themed art, clown lamps, etc. Skyrise Tower rooms offer showers only in the bath. All rooms here have safes and color TVs with in-house information and gaming stations. Circus Tower rooms are larger and do offer tub baths; however, all the hotel's accommodations are attractive. You get a lot for your hotel dollar here. The Manor section comprises five white three-story buildings out back fronted by rows of cypress. Manor rooms are being totally renovated as this book goes to press, so they should be in tip-top shape by the time you read this. Manor guests can park at their doors, and a gate to the complex that can be opened only with a room key assures security. All sections of this vast property have their own swimming pools and casino areas, and both towers offer covered parking garages.

Dining   Very popular with locals is the hotel's elegant candlelit **Steak House,** its cherry-paneled walls hung with gilt-framed oil landscapes and other pastoral scenes. Shelves of books and green glass chandeliers create a clubby look. There's an open exhibition kitchen where sides of beef are displayed, and a plush lounge adjoins. The menu features hefty portions of succulent mesquite-grilled aged midwestern beef (top sirloin, porterhouse, New York strip, filet mignon), lamb chops, prime rib, lobster, mesquite-broiled chicken, or surf and turf—all served with soup or salad, huge baked potatoes, cheddar cheese sauce, and dark, sweet bread. There's cheesecake for dessert. Dinner only; entrées $12–$20.

The very reasonably priced **Pink Pony** is Circus Circus's cheerful bubble-gum pink and bright red 24-hour coffee shop with big paintings of clowns on the walls and pink pony-motif carpeting. It offers a wide array of coffee shop fare, including a number of specially marked heart-smart (low-fat, low-cholesterol) items.

The **Skyrise Dining Room,** another festive 24-hour facility in the Skyrise Tower, has bright red chairs and booths, lots of decorative brass trim, and walls hung with old-fashioned circus posters. Its menu is similar to the Pink Pony's. A 16-ounce prime rib dinner here is just $6.95.

There's a brass-railed **Pizzeria** in the main casino, a cheerful setting with roomy red and green booths and red or yellow tables. Hung with colorful banners, it offers pies with a choice of 20 toppings.

In addition there are seven casino bars throughout the Circus Circus complex, most notable of which is the carousel-themed **Horse-A-Round Bar** on the midway level. And speaking of the midway level, don't forget **McDonald's.** The Circus Buffet is detailed in Chapter 6.

Services Limited room service (continental breakfast and drinks only), shoeshine.

Facilities Casinos, wedding chapel, tour and show desks, car-rental desk, unisex hairdresser, two swimming pools, two video game arcades, shops (see Chapter 10).

Adjacent to the hotel is **Circusland RV Park,** with 421 full-utility spaces and up to 50-amp hookups. It has its own 24-hour convenience store, swimming pools, saunas, Jacuzzis, kiddie playground, fenced pet runs, video game arcade, and community room. Rate is $10 per night.

EXCALIBUR, 3850 Las Vegas Blvd. S., at Tropicana Ave., Las Vegas, NV 89109. Tel. 702/597-7777 or toll free 800/937-7777. Fax 702/597-7040. 4,032 rms. A/C TV TEL
$ Rates: For up to four people: Sun–Thurs $39, Fri–Sat $59–$69. Children under 12 free in parents' room, children over 12 pay $7 weekends only. AE, CB, DC, MC, V. **Parking:** Free (self and valet).

The largest resort hotel in the world, Excalibur (aka "the Realm"), is a gleaming white turreted castle complete with moated drawbridge, battlements, and lofty towers. In this Arthurian fantasy world, cocktail waitresses and dealers wear medieval garb, the casino is festooned with armor and heraldic banners, and knights, jesters, madrigal singers, and dancing "bears" roam the premises. The second floor comprises the hotel's Medieval Village— site of Excalibur's restaurants and quaint shops along winding streets and alleyways. On the village's Jester's Stage, jugglers, puppeteers, and magicians delight guests with free 20-minute performances throughout the day. Another unique Excalibur feature is the Fantasie Faire, down a level from the casino, where colorful stalls and gypsy wagons are laden with international gifts and folk art. The Faire also offers crafts demonstrations and has a large video game arcade, dozens of medieval-themed carnival games, and two "magic motion machine" theaters featuring high-tech visual thrills—simulated bobsled, rollercoaster, and runaway train adventures enhanced by hydraulically activated seats that synchronize with on-screen action.

There's enough to entertain kids for hours while mom and dad enjoy the casino.

Rooms keep to the Arthurian-legend motif with walls papered to look like stone castle walls. Oak furnishings are heraldically embellished, torchier sconces frame the mirror, your bedspread is fleur-de-lis themed, and prints of jousting knights adorn the walls. The cheerful color scheme is essentially turquoise and coral.

Dining Camelot is the Excalibur's gourmet restaurant, about which more in Chapter 6.

Sir Galahad's, a prime rib restaurant, occupies a candlelit "castle" chamber with massive oak beams and wrought-iron candelabra chandeliers overhead. Seating is in large tapestried booths; Tudor-style walls are embellished with crossed swords, patinized torchiers, and heraldic crests; and lace-curtained windows are framed by gold-tasseled burgundy brocade drapes. The menu features prime rib dinners only, served with beef-barley soup or salad, homemade mashed potatoes, creamed spinach, Yorkshire pudding, and creamed horseradish. A la carte desserts include English trifle. Dinner only; entrées $8.95–$13.95.

Lance-A-Lotta Pasta is a flamboyantly Italian dining room, with interior awnings and street lamps, fluted columns, and whimsical wall decorations that include a doll carriage, a pitchfork, a sled, immense garlic cloves, and other assorted paraphernalia. Bunches of grapes, strands of pasta, cheeses, and peppers are suspended overhead. Tables are set with green and white striped cloths and red napkins. And festive Italian music sets the mood. The menu lists pizzas and pastas, subs and hero sandwiches. Open lunch and dinner; all entrées under $5 at lunch, under $8 at dinner.

Equally festive is **Oktoberfest,** designed to resemble a German village street scene with colorful flower boxes adorning the backlit windows of Tudor-style house facades. Once again there are interior awnings and tapestried booths—here at sturdy oak trestle tables. Bavarian music is provided by a live oompah-pah band at dinner. In good weather you can dine in the adjoining outdoor beer garden with umbrella tables amid trees and flowers in big terra-cotta pots. The menu offers bratwurst and sauerkraut, schnitzel, sauerbraten, and goulash, among other specialties, and there's black forest cake for dessert. Open for dinner and weekend champagne brunches; dinner entrées $3.95–$10.95, champagne brunch $7.95.

The **Sherwood Forest Café,** its entrance guarded by a sentry of lavender dragons (kids love to climb on them), is Excalibur's 24-hour facility. In heraldic mode, it has leaded-glass windows, wrought-iron candelabra chandeliers, faux stone walls, and adornments that include banners, crests, and cannons. The menu offers the usual Vegas coffee shop mix of sandwiches, burgers, salads, and serious entrées, but there are some unexpected desserts such as brioche Romanoff—a fresh-baked sweet brioche filled with Grand Marnier–marinated strawberries.

Another heraldic dining room, the **Round Table Buffet,** is detailed in Chapter 6. Other facilities include three snack bars named **Robin Hood** (in the Medieval Village), **Hansel & Gretel** (in Fantasie Faire), and **Little John's** (in the casino). The **Village Pub** is an Alpine-themed bar in Medieval Village; the **Minstrel's Thea-**

tre Lounge, off the casino, offers live entertainment nightly (during the day movies and sporting events are shown on a large-screen TV); a circular bar called **King's Pavilion** serves the high-stakes slot area; and a snack and cocktail bar serves the North pool.

Services   Limited 24-hour rooms service (continental breakfast and pizza only), free gaming lessons, shoeshine.

Facilities   Casino, tour and show desks, a state-of-the-art video game arcade), wedding chapel (you can marry in medieval attire), unisex hairdresser, car-rental desk, a parking lot that can accommodate RVs, shops (see Chapter 10). There are two swimming pools. The North pool follows a circular path around a sun-deck island, the South Pool is larger and has more shaded area if you should want to move out of the sun.

WESTWARD HO MOTEL & CASINO, 2900 Las Vegas Blvd. S., between Circus Circus and Convention Center Drs., Las Vegas, NV 89109. Tel. 702/731-2900 or toll free 800/634-6803. 656 rms, 121 suites. A/C TV TEL
$ Rates: $24–$49 single or double (sometimes higher holidays), $76 suite. Extra person $10. Children under 18 free in parents' room. MC, V. **Parking:** Free at your room door.
Very centrally located on the Strip (right next door to Circus Circus), the Westward Ho is fronted by a vast casino, with rooms in two-story buildings extending out back for several city blocks. In fact, the property is so large that a free shuttle bus goes back and forth between rooms and the casino on a continual basis 24 hours a day. Three swimming pools and three whirlpool spas are necessary to serve all areas.

Rooms are clean and adequately furnished no-frills motel units. A good buy here: two-bedroom suites with 1½ baths, living rooms with sofa beds, and refrigerators; they sleep up to six people.

There's a 24-hour restaurant in the casino under a stained-glass skylight dome. It serves buffet breakfasts ($1.49), lunches ($3.99), and dinners ($4.99), in addition to an à la carte menu featuring traditional coffee shop fare and a $3.95 steak dinner. Other facilities include a tour desk, free airport shuttle, a gift shop, a casino lounge where a three-piece country band entertains Monday to Saturday from 7pm–1am, and a deli in the casino serving sandwiches, ribs, and half-pound extra-long hot dogs.

ON THE STRIP/NONCASINO HOTELS

ALGIERS HOTEL, 2845 Las Vegas Blvd. S., between Riviera Blvd. and Sahara Ave., Las Vegas, NV 89109. Tel. 702/735-3311 or toll free 800/732-3361. Fax 702/792-2112. 103 rms, 2 suites. A/C TV TEL
$ Rates: $35–$65 single or double. Extra person $5. Children under 12 free in parents' room. AE, CB, DC, DISC, MC, V. **Parking:** Free (self).
A senior citizen on the Strip, the Algiers opened in 1953. However, a recent multimillion dollar renovation—including landscaping (note pretty flower beds out back) and a new facade with a 60-foot sign—has brought rooms and public areas up to date. There's no casino here, though you can play video poker in the bar. The Algiers's

neat two-story, aqua-trimmed peach stucco buildings center on a medium-sized pool and palm-fringed sun deck. Nice-sized rooms are clean and spiffy looking, with birch-wood-look paneling, light-wood furniture, and brand-new teal carpets. All have dressing areas.

The cozy Algiers Restaurant & Lounge is a local hangout frequented by state and city politicians and journalists. It has a copper-hooded fireplace and walls hung with historic Las Vegas photographs of pretower Strip hotels (Dunes, Sands, Flamingo), Liberace cutting the ribbon at the opening of the Riviera, Clara Bow and Joey Adams with the owner of the now-defunct Thunderbird, and many more. A glassed-in café overlooks the pool. The restaurant serves all meals, including many steak and seafood specialties, barbecued baby back ribs, and low-calorie items. There are souvenir shops, a jeweler, and a car-rental office out front. Also on the premises is the famed Candlelight Chapel, where many celebrities have tied the knot over the last three decades. Local calls are free and you can park at your room door. Room service is offered during restaurant hours.

The Algiers is a good choice for families—right across the street from Circus Circus with its many child-oriented facilities and a half block from Wet 'N Wild.

CENTER STRIP INN, 3688 Las Vegas Blvd. S., at Harmon Ave., Las Vegas, NV 89109. Tel. 702/739-6066 or toll free 800/777-7737. Fax 702/736-2521. 86 rms, 6 suites. A/C TV TEL

$ Rates (including continental breakfast): Sun–Thurs $29.95 single, $39.95 double, Fri–Sat and holidays $49.95–$89.95 single or double. Extra person $5, children 13 and under free. Mention you read about the Center Strip in Frommer's for a $5 discount Sun–Thurs. AE, CB, DC, DISC, ER, MC, V. **Parking:** Free at your room door.

This centrally located little motel is owned and operated by Robert Cohen, who is usually on the premises making sure guests are happy. He's a bit of an eccentric, and his hotel doesn't fit into any expected budget-property pattern. Rooms, for instance, have VCRs, and a selection of about 1,000 movies can be rented for just $2 each. Local calls and use of a Fax machine are free. Rates include continental breakfast (danish, doughnuts, pastries, juice, and coffee), and free coffee is available in the lobby all day. The desk often has coupons for free breakfasts at the El Cortez Hotel downtown. Also available at the front desk: irons, hair dryers, and gratis bath amenities (lotion, shampoo, conditioner, talc, suntan lotion, nail polish remover, even a toothbrush).

Rooms, housed in two-story white stucco buildings, are standard motel units with oak-look furnishings, but they do have small refrigerators, in-room safes, AM/FM clock radios, and color cable TVs offering free Showtime movies.

There's no on-premises restaurant, but a 24-hour Denny's adjoins, numerous hotel restaurants are within easy walking distance, and you can have pizza delivered to your room. Facilities include a swimming pool and sun deck and a car-rental desk; the front desk can arrange tours.

Future plans call for a new building to house 45 luxury suites with full kitchens and Jacuzzis. Cohen also operates two downtown properties where rates begin at just $19.95 per room.

CONVENTION CENTER AREA/ A NONCASINO HOTEL

VILLA ROMA, 220 Convention Center Dr., between the Strip and Paradise Rd., Las Vegas, NV 89109. Tel. 702/735-4151 or toll free 800/634-6535. Fax 702/735-5211. 100 rms. A/C TV TEL

$ Rates: Single or double $25–$55 Sun–Thurs, $35–$65 Fri–Sat. Extra person $5. Children under 12 free in parents' room. AE, CB, DC, MC, V. **Parking:** Free at your room door.

Just a half block from the Strip, Villa Roma adjoins the Wild West–themed Silver City Casino—the only totally nonsmoking gambling hall in town. Spacious rooms are clean and decently furnished. They're typical motel accommodations with cream-colored walls and dark-wood pieces. AM/FM clock radios and in-room coffee makers are provided, and local calls are free. There's a small pool on the premises, and though the motel has no restaurant, many are within easy walking distance. The front desk can arrange tours to nearby sights.

NEAR THE STRIP/A CASINO MOTEL

SUPER 8 MOTEL, 4250 Koval Lane, just south of Flamingo Rd., Las Vegas, NV 89109. Tel. 702/794-0888 or toll free 800/800-8000. 294 rms, 6 suites. A/C TV TEL

$ Rates: Sun–Thurs $32.88 for one person, $35.88–$40.88 for two people; Fri–Sat $46.88 for one, $50.88–$52.88 for two. Rates may be higher during holidays and conventions. Extra person $4. Children 12 and under free in parents' room. Pets $5 per night. AE, CB, DC, DISC, JCB, MC, V. **Parking:** Free (self).

Billing itself as "the world's largest Super 8 Motel," this friendly property occupies a vaguely Tudor-style stone and stucco building. Coffee is served gratis each morning in a pleasant little lobby furnished with comfortable sofas and wing chairs, and you can help yourself to fresh-popped popcorn all day from a machine in the casino.

Rooms are clean and well maintained. They're standard motel units decorated in three color schemes (burgundy/gray, forest green, or navy/muted blues), with cream stucco walls, oak furnishings, and bedspreads and drapes in splashy floral prints. Some rooms have safes and/or water beds. All offer remote-control color cable TVs with free movie channels and Spectravision pay-movie options.

Dining The **Ellis Island Restaurant** has a nautical decor comprised of tufted red leather booths, dark-wood beams and paneling, and a few seagoing artifacts such as ship models and steering wheels on display. Open around-the-clock, it offers typical coffee shop fare at reasonable prices, including a soup and salad bar at lunch and dinner and an all-you-can-eat Sunday brunch with unlimited champagne for $7.95. In the adjoining bar—a librarylike setting with shelves of books and green marble tables—sporting events are aired on TV monitors. There's also a bar in the casino with a karaoke machine.

Services   24-hour room service.

Facilities   Casino (race book and 50 slot/poker/21 machines), small kidney-shaped pool/sun deck and adjoining whirlpool, gift shop, car-rental desk, tour desk, unisex hair salon, small video game arcade, coin-op washers/dryers.

NEAR THE STRIP/A NONCASINO MOTEL

MOTEL 6, 195 E. Tropicana Ave., at Koval Lane, Las Vegas, NV 89109. Tel. 702/798-0728. 880 rms. A/C TV TEL

$ Rates: $27.99 one person. Extra person $6. Children under 18 free in parents' room. AE, CB, DC, DISC, MC, V. **Parking:** Free at your room door.

Fronted by a vast neon sign, Las Vegas's Motel 6 is the largest in the country, and it happens to be a great budget choice. Most Motel 6 properties are a little out of the way, but this one is very close to major Strip casino hotels. It has a big, pleasant lobby, and rooms, housed in two-story cream stucco buildings, are clean and attractively decorated with brown carpeting, white walls, and forest-green bedspreads. Some rooms have showers only, others tub/shower baths. Local calls are free and your TV has a free movie station. Three restaurants (including a 24-hour Carrows; see La Quinta above) adjoin, one of them in a casino. On-premises facilities include a large well-stocked gift shop, a tour desk, a nice-sized swimming pool in an enclosed courtyard, a smaller pool serving rooms out back, and coin-op washers and dryers.

DOWNTOWN/CASINO HOTELS

CALIFORNIA HOTEL/CASINO & RV PARK, 12 Ogden Ave., at First St., Las Vegas, NV 89101. Tel. 702/385-1222 or toll free 800/634-6255. Fax 702/388-2660. 600 rms, 50 suites. A/C TV TEL

$ Rates: Single or double $40 Sun–Thurs, $50 Fri–Sat, $60 holidays. Extra person $5. Children 12 and under free in parents' room. AE, CB, DC, DISC, MC, V. **Parking:** Free (self and valet).

This is a hotel with a very unique personality. California-themed, it markets mostly in Hawaii, and since 85% of the guests are from the "Aloha State," it offers Hawaiian entrées in several of its restaurants and even has an on-premises food store specializing in Hawaiian foodstuffs. You'll also notice that dealers are wearing colorful Hawaiian shirts. Of course, all are welcome to enjoy the aloha spirit here.

Rooms, however, do not reflect either state. Decorated in contemporary-look burgundy/mauve or apricot/teal color schemes, they have mahogany furnishings and attractive marble baths. In-room safes are a plus, and TVs have keno channels.

Dining   Decorated in forest green, with redwood paneling and a massive stone fireplace, the **Redwood Bar & Grill** looks like an elegant ski lodge. It has tapestried armchairs and booths at candlelit bare oak tables, and green-shaded gaslight-style fixtures provide soft lighting. There's piano bar entertainment in the adjoining lounge. The menu features steak, chops, prime rib, and seafood along with a few diverse entrées such as apricot chicken. You might begin your meal with crab wontons, have a combination filet mignon and lobster entrée, and finish with apple walnut pie. Dinner only; most entrées $12.95–$24.95.

The brick-floored **Pasta Pirate** evokes a coastal cannery warehouse with a corrugated-tin ceiling and exposed overhead pipes. Tables are candlelit, walls hung with neon signs and historic pages from the *San Francisco Chronicle*. You can design your own pasta dish—"first you picka you pasta, then you picka you sauce" (don't blame me, I'm quoting the menu). It comes with salad and a glass of wine. Or opt for mesquite-grilled salmon, filet mignon, tuna, shrimp, or succulent lobster tail—all served with soup or salad, pasta, stir-fried veggies, and a glass of wine. You can see food preparation going on in a display kitchen. Dinner only; pasta dinners $8, entrées $12–$20.

The **Market Street Café** is the requisite 24-hour facility. This one is rather charming, its walls hung with old-fashioned shop signs and historic photographs of San Francisco. The menu lists all the expected coffee shop fare, including Hawaiian items and specially marked "heart-smart" choices. A noteworthy special is the 18-ounce porterhouse steak dinner for $10.95, including soup or salad bar, vegetables, potatoes, and roll and butter.

The **Cal Club Snack Bar** is a casual cafeteria with an ice-cream parlor decor—a black-and-white checkerboard floor and chrome-rimmed tables. It does serve ice-cream sundaes, along with Hawaiian soft drinks (flavors like guava and island punch) and Chinese/ Japanese snack fare—sushi, egg rolls, wonton soup, tempura.

There are two 24-hour casino bars, the **Main Street Bar** and the **San Francisco Pub. Dave's Aloha Bar** on the mezzanine level is a tropical setting for exotic cocktails, liqueur-spiked coffees and ice-cream drinks, and international beers.

Services Room service (breakfast only).

Facilities Casino, car-rental desk, small rooftop pool, small video game arcade, shops (gift shop, chocolates). A food store called **Aloha Specialties** carries kimchee, saimin, macadamia nuts, curries, and numerous flavors of jerky (beef, buffalo, sweet pork, and so on); there are a few umbrella tables outside where these victuals might be consumed.

The California also has an attractively landscaped 222-space RV park with pull-through spaces; 192 spaces offer full hookup, and 30 provide electric and water. Facilities include restrooms, showers, a coin-op laundry, dog run, convenience store, swimming pool, and whirlpool. Rate is $12 a night.

EL CORTEZ HOTEL & CASINO, 600 Fremont St., between 6th and 7th Sts., Las Vegas, NV 89101. Tel. 702/385-5200 or toll free 800/634-6703. 108 rms, 200 minisuites. A/C TV TEL

$ Rates: $23–$28 single or double, $32–$40 minisuite. Extra person $3. AE, CB, DC, DISC, JCB, MC, V. **Parking:** Free (self and valet).

This small hotel is popular with locals for its casual just-folks Downtown atmosphere and its frequent big-prize lotteries (up to $50,000) based on social-security numbers. The nicest accommodations are the enormous minisuites in the newer 14-story tower. Decorated in cool earth tones with sienna and teal accents, they have oak furnishings and attractive leaf-print bedspreads and drapes. Some are just exceptionally large king-bedded rooms with sofas; others have separate sitting areas with sofas, armchairs, and tables plus small dressing areas. Rooms in the original building are furnished more traditionally and with less flair—however, they cost less. Local calls cost just 25¢.

Roberta's Café, a pretty candlelit restaurant decorated in sienna and teal, has tulip-motif fabric wall coverings and etched-glass panels. A pink glow emanates from recessed lighting in a cove ceiling. The menu features charbroiled steaks, prime rib, southern-fried chicken, barbecued baby back ribs, and seafood entrées such as jumbo crab legs and rainbow trout amandine—all served with soup or salad, baked potato, hot rolls and butter, and coffee. There's cheesecake for dessert. Dinner only; most entrées $5.95–$10.95.

There's also a large 24-hour coffee shop called the **Emerald Room** featuring a bacon-and-eggs breakfast with hash browns, toast, and coffee for $1. A soup-to-nuts 18-ounce porterhouse steak dinner is $6.45 here, many other full dinners are $4–$6, and Mexican combination platters are an option. Four bars serve the casino.

On-premises facilities include a small video game arcade, a beauty salon, a gift shop, and a barbershop.

Under the same ownership is **Ogden House,** right across the street, with rooms for just $18 a night.

FITZGERALD'S CASINO/HOTEL, 301 E. Fremont St., at Third St., Las Vegas, NV 89101. Tel. 702/388-2400 or toll free 800/274-LUCK. Fax 702/388-2181. 652 rms. A/C TV TEL

$ Rates: Single or double Sun–Thurs $24–$42, Fri–Sat $45–$90. Extra person $10. Children under 12 free in parents' room. AE, CB, DC, DISC, MC, V. **Parking:** Free (self and valet).

At 34 stories the tallest building in Nevada, Fitzgerald's is Irish themed with pieces of the actual Blarney stone from County Cork at various points in the casino (rub them for luck) and a four-leaf clover logo. There's a little museum of luck on the premises with a two-tailed lizard and other symbols of good fortune. And even rooms—decorated in rust and forest green with dark-stained oak furnishings—look a bit like leprechaun habitats. All have remote-control TVs with pay-movie options. Corner rooms offer great two-sided views, and 34 rooms have Jacuzzis and sofas.

Dining Oak-paneled and oak-beamed, the American-nostalgia-themed **Cassidy's** has a handsome interior, like the rooms done up in rust and forest green. Cream stucco walls are hung with photographs of America the way it used to be—old cafés, barns, fire stations, diners, and roadhouses. An eclectic lunch menu lists

Irish mulligan stew, Mexican fajitas, and fettuccine Alfredo, along with salads and sandwiches. At dinner, mesquite-grilled steaks, seafood, and pasta dishes are highlighted. Open lunch and dinner; lunch entrées $4.95–$6.95, most dinner entrées $8–$13.

Molly's Country Kitchen is the 24-hour coffee shop, and a very attractive one it is, with booths and chairs upholstered in charcoal gray and planters of greenery creating intimate seating areas. Inexpensive meals include fried pork chops with pan gravy and applesauce, served with corn chowder soup, homemade whipped potatoes, coleslaw, and biscuits for $5.95.

Fitzgerald's also offers buffets at all meals (breakfast $3, lunch $4, dinner $5). There's a **McDonald's** on the casino floor, and three bars serve the casino, one of them featuring lounge acts.

Services   Room service 6am–2pm and 5–11pm, complimentary gaming lessons.

Facilities   Casino, tour and show desks, car-rental desk, health club (1/17-mile running track, weight room, Universal multistation machine, treadmill, exercise bike), gift shop.

FOUR QUEENS, 202 E. Fremont St., at Casino Center Blvd., Las Vegas, NV 89101. Tel. 702/385-4011 or toll free 800/634-6045. Fax 702/383-0631. 682 rms, 38 minisuites. A/C TV TEL

$ Rates: Single or double $47 Sun–Thurs, $57 Fri–Sat; minisuites $85–$95. Extra person $8. Children under 12 free in parents' room. AE, CB, DC, DISC, MC, V. **Parking:** Free (self and valet).

Opened in 1965 as a nonhotel casino, the Four Queens has evolved over the decades into a major Downtown property occupying an entire city block. Its attributes include an on-premises museum, good restaurants, and a cheerful, brightly lit casino featuring the world's largest slot machine (over nine feet high and almost 20 feet long; six people can play it at one time).

Notably attractive rooms are housed in 19-story twin towers. Especially lovely are the minty-green North Tower rooms with white-painted brass bed frames, very pretty floral-print bedspreads and wallpapers, gaslight-style bed lamps, lace-curtained windows, and gilt-framed impressionist prints on the walls. South Tower rooms are decorated in earth tones with dark-wood furnishings, leaf-design bedspreads and drapes, and wallpapers in small floral prints. Minisuites, decorated in traditional styles, have living rooms (separated from bedrooms by a trellised wall) and dining areas, double-sink baths, and dressing areas. All accommodations offer AM/FM alarm-clock radios and color cable TVs with in-house information and pay-movie channels.

Dining   Hugo's Cellar is a plush continental restaurant with an oak-beamed ceiling, exposed brick walls hung with gilt-framed landscape paintings, candlelit white-linened tables, and seating in spacious booths illuminated by amber-bulbed sconces. Entrées are served with a fabulous table-side salad bar, baked lavash with cheese and crusty French bread, fresh vegetables, potato skins with sour cream and chives or red parsley potatoes, sorbet between courses, and a complimentary dessert of light and dark chocolate-dipped fruits with fresh whipped cream. Bottled mountain water is served gratis. Possible entrées: jumbo shrimp stuffed with seasoned crabmeat, sautéed chicken breast with basil and pine nuts in cream sauce, charbroiled steaks and prime ribs, roast rack of lamb with Indonesian spices, and anise-rubbed roast duck flamed in Grand Marnier. Every woman is given a red rose as she is seated. Dinner only; entrées $20–$30.

Magnolia's Veranda, a 24-hour dining facility overlooking the casino, has three sections. The veranda part is a casual café with an oak-beamed ceiling, stained-glass skylight panels, lots of hanging plants, and seating in large peacock chairs. The adjoining courtyard, with Casablanca fans overhead, is simply the nonsmoking area. And there's also a rather elegant crystal-chandeliered section decorated in peach and verdigris, with etched-glass booth dividers and murals of New Orleans on the walls. The same menu is offered throughout. In addition to the requisite coffee shop fare, Magnolia's offers Hawaiian specialties such as teriyaki chicken and broiled mahimahi. And a great deal is the $8.95 prime rib dinner served from 6pm–2am; you get $5 back in slot machine tokens.

The **Snack Shoppe** overlooking the casino offers ice cream and sundaes, sandwiches, hot dogs, tacos, and other light fare. **Hugo's** has a cozy lounge with a working fireplace, live music (including many big-name performers) is featured in the **French Quarter Lounge,** and two bars serve the casino.

Services   24-hour room service.

Facilities   Casino, gift shop, car-rental desk, tour and show desks, small video game arcade. The very entertaining **Ripley's Believe It or Not! Museum** is on the premises, complete with a chamber of horrors, a toilet carved from a walnut, a two-headed calf, and over a thousand other fascinating oddities (details in Chapter 7).

SAM BOYD'S FREMONT HOTEL & CASINO, 200 E. Fremont St., between Casino Center Blvd. and 3rd St., Las Vegas, NV 89101. Tel. 702/385-3232 or toll free 800/634-6182. Fax 702/385-6229. 428 rms, 24 suites. A/C TV TEL

$ Rates: Single or double $25–$36 Sun–Thurs, $52 Fri–Sat, $60 holidays. Extra person $8. Children under 12 free in parents' room. AE, CB, DC, DISC, JCB, MC, V. **Parking:** Free (self and valet).

Under the same ownership as the Stardust, the Fremont was the first high-rise in downtown Las Vegas when it opened in 1956. Wayne Newton got his start here, singing in the now-defunct Carousel Showroom.

Its tower rooms were recently renovated in two decorator schemes—forest green/rust/cream with floral-print drapes and bedspreads or burgundy/mauve/muted blue with paisley-print fabrics. All have neutral-toned striped wallpapers and offer in-room safes and remote-control color cable TVs with house-information channels and pay-movie options.

Dining   Tony Roma's, A Place for Ribs has a branch here. If you're not familiar with this national chain, it offers scrumptious barbecued chicken and smoky, fork-tender baby back ribs. Juicy charbroiled steaks and fresh seafood are additional options. All entrées come with coleslaw and baked potato, fries, or ranch-style beans. A children's menu is a plus. This is a handsome restaurant, with seating amid planters of greenery and oak-wainscoted forest-green walls hung with historic photographs of Las Vegas. Dinner only; entrées $5.45–$12.95.

The **Overland Stage Café,** a comfortable western-themed 24-hour facility with dark-green leather booths, is decorated with murals of cowboys and stagecoaches, displays of miniature stagecoaches, and western paintings. In addition to the requisite coffee shop fare, it offers an extensive Chinese menu from 11am–2am. Many low-priced specials here, too—for example, a $5.95 prime rib dinner. A small snack bar adjoins.

The Fremont has great buffets (see Chapter 6 for details). Lounge acts appear nightly in **Roxy's,** which, along with the **Keno Bar** and **Jake's bar,** serves the casino.

Services Room service at breakfast only.

Facilities Casino, 24-hour gift shop. Guests can use the swimming pool and RV park at the nearby California Hotel, another Sam Boyd enterprise.

SHOWBOAT, 2800 Fremont St., between Charleston Blvd. and Sahara Ave., Las Vegas, NV 89104. Tel. 702/385-9123 or toll free 800/826-2800. Fax 702/383-9283. 475 rms, 7 suites. A/C TV TEL

$ **Rates:** Single or double $26–$45 Sun–Thurs, $30–$65 Fri–Sat, $65 holidays; suites $85–$215. Extra person $8. Children under 12 free in parents' room. AE, CB, DC, DISC, MC, V. **Parking:** Free (self and valet).

Despite its slightly off-the-beaten-track location, this riverboat-themed hotel is very popular for its extensive facilities, friendliness, and totally delightful interior. The Showboat welcomes guests into a charming lobby adorned with flower boxes, murals of Mississippi plantations and riverboats, and stunning Venetian-glass chandeliers. Beautiful oil paintings of the Old South also embellish the cheerful peach and lavender flower-bedecked casino.

The Showboat has a long history in this town. Opened in 1953, it was the first hotel to offer buffet meals—let alone bowling alleys. Today its gorgeous 24-hour bingo parlor is famous—for its flower garden murals and for the highest payouts in town. And the bowling alley—North America's largest—hosts major PBA tournaments.

Spacious rooms are very pretty, with mahogany furnishings in traditional styles, striped wallpapers, and floral-print fabrics that harmonize nicely with the burgundy, teal, or cocoa carpeting. Paintings and lamps are riverboat themed. Baths have dressing areas, and your TV is a remote-control cable color set with pay-movie options.

Dining The **Plantation** keeps to the garden theme. One room evokes a veranda with wooden plank floors and white porch railings backed by exquisite botanical murals. Candlelit tables are covered in pale pink linen. The other dining area is more elegant, with Palladian windows and mirrors and ornate Victorian chandeliers. Together they comprise a lovely setting in which to enjoy mesquite-grilled steaks, prime rib, chops, and seafood specialties such as sautéed Alaskan crab legs. Dinner only; entrées $7.95–$13.95.

Di Napoli diverges from the Old South theme, though it, too, is done in pastel hues (peach and apricot) and has a flower-filled fountain and a grape arbor painted on the ceiling. However, Roman wall frescoes, columns, and classical statuary set the tone for this charming candlelit dining room. The menu features California-influenced southern Italian cuisine, including pizzas topped with goat cheese, sun-dried tomatoes, roasted peppers, pine nuts, and fresh basil. And, Naples being a seaport, there are seafood specialties such as lobster sautéed with garlic, shallots, and white wine served over linguine with a spicy tomato sauce. Dinner only; most entrées $6.95–$14.95.

We're back to the theme at the charming peach-walled 24-hour **Showboat Coffee Shop,** wherein you'll find more riverboat/plantation murals and lots of lacy white trim. It serves everything from light fare to full meals, including Chinese specialties.

There's also a very good buffet here (details in Chapter 6). A snack bar and a bar/lounge are located in the bowling alley. And six bars serve the casino, including the **Mardi Gras Lounge,** featuring big-name groups from the '50s nightly.

Services   24-hour room service, shoeshine.

Facilities   Casino, gift shop, beauty salon/barbershop, 24-hour bowling alley with 106 lanes, bowling pro shop, video game arcade. The Showboat has an Olympic-size swimming pool in a courtyard setting. There's an in-house babysitting center where you can drop off kids age 2–7 at no charge for up to three hours a day. It has TV tapes, a slide, toys, art supplies, and games, and staff members play with the kids and read them stories.

5. HOSTELS

There are two hostels in town, and they're especially fun places for young people. They attract an international clientele, most of them under 30, with a sprinkling of aging hippies. Women traveling alone should be aware that these facilities—though conveniently located (the Sahara Hotel is just a few blocks away)—are in a rather sleazy part of town—the stretch of Las Vegas Boulevard South between the Strip and Downtown. It's not wise for women—probably not wise for anyone—to walk around this area alone at night.

Note: For hostels, July and August are the busiest months, though they happen to be the slowest in the rest of town. Hence, if you want to stay at a hostel because you like hosteling as a way of life, reserve a few weeks in advance. On the other hand, if you're only staying at a hostel to save money, try bargaining with Strip hotels in their off-season; you might obtain very low rates.

AYH HOSTEL, 1236 Las Vegas Blvd. S., between Charleston and Oakey Blvds., Las Vegas, NV 89104. Tel. 702/382-8119. Capacity: 85 people. A/C

$ Rates: $11.50 per night in four-person dorm with shared bath ($8.50 for AYH members), $25 in a private room with bath ($22 for members). No credit cards. **Parking:** Free.

The AYH hostel here offers mostly dorm accommodations in little cottages surrounding a lawn. Reasonably clean, they're on the Spartan side, though they do have carpeted floors, a few sticks of furniture (a lamp and table), and closets. Beds are narrow single cots or bunks. Half the rooms have color TVs. Most baths have showers only. Sheets, a blanket, and pillowcases are provided free; an extra sheet is $1, towels 50¢ each. You can rent a locker for 75¢ a day, and there are coin-op washers and dryers.

However, no one stays at a hostel for its luxury digs. The fun part involves meeting people and hanging out. For this purpose, there are two lounges offering TVs, cassette players, games, a small library. A fully equipped community kitchen has an adjoining dining area. Barbecues are frequent happenings out back on a tree-shaded lawn with picnic tables and chaise longues. And the hostel arranges day trips to Hoover Dam, Red Rock Canyon, Mount Charleston, and Valley of Fire.

Every night you stay at an AYH hostel gives you credit towards membership; ask for details at the desk. There's a 3-night maximum stay when the hostel is very full (usually summer only).

INDEPENDENT YOUTH HOSTEL, 1208 Las Vegas Blvd. S., between Charleston and Oakey Blvds., Las Vegas, NV 89104. Tel. 702/385-9955. Capacity: 60 people. A/C
$ Rates: (including continental breakfast) $8.95 in a dorm room with shared bath accommodating 4–6 people, $19.90 for a private room with shared bath. No credit cards. **Parking:** Free.

Very similar to the above, this unaffiliated hostel also offers clean but Spartan rooms, here in a two-story building. Upstairs rooms are a tad nicer, with balconies and polished pine floors (ceramic tile downstairs). You get a free sheet and pillowcase and pay $1 for a top sheet, blanket, and towels. Guests get acquainted over complimentary breakfast (fresh fruit, cereal, tea, and coffee); gratis coffee, tea, and lemonade are available in the lounge throughout the day. There are two lounges offering TV, VCR (and tapes), a stereo, books, and games. Other facilities include barbecue grills/picnic tables/chaise longues out back, coin-op washers and dryers, a fully equipped kitchen, bicycle racks and lockup, and locker rental (75¢). This hostel also runs day trips to all the above-mentioned attractions, plus Bryce, Zion, and Grand canyons, and the friendly office is knowledgeable about local sights and restaurants.

LAS VEGAS DINING

Many people consider Las Vegas a great restaurant town. It all depends on your point of view. From the vantage point of value for your money it's unbeatable. You can enjoy veritable food orgies at low-priced buffets, many of them offering incredible arrays of good, fresh food, creatively prepared and attractively displayed. At weekend brunch buffets, champagne flows freely as well. And speaking of drinks, they're free at gaming tables in the casinos.

Nor are buffets the only game in town. At many casino-hotel restaurants full dinners are well under $10. At the El Cortez, for instance, a soup-to-nuts dinner with an 18-ounce porterhouse steak entrée is $6.45. And the same hotel features a $1 breakfast of bacon and eggs with hash browns, toast, and coffee. To locate budget fare, check local newspapers (especially Friday editions) and free magazines (such as *Vegas Visitor* and *What's On in Las Vegas*) that are given away at hotel reception desks. Sometimes these sources also yield money-saving coupons.

Now for the negatives. In terms of sophisticated dining, Las Vegas is about 20 years behind the times. Basically this is a steak and potatoes kind of town. With a few exceptions (most notably the Palace Court at Caesars), Las Vegas bastions of haute cuisine serve everything flambé in cognac cream sauce and feature cherries jubilee and bananas Foster for dessert. Culinary concepts that took hold in close-by California over a decade ago have yet to dent the dining scene here. And the low-priced ethnic eateries you find in most big towns are sparse. Not that I really mind. Las Vegas dining rooms are gorgeous and plushly comfortable, service is gracious, and, lets face it, there are many worse things than cognac cream sauce or a really good steak. Also, it does look like things are beginning to change. L.A. restaurateur Wolfgang Puck is opening a branch of his famed Spago at Caesars (in the Forum Shops) shortly after this book goes to press, and, speaking of ethnic fare, New York's Carnegie Deli will be opening at the same location. The city's culinary future looks bright. At all of the carefully selected restaurants in this chapter, I guarantee you a first-rate meal and a very pleasurable dining experience.

The below-listed establishments comprise a mix of exceptional hotel dining rooms and noteworthy free-standing restaurants. Among the latter, Las Vegas offers many fewer cheap eateries than other cities; they simply can't compete with casino hotels that use inexpensive food to draw in gamblers. Most Las Vegas visitors do eat in hotels, and in the hotel section of this book (Chapter 5), you'll find dozens of restaurants described at all price levels. Please peruse that chapter as well for dining choices.

Note: Restaurants are arranged alphabetically by location within price categories. My personal favorites are starred, and those offering especially good value are marked by a $ sign.

---

1. VERY EXPENSIVE

We're talking $100-plus for a meal for two. We're also talking the kind of ambience that makes for a memorable evening. Go ahead and splurge at least once. It's probably less expensive than an evening in the casino.

ON OR NEAR THE STRIP

BACCHANAL, Caesars Palace, 3570 Las Vegas Blvd. S., just north of Flamingo Rd. Tel. 734-7110.
   Cuisine: ROMAN ORGY CONTINENTAL. **Reservations:** Essential. **Parking:** Free (self and valet).
$ Prices: $65 prix fixe, plus tax and gratuity. AE, MC, V.
   Open: Tues–Sat 6–11pm with seatings at 6–6:30pm and 9–9:30pm.

Its pedimented doorways guarded by golden lions, Bacchanal is an archetypal Las Vegas experience—an imperial Roman feast with comely "wine goddesses" in harem-girl attire performing sinuous belly dances, decanting wine from shoulder height into ornate silver chalices, and—believe it or not—massaging male diners and feeding them grapes! When not performing, the goddesses repose gracefully around a fountained pool centered on a gold statue of a graceful wine-pouring Venus. During interludes between belly dance acts, beautiful harp music sets a celestial tone. The setting is palatial: White-columned walls are backed by murals of ancient Rome; an azure ceiling suggests an open sky, with a grape arbor looping from beam to beam; and crystal torchiers provide romantic lighting. The dramatic focus of the evening is a thunder and lightning storm caused by Zeus to herald the arrival of Caesar and Cleopatra. Caesar makes a short speech, and the royal pair tour the room greeting diners. Abandon all reality, ye who enter here.

Dinner is a sumptuous multicourse feast, including unlimited wine and champagne. Your first course, presented in a silver and brass étagère, offers a selection of crudités with a creamy herb dip and an assortment of fresh and dried fruits. This is followed by a cold seafood medley (shrimp, scallops, and crab claws) in a tangy vinaigrette and soup du jour served in hollowed out bread. A pasta course varies nightly—perhaps fettuccine Alfredo or spinach tortellini in lobster sauce. Next comes a salad—a Caesar salad, of course. Entrée choices ("the finest procession of bounties from the woodlands of Rome") include filet mignon, roast prime rib, and Long

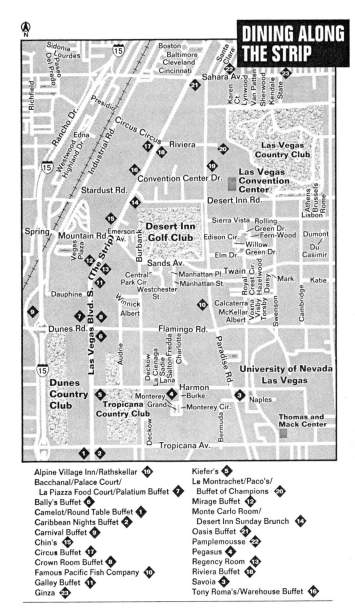

DINING ALONG THE STRIP

Map labels (clockwise/as shown):

Sidonia, Lourdes, Del Prado, Paseo, Richfield, Rancho Dr., Presidio, Circus Circus, Industrial Rd., Edna, Westwood, Highland Dr., Vegas Plaza, Mountain Rd., Emerson Av., Burbank, Las Vegas Blvd. S. (The Strip), Dauphine, Spring, Winnick, Albert, Audrie, Deckow, La Cienaga, Sadie, Salton, Fredda, Lana, Charlotte, Monterey, Grand, Burke, Monterey Cir., Deckow

Boston, Baltimore, Cleveland, Cincinnati, Sahara Av., Santa Clara, Karen Ct., Lynwood, Van Patten, Sherwood, Kendale, State, Riviera, Convention Center Dr., Desert Inn Rd., Stardust Rd.

Las Vegas Country Club, Las Vegas Convention Center, Athens, Brussels, Lisbon, Rome, Dumont, Du Casimir, Katie, Cambridge, Mark

Desert Inn Golf Club, Sierra Vista, Rolling Green Dr., Fern-Wood, Willow, Green Dr., Edison Cir., Elm Dr., Sands Av., Central Park Cir., Manhattan Pl., Manhattan St., Westchester St., Twain, Calcaterra, McKellar, Albert, Royal Crest Cir., Voxna, Visby, Hazelwood, Torsby, Daisy, Swenson

Dunes Rd., Flamingo Rd., Paradise Rd., University of Nevada Las Vegas, Harmon, Naples, Thomas and Mack Center, Tropicana Country Club, Tropicana Av., Dunes Country Club

Legend:

Alpine Village Inn/Rathskellar 19	Kiefer's 5
Bacchanal/Palace Court/ La Piazza Food Court/Palatium Buffet 7	Le Montrachet/Paco's/ Buffet of Champions 20
Bally's Buffet 6	Mirage Buffet 12
Camelot/Round Table Buffet 1	Monte Carlo Room/ Desert Inn Sunday Brunch 14
Caribbean Nights Buffet 2	Oasis Buffet 21
Carnival Buffet 9	Pamplemousse 22
Chin's 15	Pegasus 4
Circus Buffet 17	Regency Room 13
Crown Room Buffet 8	Riviera Buffet 18
Famous Pacific Fish Company 10	Savoia 3
Galley Buffet 11	Tony Roma's/Warehouse Buffet 16
Ginza 23	

Island duckling à l'orange, along with nightly specials such as rack of lamb or stuffed Cornish game hen. They're served with varying side dishes such as herbed potatoes and broccoli hollandaise. The dramatic finale—a flaming dessert of vanilla ice cream topped with liqueur-soaked fresh fruits—is accompanied by petits fours and tea or coffee.

THE MONTE CARLO ROOM, The Desert Inn, 3145 Las

**Vegas Blvd. S., between Desert Inn Rd. and Sands Ave.
Tel. 733-4444.**
Cuisine: FRENCH. **Reservations:** Recommended. **Parking:**
Free (self and valet).
$ Prices: Appetizers $10–$11, entrées $26–$37. Prix-fixe dinner
$35. AE, CB, DC, DISC, JCB, MC, V.
Open: Thurs–Mon 6–11pm.

The delightful Monte Carlo Room is equally renowned for its
sublime setting and fine French cuisine. The main dining room is
romantically decorated in shades of tawny peach, with Palladian
windows overlooking the palm-fringed pool and charming murals of
Greek youths and nymphs lolling in a classical setting framed by rose
bowers. The ceiling is painted with cupids frolicking amid fluffy
clouds punctuated by crystal candelabra chandeliers suspended from
ornate medallions. And diners are comfortably ensconced in tapestried banquettes at peach-clothed tables illumined by white taper
candles or pink-shaded crystal lamps. A second dining room is
similar, though the windows are replaced by Palladian mirrors. The
Monte Carlo is a major celebrity venue. Sinatra comes in whenever
he's in town, and when Esther Williams had a birthday party here
(attended by Debbie Reynolds, Ann Miller, and June Allyson) a teddy
bear that sings "Happy Birthday" was acquired for the occasion;
since then this birthday bear has been a Monte Carlo tradition.

Your meal begins with a complimentary hors d'oeuvre of tuna
croquette in lobster thermidor sauce. An excellent appetizer choice is
coquille de la marée—chunks of fresh lobster, shrimp, and scallops
in an Armagnac cream sauce topped with browned duchesse potatoes. Shrimp scampi has never been more scrumptious—tender, juicy
jumbo shrimps are flamed with cognac and served with a garlicky
cream sauce garnished with red and green pepper strips. Soup choices
include a traditional french onion served in a huge scooped-out
Bermuda onion and a thick, velvety cognac-laced lobster bisque, full
of rich flavor, served in a scooped-out round loaf of bread. The house
salad—a mix of radicchio, frisé, butter lettuce, and watercress tossed
with artichoke hearts and mushrooms in a walnut-pistachio vinaigrette, makes a refreshing interlude, as does the sorbet served
between courses.

For your entrée, there's roasted Nevada quail stuffed with foie
gras, wild rice, and pignolia nuts; it's served on a bed of crunchy wild
rice in a rich red wine truffle sauce and garnished with garlic-toast
points, artichoke hearts, and quail eggs. Or consider a superb fresh
sea bass with lemon and lime beurre blanc. Simple steaks and chops
are additional options. A melange of vegetables and a potato dish
(perhaps pommes Monte Carlo—thin-sliced potatoes layered with
cheeses and oven browned) accompany entrées. There's an extensive
wine list, including a good selection of French and California
champagnes, wines of the great French chateaux, German Rhine
wines and Moselles, even Japanese plum wines and saké. Consult the
sommelier for suggestions. Flaming table-side preparations are a
specialty, and that extends to desserts such as crêpes Suzette and
cherries jubilee. However, I recommend the vanilla soufflé (order
with your main course) smothered in crème anglaise and Grand
Marnier sauce.

LE MONTRACHET, Las Vegas Hilton, 3000 Paradise Rd. Tel. 732-5111.
Cuisine: FRENCH. **Reservations:** Essential. **Parking:** Free (self and valet).
$ Prices: Appetizers $8–$18.50, entrées $23–$35. AE, CB, DC, DISC, JCB, MC, V.
Open: Wed–Mon 6–11pm.

This ultraelegant French restaurant seats diners under a dome bathed in flattering pink light, an effect enhanced by shaded Chinese lamps casting a soft glow on white-linened tables. Said tables are beautifully appointed with fine crystal and silver and graced with bowls of roses. Richly paneled mahogany walls are hung with gilt-framed landscape and still-life paintings. A crystal chandelier and beveled mirrors add sparkle. And the room centers on a templelike circle of massive walnut columns wherein a large floral centerpiece graces an ornate marble table. The color scheme utilizes soft earth tones.

Dishes are exquisitely presented and prepared. You might begin with chilled duck fois gras served on toast points or a mix of lobster mousse and chunks of lobster wrapped in flaky strudel dough and garnished with champagne sauce and sturgeon caviar. There are also nightly specials. On a recent visit I enjoyed a superb tenderloin of quick-sautéed herbed rabbit in noisette butter served on spinach leaves. Also recommendable are a creamy lobster bisque with tangy-sweet garlic croutons and la salade "Le Montrachet"—a refreshing melange of Belgian endive, hearts of palm, watercress, julienned beets, and radicchio in a Dijon/red wine vinegar dressing. Entrée choices include thin-sliced Scottish salmon in a red wine-spiked lobster sauce served with fresh vegetables and a timbale of shredded potato sautéed with shallots. Other possibilities are a classic entrecôte au poivre in cognac cream sauce and roasted double breast of chicken marinated in chardonnay wine and rosemary, stuffed with wild rice and chopped duck liver, and served with Madeira sauce. Sorbets are served between courses, most uniquely a sweet basil sorbet that is very refreshing to the palate (request it). There are stunning desserts such as a cakey chocolate cup filled with homemade vanilla ice cream and toasted almonds, topped with fresh seasonal berries and strawberry coulis; it's served on a bed of crème à l'anglaise marbelized with chocolate and raspberry and garnished with fresh mint. Or you might opt for a Swiss chocolate soufflé with crème à l'anglaise and cointreau. Le Montrachet's wine cellar stocks over 400 wines from vineyards spanning the globe.

PALACE COURT, Caesars Palace, 3570 Las Vegas Blvd. S., just north of Flamingo Rd. Tel. 734-7110.
Cuisine: FRENCH. **Reservations:** Essential. **Parking:** Free (self and valet).
$ Prices: Appetizers mostly $11–$19.50, entrées $28–$40. AE, MC, V.
Open: Nightly 6–11pm; Fri–Sat there are specified seatings at 6, 6:30, and 9:30pm.

Reached via a crystal-ceilinged bronze elevator—or an elegant brass-balustraded spiral staircase—the circular Palace Court is as opulent as a Venetian palazzo. The centerpiece of the room is a towering stained-glass skylight dome (an orange and yellow sunburst) 36 feet in diameter. It shelters a grove of ficus trees flanked by classical statuary and flower beds. White-lattice windows draped with peach balloon curtains overlook the hotel's Pompeiian-inspired swimming pool and mountains beyond. On the opposite wall is a charming mural of the French countryside. White-linened tables— appointed with gold and white Lenox china, vermeil flatware, and hand-blown crystal—are softly lit by shaded brass candle lamps. And the room is further enhanced by bountiful flower arrangements in terra-cotta urns.

Chef Arnauld Briand was a darling of New York food critics at Le Bernadin and other East Coast bastions of haute cuisine. His culinary creations are magical, his presentations exquisite. If you're planning just one big dinner bash at a top Las Vegas restaurant, this is the place. An appetizer of smoked salmon (sliced to translucent thinness and layered with equally thin slices of lime) makes a good beginning. Seafood ravioli (delicate wonton skins stuffed with salmon and sturgeon) is served with two sauces—lobster bisque and white wine with cream and chives. And shrimp scampi is artfully arranged around a mound of couscous dotted with infinitesimally fine choppings of carrot and zucchini—an epiphany of color and texture. Also noteworthy: a velvety Armagnac-laced bisque replete with chunks of tender lobster and a salad comprised of oak-leaf lettuce and French chicory tossed with crunchy morsels of bacon, crumbled Roquefort, and walnuts, in a light creamy vinaigrette. Sorbets are served between courses in frosted glass lilies.

Among entrées, a Briand specialty is fresh salmon wrapped in a crispy crust of thin-sliced potatoes; it's served atop a gossamer bed of zucchini, with sauces (the same duo that graced the seafood ravioli mentioned above) separated by a wheel of asparagus spears. Blush-pink slices of roast duck come layered on braised endive and sauced with a mix of fresh herbs, burgundy, and pink and green peppercorns; a silver panier of pommes soufflés accompanies this entrée. There's a very extensive, recherché wine list, with 23 by-the-glass selections; consult the sommelier for assistance. Chocolate-dipped and sugar-glazed strawberries are served gratis at the conclusion of your meal. However, that doesn't mean you should bypass dessert. Choices include ambrosial soufflés and a totally satisfying flourless chocolate truffle cake topped with homemade hazelnut ice cream. Coffee made from fresh Kona beans is brewed at your table in a glass Hellem pot from France over an alcohol flame—another lovely presentation.

End your evening over après-dinner drinks in the romantic adjoining piano bar/lounge. Overlooking the pool, this plushly furnished venue is under a stained-glass skylight that retracts for a view of open starlit sky. Off the lounge is an intimate crystal-chandeliered European-style casino for high-stakes players only.

PEGASUS, Alexis Park Resort, 375 E. Harmon Ave, between Koval Lane and Paradise Rd. Tel. 796-3300.
   Cuisine: FRENCH. **Reservations:** Essential. **Parking:** Free (self and valet).

$ Prices: Appetizers $7.50–$25, entrées $23–$38. AE, DC, MC, V.

Open: Nightly 6–9:30pm.

This low-key luxury resort draws many visiting celebrities and Strip headliners, and its premier restaurant is a fitting venue for such upscale clientele. Pegasus has an almost celestial ambience. Its harp music, its mist of diffused lighting playing on etched mirrors, and its splashing fountains combine to make me feel like I'm dining in an underwater kingdom. Planters of greenery, pots of ferns, and a large floral centerpiece enhance this serene setting, as does a wall of arched windows overlooking a fountained rock garden.

Flambé table-side preparations are featured, and sorbets are served between courses. You might begin with a seafood salad—shrimp, scallops, and lobster—flamed with cognac and tossed with Boston lettuce vinaigrette. Among the soups two splendid velvety choices are a cognac-laced lobster bisque and chilled avocado cream soup served in a scooped-out coconut. And fresh-shucked oysters Rockefeller here elevate this dish to its delicate apogee. The featured entrée is Maine lobster sautéed with black truffles in a Madeira/bordelaise sauce; crowned with almond meringue baked to a golden brown, it is dramatically presented in a flaming veil of fire. Also excellent are boneless quail served with Madeira sauce and wild rice and salmon layered with spinach en croûte in a citrusy white wine–flavored dill sauce. A daily game special is offered each evening. When I last visited it was tenderloin of rabbit battered in coconut and sautéed in a chambord cream sauce. Entrées come with fresh steamed seasonal vegetables (you can have them plain or topped with hollandaise) and rice or fancy potato dishes. Dessert options include flambé selections such as bananas Foster and cherries jubilee along with pastries and cakes from the cart. There's an extensive wine list (mostly French and Californian) with options in varying price ranges, and seven or eight premium wines are offered by the glass each night.

DOWNTOWN

ANDRE'S, 401 S. 6th St., at Lewis Ave. (between Fremont St. and Charleston Blvd.). Tel. 385-5016.

Cuisine: FRENCH/CONTINENTAL. **Reservations:** Recommended. **Parking:** Free (valet).

$ Prices: Appetizers $9.75–$18.75 (an ounce of beluga caviar is $65), entrées $18.75–$32. AE, CB, DC, MC, V.

Open: Nightly 6–10pm.

Owner-chef Andre Rochat has created a rustic country-French setting in a converted 1930s house. Low ceilings are crossed with rough-hewn beams and wainscoted stucco walls, imbedded with straw, are hung with provincial pottery and copperware. Seating is in tapestried chairs and banquettes at lace-clothed tables adorned with fresh flowers. And soft lighting emanates from candles and sconces. In addition to a warren of cozy interior rooms, there's a lovely ivy-walled garden patio under the shade of a mulberry tree. This is a major celebrity haunt, where you're likely to see Wayne Newton,

**FROMMER'S SMART TRAVELER:
RESTAURANTS**

1. By taking advantage of low-priced buffet meals and casino-hotel restaurant specials, you can dine sumptuously for next to nothing.
2. Peruse local papers and free visitor publications distributed at hotel reception deks. They list all the buffets in town and frequently contain coupons for restaurant discounts and two-for-the-price-of-one meals.
3. Patronize hotel coffee shops. They offer very tasty fare in pleasant surroundings at moderate prices.
4. Go to an occasional dinner show, especially if you're not a drinker. The surcharge for a full meal instead of two drinks is very reasonable at most showrooms.
5. Dine in the wee hours. Incredibly low-priced specials are offered by casino-hotel restaurants to keep late-night wagerers awake. For example, the Golden Nugget serves a $2 meal of steak and eggs, with home fries, biscuits, and gravy, from 11pm to 5am.

Dolly Parton, Frank Sinatra, and other Strip headliners. I was in one night when Tom Hanks, Steven Spielberg, and James Spader joined some pals for a bachelor party.

The menu changes daily. On a recent visit, appetizers included jumbo sea scallops rolled in crunchy macadamia nut crust with citrus beurre blanc. Slices of crayfish and scallop sausage came with a spicy rémoulade. And escargots in garlic butter were stuffed with artichokes and sautéed spinach into a puff pastry crust. Sorbets are served between courses. An entrée of poached Norwegian salmon in scallion-studded beurre blanc was served with angel hair pasta in a coarsely chopped tomato sauce with a nuance of garlic. And a fan of pink, juicy slices of sautéed duck came with a confit of port wine and onions. A medley of vegetables—perhaps pommes lyonnaise, asparagus, broccoli hollandaise, and baby carrots—accompanies each entrée. For dessert, I love Andre's classic fruit tarts—flaky butter crusts, layered with Grand Marnier custard, topped with fresh plump berries. An extensive wine list (over 600 labels) is international in scope and includes many rare vintages; consult the sommelier.

ELAINE'S, Golden Nugget, 129 E. Fremont St. at Casino Center Blvd. Tel. 385-7111.
   Cuisine: CALIFORNIA-INFLUENCED CONTINENTAL. **Reservations:** Recommended. **Parking:** Free (self and valet).
$ Prices: Appetizers $8.75–$12.50, entrées $18.50–$29.50. AE, CB, DC, DISC, JCB, MC, V.
   Open: Thurs–Mon 6–10:30pm.

Up an elegant brass-railed spiral staircase, entered via a stunning marble-floored courtyard, Elaine's is a gem—and a glittering one at that. Its ornate interior has intimate curtained booths, beveled mirrors adorned with gilt sconces and cupids, and an oak-beamed leather ceiling painted to look like a sky at sunset. The room centers on a hand-blown Venetian-glass chandelier and a Monet-like impressionist painting. It's a lovely setting—softly lit and enhanced by a backdrop of classical music.

Appetizers here deserve serious consideration. An exquisite mix of sea scallops and shaved Maui onions are lightly dusted in flour, crisp fried, and deglazed with chardonnay. Escargots in garlic butter-champagne sauce nestle in fresh-baked brioche. And shrimp Victoria—served on onions caramelized in balsamic vinegar with two sauces (red pepper coulis and tarragon cream)—yields a wonderful melange of flavors. Another possibility is very rich red onion soup spiked with burgundy wine and topped with a thick layer of fontina cheese and sourdough croutons. Entrées—which arrive at your table in gleaming silver cloches—include rack of lamb basted with English mustard and honey and broiled Norwegian salmon topped with macadamia nuts, thyme butter, white wine, and shallots. Char-grilled Cajun shrimp with spicy red sauce is served with delicious rice studded with finely diced vegetables and roasted pecans. Steaks, chops, and prime rib are also offered. Entrées come with potatoes du jour and an array of crisp, fresh vegetable. Two desserts are standouts: a scrumptious apricot soufflé with chantilly cream (order with your entrée) and something called a horn of plenty—a cookie shell brushed with chocolate, filled with fresh berries, and served on sabayon sauce garnished with fresh mint. The wine list is international in scope, and four premium wines are offered nightly by the glass.

2. EXPENSIVE

Herein, more luxurious venues for anything from an impressive business dinner to a romantic evening on the town. Depending on what you order, you could manage a dinner at some of these restaurants in the moderate price range. Dinner entrées average $11–$20.

ON OR NEAR THE STRIP

CAMELOT, Excalibur Hotel, 3850 Las Vegas Blvd. S., at Tropicana Ave. Tel. 597-7777, ext. 7449.
   Cuisine: CONTINENTAL. **Reservations:** Recommended. **Parking:** Free (self and valet).
$ Prices: Appetizers $4.75–$7.75, pastas $3.75–$5.25, entrées $10.95–$18.75. AE, CB, DC, DISC, MC, V.
   Open: Sun–Thurs 6–11pm, Fri–Sat 5pm–midnight.
Named for the legendary English town where King Arthur presided over his court and Round Table, the Excalibur offers gourmet dining in a rustic castle setting. Stone walls are hung with copies of medieval tapestries. Ivied stone archways—some embellished with crossed swords—create intimate dining areas, and murals of Camelot's pristine lakes and verdant forests form an idyllic backdrop. Diners are

comfortably ensconced in floral-tapestried armchairs at white-linened tables illumined by shaded silver paraffin lamps.

Food presentations are notably attractive, service deft and gracious. Sous-chef Sergio Verduzco previously worked with Paul Prudhomme, hence a shrimp etouffée has found its way onto the roster of appetizers. This tasty stewed shrimp dish, served with spicy Cajun red sauce, is arranged around a mound of Spanish rice studded with peas and pimientos. Inexpensive pasta dishes are also good beginnings—perhaps lobster-filled ravioli in a saffroned butter-cream sauce sprinkled with caviar or white and green fettuccine tossed with salmon and peas in white wine sauce. Among the entrées, chicken Merlin is a classic coq au vin in a zinfandel wine sauce. Also very recommendable is sautéed fresh Pacific salmon served on julienne vegetables in a brandy cream sauce flavored with lobster stock. Steaks and rack of lamb are additional options. Main courses include an excellent salad of assorted lettuces—radicchio, oak leaf, butterleaf, and endive—tossed with tomato wedges, artichoke hearts, and hearts of palm in a creamy Dijon vinaigrette. You also get freshly baked bread, seasonal vegetables, and a potato dish—perhaps roasted Parisienne potatoes with butter and fresh herbs. Camelot's wine list is international in scope, with a predominance of California vintages. Dessert selections include four sorbets (kiwi, raspberry, lemon, and cantaloupe) served on a chocolate palette complete with chocolate paintbrush. And carrot cake here is an excellent representative of its genre slathered with creamy, delicious icing. But the pièce de résistance is a tiramisù torte—espresso-soaked layers of cake and marscapone cream topped with powdered cocoa and served afloat praline crème anglaise marbelized with raspberry.

CHIN'S, 3200 Las Vegas Blvd. S., just off the Strip in the Fashion Show Mall (turn at the Frontier sign). Tel. 733-8899.
Cuisine: CANTONESE. **Reservations:** Recommended. **Parking:** Free (self and valet).
$ Prices: Appetizers $5–$13.50, entrées $7.95 lunch, $12–$24 dinner. AE, CB, DC, MC, V.
Open: Mon–Sat 11am–10pm, Sun noon–10pm.

Chin's offers a tranquil contrast to the neon overkill of the Strip. Its very understated decor is almost stark, with bare white walls and white-clothed tables. During the day a single tulip in a vase graces each table; at night it is removed and replaced by a glass oil candle. A narrow band of recessed pink lighting is practically the sole adornment, except in the bar where a lush tropical garden flourishes under a pyramidal skylight. Seating is in comfortable mauve velvet-upholstered armchairs and banquettes. Nightly except Sunday and Monday a pianist plays mellow classics—Cole Porter and the like. I believe you'll find, as I did, that what at first seems a too-cool setting, is actually aesthetically refined and soothing.

Chin's cuisine is as pleasing as its ambience—on a par with the finest Chinese restaurants of New York and California. Not-to-be-missed appetizers—served with a trio of sauces—include crispy spring rolls stuffed with finely chopped chicken and vegetables;

heavenly shrimp puffs (minced shrimp and mildly curried cream cheese wrapped in wonton skins and deep fried), and a Chinese chicken salad that is a crunchy mix of crisp-fried chicken strips and lettuce tossed with rice noodles, sesame seeds, and coriander in a light dressing with a tang of mustard. At lunch this scrumptious salad is offered as a main course. There are a number of highly recommendable dinner entrées: chunks of tender orange roughy wok-fried in black pepper sauce with onions and red and green peppers; barbecued pork fried rice—here a culinary masterpiece comprising a mound of savory rice studded with morsels of pork, crisp scallions, peas, and very finely chopped carrots and onions; Chin's beef—thin slices of wok-sauteed beef that has been marinated for 24 hours in a secret sauce, tossed with rice noodles; and strawberry chicken—tender slices of fresh chicken deep-fried in a battered crust served with strawberry sauce and fresh strawberries. A small, but carefully constructed, wine list is composed of French and California wines selected to complement Chinese cooking. Do order crispy pudding for dessert—a refreshing batter-dipped egg custard splashed with Midori, a melon liqueur.

THE FAMOUS PACIFIC FISH COMPANY, 3925 Paradise Rd., at Corporate Dr. (between Flamingo Rd. and Sands Ave.). Tel. 796-9676.
Cuisine: SEAFOOD. **Reservations:** Recommended. **Parking:** Free.
$ Prices: Appetizers and light meals $4.95–$7.95; entrées $5.25–$10.95 lunch, $12.95–$19.95 dinner. AE, CB, DC, DISC, MC, V.
Open: Mon–Thurs 11am–10pm, Fri–Sat 11am–11pm, Sun 4–10pm.

The Famous Pacific Fish Company is a nautically themed warehouse of a restaurant. Under its lofty skylit ceiling are exposed pipes, rough-hewn rafters draped with fishnet, and a weathered fishing dinghy or two. Sunlight streams in through many windows, exposed-brick walls are hung with black-and-white nautical photographs, and rusty boat propellers, lobster traps, buoys, and ship models are displayed here and there. For all that, the FPFC manages a cozy charm, with planters of greenery and intimate seating areas comprised of upholstered booths at oak tables. Carpeting keeps the noise level down. There's a large and comfortable bar/lounge area (a popular happy hour haunt) and a gorgeous outdoor patio with pink-clothed candlelit tables, the latter kept warm by space heaters in winter and cooled by misters in summer.

Fresh fish is flown in from both coasts and grilled over mesquite charcoal. Everything here is made from scratch. Your meal begins with a complimentary serving of lavash and smoked salmon dip. Appetizer recommendations include oysters Rockefeller (topped with spinach, bacon, onion, and garlic and baked to a light crust with hollandaise sauce) and angels on horseback (plump oysters and crunchy water chestnuts wrapped in bacon and baked in wine and garlic butter). Soups here also merit attention, especially the spicy gumbo—a hearty combination of sautéed chicken, andouille sausage, shrimp, and oysters in a savory broth. Shrimp cha cha cha—jumbo shrimp stuffed with crabmeat and topped with jalapeño hollandaise—can be ordered as an appetizer or entrée. Other good entrée choices include a platter of shrimp and crab sautéed in garlic butter and served atop fettuccine Alfredo; mesquite-grilled Atlantic salmon smothered in Dijon cream sauce; and freshly cut swordfish steak, sautéed with rosemary, garlic, and wine and served with a light parmesan cream sauce. All entrées come with soup, salad, or coleslaw (here a rough-chopped mix of cabbage and peanuts tossed in poppy-seed dressing); chicken stock flavored rice or potato (opt for the twice-baked potato—scooped out, mixed with bacon/chives/butter/onions/sour cream/parmesan, and topped with melted cheddar); fresh-baked sourdough bread; and a medley of fresh vegetables. Lighter fare, including sandwiches and salads, is available at lunch. The wine list highlights California wines, all of which are available by the glass. Desserts include an ultrarich Grand Marnier white chocolate cheesecake and banana chocolate chip layer cake slathered with chocolate icing.

KIEFER'S, The Carriage House, 105 E. Harmon Ave., between Las Vegas Blvd. S. and Koval Lane. Tel. 739-8000.
Cuisine: STEAK/SEAFOOD/PASTA. **Reservations:** Recommended. **Parking:** Free.

 FROMMER'S COOL FOR KIDS:
RESTAURANTS

Buffets (see "Specialty Dining," later in this chapter) Cheap eats for the whole family. The kids can pick what they like, and there are usually make-your-own-sundae machines.

Tony Roma's—A Place for Ribs (see p. 130) The food is great, the setting is comfy, and children's entrées are just $4.95.

Pink Pony (see p. 97) The bubble-gum pink, circus-motif, 24-hour coffee shop at Circus Circus Hotel/Casino will appeal to kids. And mom and dad can linger over coffee while the kids race upstairs to watch circus acts and play carnival games. There's also a McDonald's at Circus Circus.

Sherwood Forest Café (see p. 99). Kids love to climb on the lavender dragons fronting this 24-hour coffee shop at the Excalibur. And, as at Circus Circus, they can enjoy numerous child-oriented activities while you're on the premises.

Magnolia's Veranda (see p. 107). After a meal at the Four Queens' very attractive 24-hour coffee shop, the kids can tour the fascinating **Ripley's Believe It or Not! Museum** on the premises.

$ Prices: Appetizers $4.95–$8.95, Light entrées $6.95–$9.95, full entrées $12.95–$18.95. AE, CB, DC, MC, V.

Open: Nightly 5–11pm.

Perched on the ninth floor of a resort hotel, Kiefer's offers a romantic setting with superb views of the neon Las Vegas skyline from a wall of windows. Its low-key peach-toned interior features potted ficus trees and seating on plush sofas and bamboo chairs upholstered in raw silk. Candlelit tables are draped in cream linen cloths with peach napery, and sconce lighting casts a rosy glow. Tuesday through Saturday, a pianist entertains in an adjoining lounge with a small dance floor. After your meal, adjourn to this simpatico piano bar for dessert or after-dinner drinks.

Appetizers of crisp-fried calamari served with spicy cocktail sauce or oysters Rockefeller make a good beginning. And you could make a light meal of entrées such as Chinese chicken salad, shrimp Louie, or seafood gumbo, perhaps with a glass of wine and dessert. Heartier entrées include tender boneless chicken breasts sautéed in butter with fresh garlic, dill, and artichoke hearts; sliced tenderloin of beef in a burgundy-based brown sauce with fresh mushrooms, shallots, diced tomatoes, and garlic butter; and squid ravioli stuffed with lobster and garnished with sautéed mushrooms and snow peas in a delicate champagne cream sauce. Blackened fresh Norwegian salmon is a house specialty. Entrées come with a Caesar or hot spinach salad, a medley of fresh vegetables nuanced with garlic, and rice pilaf or buttered red potatoes garnished with parsley. For dessert a Snickers bar cake is rather fun. Over 20 wines are offered by the glass.

PAMPLEMOUSSE, 400 E. Sahara Ave., between Santa Paula and Santa Rita Drs., just east of Paradise Rd. Tel. 733-2066.

Cuisine: FRENCH. **Reservations:** Essential. **Parking:** Free limited parking on premises, plentiful street parking in the area.

$ Prices: Appetizers $4.50–$9.50, entrées $17.50–$24.50. AE, CB, DC, DISC, MC, V.

Open: Two seatings nightly at 6–6:30pm and 9–9:30pm.

Evoking a cozy French countryside inn, Pamplemousse is a series of low-ceilinged rooms and intimate dining nooks with rough-hewn beams, multipaned windows, and walls hung with copperware and provincial pottery. Candlelit tables, beautifully appointed with Villeroy & Boch show plates and posies of fresh flowers, are draped in pale-pink linen. Classical music or light jazz plays softly in the background. It's all very charming and un-Vegasy. There's additional seating in a small garden sheltered by striped tenting. The restaurant's name, which means grapefruit, was suggested by the late singer Bobby Darin, one of the many celebrity pals of owner Georges La Forge. Strip headliners Wayne Newton, Siegfried & Roy, and Englebert Humperdinck are regulars, and Robert Goulet celebrated a recent birthday here.

There's no printed menu. The chef prepares four or five appetizers and entrées each night which are recited by your waiter. Your meal here begins with a large complimentary basket of crudités (about 10 different crisp, fresh vegetables), a big bowl of olives, and—a nice country touch—a basket of hard-boiled eggs. On my last visit there were such tantalizing appetizers as lightly floured bay scallops sautéed in buttery grapefruit sauce and soft-shell crab in a butter cognac sauce with fresh herbs and a nuance of Dijon mustard. Entrées included crispy slices of duck breast and banana in a sauce of orange, honey, dark rum, and crème de banane (corn-fed duck, raised to the restaurant's specifications at a Wisconsin farm, is a specialty here). Another offering the same evening was fresh Norwegian salmon, seared crisp on the outside, juicy pink and tender on the inside, in a light orange beurre blanc with a touch of curry. And there's always a steak and one other meat or poultry dish. Entrées are served with a medley of fresh vegetables. Dessert might be homemade dark chocolate ice cream with praline in a sabayon sauce or a classic fruit tart. A very extensive, well-rounded wine list complements the menu.

SAVOIA, 4503 Paradise Rd., at Harmon Ave. (in the St. Tropez Plaza). Tel. 731-5446.
   Cuisine: STEAK/SEAFOOD/PASTA. **Reservations:** Recommended. **Parking:** Free.
$ **Prices:** Appetizers $4.25–$8.50; entrées $5.50–$10.25 lunch, $10.50–$24.50 dinner. AE, CB, DC, DISC, MC, V.
   Open: Lunch Mon–Fri 11am–5:30pm; dinner Sun–Wed 5:30–11pm, Thurs–Sat 9pm–2am.

This second Georges La Forge enterprise (see Pamplemousse above) is a stunning restaurant—a light and airy setting with glossy cream walls and seating areas defined by planters of greenery. Plum carpeting harmonizes nicely with candlelit tables clothed in mauve linen, and soft opalescent lighting emanates from kite-shaped fixtures in pale peach and aqua tints. A warm glow also comes from a ceramic-tiled oak-burning oven hung with copper pots and pans. There's additional seating on a candlelit patio under a weeping willow tree. Thursday through Saturday nights dinner is enhanced by live jazz, and frequently singers from Strip extravaganzas drop by after late shows and take the mike. Showroom headliners Robert Goulet, Paul Anka, and Englebert Humperdinck dine here regularly, and Savoia was chosen by the Las Vegas cast of *Cats* when they threw a party for Andrew Lloyd Webber. It's a lively place, always crackling with excitement.

   A complimentary hors d'oeuvre of eggplant caviar with croutons is served when you sit down. The menu features first-rate cuts of meat and fresh fish, expertly prepared and beautifully presented. Not on the menu, but usually available as an appetizer (or entrée), is lobster-filled black ravioli (made from squid pasta) in a bisque sauce. Another good beginning is fresh Yucatán duck sausage in tequila-spiked herbed beurre blanc served with paper-thin pineapple slices. For the main course consider a mixed grill of baby lamb chops, duck sausage, and filet mignon. It comes with a choice of sauces—a superb béarnaise, tangy diablo made with grainy mustard and cognac, or a cream- and Armagnac-based green peppercorn (ask for all three). Fresh grilled Norwegian salmon is brushed with a caramelized orange honey mustard finish. And the house specialty is "hobo" steak—a juicy 28-ounce center cut prime New York steak baked in the oak-burning oven. Entrées include whipped duchesse potatoes, a medley of fresh vegetables, and a bountiful table-side salad bar with

Caesar or creamy vinaigrette dressing. There's an extensive wine list, including many rare wines from La Forge's private cellar and an ample number of by-the-glass selections. The lunch menu adds pizzas, pasta and seafood salads, and sandwiches. Desserts include Grand Marnier and strawberry soufflés and a lovely crème brûlée garnished with Irish cream, fresh strawberries, and grated lemon rind.

There's a handsome bar/lounge—a simpatico setting for drinks and light fare on jazz nights; other times sporting events are shown on a large-screen TV.

THE TILLERMAN, 2245 E. Flamingo Rd., at Channel 10 Dr. (just west of Eastern Ave.). Tel. 731-4036.
Cuisine: STEAK/SEAFOOD. **Reservations:** Not accepted.
Parking: Free.
$ Prices: Appetizers $5.50–$11.95, entrées $14.95–$23.95. AE, CB, DC, DISC, MC, V.
Open: Nightly 5–11pm.

Ask any local for a list of favorite restaurants, and you can be sure the Tillerman will be on it. How can you go wrong offering flawless food in a stunning arboreal setting? The restaurant's verdant plant-filled interior is under an oak-beamed, 40-foot cathedral ceiling with retractable skylights open to a starry sky. Candlelit dining areas offer seating amid a grove of ficus trees, their woodsy ambience enhanced by exquisite oak paneling and tree-trunk pillars. A circular stained-glass window makes a lovely focal point. There's additional seating on the mezzanine level, where diners enjoy treetop views. All the top Strip performers are regular Tillerman customers.

Owner Bob Kapp personally inspects every piece of meat and fish that comes into the restaurant, and his food sources are worldwide. The menu is likely to offer Chilean sea bass, Norwegian salmon, Australian lobster, farm-raised mussels from Washington State, and Chesapeake Bay oysters, among others. Of equal quality is his dry-aged prime beef, cut on the premises.

Your meal begins with a relish tray and a basket of delicious oven-fresh breads. Also complimentary is a lazy Susan salad bar served at your table with a choice of homemade dressings, including a memorable chunky blue cheese. The menu features superb cuts of meat and fish, lightly sauced to enhance, not smother, natural fresh flavors. Portions are immense, so appetizers are really not necessary, but, then again, they're too good to pass up. Especially notable: ultrafresh plumply red medallions of yellowfin tuna blackened and served very rare in spicy mustard sauce. If you're a sushi aficionado, this is a must. Meat entrées include prime center cut New York strip steak, fork-tender filet mignon, and prime rib. And there are at least a dozen fresh fish/seafood specials each night. On a recent visit I had a piece of snowy-white halibut, charcoal-broiled to perfect brownness and brushed with pecan pesto. Other possibilities that night included blackened sea bass, rainbow trout amandine, and sea scallops sautéed in a light dill Dijon cream sauce. By the way, if you're watching your weight and/or cholesterol intake, this is one restaurant that will happily prepare food without any oils or fats. Entrées come with a white and wild rice mixture tossed with slivered almonds and chives and fresh vegetables (perhaps thick asparagus spears). Homemade desserts—such as light cheesecake with fresh raspberry sauce or Bavarian cream with strawberries and bananas—change nightly. The wine list highlights California selections and offers six premium wines by the glass each night.

Note: Since the Tillerman doesn't take reservations, arrive early to avoid a wait for seating . . . or plan a predinner cocktail in the cozy oak-paneled lounge with a working fireplace.

3. MODERATE

The following selections are the restaurants most of us prefer for everyday dining. They all offer excellent meals at reasonable prices, in many cases with a fair amount of ambience thrown in for good measure. Once again, depending on what you order, you could manage an inexpensive dinner at some of these restaurants. Dinner entrées average $7 to $15.

NEAR THE STRIP

ALPINE VILLAGE INN, 3003 Paradise Rd., between Riviera Blvd. and Convention Center Dr. Tel. 734-6888.
   Cuisine: SWISS GERMAN. **Reservations:** Recommended.
   Parking: Free (valet and self).
$ Prices: Prix-fixe dinners only, $13.25–$16.50; children's portions (under 12 only) about half price. AE, CB, DC, DISC, MC, V.
   Open: Nightly 5–11pm.

A Las Vegas tradition since 1950, this extremely popular family restaurant does not subscribe to the less-is-more theory of interior design. Fresh white napery and red napkins make an immediate cheerful impact. Walls are painted with murals of snowy Alpine scenery, an effect enhanced by snow-covered chalet roofing, twinkling Christmas tree lights, and miniature ski lifts on cables strung across the ceiling. There are Swiss and Austrian cowbells, mounted deer heads, and window boxes filled with geraniums. And the very efficient waitstaff is in Tyrolean costume. Seating is in comfortable burgundy leather booths lit by amber wall lamps.

Prepare for your meal here by eating almost nothing all day. Dinner is a multicourse feast beginning with a big pewter bowl of crudités served with herbed cottage cheese dip and crackers. Next comes a steaming bowl of savory Bavarian chicken soup thickened with a purée of fresh vegetables; a pewter kettle of it is left on your table, so you can ladle out as much as you like. A basket of fresh-baked breads includes scrumptious hot cinnamon rolls (iron discipline is required not to fill up on these). A salad comes with house dressing—paprika-flavored blue cheese vinaigrette. As an entrée, I recommend the roast duckling with sausage stuffing served over wild and brown rice (it comes with a side dish of orange and cherry sauces) or roast tender chicken with chestnut dressing. Accompanying it is an array of vegetables (red cabbage, sauerkraut, and string beans tossed with bacon and onions) and choice of potato—crisp potato pancakes, dumplings, a baked potato, puréed sweet potatoes (mixed with coconut, rum, and marshmallows), or Swiss Rösti potatoes (shredded potato mixed with onion, bacon, eggs, and spices, fried in a pancake, and garnished with grated parmesan). If you'd like more than one of the above selections, waiters generally comply. The finale: homemade apple or peach strudel, served warm (topped with vanilla ice cream if you so desire). Tea or coffee is included. The wine list offers wines by the glass and a goodly selection of beers, 19 varieties of schnapps, and exotic cocktails.

After dinner, if you can still move, check out the adjoining gift shop's selection of cuckoo clocks, crystal, beer steins, music boxes, cowbells, and Hummel figures. There's also a bar/lounge and a separate downstairs restaurant called the Rathskellar (details below).

GINZA, 1000 E. Sahara Ave., between Paradise Rd. and Maryland Pkwy. Tel. 732-3080.

Cuisine: JAPANESE. **Reservations:** For large parties only. **Parking:** Free in lot out back.
$ Prices: Appetizers $2.25–$8, entrées $6–$14.50. AE, MC, V.
Open: Tues–Sun 5pm–1am.

For almost two decades this charming little restaurant has drawn a devoted clientele of local Japanese and Japanese food aficionados. There's a sushi bar in the front room, and the main dining area has shoji-screened windows, tables sheltered by shingled eaves, rice paper-style lighting fixtures, and cream walls adorned with Japanese fans, paintings, and prints. Four spacious red leather booths are the sole concession to Las Vegas style.

You might begin with a shared appetizer of tempura shrimp and vegetables. Entrées—such as beef, chicken, or salmon sprinkled with sesame seeds in a thick teriyaki sauce—come with soup (miso or egg flower), sunomono (a vinegared Japanese salad), and green tea. Sushi is a highlight, and there are about 30 à la carte selections to choose from. Be sure to try an appetizer or entrée portion of Ginza's unique Vegas rolls—salmon, tuna, yellowtail, and avocado rolled with seaweed in sesame-studded rice and quickly deep-fried so the sesame seeds form a scrumptious crust. It's served with lemon soy sauce. Also delicious are seaweed-wrapped California rolls filled with crabmeat, avocado, and cucumber and topped with salmon caviar. All the fish is very fresh, and everything here is made from scratch. A bottle of saké is recommended. For dessert there's lemon sherbet or ginger and green tea ice cream.

PACO'S, Las Vegas Hilton, 3000 Paradise Rd. Tel. 732-5667.

Cuisine: MEXICAN. **Reservations:** Recommended. **Parking:** Free (self and valet).
$ Prices: Appetizers mostly $5–$7.95, entrées $7.50–$15.95. AE, CB, DC, DISC, JCB, MC, V.
Open: Fri–Tues 6–11pm.

This gorgeous Mexican restaurant opened in 1991 and was immediately a hit. Charmingly decorated in soft southwestern hues, with weathered driftwood beams overhead, it has cream stucco walls hung with photographs of old Mexico, colorful serapes, and antique mirrors in hand-carved frames resurrected from old Spanish haciendas. Pots of cactus, Mexican papier-mâché animals, hand-painted pottery, saddles, and spurs are on display, and appropriate music enhances the south-of-the-border ambience.

Chef Miguel Barajas learned the basics of Mexican cookery from his grandparents (they owned a few small restaurants in Guadalajara) and refined his skills at a San Francisco culinary academy. His kitchen turns out highly authentic dishes. You're immediately served a basket of fresh yellow and red chili corn chips with salsa when you sit down. There are two especially noteworthy appetizers: Mexicali skins—three crisp potato skins, one topped with beans, one with shredded spicy beef, and one with shredded spicy chicken—come smothered with melted cheddar and Monterey Jack cheeses and garnished with sour cream and guacamole. Equally scrumptious are taquitos—deep-fried crispy golden corn tortillas stuffed with seasoned shredded chicken or beef and served with sour cream and guacamole. Do opt for Paco's salad of crisp greens tossed with cheeses, avocado wedges, and very thinly sliced red onions in avocado ranch dressing. For an entrée, you can't go wrong with lime-marinated beef, chicken, or shrimp fajitas (combinations available) served sizzling on a cast-iron platter with all the fixings—flour tortillas, red and green peppers, cilantro and onions, sour cream, guacamole, Spanish rice, and refried beans. Also excellent are enchiladas del mar—corn tortillas rolled around crabmeat, shrimp, and scallops, topped with melted cheeses, and served in a light cream sauce with Spanish rice and an Anaheim chili stuffed with julienned steamed carrots. And carne asada—grilled New York steak—also comes topped with a roasted Anaheim chili plus side dishes of cheese enchiladas, refried beans, Spanish rice, and flour tortillas. If you have room for dessert, the margarita pie (tequila-flavored lime mousse on a chocolate cookie crust with meringue topping) is marvelously light and delicious. Also a winner, but a more filling one, is a crispy taco-shaped chocolate shell filled with Kahlúa mousse and served atop rich caramel sauce. There's a full bar, its offerings including frosty pitchers of fruit (strawberry, peach, melon, or black raspberry) margaritas and daiquiris.

4. INEXPENSIVE

Take the family. All of these inexpensive eateries offer extremely pleasant settings and affordable prices. Most have children's menus. Dinner entrées average $5 to $10.

CHILI'S GRILL & BAR, 2590 S. Maryland Pkwy., between Sahara and Karen Aves., in the Sahara Town Square Shopping Center. Tel. 733-6402.
  Cuisine: SOUTHWESTERN. **Parking:** Free.
$ Prices: Appetizers $4.45–$5.95, entrées $4.75–$9.95. AE, CB, DC, DISC, MC, V.

Open: Mon–Thurs 11am–10pm, Fri–Sat 11am–11pm, Sun 11:30am–10pm.

Chili's is a national chain, based in Texas, offering superior "bowls of red" and other southwestern specialties. This branch is a sunny, brick-floored restaurant with many plants flourishing in the light streaming in through numerous windows. Seating is in comfortable rust leather- and ultrasuede-upholstered booths. Ceramic-tiled tables are under hanging lamps made from old copper chili pots. Wainscoted gray-green walls are adorned with framed posters and photographs of chili cook offs. And slowly whirring fans are suspended from the forest-green ceiling. You can also eat in the lively bar area, where the TV is always tuned to sporting events. The setting is rustic and casual, but very comfortable. This is a great choice for family dining.

The same menu is offered all day. Chili is, of course, a specialty, available with or without beans. Equally popular are the fabulous half-pound burgers, made from fresh-ground beef and sandwiched with mustard, lettuce, tomato, onion, pickle, and mayonnaise (let the waiter know if you don't want all that). They come with home-style fries made from scratch, and various toppings (I like cheese and chili). Another big item is fried chicken with country gravy, served with homemade mashed potatoes (with skins), corn on the cob, and Texas toast. Recently, Chili's added a few lighter, health-conscious items to its menu, such as grilled tuna served with tortillas, aioli and salsa dressing, rice, cabbage, and a spicy pinto-bean soup. You can even get a plate of steamed vegetables here. Similarly, desserts run the gamut from a brownie topped with ice cream, hot fudge, chopped walnuts, and whipped cream to frozen yogurt. A children's menu, listed on a place mat with games and puzzles, offers full meals for $2.45, including "bottomless fountain drinks."

LA PIAZZA FOOD COURT, Caesars Palace, 3570 Las Vegas Blvd. S., just north of Flamingo Rd. Tel. 731-7110.

Cuisine: FOOD COURT. **Parking:** Free (self and valet).

$ Prices: $5–$10 for a complete meal. AE, DISC, MC, V.

Open: Mon–Thurs 11am–11pm, Fri 11am–midnight, Sat 9am–midnight, Sun 9am–11pm.

Essentially an upscale version of a cafeteria, this is a great choice for families. Food stations are along an attractive arched walkway lit by pink neon, and the brass-railed dining area, under massive domes, is rather elegant with gold-topped columns and comfortable upholstered seating. The food is top quality—terrific deep-dish pizzas, an excellent salad bar, fresh-baked pies and cakes, sushi, smoked fish, immense burritos, Chinese stir-fry, deli, Häagen-Dazs bars, and a selection of beverages that includes herbal teas, wine, beer, espresso, and cappuccino. There's something for every dining mood. Waffle cones are baked on the premises, creating a delicious aroma.

THE RATHSKELLAR, 3003 Paradise Rd., between Riviera Blvd. and Convention Center Dr. Tel. 734-6888.

Cuisine: GERMAN/AMERICAN. **Reservations:** Recommended. **Parking:** Free (valet and self).

$ Prices: Most entrées $4.95–$10.75. AE, CB, DC, DISC, MC, V.

Open: Nightly 5–11pm.

The Rathskellar is a rollicking downstairs adjunct to the Alpine Village Inn (see above)—a cozy beer hall, with red-and-white checkered tablecloths and a floor strewn with peanut shells (there are bowls of peanuts on every table). A pianist and singer entertain nightly, and everyone sings along. The menu offers unique specialties such as German pizza (topped with sauerbraten, ham, and mozzarella cheese), buffalo-meat burgers, and a game sausage plate of venison, pheasant, and rabbit bratwursts served on sauerkraut with German potato salad. If you aren't feeling especially adventurous, a regular hamburger with french fries and a hot turkey sandwich are also options. There's an extensive children's menu; this is a family place.

RICARDO'S, 2380 Tropicana Ave., at Eastern Ave. (northwest corner). Tel. 798-4515.

Cuisine: MEXICAN. **Reservations:** Recommended. **Parking:** Free.

$ Prices: Appetizers $2.50–$6.50, entrées $5.50–$10.95; lunch buffet $6.75; children's plates $3.25, including milk or soft drink with complimentary refills. AE, CB, DC, MC, V.

Open: Mon–Thurs 11am–11pm, Fri–Sat 11am–midnight, Sun noon–10pm.

This hacienda-style restaurant is a great favorite with locals. It has several stucco-walled dining rooms separated by arched doorways—all of them lovely, with candlelit oak tables and booths upholstered in Aztec prints. There's a plant-filled greenhouse area, with Saltillo tile floors and rotating bamboo fans overhead. A tiered terra-cotta fountain and a mission bell grace a garden room with a lofty pine-beamed ceiling. And yet another area has a ceramic-tiled fireplace (ablaze in winter) and a dark-wood coffered ceiling. Strolling Mexican musicians entertain at night.

Start off with an appetizer of deep-fried battered chicken wings served with melted Monterey Jack (ask for jalapeños if you like your cheese sauce hotter). Nachos smothered with cheese and guacamole are also very good here. For an entrée, you can't go wrong with chicken, beef, or pork fajitas served sizzling on a hot skillet atop sautéed onions, mushrooms, and peppers. It comes with rice and beans, homemade tortillas, a selection of salsas, guacamole, and tomato wedges with cilantro. All the usual taco/enchilada/tamale combinations are listed, along with a variety of burritos. A delicious dessert is helado Las Vegas—ice cream rolled in corn flakes and cinnamon, deep-fried, and served with honey and whipped cream. If that's too much, a simple flan with Kahlúa might hit the spot. And do order a pitcher of Ricardo's great margaritas. The same menu is offered all day, but a buffet is an option at lunch. The kid's menu—on a place mat with games and puzzles—features both Mexican and American fare.

There's another Ricardo's in the Meadows Mall (tel. 870-1088). It's open Monday to Thursday 11am to 10pm, Friday to Saturday 11am to midnight, Sunday 11am to 8pm.

TONY ROMA'S—A PLACE FOR RIBS, Stardust Resort &

Casino, 3000 Las Vegas Blvd. S., at Convention Center Dr. Tel. 732-6111.
Cuisine: BARBECUE. **Reservations:** Not accepted. **Parking:** Free (self and valet).
$ Prices: Appetizers $4.25–$6.95, entrées $8.25–$12.95. Children's entrées $4.95. AE, CB, DC, DISC, MC, V.
Open: Sun–Thurs 5–11pm, Fri–Sat 5pm–midnight.

Tony Roma's is a deservedly popular national chain, and the company has voted this Stardust location the very best of its 140 franchises in terms of service, food quality, and cleanliness. It's a very comfortable eatery, with seating in leather-upholstered captain's chairs and wood-paneled walls hung with historic photographs of Las Vegas. A tub with brass faucets sits outside, so you can wash your sticky fingers on exiting.

This is a great choice for family dining. The house specialty is meaty, fork-tender baby back ribs barbecued in tangy sauce, but you can also opt for big, juicy beef ribs, honey- and molasses-basted Carolina-style pork ribs, or spicy Cajun ribs. A sampler plate is available. There are also hearty platters of barbecued shrimp or chicken, burgers, catch of the day, steaks, and salads. Do opt for a side order of onion rings (served in a loaf). Entrées come with coleslaw and a choice of baked potato, french fries, or ranch-style beans. The children's menu lists a choice of four meals in a basket—ribs, burgers, chicken fingers, or chicken drumstick and thighs, all served with fries. For dessert there are fresh-baked chocolate, coconut, and banana cream pies, and all bar drinks are available.

5. SPECIALTY DINING

BUFFETS & SUNDAY BRUNCHES

Las Vegas is famous for its lavish low-priced buffets. These abundant all-you-can-eat meals—devised by casino hotels to lure guests to the gaming tables—range from lackluster steam-table provender to lovingly prepared and exquisitely presented banquets with free-flowing champagne. Similarly, the settings for buffet meals run the gamut from fluorescent-lit rooms that look like bingo parlors to plush, softly illumined precincts. There are close to three-dozen hotel buffets in town, the most noteworthy of which are detailed below.

Note: These cheap eats are extremely popular. Arrive early (before opening) or late to avoid a long line, especially on weekends.

✪ **BALLY'S** Located at 3645 Las Vegas Blvd. S. (tel. 739-4651), Bally's is the scene of the ultraluxurious **Sterling Sunday Brunch** served in the crystal-chandeliered Caruso's. Reached via a marble staircase, this is an opulent dining room, with gilt-framed mirrors and crystal sconces on sienna velvet-covered walls. You're seated in roomy silk damask–upholstered chairs at elegantly appointed white-linened tables. Flower arrangements and ice sculptures of swans and fish grace lavish buffet spreads tended by white-hatted chefs. A pianist entertains. There's an omelet station with an array of fillings including New Zealand lobster tail, an extensive—and very excellent—sushi bar, a carving station, and a lavish dessert table. You might opt for smoked fish with bagels and cream cheese or help yourself from a mound of fresh shrimp. Entrées vary weekly. On my last visit the possibilities included rolled chicken stuffed with pistachios and porcini mushrooms, beef tenderloin, steak Diane, roast halibut, duck breast with mango, and penne florentine with pine nuts and smoked chicken in vodka sauce. Of course there are deli and breakfast meats, many vegetables and scrumptious salads, waffles, cheeses, fruits, and side dishes such as stuffed potatoes with caviar and sour cream. Everything is delicious and beautifully presented, and champagne flows freely.

Sunday brunch, including unlimited champagne, is served 9am to 2:30pm. Adults pay $22.95, children 12 and under pay $10.95. Reservations suggested.

Bally's also offers the **Big Kitchen Buffet,** not as lavish as the above but still a gorgeous spread served in a plush carpeted and crystal-chandeliered room with comfortable upholstered armchair seating. Everything is very fresh and of the highest quality. There's a prime rib carving station, a bountiful salad bar, a good choice of fruits and vegetables, entrées (perhaps fried chicken, Swiss steak, and a catch of the day), pasta and rice dishes, redskin potatoes, cold cuts, fresh-baked desserts, and homemade ice cream. The earlier meal includes breakfast fare and all-you-can-eat shrimp, while the dinner buffet adds Chinese selections.

Brunch daily 7:30am to 2:30pm ($5.95). Dinner nightly 4:30 to 10pm ($10.95).

✪ THE PALATIUM BUFFET AT CAESARS PALACE 3570

Las Vegas Blvd. S. (tel. 731-7110), proffers daily feasts fit for an emperor adjacent to the race and sports book in the Olympic Casino. Named for the 2nd-century meeting place of Rome's academy of chefs, this elegant dining room—with white-linened tables, murals of ancient Rome, and a peach-russet color scheme enhanced by gleaming brass accents—is fronted by an imposing colonnaded pediment. Selections at lunch and dinner include elaborate salad bars, carving stations for roast meats and poultry, a wide array of entrées, fresh-baked breads, desserts, and much, much more. The evening meal includes an elegant seafood station and often highlights Italian, Mexican, and other ethnic specialties. Especially lavish are weekend brunches with omelet stations (in addition to egg dishes), breakfast meats, fresh-squeezed juices, potatoes prepared in various ways, pastas, rice casseroles, carved meats, cold shrimp, smoked salmon, and a waffle and ice-cream sundae bar (they also make flaming desserts like bananas Foster) in addition to two dessert islands spotlighting cakes and pastries. That's not the half of it.

Breakfast Monday to Friday 7 to 11am ($6.25). Lunch Monday to Friday 11:30am to 2:30pm ($7.75). Dinner nightly 4:30 to 10pm ($10.95). Saturday brunch 7:30am to 2:30pm ($9.95). Sunday brunch, including unlimited champagne, 8:30am to 2:30pm ($13.50 for adults, $10.50 for children 7 to 12, under 6 free).

⑤ CIRCUS CIRCUS The **Circus Buffet at Circus Circus,**

2880 Las Vegas Blvd. S. (tel. 734-0410), takes place in a large, cheerful room decorated with whimsical big-top themed paintings and pink-and-white canvas tenting. Food at all meals is fresh, cheap, and abundant (45 items at each meal), and plates are oversized to hold plenty of it. At dinner, for instance, there's a carving station (roast beef and ham), along with numerous entrées (fried fish, fried chicken, lasagne, egg rolls, sweet-and-sour pork, barbecued beef and chicken, and Salisbury steak on a recent visit). Side dishes include a big salad bar, rice and potato dishes, vegetables, and desserts, plus a make-your-own-sundae station and beverages. There are nightly specials—Italian, barbecue, Mexican, seafood, and soon. Four serving lines keep things moving along quickly. At breakfast, fresh-squeezed orange juice is a plus, not to mention oven-fresh biscuits, cheese blintzes, pancakes, and waffles. All that is also served at brunch along with hot entrées.

Breakfast daily 6 to 11:30am ($3). Brunch daily noon to 4pm ($3). Dinner nightly 4:30 to 11pm ($4).

DESERT INN The **Sunday Champagne Brunch Extraordinaire at the Desert Inn,** 3145 Las Vegas Blvd. S. (tel. 733-4444), takes place in the Crystal Room, the hotel's plus headliner theater. Buffet selections include an array of delicious salads, cold shrimp and snow crabs, bagels and Nova lox, creamed herring, a roast beef carving station, an omelet and waffle station, cheese blintzes, egg dishes and breakfast meats, potatoes and fresh vegetables, rice pilaf, fresh fruit, and about half a dozen hot entrées (perhaps fried chicken, catch of the day, seafood Newburg, beef Stroganoff, corned beef hash, and braised pork chops). A dessert table is laden with cakes, pies, pastries, mousses, and other treats, and champagne is unlimited.

Brunch is served from 9am to 2pm. Adults pay $9.95, children age 3 to 10 $6.96, under 3 free.

☉ EXCALIBUR The **Round Table Buffet at Excalibur,** 3850 Las Vegas Blvd. S. (tel. 597-7777), occupies, like all facilities here, a medieval setting. Crossed swords and paintings of knights in armor adorn castlelike faux stone walls, and lighting emanates from vast wrought-iron candelabra chandeliers overhead. The fare served isn't fancy, but it's freshly made, abundant, and cheap. Breakfast features fresh-squeezed orange juice and eggs Benedict, along with all the expected morning meal components. Lunch and dinner offer a number of hot and cold entrées (fried chicken, fried fish, stuffed cabbage, stuffed shells, and barbecued baby back ribs on a recent visit), along with dozens of salads, soup, rice and potato dishes, vegetables, fresh fruits, desserts, beverages, and a make-your-own sundae bar. At dinner there's a roast beef and turkey carving station. Plates are oversized, so you don't have to make as many trips to the buffet tables.

Breakfast daily 7 to 11am ($2.99). Lunch daily 11am to 4pm ($3.99). Dinner nightly 4 to 10pm ($4.99).

FLAMINGO HILTON At the **Flamingo Hilton's Crown Room Buffet,** 3555 Las Vegas Blvd. S. (tel. 733-3111), you can dine indoors in a pleasant room under an octagonal stained-glass skylight

and globe chandelier fans or al fresco, poolside, at umbrella tables on
the terrace. Dinners have monthly changing ethnic themes—Italian,
Mexican, German, and so on—in addition to a full panoply of
American dishes. A new, infinitely more lavish buffet room is in the
works at this writing and may be in place as you read this; check it
out.

Breakfast daily 6:30am to noon ($3.95). Dinner nightly 4 to
9:30pm ($5.95).

✪ **THE FREMONT** The **Paradise Buffet at the Fremont,**
200 E. Fremont St. (tel. 385-3232), is served in a very attractive
tropically themed room. Diners sit in spacious booths amid lush
jungle foliage—birds of paradise, palms, and bright tropical
blooms—and the buffet area is surrounded by a "waterfall" of Tivoli
lighting under a reflective ceiling. Island music, enhanced by bird
calls and the sound of splashing waterfalls, helps set the tone. Meals
here are on the lavish side. A typical dinner features a carving station
with three meats (perhaps roast suckling pig, top round, and roast
turkey) and six hot entrées (beef Stroganoff, barbecued Thai chicken,
fettuccine Alfredo, eggplant parmigiana, salmon ovals with lemon
butter, and shrimp fried rice on a recent visit). Fresh salads, soup, cold
cuts, herring in cream sauce, vegetables, rice and potato dishes, and
desserts ranging from bakery-fresh pies and cakes to make-your-own
sundae fixings round out the offerings.

Tuesday and Friday nights the buffet is renamed the **Seafood
Fantasy** and food tables, adorned by beautiful ice sculptures, are
laden with Maine lobster claws, crab legs, shrimp, raw oysters,
smoked salmon, oysters Rockefeller, clams, and entrées such as
lobster Thermidor, calamari, cioppino, and Cajun red snapper—all
in addition to the usual meat carving stations and a few nonseafood
entrées. It's great! And finally, the Fremont has a delightful champagne Sunday brunch served by "island girls" in colorful sarongs. It
includes not only unlimited champagne, but a full carving station,
smoked fish and herring with bagels and cream cheese, an omelet
station, and flaming desserts such as cherries jubilee.

Breakfast Monday to Friday 7am to 10:30pm ($3.95). Lunch
Monday to Friday 11am to 3pm ($4.95). Dinner Sunday, Monday,
Wednesday, and Thursday 4 to 10pm and Saturday 4 to 11pm
($7.95). Seafood Fantasy Tuesday 4 to 10pm and Friday 4 to 11pm
($10.95). Champagne brunch Saturday to Sunday 7am to 3pm
($5.95).

✪ **GOLDEN NUGGET** The **buffet at the Golden Nugget,**
129 E. Fremont St. (tel. 385-7111), has often been voted No. 1 in Las
Vegas. Not only is the food fresh and delicious, it's served in an
opulent dining room with marble-topped tables amid planters of
greenery and potted palms. Mirrored columns, beveled mirrors,
etched glass, and brass add sparkle to the room, and swagged
draperies provide a note of elegance. Most of the seating is in plush
booths. Lunch and dinner feature carving stations (turkey, roast beef,
ham) plus five or six entrées (perhaps Calcutta chicken in a curry fruit
sauce, sliced leg of lamb, whitefish in salsa, seafood scampi, beer-
battered cod, and linguine alla carbonara). Buffet tables are also
laden with an extensive salad bar (about 50 items), fresh fruit, and

marvelous desserts including Zelma Wynn's (Steve's mother) famous bread pudding. Every night crab legs, sushi, or jumbo shrimp is featured. Most lavish is the all-day Sunday champagne brunch, which adds items like eggs Benedict, blintzes, pancakes, creamed herring, and smoked fish (Nova, whitefish, trout, and so on) with bagels and cream cheese. *Note:* This stunning buffet room is also the setting for a $2 late-night meal of steak and eggs with home fries and biscuits with gravy; it's served 11pm to 5am.

Breakfast Monday to Saturday 7 to 10:30am ($4.75). Lunch Monday to Saturday 10:30am to 3pm ($7.50). Dinner Monday to Saturday 4 to 10pm ($9.95). Sunday brunch, including unlimited champagne, 8am to 10pm ($9.95, half price for children under seven).

HARRAH'S The **Galley Buffet at Harrah's,** 3475 Las Vegas Blvd. S. (tel. 369-5000), is served in a red-white-and-blue Americana-themed room. A lavish food display under a stained-glass skylight, it features the full panoply of hot and cold entrées, an excellent salad bar, a prime rib and roast turkey carving station (at dinner), and a make-your-own-ice-cream-sundae station in addition to an array of homemade desserts.

Breakfast daily 7 to 11am ($3.80). Lunch daily 11am to 5pm ($4). Dinner nightly 5 to 11pm ($5.95).

LADY LUCK The **Lady Luck Buffet,** 206 N. Third St. (tel. 477-3000), is served in a very pretty garden-themed room with trellised dividers separating comfortable leather booths and leaf-design chandeliers overhead. Dinner includes a carving station (roast beef and baked ham) and a choice of hot entrées (perhaps baked sea perch, teriyaki chicken, baked lasagne, Hungarian goulash, home-made meat loaf, and pasta primavera). Frequently, there are Chinese, Mexican, and Italian specialties as well. You can choose from about 20 fresh salads and a nice assortment of oven-fresh desserts.

Breakfast daily 6 to 10:30am ($2.50). Lunch daily 11am to 3pm ($4). Dinner nightly 4 to 11pm ($5).

✪ LAS VEGAS HILTON The **Buffet of Champions at the Las Vegas Hilton,** 3000 Paradise Rd. (tel. 732-5111), is served in a beautiful gardenlike dining room with pristine white trellising, big planters of flowers, and magnificent white wrought-iron chandeliers and sconces. As the name implies, the room—located near the casino entrance to the race and sports SuperBook—is equally sports themed. Cream walls are adorned with very attractive murals and photographs of hockey, football, boxing, and horse racing, and there are bookshelves stocked with sporting literature. All in all, it's one of the loveliest buffet rooms in town. And the fare is fresh and delicious. The tempting array includes a roast beef and turkey carving station; hot entrées such as crab cakes, roast chicken, and pot roast, along with Chinese dishes; gorgeous salads and fresh fruits; many fresh vegetables; and a good selection of homemade desserts plus an ice cream/frozen yogurt sundae station.

Breakfast Monday to Friday 7 to 9:30am ($6.25). Lunch Monday to Friday 11am to 2:30pm ($7.25). Dinner nightly 5 to 10pm ($9). Saturday to Sunday brunch, including unlimited champagne, 8am to 2:30pm ($8.50).

MIRAGE The **Mirage Buffet,** 3400 Las Vegas Blvd. S. (tel. 791-7111), offers lavish spreads in a lovely garden-themed setting with palm trees, a plant-filled stone fountain, and seating under verdigris eaves and domes embellished with flowers. All meals except breakfast feature a carving station (fresh roast turkey and honey-baked ham at lunch, those plus prime rib at brunch and dinner). A typical Mirage buffet meal offers a choice of about a dozen hot entrées, always including a fresh catch of the day and a pasta dish; other selections might range from roast chicken stuffed with wild rice to braised Korean short ribs of beef. The chefs are very creative with salads, offering about 25 at each meal—choices such as Thai beef, seafood, Niçoise, taboulleh, Chinese chicken, Creole rice, and tortellini. At brunch champagne flows freely and a scrumptious array of smoked fish is added to the board, along with items like fruit-filled crêpes and blintzes. And every meal features a spectacular dessert table (the bread pudding in bourbon sauce is especially notable). Should healthy eating be a concern there are many light items to choose from, including sugar- and fat-free puddings. And on Sundays a nonalcoholic sparkling cider is a possible champagne alternative.

Breakfast Monday to Saturday 7 to 10:30am ($5.75). Lunch Monday to Saturday 11am to 3pm ($8). Dinner Monday to Saturday 3 to 9:30pm ($9.50). Sunday brunch 7am to 9:30pm ($12.50). Children under four free, half price for children ages four to nine.

RIO The **Carnival Buffet at the Rio,** 3770 W. Flamingo Rd. (tel. 252-7777), takes place in a festively decorated room with variegated wide sequined ribbons looped overhead and seating amid planters of lush faux tropical blooms. Chairs and booths are in bright tropical hues—green, purple, red, orange, and turquoise. It's a very good buffet, featuring a prime rib carving station (at dinner), pasta dishes, hot entrées, crisp salads, oven-fresh pastries, even a frozen-yogurt machine. Sunday night buffets feature ribs.

Breakfast Monday to Friday 7 to 10:30am ($3.50). Lunch Monday to Friday 11am to 2:30pm ($4.55). Dinner nightly 4 to 10pm ($6.70). Saturday to Sunday brunch 7am to 2:30pm ($5.60).

RIVIERA The **Riviera Buffet,** 2901 Las Vegas Blvd. S. (tel. 734-5110), offers good value for your money. It's served in an attractive turquoise/mauve/burgundy room on the second floor near the shopping arcade. Brunch daily 7am to 3pm ($4.95). Dinner daily 4:30 to 11pm ($6.95).

SAHARA The **Oasis Buffet at the Sahara,** 2535 Las Vegas Blvd. S. (tel. 737-2111), is a vast spread served in an attractive room with a wall of windows overlooking the pool and brass palm trees shading the food display tables. It's not fancy fare, but it is abundant, fresh, and tasty. A typical dinner buffet, for instance, will feature a ham and baron of beef carving station, dozens of salads, about eight hot entrées (usually including one or two ethnic dishes each night such as tacos and burritos, Chinese stir fry, or bratwurst and sauerkraut), vegetables, rice, mashed potatoes, a big dessert display of oven-fresh pies and cakes, and beverages.

Breakfast Monday to Saturday 7:30 to 10:30am ($4.95). Lunch

Monday to Saturday 11:30am to 2:30pm ($5.95). Dinner nightly 4 to 10:30pm ($6.95). Sunday brunch 8:30am to 2:30pm ($6.95). Children under 12 pay half price for all buffets.

SANDS At lunchtime, the **Regency Room at the Sands,** 3355 Las Vegas Blvd. S. (tel. 733-5000), becomes the "Regency Ristorante," serving all-you-can-eat Italian buffet meals in elegant surroundings. The room is richly oak paneled, with crystal chandeliers, white-linened tables, and seating in semicircular black tufted-leather booths. The buffet consists of several hot entrées (on my last visit these included halibut with basil cream sauce, sausage and peppers, chicken cacciatore, vegetable lasagne, and penne in marinara cream sauce), antipasto and seafood salads, oven-fresh breads (Italian loaf, foccacia with onions and garlic, and bruschetta with tomato, parmesan, and garlic), and a wide array of desserts such as strawberry tarts, cannolis, eclairs, and cheesecake.

Served daily 11:30am to 3pm ($6.95).

Also keep in mind the Sands' other low-priced food specials: An early bird dinner served from 4 to 6pm at the House of Szechwan is $6.95, and a full prime rib dinner served from 11am to 2am in the Garden Terrace is $4.95.

SHOWBOAT The **Captain's Buffet at the Showboat,** 2800 Fremont St. (tel. 385-9123), occupies a cheerful New Orleans garden-themed room. Centered on a gazebo, it's decorated in raspberry and peach and adorned with lovely still-life paintings of flowers and fruit. There are stunning floral-motif chandeliers overhead; seating is in booths with trellised dividers or at umbrella tables. Lunch and dinner menus offer entrées such as chicken picatta, broiled salmon, smoked barbecued Cornish game hens, veal breast stuffed with pistachios, tortellini primavera, and charbroiled tenderloin. All that is in addition to a carving station serving up roast beef, turkey, and honey-glazed ham. These items are complemented by an extensive salad bar, a vast selection of pastries, and a build-your-own ice-cream (or frozen-yogurt) sundae bar. Seafood buffets Wednesday and Friday evenings feature stuffed crab, fried shrimp, bouillabaisse, crab legs, raw shrimp, and more. And weekend brunch buffets include an omelet station, fruit-stuffed pancakes, and smoked fish with bagels and cream cheese. The Showboat was the innovator of Las Vegas hotel buffets, and its buffets are still among the best in town.

Lunch Monday to Friday 10am to 3:30pm ($4.45). Dinner Monday, Tuesday, and Thursday 4:30 to 10pm, Saturday to Sunday 4 to 10pm ($6.45). Seafood Spectacular dinner Wednesday and Friday 4:30 to 10pm ($7.45). Saturday to Sunday brunch 8am to 3pm ($5.45).

STARDUST The **Warehouse Buffet at the Stardust,** 3000 Las Vegas Blvd. S. (tel. 732-6111), features, as the name suggests, a raftered warehouse decor, with big restaurant cans of olive oil and chili, sacks of flour, crates of apples, and other provender on display. Tables are covered in laminated burlap potato sacking. It's a pleasant setting for very good buffet meals, featuring a carving station (roast beef, ham, and turkey), a wide array of salads and hot and cold entrées, fresh fruits, and many fresh-baked breads and cakes. You can also pump your own ice cream.

Breakfast Monday to Saturday 7 to 10:30am ($4.95). Lunch Monday to Saturday 10:30am to 3pm ($5.95). Dinner nightly 4 to 10pm ($7.95). Sunday brunch 7am to 3:30pm ($6.95).

TROPICANA The **Caribbean Nights Buffet at the Tropicana,** 3801 Las Vegas Blvd. S. (tel. 739-2222), takes place in a verdant setting with seating at glossy butcher-block tables amid planters of lush greenery. Peach walls are adorned with paintings of tropical flowers. Caribbean fare is featured. Dinner, for instance, always includes a carving station (prime rib and leg of pork), along with five or six entrées (perhaps chicken teriyaki, glazed pork ribs, pork and banana stew, blackened red snapper, Cajun chicken, and steamed clams), stir-fried veggies, saffron rice, salads, and a wide selection of desserts, including bananas Foster. Brunch also offers a carving station (prime rib, roast pork, roast turkey), an omelet station, smoked fish, about a dozen salads, breakfast meats, hash browns, hot entrées (perhaps chicken stuffed with fruit, red snapper in dill butter sauce, beef stroganoff with fettuccine, and steamed clams), and at least a dozen homemade desserts.

Dinner Friday to Saturday 4 to 10pm ($8.95). Saturday to Sunday brunch 8am to 2pm ($5.95).

A lavish **Sunday buffet brunch** is also served from 9:30am to 2pm in Rhapsody, the Trop's crystal-chandeliered gourmet room. This very elegant precinct offers plush seating in burgundy and teal velvet booths and armchairs and has a wall of windows overlooking the swimming pool, waterfalls, and tropical foliage. The spread is more haute than the above; it includes a sushi bar and unlimited champagne. Price is $17.95, $10.95 for children age 10 and under.

CHAPTER 7

WHAT TO SEE & DO IN LAS VEGAS

Las Vegas is unlike any other tourist mecca. Here the main attraction is gambling, and if you're staying at one of the casino megahotels, you have not only casino gaming, but accommodations, dining, sightseeing, sports facilities, and entertainment under one roof. The more lavish the hotel, the more Disneyesque its attractions—from the erupting volcano and white tiger habitat at the Mirage to Caesars' Omnimax movies and talking Roman statues. Just strolling the Strip—especially at night when every hotel is spectacularly illuminated in multihued neon—is a mind-boggling experience. There's nothing quite like it anywhere else in the world.

But there's much more to a Las Vegas vacation than gaming action and headliner entertainment. There are many other attractions here, ranging from the sublime (magnificent vistas like Red Rock Canyon and Valley of Fire) to the slightly ridiculous (the Liberace Museum). Nearby Hoover Dam is a major sightseeing venue in its own right, and Lake Mead is one of several pristinely beautiful recreation areas. Nevada, and neighboring Arizona, offer stunning scenery, whether you venture just outside Las Vegas or all the way to the Grand Canyon. You can study ancient petroglyphs and learn about Native American cultures dating back 12,000 years, visit ghost towns, raft the Colorado River, hike or ride horseback through canyons, even ski in winter. To my mind, the ideal Las Vegas vacation combines the glitz and glitter of casino hotels with explorations of the area's majestic canyons and desert wilderness. The latter is the perfect antidote to the former. In this chapter, all sightseeing options are described in detail. Check them out, and plan an itinerary that suits your interests.

SUGGESTED ITINERARIES

Itineraries suggested here are for adult travelers. If you're traveling with kids, incorporate some of the "Cool for Kids" suggestions listed below. Activities sketchily described in these itineraries are detailed elsewhere in this chapter.

IF YOU HAVE 1 DAY   Go to the Mirage, get tickets for *Siegfried & Roy* for the evening, and spend as much time as you like gambling in the casino. While you're here, see the rain forest, tiger and dolphin habitats, and aquarium. Head next door to Caesars, entering via the Forum Shops People Mover. Peruse shops and statuary, see an IMAX film. Consider spending some time at your hotel swimming pool during the day. Enjoy a leisurely preshow dinner at one of the many restaurants at Caesars or the Mirage (details in Chapter 5).

IF YOU HAVE 2 DAYS   Follow the above plan on the first day; you may wish to procure show tickets for additional days at the outset. On the second day, get up early and after breakfast drive out to Red Rock Canyon. The panoramic 13-mile Scenic Loop Drive is best seen early in the morning when there's little traffic. If you're so inclined, spend some time hiking here. Have lunch at nearby Bonnie Springs Ranch. After lunch enjoy a guided trail ride into the desert wilderness. (See Chapter 12, "Easy Excursions from Las Vegas," for details on the above.) Return to town and loll by the pool with a good book. Suggested evening show: *Enter the Night* at the Stardust.

IF YOU HAVE 3 DAYS   Follow the above itinerary for your first two days. On the third day, plan a tour to Hoover Dam. Leave early in the morning. Return to Las Vegas after lunch via Valley of Fire State Park, stopping at the Lost City Museum in Overton en route (see Chapter 12 for details). At night, if you still have energy, hit the casinos and/or catch another show—either a headliner favorite or *Splash* at the Riviera. Another option: a romantic evening at the Palace Court piano bar at Caesars Palace (have dinner here first if you feel like splurging). The Desert Inn's Star Lite Theatre lounge is another elegant spot for cocktails and dancing to live music.

IF YOU HAVE 5 DAYS OR MORE   Choose among the above suggestions in planning your first three days. On the fourth day, instead of returning from your Hoover Dam trip the same day, spend overnight—or longer—at the charming Lake Mead Lodge. Take a dinner cruise on the *Desert Princess,* and spend part of the next day enjoying Lake Mead's many recreational facilities before returning to town via Valley of Fire State Park.

As you plan any additional days, consider excursions to other nearby attractions such as Mount Charleston, Goodsprings, and the Grand Canyon. Inquire about interesting tours at your hotel sightseeing desk. And visit local museums.

1. ATTRACTIONS IN LAS VEGAS

Many of the most fascinating attractions are located outside the Strip/Downtown area. Without leaving Las Vegas proper, your options are as follows:

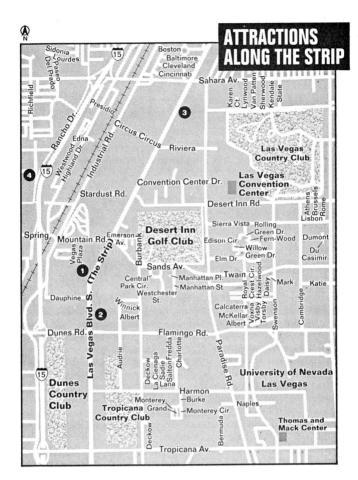

Dolphin Habitat ❶
Imperial Palace
  Auto Collection ❷
Scandia Family
  Fun Center ❹
Wet 'n Wild ❸

BETHANY'S CELEBRITY DOLL MUSEUM, 1775 E. Tropicana Ave., at Spencer St. (next door to the Liberace Museum). Tel. 798-3036.

Opened in mid-1992, this is, according to the owners, the first museum in the world dedicated to celebrity dolls. Rich Little and Debbie Reynolds attended the opening and unveiled their doll look-alikes. The display includes fictional characters that run the gamut from *Alice in Wonderland* to the entire cast of *Gone With the*

Wind, as well as an incredible number of stage and screen-luminary replicas. Among the latter: Elvis, Clark Gable, Marlene Dietrich, John Wayne, the Beatles, Bette Davis, Captain Kangaroo, Michael Jackson, Bill Cosby, Lucille Ball, Redd Foxx, Sonny and Cher, Carmen Miranda, Katharine Hepburn, Vanna White, and Peewee Herman. Some dolls are attired in movie and TV costumes, among them Liza Minnelli (*Cabaret*), Audrey Hepburn (*Breakfast at Tiffany*), Leslie Caron (*Gigi*), Grace Kelly (*To Catch a Thief*), Marilyn Monroe (*Some Like It Hot*), Linda Evans and Joan Collins (as *Dynasty*'s Krystle and Alexis), and Johnny Depp (*Edward Scissorhands*). There are presidents and president's wives, Princess Di as a happy bride (who knew?), and famous authors such as Shakespeare and Mark Twain. Even Barbie merits some shelf space. Lots of fun browsing here.

Admission: $3 for adults, $1.50 for seniors and children 12 and under.

Open: Mon–Sat 10am–5pm, Sun 1–5pm.

THE DOLPHIN HABITAT, The Mirage, 3400 Las Vegas Blvd. S. Tel. 791-7111.

This is no theme park exhibit. The Mirage's dolphin habitat was designed to provide a healthy and nurturing environment and to educate the public about marine mammals and their role in the ecosystem. Mirage owner Steve Wynn is a dedicated environmentalist whose hotel restaurants serve only dolphin-safe tuna and boycott Icelandic fish in protest of that nation's whaling practices. No fur is sold in Wynn's hotel boutiques. Specialists worldwide were consulted in the creation of the habitat, which was designed to serve as a model of a quality secured environment. The pool is more than four times larger than government regulations require, and its 1.5 million gallons of man-made sea water are cycled and cleaned once every two hours. The habitat houses six Atlantic bottlenose dolphins in a lush tropical setting. The facility offers visitors the opportunity to watch dolphins frolicking from above- and below-water viewing areas, and the 15-minute tour is entertaining and informative to adults and children alike. A highlight is a video of a resident dolphin (Duchess) giving birth (to Squirt) underwater. After the tour you can stay in the area and continue observing the dolphins.

While you're at the Mirage visit the royal white tiger habitat and see the 53-foot, 20,000-gallon simulated coral reef aquarium behind the registration desk. The latter accommodates 1,000 fish and sea creatures—including sharks and rays—indigenous to the Caribbean, Hawaii, Tonga, Fiji, the Red Sea, the Marshall Islands, and Australia.

Admission: $3. Children under 3 free. Children 12 or under must be accompanied by an adult.

Open: Mon–Fri 11am–7pm, Sat–Sun and holidays 9am–7pm.

ETHEL M CHOCOLATES, 2 Cactus Garden Dr., just off Mount Vista and Sunset Way in the Green Valley Business Park. Tel. 458-8864.

Just a 15-minute drive (six miles) from the Strip is the ultra-modern Ethel M Chocolate factory, a tourist attraction that draws about 1,800 visitors a day. Ethel Mars began making fine chocolates in a little candy kitchen around the turn of the century and her small

enterprise evolved to produce not only dozens of varieties of superb boxed chocolates but some of the world's most famous candies—M&M's, Milky Way, 3 Musketeers, and Mars bars.

On a self-guided tour of the plant, you'll see the candy-making process from a glass-enclosed viewing aisle. All of the equipment is marked to aid visitor comprehension. "Kitchen" procedures include the cooking of buttery cream fillings in immense copper kettles, the hand-sorting of nuts, grinding of fresh peanut butter, and fudge making. In one production-line process little creamy centers are bathed in chocolate and decorated with Ethel M's trademark swirls. On another line chocolate is deposited into molds, vibrated to eliminate air bubbles, cooled, filled (with nuts, creams, and/or liqueurs), and hand boxed. There are actually employees whose job involves the "arduous" task of tasting for quality control. Depending on what's being made the day you visit, you may observe all or little of the above; however, you will see it all in informative video presentations shown along the aisle. Lithographs on the opposite wall depict candy making in the 1700s as shown in Diderot's first French *Encyclopedia*. The tour winds up in an attractive gift shop where you can sample a free piece of candy (my favorite is almond butter krisp) and purchase chocolates that can be delivered anywhere in the United States.

Also on the premises is a 2.5-acre garden displaying 350 species of rare and exotic cacti with signage provided for self-guided tours. To get here drive east on Tropicana Avenue, make a right on Mountain Vista, then go two miles to Sunset Way and turn left into Green Valley Business Park. Ethel M is conveniently visited en route to or from Hoover Dam.

Admission: Free.

Open: Daily 8:30am–7pm. **Closed:** Thanksgiving Day and Christmas.

THE IMPERIAL PALACE AUTO COLLECTION, Imperial Palace Hotel, 3535 Las Vegas Blvd. S. Tel. 731-3311.

This fascinating museum on the fifth floor of the Imperial Palace Hotel displays, on a rotating basis, some 750 antique, classic, and special-interest vehicles spanning more than 100 years of automotive

FROMMER'S FAVORITE
LAS VEGAS EXPERIENCES

Strolling the Strip After Dark You haven't really seen Las Vegas until you've seen it at night. It's the world's greatest sound and light show.

A Creative Adventures Tour All of the nearby natural attractions described in this chapter are favorite experiences. Char Cruze (see "Organized Tours" below) provides personalized tours that unlock the mysteries of the desert canyons and make regional history come vibrantly alive. I can't think of a better way to spend a day than exploring canyons with her.

Mount Charleston Especially in summer, this scenic drive to the mountains, culminating at a charming restaurant nestled in a pine forest, is a delight. Spend the day here hiking, horseback riding, or just kicking back.

Dinner at the Palace Court This stunning French restaurant at Caesars Palace offers the best food in Las Vegas, graciously served in opulent surroundings. Plan after-dinner drinks at the adjoining piano bar, where a retracting skylight opens to starry skies—one of the most romantic spots in town.

Siegfried & Roy I'd as soon miss their show at the Mirage as go to India and skip the Taj Mahal. See it!

Sunday Champagne Brunches Especially leisurely and lavish are those featured at Bally's, Caesars Palace, and the Golden Nugget.

history. It's one of the premier collections of its kind. Some 200 vehicles—enhanced by mannequins and period tableaux—are on exhibit at any given time in a plush showroom setting. Within that setting is a 15,000-square-foot room housing the world's largest collection of Model J Duesenbergs, including cars once owned by James Cagney, chewing-gum magnate Phillip K. Wrigley, boxing champion Max Baer, heiress Doris Duke, Father Divine, Tyrone Power, and others. The Duesenbergs alone (there are 25 of them, built between 1929 and 1937) are valued in excess of $50 million. The Duesenberg Room also features a cocktail lounge with 1880s Brunswick furnishings.

In President's Row, JFK's 1962 "bubbletop" Lincoln Continental, Lyndon Johnson's 1964 Cadillac, Eisenhower's 1952 Chrysler Imperial 20-foot-long parade car, Truman's 1950 Lincoln Cosmopolitan with gold-plated interior, FDR's unrestored 1936 V-16 Cadillac, and Herbert Hoover's 1929 Cadillac are on display. Adolf Hitler's armored bulletproof and mineproof 1936 Mercedes-Benz 770K (the parade car in which he rode with Mussolini on June 18, 1940), Mussolini's 1939 Alfa Romeo (which he later gave to his mistress, Carlotta Petacci), Hirohito's 1935 Packard, Czar Nicholas II's 1914 Rolls-Royce, former Mexican president Lazaro Cardenas's black 1939 V-12 Packard (armor plated to resist 50-caliber machine gun bullets), and Argentinean strongman Juan Peron's 1939 straight-8 Packard, are displayed in Dictator's Row. And elsewhere in the collection are cars that belonged to Pope Paul VI, the King of Siam, and Queen Wilhemina of the Netherlands.

Commercial vehicles of bygone days include antique buses, military transport, taxis (among them, the 1908 French model that appeared in the movie version of *My Fair Lady*), gasoline trucks, fire engines, delivery trucks and vans, dump trucks, and pickup trucks. Other highlights are Al Capone's 1930 V-16 Cadillac, Elvis Presley's powder blue 1976 Cadillac Eldorado, Liberace's pale-cream 1981 Zimmer (complete with candelabra), W. C. Fields's black 1938 Cadillac V-16 touring sedan with built-in bar, Caruso's 1920 green and black Hudson, Howard Hughes's 1954 Chrysler (because of his phobia about germs, Hughes installed a special air-purification system that cost more than the car itself!), a 1947 Tucker (one of only 51 manufactured before the company went out of business), a 1977 Safarikar with an all-leather exterior and doors that can be extended to ward off attacking jungle animals, and motorcycles that belonged to Steve McQueen, Clark Gable, and Sammy Davis, Jr. A gift shop on the premises carries a wide selection of automotive books, model kits, and memorabilia.

Admission: $6.95 adults, $3 seniors and children under 12, children under 5 free.

Open: Daily 9:30am–11:30pm.

LIBERACE MUSEUM, 1775 E. Tropicana Ave., at Spencer St. Tel. 798-5595.

This is an only-in-Vegas phenomenon—an entire museum devoted to the career memorabilia of "Mr. Showmanship," Walter Valentino Liberace. Three exhibit areas house his spectacular cars (he owned over 50 automobiles), antique and custom-made pianos, dazzling costumes and capes, glittering stage jewelry, miniature piano collection (over his lifetime he was given more than 3,000 of these by fans), honorary degrees and awards, musical arrangements, and photographs. There's also a re-creation of his office (which contains an inlaid ormolu Louis XV desk originally owned by Czar Nicholas II of Russia) and ornate bedroom suite. Visitors are greeted at a piano-shaped desk.

Among the fabulous pianos on display here are a 19th-century hand-painted concert grand piano that Chopin played at Versailles, an 1863 rosewood Steinway with African ivory keys, George Gershwin's Chickering concert grand, and Liberace's own mirror-tiled Baldwin concert grand. Then there are the cars, among them a mirrored white Rolls-Royce Phantom V (one of seven made) with a design of galloping horses etched into the mirror tile; a 1975 English cab painted in black and white houndstooth; a 1927 gold Custom Bradley GT, a shocking-pink mirror-tiled Volkswagen with a Rolls-Royce front (it went with his pink fur-trimmed pink-sequined cape); a rhinestone-covered car designed to match a similarly bejeweled piano and costume; and the glittering red, white, and blue bicentennial Rolls-Royce that Liberace drove onstage at Radio City in 1976 (he wore matching red-, white-, and blue-spangled hot pants and boots). Dozens of furred, feathered, beaded, sequined, and bejeweled costumes include a Czar Nicholas uniform with 22-karat-gold braiding and a blue velvet cape styled after the coronation robes of King George V and covered with $60,000 worth of rare chinchilla!. There are photographs of Liberace with Elvis, Barbra, Debbie Reynolds, Ronald Reagan, and many other celebrities. A collection of his crystal, silver, and china includes a set of 22-karat gold-banded Moser crystal glasses from Czechoslovakia—a magnificent service for 12 with 14 glasses for each setting. It is one of only two such handmade collections; the other is owned by Queen Elizabeth. Among the jewelry on display is a candelabra ring with platinum candlesticks and diamond flames and a spectacular piano-shaped ring containing 260 diamonds with keys made of ivory and black jade (a gift from Barron Hilton). Other notable exhibits: a gold replica of Liberace's hands made by the Disney studios, his famed candelabras, and a $50,000 50.6-pound rhinestone—the world's largest—presented to him at Caesars Palace by the grateful Austrian firm that supplied all his costume stones. There's a gift shop on the premises where you can buy anything from minature crystal grand pianos to Liberace logo thimbles, along with performance videos, cassettes, and CDs. The museum is 2½ miles east of the Strip on your right. While you're here, visit the adjoining Bethany's Celebrity Doll Museum (details above).

Admission: $6.50 for adults, $4.50 for seniors over 60, $3.50 for students, $2 for children under 12.

Open: Mon–Sat 10am–5pm, Sun 1–5pm.

RIPLEY'S BELIEVE IT OR NOT! MUSEUM, Four Queens Hotel, 202 E. Fremont St. Tel. 385-4011.

This massive exhibit of over 1,500 oddities, curiosities, and fascinating artifacts from far-away places is a delightful way to spend an hour or two. It all began in 1918, when sports cartoonist Robert Ripley created an "oddities in sports" feature called "Champs and Chumps" for the *New York Globe*. Financed by Hearst's King Features Syndicate, he was soon encouraged to travel the world in search of bizarre items. Over his lifetime, Ripley visited 198 countries, always returning with bundles of material. He soon began showing his burgeoning collection—ranging from shrunken heads to medieval torture instruments—in traveling shows nationwide. After Ripley's death in 1949, the collection was cataloged, and, with later additions, it has filled a dozen museums in the United States and Canada, of which this Las Vegas facility is the largest.

Among the miscellanea on display here in exhibits and detailed tableaux: a replica of Lincoln's log cabin made entirely of pennies, the death mask of John Dillinger, a ball of twine two feet in diameter, torture devices such as the iron maiden (a spiked cage used during the Spanish Inquisition), Shah Aga Mohammed Khan (an 18th-century Persian ruler who once blinded 35,000 men—the entire population of a vanquished city), a cannibal necklace made of human bones, Ubangis with wooden plates in their lips, a Pakistani fakir who wore 670 pounds of chains for 13 years, a man who ate an 11-inch birch log to win a $10,000 prize, a Hindu reclining on a bed of nails, a toilet carved from a walnut, a two-headed calf, and a replica of a space shuttle constructed of 77,069 matchsticks. This being Las Vegas there is a room devoted to gambling-related exhibits such as a roulette table made of 14,000 jelly beans, a 50-story house of cards, and a pair of dice a gambler used at Binion's Horseshoe Casino on a million dollar bet (he lost). A favorite of mine is "the human unicorn"—a Chinese man with a 13-inch horn growing out of his head. He is shown placidly seated over tea with an 18-year-old Austrian lady who has grown a 4-inch beard! Perhaps he was one of her suitors; she is said to have received many marriage proposals. Not so lucky the young Banda tribeswomen of Zaire, who are not deemed eligible for marriage until they have eaten an entire raw unplucked chicken without breaking a single bone (the things we do for love). Exhibits are enhanced by sound effects and thematic settings such as a cavelike passage with a real waterfall.

Admission: $4.95 for adults, $3.95 for seniors (50 and over), $2.50 for children under 13, children 5 and under free.

Open: 9am–midnight Sun–Thurs, 9am–1am Fri–Sat.

SCANDIA FAMILY FUN CENTER, 2900 Sirius Ave. (enter on Rancho Dr. between Sahara Ave. and Spring Mountain Rd.). Tel. 364-0070.

This family amusement center just a few blocks off the Strip offers three 18-hole miniature golf courses, a state-of-the-art video arcade with 225 machines, miniature car racing, bumper boats, and automated softball- and baseball-pitching machines for batting practice.

Admission: Free, but there's a fee to play each game. Miniature golf costs $5 for 18 holes, children under 5 free. Car racing and bumper boats are $4 per ride; children shorter than height regulations (54″ for race cars, 46″ for boats) can ride free with an adult. And batting practice costs $1.25 for 20 pitches. Super Saver Coupons ($11) entitle you to a round of miniature golf, two rides, and 12 video games. There's also a Ride Package offering five rides for the price of four.

Open: Sept–early June Sun–Thurs 10am–11pm, Fri–Sat 10am–midnight; June–end of Aug Sun–Thurs 10am–midnight, Fri–Sat 10am–1am.

WET 'N WILD, 2601 Las Vegas Blvd. S., just south of Sahara Ave. Tel. 737-3819.

When temperatures soar, head for this 26-acre water park right in the heart of the Strip and cool off jumping waves, careening down steep flumes, and running rapids. Among the highlights: Surf Lagoon, a 500,000-gallon wave pool; Bonzai Boggan, a roller coaster–like water ride (aboard a plastic sled, you race down a 45-degree angled chute and skip porpoiselike across a 120-foot pool); Der Stuka, the world's fastest and highest water chute; Raging Rapids, a simulated white-water rafting adventure on a 500-foot-long river; Lazy River, a leisurely float trip; Blue Niagara, a thrilling descent inside intertwined looping tubes from a height of six stories; and Willy Nilly, a hydra-hurricane that propels riders on inner tubes around a 90-foot-diameter pool at 10 miles per hour. The newest—and most dramatic—attraction is the Black Hole, an exhilaratingly rapid space-themed flume descent in the dark enhanced by a bombardment of colorful fiber-optic star fields and spinning galaxy patterns en route to splashdown. There are additional flumes, a challenging children's water playground, and a sunbathing area with a cascading waterfall, as well as lawn games (volleyball, horseshoes), video and arcade games, and a picnic area. Food concessions are located throughout the park, and you can purchase swimwear and accessories at the gift shop.

Admission: $16.95 adults, $13.95 children under 10, under 3 free. Parking is free.

Open: The season and hours vary a bit from year to year. Basically, the park is open daily mid-Apr–mid-June and Sept 10am–5 or 6pm, early June–end of Aug 10am–8pm.

2. COOL FOR KIDS

Las Vegas used to be an adults-only kind of town. These days, it's actively pursuing the family-travel trade and offering dozens of child-oriented activities. In addition to the below-listed attractions, a *Wizard of Oz*–themed amusement park and a major casino hotel based on *Treasure Island* (which will bring pirate battles to the Strip) are in the works. Here's a rundown on the current kid-pleasers both in town and afield:

Circus Circus (see p. 96) has ongoing circus acts throughout the day, a vast pinball and video game arcade, and dozens of carnival games on its mezzanine level. The **Excalibur Hotel** (see p. 98) also offers video and carnival games, plus thrill cinemas and free shows (jugglers, puppets, and so on). **IMAX movies at Caesars Palace** (see p. 52) are a thrill for everyone in the family; a video game arcade adjoins the IMAX theater. Animated talking statues in the Forum

Shops area are also a kick. **Ripley's Believe It Or Not! Museum** at the Four Queens Hotel (*see p. 146*) contains 1,5142exhibits ranging from shrunken heads to a 50-story house of cards.

Other unusual diversions in town include **Ethel M Chocolates** (*see p. 142*), where you will tour a candy-making factory and avail yourselves of free samples; **Bethany's Celebrity Doll Museum** (*see p. 141*), the world's first museum dedicated to doll replicas of the rich and famous; and the **Dolphin Habitat at the Mirage** (*see p. 142*), which offers an educational and fun 15-minute tour. While you're here, see the tigers and the sharks; at night, the volcano eruption is a must.

Perhaps the best places for kids to burn off energy in town are **Wet 'n Wild** (*see p. 148*), where you'll find flumes, wave pools, simulated white-water rafting, and other splashy thrills, and the **Scandia Family Fun Center** (*see p. 147*), where kids can flit between the miniature golf course, video arcade, bumper boats, miniature car racecourse, and batting cages.

Some of the famed **casino hotel shows** are appropriate for children, including *King Arthur's Tournament* at the Excalibur, *Siegfried & Roy* at the Mirage, and *Melinda, First Lady of Magic* and *Pacific Rim Island Magic Dinner Show* at the Sahara).

Beyond city limits is **Bonnie Springs Ranch/Old Nevada** (*see p. 219*), with trail and stagecoach rides, a petting zoo, old-fashioned melodramas, stunt shootouts, a Nevada-themed wax museum, crafts demonstrations, and more; and **Lake Mead** (*see p. 210*), which has great recreational facilities for family vacations. Finally, there are a number of **organized tours** (*see p. 150*) you can take to Grand Canyon and other interesting sights in southern Nevada and neighboring states—they can be great family fun. Check with your hotel sightseeing desk.

3. ORGANIZED TOURS

Just about every hotel in town has a sightseeing desk offering a seemingly infinite number of tour options in and around Las Vegas. You're sure to find a tour company that will take you where you want to go.

GRAY LINE Gray Line (tel. 384-1234) features a particularly comprehensive tour roster that includes:

- 5½- and 7-hour city tours combining visits to nearby museums with peeks at stars' homes and a bit of Las Vegas history.
- A Las Vegas nightclub tour that begins with a dinner show (the *Folies Bergère* or *King Arthur's Tournament*) and winds up with a bus tour of the Strip and Glitter Gulch at night.
- Full-day excursions to Laughlin, Nevada, an up-and-coming mini–Las Vegas 100 miles south with casino hotels on the banks of the Colorado River.
- 5-, 6-, and 7-hour excursions to Hoover Dam and Lake Mead, the longest of them including a visit to Ethel M Chocolate Factory.

- An 8-hour excursion to Red Rock Canyon, including a visit to the University of Nevada Museum of Natural History.
- An 8-hour excursion to the Valley of Fire that includes lunch at a Lake Mead resort and a drive by Wayne Newton's Ranch.
- A Lake Mead sightseeing excursion and dinner cruise aboard a Mississippi-style paddle wheeler.
- A full-day river-rafting tour on the Colorado River from the base of Hoover Dam through majestic Black Canyon.
- A morning or afternoon air tour (and you thought they only had buses) of Grand Canyon.
- A full-day land tour of Hoover Dam and air tour of Grand Canyon.
- A 10-hour Grand Canyon excursion that includes "flightseeing" and river rafting on the Colorado.
- An overnight trip to Grand Canyon.
- A tour combining "flightseeing" over Hoover Dam and the Grand Canyon and the Lake Mead dinner cruise.

Call for details or inquire at your hotel sightseeing desk.

THE GRAND CANYON   Generally, tourists from Las Vegas don't drive 300 miles to Arizona to see the Grand Canyon, but there are dozens of sightseeing tours departing from the city daily. In addition to the **Gray Line** tours described above, the major operator, **Scenic Airlines** (tel. 739-1900), runs deluxe, full-day guided air-ground tours for $179 per person ($139 for children 2 to 11) the price includes a bus excursion through the National Park, a flight over the canyon, lunch, and a screening of the IMAX movie *Grand Canyon—the Hidden Secrets.* All Scenic tours include "flightseeing." The company also offers both full-day and overnight tours with hiking. And though all Scenic tours include hotel pick up and drop off, if you take the Premium Deluxe Tour ($209 for adults, $159 for children) you'll be transported by limo. Scenic also has tours of Monument Valley and Los Angeles.

INDIVIDUALIZED TOURS   A totally different variety of tours is offered by Char Cruze of **Creative Adventures** (tel. 361-5565). Char, a charming fourth-generation Las Vegan (she was at the opening of the Flamingo), spent her childhood riding horseback through the mesquite and cottonwoods of the Mojave desert, discovering magical places you'd never find on your own—or on a commercial tour. Char is a lecturer and storyteller as well as a tour guide. She has extensively studied southern Nevada's geology and desert wildlife, its regional history and Native American cultures. Her personalized tours—enhanced by fascinating stories about everything from miners to mobsters—visit haunted mines, sacred Paiute grounds, ghost towns, canyons, and ancient petroglyphs. Depending on your itinerary, the cost is about $100 a day if you use your own car (more, depending on the number of people, if rental transportation is required). It's a good idea to make arrangements with her prior to leaving home.

4. SPORTS & RECREATION

Bring your sports gear to Las Vegas. The city and surrounding areas offer unexampled opportunities for sportive recreation. Just about every hotel has a large swimming pool and health club, tennis courts abound, and there are many highly rated golf courses. All variety of water sports are offered at Lake Mead National Recreation Area, there's rafting on the Colorado, horseback riding at Mount Charleston and Bonnie Springs, great hiking in the canyons, and much, much more. Do plan to get out of those smoke-filled casinos and into the fresh air once in awhile. It's good for your health and your finances.

Note: When choosing a hotel, check out its recreational facilities, all listed in Chapter 5.

ACTIVE SPORTS

BICYCLING   City Streets (tel. 596-2953) in nearby Henderson rents 21-speed mountain bikes and offers free delivery to all Downtown and Strip hotels. Rates are $25 a day, $20 for a half day, and you must show a major credit card (American Express, Master Card, or Visa). You also have to be at least five feet tall (or close to it) to rent (they don't have children's bikes), and one member of your party must be 18 or older. Inquire about City Streets' bike trips to Red Rock Canyon and other good biking areas.

In Mount Charleston you can rent from **Mountaintop Bicycles** at the Restaurant and Lounge (tel. 872-5641 or 252-0646). They, too, rent 21-speed mountain bikes, but also have kids' bikes. Rates are $30 a day, $20 for a half day, and you must show a major credit card (American Express, Master Card, or Visa). At least one member of your party must be 18 or older. Hotel delivery in Las Vegas is available for a fee. Rentals include helmets, water bottles, and maps.

BOWLING   The Showboat Hotel & Casino, 2800 E. Fremont St. (tel. 385-9153), is famous for housing the largest bowling center in North America—106 lanes—and for being the oldest stop on the Professional Bowlers Tour. Its alleys are looking spiffier than ever due to a recent renovation in which lanes were resurfaced, new carpeting and brighter lighting installed, and furnishings upgraded. A fifties diner-themed eatery also opened recently. Open 24 hours.

CAMPING   A free comprehensive guide to campsites and RV parks in Nevada (including many in Las Vegas and Lake Mead National Recreation Area) is available from the **Nevada Commission on Tourism,** Capitol Complex, Carson City, NV 89710 (tel. 702/687-4322 or 800/237-0774).

FISHING   One doesn't usually think of fishing in the desert, but there are lakes. Closest to Las Vegas are the lakes in **Floyd R. Lamb State Park,** 9200 Tule Springs Rd. (tel. 486-5413). The park is about 15 miles from the Strip. To get there take I-15 to U.S. 95 north, get off at the Durango exit and follow the signs. The lakes are stocked with catfish, trout, bluegill, sunfish, and large-mouth bass. You will need your own gear, bait, and tackle, as well as a Nevada fishing license, which is available at any sporting goods store (check the Las Vegas *Yellow Pages*). There's also fishing at Lake Mead (see listing in Chapter 12 for details).

GOLF There are dozens of local courses, including two very challenging ones—the Desert Inn Country Club (which hosts three major PGA tournaments each year) and the Dunes Country Club. Beginner and intermediate golfers might prefer the other courses listed.

The **Angel Park Golf Club,** 100 S. Rampart Blvd. (tel. 254-4653), a 36-hole, par-71 public course, was designed by Arnold Palmer. Yardage (Palm Course): 6,743 championship, 6,120 regular, 4,790 ladies; (Mountain Course) 6,722 championship, 6,235 regular, 5,147 ladies. Facilities: pro shop, nightlit driving range, 18-hole putting course, restaurant, snack bar, cocktail bar, beverage cart.

The **Black Mountain Country Club,** 501 Greenway Rd., in nearby Henderson (tel. 565-7933), is an 18-hole, par-72 semiprivate course requiring reservations four days in advance. Yardage: 6,541 championship, 6,223 regular, 5,505 ladies. Facilities: pro shop, putting green, driving range, restaurant, snack bar, and cocktail lounge.

The **Craig Ranch Golf Club,** 628 W. Craig Rd. (tel. 642-9700), is an 18-hole, par-70 public course. Yardage: 6,001 regular, 5,221 ladies. Facilities: driving range, pro shop, putting green, and snack bar.

The **Desert Inn Country Club,** 3145 Las Vegas Blvd. S. (tel. 733-4290), gets the nod from champions. It's an 18-hole, par-72 resort course. Yardage: 7,111 championship, 6,633 regular, 5,809 ladies. Facilities: driving range, putting green, pro shop, and restaurant. You can reserve two days in advance. This is the most famous and demanding course in Las Vegas. *Golf Digest* calls it one of America's top resort courses. The driving range is open to the public, but you must stay at the Desert Inn to play the course.

The **Desert Rose Golf Club,** 5483 Club House Dr. (tel. 431-4653), is an 18-hole, par-71 public course. Yardage: 6,600 championship, 6,135 regular, 5,458 ladies. Facilities: driving range, pro shop, restaurant, and cocktail lounge.

The **Dunes Country Club,** 3650 Las Vegas Blvd. S. (tel. 737-4746), is an 18-hole, par-72 resort course. Yardage: 7,240 championship, 6,571 regular, 5,982 ladies. Facilities: clubhouse, putting green, pro shop, coffee shop, and cocktail lounge.

The **Las Vegas Municipal Golf Course,** 4349 Vegas Dr. (tel. 646-3003), is an 18-hole, par-72 course. Yardage: 6,335 regular, 5,734 ladies. Facilities: lighted driving range, pro shop, coffee shop, and cocktail lounge.

The **Riviera,** 2901 Las Vegas Blvd. S. (tel. 792-9700), doesn't have a golf course, but it does offer an interesting alternative called Par T Golf—video simulations of seven world-class championship courses projected on a large screen. You can choose simulated play at courses ranging from Pebble Beach in California to the Club de Bonmont in Switzerland. As your ball races down the fairway a computer analyzes how far, and how straight, you hit it. Open daily 8am to 2am.

The **Sahara Country Club,** 1911 Desert Inn Rd. (tel. 796-0016), is an 18-hole, par-71 public course. Yardage: 6,815 championship, 6,418 regular, 5,761 ladies. Facilities: pro shop, restaurant, and cocktail lounge.

HEALTH CLUBS   Almost every hotel in Las Vegas has an on-premises health club. Facilities, of course, vary enormously. Full descriptions are given of each club in hotel facilities listings in Chapter 5.

But none offers the amazing range of facilities you'll find at the **Las Vegas Sporting House,** 3025 Industrial Rd., right behind the Stardust Hotel (tel. 733-8999). Opened in 1978, this posh club is ultraluxurious. UNLV teams and many athletes and Strip headliners work out here, among them Siegfried (of Siegfried & Roy), Julius Irving, and Andrew Dice Clay. Facilities include: 12 racquetball/handball courts; two squash courts; two outdoor Har-tru tennis courts (lit for night play); a full gymnasium for basketball and volleyball; an outdoor pool and sunbathing area; a 25-meter, five-lane indoor pool for lap swimming; indoor and outdoor jogging tracks; 10 treadmills; nine stair machines; free weights; full lines of Cybex, Universal, and David machines, along with some Nautilus equipment; sauna, steam, and Jacuzzi; a pro shop; men's and women's skin care and hair salons; a tanning salon; massage; free babysitting service while you work out; restaurant, bar, and lounge. Aerobics classes are given at frequent intervals throughout the day. Cost for a single visit is $15 if you're staying at a local hotel; reduced weekly and monthly rates are available. Open daily 24 hours.

HORSEBACK RIDING   The **Mount Charleston Riding Stables** (tel. 872-7009, 386-6899 from Las Vegas), under the auspices of the Mount Charleston Restaurant & Lounge, offer glorious scenic trail rides to the edge of the wilderness. As many as 20 rides a day depart from stables on Kyle Canyon Road. Weekday rates are $18 per hour, $32 for two hours, $44 for three hours; weekend and holiday rates are $22 per hour, $35 for two hours, and $45 for three hours. The stables also offer sleigh rides in winter and hayrides in summer.

Riding stables at **Bonnie Springs Ranch** (tel. 875-4191) also offer guided trail rides daily. Rates are $15 per hour.

And there's also riding at **Floyd R. Lamb State Park** (tel. 486-5413), 15 miles northwest of the Strip off U.S. 95. Guided trail rides are offered daily. Rates are $18 an hour.

HIKING   Except in summer, when temperatures can reach 120 degrees in the shade, the Las Vegas area is great for hiking. Optimum hiking season is November through March. Great locales include the incredibly scenic Red Rock Canyon, Valley of Fire State Park, and Mount Charleston (see individual listings in Chapter 12 for details).

JET SKIING   **Team Loomis** (tel. 434-1156) offers jet ski rides on Lake Mead and the Colorado River. You must be at least 12 to participate. Hotel pick ups can be arranged. Call for details.

DESERT HIKING TIPS

Hiking in the desert is very rewarding, but it can be dangerous. Some safety tips:

1. It's preferable not to hike alone.
2. Carry plenty of water and drink it often. Don't assume spring waters are safe for you to drink. A gallon of water per person per day is recommended for hikers.
3. Be alert to signs of heat exhaustion (headache, nausea, dizziness, fatigue, and cool, damp, pale, or red skin).
4. Gauge your fitness accurately. Desert hiking may involve rough or steep terrain. Don't take on more than you can handle.
5. Check weather forecasts before starting out. Thunderstorms can turn into raging flash floods extremely hazardous to hikers.
6. Dress properly. Wear sturdy walking shoes for rock scrambling, long pants (to protect yourself from rocks and cactus), a hat, sunscreen, and sunglasses.
7. Carry a small first-aid kit.
8. Be careful when climbing on sandstone, which can be surprisingly soft and crumbly.
9. Don't feed or play with animals, such as wild burros in Red Rock Canyon.
10. Keep alert to snakes and insects. Though they're rarely encountered, you'll want to look into a crevice before putting your hand into it.
11. Visit park or other information offices before you start out and acquaint yourself with rules and regulations and any possible hazards. It's also a good idea to tell them where you are going, when you will return, how many are in your party, and so on. Some park offices offer hiker-registration programs.
12. Follow the hiker's rule of thumb: "Take only photographs, and leave only footprints."

RACQUETBALL   Courts can be found in several locations around town.

The **Las Vegas Athletic Club East,** 1070 E. Sahara Ave., at Maryland Parkway (tel. 731-7110), has seven courts open 24 hours a day, seven days a week. Rates: $10 per person, per visit; $25 per week. Call to reserve a court.

The **Las Vegas Athletic Club West,** 3315 Spring Mountain Rd., between I-15 and Valley View Boulevard (tel. 362-3720), has eight courts open weekdays 5am to 10pm, weekends 8am to 8pm. Rates: $10 per person, per visit; $25 per week.

The **Las Vegas Sporting House,** 3025 Industrial Rd., right behind the Stardust Hotel (tel. 733-8999), has 12 racquetball/

handball courts open 24 hours a day, seven days a week. Rates: $15 per visit if you're staying at a local hotel.

The **University of Nevada, Las Vegas (UNLV),** 4505 Maryland Pkwy., just off Harmon Avenue (tel. 739-3150), has eight racquetball courts open weekdays 6am to 9:45pm, Saturdays 8am to 8pm, and Sundays 10am to 6pm. Rates: $2 per hour. Call before you go to find out if a court is available. You have to pick up a guest pass in the Physical Education Building.

RIVER RAFTING **Black Canyon Inc.** (tel. 293-3776) offers daily raft trips on the Colorado River from February 1 through the end of November. Trips include three hours of scenic rafting and lunch. You'll see waterfalls gush from majestic canyon walls, pass tranquil coves, spy bighorn sheep on sheer cliffs, and spot blue herons, cormorants, and falcons. Knowledgeable guides provide a lot of fascinating area history and geology. Each raft is piloted by an experienced navigator. Rates, including Las Vegas hotel pick up and return are $69.95 per person, $59.95 if you drive to and from the put-in point.

ROCK CLIMBING Red Rock Canyon, just 19 miles west of Las Vegas, is one of the world's most popular rock climbing areas. In addition to awe-inspiring natural beauty, it offers everything from bouldering to big walls. If you'd like to join the bighorn sheep, Red Rock has over 1,000 routes to inaugurate beginners and challenge accomplished climbers. Experienced climbers can contact the Visitor Center (tel. 363-1921) for information.

If you're interested in learning, or improving your skills, an excellent rock-climbing school and guide service called **Sky's the Limit** (tel. 363-4533) offers programs for beginning, intermediate, and advanced climbers. No experience is needed. The school is accredited by the American Mountain Guides Association. Similar programs are offered by **Mountain Skills** (tel. 256-7078), also fully accredited.

SNOWMOBILING **Team Loomis** (tel. 434-1156) offers guided snowmobile trips in the Mount Charleston area December to April (depending on snowfall). There are half-day trips including lunch, full-day trips including lunch and dinner, and overnight trips with trailer accommodations and campfire cookouts, as well as moonlight rides. The company is very safety oriented. Helmets and safety gear are furnished. You must be at least 12 to participate. Hotel pick ups can be arranged.

TENNIS Tennis buffs should choose one of the many hotels in town that offer tennis courts. These include:

Caesars Palace (tel. 731-7110): Four outdoor hard courts, pro shop. Open to the public. Hours: 7am to 8pm daily. Rates: $25 per hour per court for nonguests, $15 for guests (you can stay longer if no one is waiting). Make reservations.

Desert Inn (733-4444): Ten outdoor hard courts (five lit for night play), pro shop. Open to the public. Hours: 8am to 8:30pm daily (6am to 10:30pm in summer). Rates: $10 per person for a daily pass (you book for an hour, but you can stay longer if no one is waiting), free for guests. Make reservations.

Flamingo Hilton (tel. 733-3111): Four outdoor hard tennis courts (all lit for night play), pro shop. Open to the public. Hours: 8am to 7pm daily. Rates: $12 per court per hour for nonguests staying at other hotels, $5 for Flamingo Hilton guests. Make reservations.

Las Vegas Hilton (tel. 732-5111): Six outdoor hard courts (all lit for night play), pro shop. Not open to the public. Hours: 6am to 10pm daily. Rates: No charge.

Riviera (tel. 734-5110): Two outdoor hard courts (both lit for night play). Open to the public, subject to availability; hotel guests have prior claim. Hours: 24 hours. Rates: No charge. No reservations.

In addition to hotels, the **University of Nevada, Las Vegas (UNLV)**, 4505 Maryland Pkwy., just off Harmon Avenue (tel. 739-3150), has a dozen night-lit tennis courts open weekdays 6am to 9:45pm, Saturdays 8am to 8pm, and Sundays 10am to 6pm. Rates: $2 per hour. Call before you go to find out if a court is available. Pick up a guest pass in the Physical Education Building.

SPECTATOR SPORTS

The **Sam Boyd Silver Bowl** at the University of Nevada, Las Vegas (UNLV), Boulder Highway and Russell Road (tel. 739-3900), is a 40,000-seat outdoor stadium. The UNLV Rebels play six football games here each year between September and November, and the stadium is also used for Motorcross events, truck and tractor pulls, high school football games, and the Las Vegas Football Bowl in December. For information, and to charge tickets, call the above number or Ticket Master (tel. 474-4000).

The **Thomas and Mack Center,** also on the UNLV campus at Tropicana Avenue and Swenson Street (tel. 739-3900), is an 18,500-seat facility used for a variety of sporting events. It is home to the UNLV's Runnin' Rebels (basketball), who play 16 to 20 games during a November to March season. Other events here include WWF wrestling matches, American Gladiators, major boxing tournaments, NBA exhibition games, rodeos, truck and tractor pulls, and major tennis matches. For information, and to charge tickets, call the above number or Ticket Master (tel. 474-4000).

Bally's' 5,000-seat Goldwyn Events Center (tel. 739-4111) sometimes hosts major boxing matches.

Caesars Palace (tel. 731-7110 or 800/634-6698) has a long tradition of sporting events, from Evel Knievel's attempted motorcycle jump over its fountains in 1967 to Grand Prix auto races. The hotel's tennis courts have been the site of many championship tournaments, and—an interesting side note—one Caesars employee used to sneak his talented son onto the courts here to practice. That was little Andre Agassi, who later legitimately played championship tournaments on those same courts. Mary Lou Retton has tumbled in gymnastic events at Caesars, and Olympians Brian Boitano and Katarina Witt have taken to the ice, as has Wayne Gretzky (he led the L.A. Kings to victory over the New York Rangers in a preseason exhibition game). In 1992 Evander Holyfield defeated Larry Holmes here—one of 60 world-championship boxing contests to take place since the hotel opened. In the spirit of ancient Rome, Caesars awards riches and honors to the "gladiators" who compete in its arenas.

The **Las Vegas Hilton** (tel. 732-5755 or 800/222-5361) has been hosting world-championship boxing matches in the vast Hilton Center since 1978, when Muhammad Ali lost his World Heavyweight Championship to Leon Spinks in a shocking upset. Since then, dozens of important bouts have taken place here, featuring boxing greats like Mike Tyson, Thomas Hearns, Larry Holmes, and numerous others.

The **Mirage** (tel. 791-7111 or 800/627-6667) features championship boxing matches several times a year.

The **Riviera** (tel. 734-5110 or 800/634-6753) features frequent championship boxing matches.

The **Sahara** (tel. 737-2111) hosts occasional major sporting events such as ESPN boxing and PRCA National Finals Rodeos.

CHAPTER 8

STROLLING AROUND LAS VEGAS

Las Vegas is a city that has to be seen by night. After dark, the town is a neon extravaganza, unrivaled anywhere else in the world. Compared to the Strip at night, even the lights of Broadway seem to be on dimmer switches. The show gets better every year as hotels vie to win the glitter wars. *Note:* Though I've only cited one food stop, all of the below-listed hotels offer a panoply of excellent restaurants and bar/lounges in all price ranges. See Chapters 6 and 11 for details.

A WALKING TOUR OF THE STRIP

Begin: Circus Circus.
End: "Four Corners" (where the Strip meets Dunes and Flamingo roads).
Time: 2–5 hours, depending on stops.
Best Time: Begin immediately after dark.

Begin on the Strip facing south at the junction of Circus Circus Drive and Riviera Boulevard. On your right is the:

1. **Circus Circus Hotel/Casino** fronted by Lucky, a 123-foot neon clown clutching a spinning pinwheel. Circus Circus stretches so far back from the Strip that a Disney World–style monorail is required to shuttle guests to the far reaches. Go in and ascend to the midway level where you can test your skill at dozens of carnival games or in a vast video game arcade. Through midnight you can also catch ongoing circus acts on this level—trapeze artists, magicians, acrobats, high-wire artists, clowns, and more. Across the street is the:

2. **Candlelight Wedding Chapel,** where for over three decades scores of celebrities have tied the knot. Among those who've said "I do" at the Candlelight's altar: Patty Duke, Bette Midler, Barry White, Tony Curtis, Sam Kinison, and Whoopie Goldberg. Best not to inquire how many of those marriages lasted. The Candlelight is one of two free-standing wedding chapels on the Strip. Next stop continuing on your left is:

3. **The Riviera Hotel & Casino,** which has a celebration-themed facade with neon stars and fireworks. The Riviera's casino is open to the street. Get a ticket out front for a free slot pull (bear

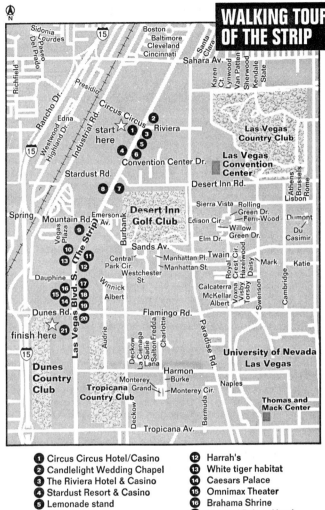

① Circus Circus Hotel/Casino
② Candlelight Wedding Chapel
③ The Riviera Hotel & Casino
④ Stardust Resort & Casino
⑤ Lemonade stand
⑥ Silver City Casino
⑦ Desert Inn
⑧ The Frontier
⑨ Treasure Island
⑩ The Mirage
⑪ Sands Hotel Casino

⑫ Harrah's
⑬ White tiger habitat
⑭ Caesars Palace
⑮ Omnimax Theater
⑯ Brahama Shrine
⑰ Imperial Palace Hotel
⑱ Flamingo Hotel
⑲ Barbary Coast
⑳ Bally's
㉑ The Dunes

left in the casino to find the machine) and you could win as much as $10,000. At worst, you'll get a logo cup as a consolation prize. Further back in the property is a wine-tasting booth (open till 10:30pm daily) operated by Lakeside Cellars, a northern California winery. You can sample five of their wines gratis. Now, suitably refreshed, return to the Strip. Note on your right that in Las Vegas even McDonald's sports a tall neon sign. And further along on the right is a long-time Strip resident (built in 1958), the:

4. **Stardust Resort & Casino,** occupying a dazzlingly lit city block fronted by a fountained plaza. Its 188-foot sign (one of the world's best-known landmarks), and several smaller signs, depict—what else—stardust. The hotel's main tower is bathed in soft blue light, accented by pink and blue neon tubing. The Stardust has always been famous for top-flight entertainment, and currently its showroom features *Enter the Night,* a lavish spectacular that is one of the best in Las Vegas. Try to see it while you're here. Across the street, in front of the **La Concha** sign, there's usually a:

5. **Fresh-squeezed lemonade stand** May to September; the lemonade is delicious, and proceeds go to charity. Adjacent to La Concha is the Old West–themed:

6. **Silver City Casino,** Las Vegas's only nonsmoking casino. I love to gamble here. In addition to supplying fresh air, Silver City is a very friendly place and minimum bets are low ($1 blackjack). Continuing on this side of the Strip, after a pretty street lined with palm trees, souvenir shops and the **Monaco Motel,** you'll come to the tastefully restrained (for Vegas) facade of the:

7. **Desert Inn,** known for its low-key elegance as "the country club hotel." Step into the casino lounge, just off the entrance, for a drink and some really good music, frequently mellow jazz. Some big names play here. You can dance to a tune or two before proceeding on your walk. Across the street is:

8. **The Frontier,** which, at this writing has been fronted by picketing strikers for close to a year. To the right of the Frontier sign is the **Fashion Show Mall.** The mall occupies about two blocks on your right, and across the street are vast parking facilities followed by an empty lot—a boring stretch. But don't worry, there's lots of excitement just ahead. During summer, there's another lemonade stand in front of the **Tam O'Shanter Motel** (on your left) should you feel the need for liquid refreshment. Back on your right is another lot where construction is in progress. It's the site of the upcoming:

9. **Treasure Island,** which like the Mirage will be Y-shaped. Steve Wynn's third Las Vegas property will have a pirate theme and be fronted by a replica of the small bay village described in Stevenson's *Treasure Island.* Once an hour a pirate ship, the *Hispaniola,* and the HMS *The Sir Francis Drake* will engage in a cannon battle, and, the company has disclosed, after much debate, the pirates will emerge victorious! Opening is set for November 22, 1993, so this may be in place as you take your tour. Now stay on your right. Coming up is:

10. **The Mirage.** After you pass its first large sign and its parking area (concealed by lush tropical plantings), you'll hit a long stretch of tiered waterfalls and tropical foliage flanking the imposing arched entranceway. Walk up this main entrance path—a palm-fringed causeway—past sculptures of cavorting dolphins and more waterfalls flowing down jagged rocks into a lagoon below. Stand in front of the hotel facing the Strip. This is the best vantage point to observe the most popular free show in town. Every 15 minutes after dark, heralded by loud rumbling and the twittering chatter of jungle birds, a volcano erupts

spewing fire 50 feet into the air and cascading down the waterfall, which is backlit in red! Now enter the hotel, its entrance fronted by gleaming brass dolphins, and stroll through the verdant tropical rain forest—a 90-foot domed atrium planted with royal palms, orchids, elephant ears, and banana trees amid lofty waterfalls, splashing streams, and serene pools. Also check out the vast 20,000-gallon coral reef aquarium behind the front desk.

REFUELING STOP   The Caribe Café, the Mirage's festive 24-hour coffee shop decorated in bright tropical colors, is a lush jungle setting designed to evoke an open-air Caribbean village. It's a great choice for anything from scrambled eggs to a full steak or prime rib dinner. Of course, you can also choose any of the other restaurants here—or opt for a tropical drink in the Lagoon Saloon, located in the rain forest.

Exit the Mirage by the same pathway you came in. Across the street, a famed Strip landmark, is the circular:

11. **Sand Hotel Casino** where in the 1950s, members of the famed Rat Pack (Frank Sinatra, Sammy Davis, Jr., Joey Bishop, and Dean Martin) appeared regularly on the Copa Room stage. Next to it is another Las Vegas landmark:

12. **Harrah's**, its facade a replica of a Mississippi riverboat complete with 185-foot smokestacks, a rotating red neon paddle wheel, and a foghorn that sounds at frequent intervals. Behind the boat, Harrah's accommodations towers are bathed in soft green light. Sometimes live Dixieland bands play out front. Back on your right is another entrance to the Mirage—a moving sidewalk into the casino. Hop aboard, because at the other end is a:

13. **White tiger habitat,** home to the royal white tigers of famed illusionists Siegfried and Roy. When they're not appearing (and disappearing) on stage, the tigers live in this palatial setting around a huge fountained pool open to the sky. There's a large viewing area for guests. Now leave the fabulous Mirage via the same moving sidewalk and board an adjacent one. This automated walkway (here dubbed a "People Mover") is heralded by a marble temple housing a golden charioteer and four horses. The sculpture is flanked by flaming torchiers and fronted by a waterfall cascading over a bas-relief of the god Neptune. This entranceway, under five coffered triumphal archways, could only lead to:

14. **Caesars Palace.** The walkway itself glides past waterfalls, fountains, and classical statuary. It arrives at a colonnaded portico, where there's usually a gladiator with sword and shield to greet you. You'll enter into the **Forum Shops** arcade (details in Chapter 10) under a simulated sky that actually changes color from fair to cloudy—like a real sky—throughout the day. Directly ahead is the **Festival Fountain** where monumental— seemingly immovable—marble sculptures of mythical Roman gods—Bacchus, Apollo, Venus, and Plutus—come to life via audio animatronic technology. Every hour on the hour (through

11pm Sunday to Thursday, midnight Friday to Saturday), they put on a Disneyesque show complete with laser lighting glittering jewel-like over cascading waters, music, and godly dialogue.

15. Come out the same door you went in by, and take the automated walkway to your left (it parallels a wide entranceway flanked by trumpeting angels atop marble columns), leading to a geodesic dome on which an exterior light show is taking place. Behind the dome, the hotel is bathed in green light. At the end of this walkway, you enter the Olympic Casino, where a large statue of Caesar points the way to the **Omnimax Theatre.** Should you need further assistance, a helmeted Roman centurion is also usually on hand. Thrilling Omnimax shows take place every hour on the hour through 10pm (through 11pm Friday to Saturday). Take a break here and catch the current show. Back on the Strip you'll come to another People Mover leading to the:

16. Brahama Shrine, an authentic replica of one of Thailand's best-known Buddhist shrines. Cast in bronze and plated in gold, it is supposed to ward off bad luck (though one can't hope wondering if Caesar's good luck and ours is linked). This temple was formally dedicated under the supervision of Buddhist monks, with a troupe of 21 Thai dancers and musicians in attendance. The four faces of the shrine represent the "four divine states of mind"—loving kindness, compassion, sympathy, and equanimity. Across the street, note the unique blue neon pagoda which is the:

17. Imperial Palace Hotel. After you're through with Caesars, consider a visit to the **Imperial Palace Auto Collection** of over 750 vehicles spanning a century of automotive history. It's open nightly till 11:30pm (details in Chapter 7). But don't cross over quite yet. Back on the Strip you'll come to yet another tall Caesars sign and the main entrance to the hotel heralded by an imposing row of cypress-lined fountains and a reflection pool worthy of Versailles. Daredevil Evel Knievel attempted to jump the fountains on a motorcycle in 1967. He failed, but his son Robbie performed the jump flawlessly in 1989. Once again board a People Mover—this time to the porte-cochere entranceway lit by pink neon and graced by copies of classical statuary. In front of the entrance stands *The Rape of the Sabines* (Giovanni Bologna, 1853). Standing as a sentinel over the fountains is the winged *Victory at Samothrace* (300 B.C.), the original of which is in the Louvre. Other gleaming white marble replicas of art treasures here include several Venuses and *David* and *Bacchus* by Michelangelo. When you've finished perusing these works, cross the street to see what has become of Bugsy Siegel's dream of "building a real class joint" in the 1940s, the:

18. Flamingo Hilton, today uniquely recognizable by its charming neon frieze of pink and orange flamingos. You have now arrived at the "Four Corners"—the very hub of Strip action. Adjacent to the Flamingo is the:

19. Barbary Coast, designed to look like a turn-of-the-century San Francisco gambling emporium. Stop in to view the casino's

$2 million worth of gorgeous stained-glass skylights, panels, and signage. Another Four Corners hotel is:

20. Bally's, across Dunes/Flamingo roads on your left, which has the most cheerful casino in town. And, finally, across the street, an immense minaret-capped sign and neon palm trees signal another long-time Strip resident,

21. The Dunes (opened in 1955), famous for its challenging golf course.

CHAPTER 9

ABOUT CASINO GAMBLING

1. HOW TO BET
2. THE CASINOS

Most people don't come to Las Vegas just to visit the Liberace Museum. The Las Vegas economy revolves around gambling, and even hotels here basically conceive of themselves as casinos with rooms. Visitors range from cautious types who play nickel slots for an hour and fret about losing a few dollars to flamboyant high rollers risking hundreds—if not thousands—of dollars on a roll of the dice, a good blackjack hand, or a spin of slot machine reels. These diverse gamblers have just one thing in common: secretly they expect to win. It's this elusive dream that keeps people coming back, trying out elaborate systems, reading books on how to beat the odds, betting excitedly when a craps table gets hot, and dropping spare change into slot machines.

Of course, there is no system that really beats the odds. And if there was, the casinos would be on it faster than you can lose a dollar at roulette. The best system is to decide how much you're willing to risk, learn the rules of any game you're playing, and, if you have the fortitude, walk away with moderate winnings. Many good players hold out for a 50% profit. Keep in mind that it's very easy to get carried away trying to recoup losses. I've personally seen tragic instances of average folks losing largish sums, and, desperate to win them back, making larger and larger bets until they've gambled away cars, homes, and savings.

The following part of this chapter tells you the basics of betting. Knowing how to play the games not only improves your odds but makes playing more enjoyable. In addition to the instructions below, you'll find dozens of books on how to gamble at all casino hotel gift shops, and most casinos actually offer free gaming lessons on the premises (see "Facilities" in hotel listings in Chapter 5). The second part of this chapter describes all the major casinos in town.

1. HOW TO BET

CRAPS

The most exciting casino action is always at the craps tables. Betting is frenetic, play fast-paced, and groups quickly bond yelling and screaming in response to the action.

THE TABLE The craps table is divided into marked areas (Pass, Come, Field, Big 6, Big 8, and so on), where you place your chips to bet. The following are a few simple directions.

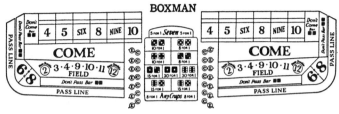

Pass Line   A "Pass Line" bet pays even money. If the first roll of the dice adds up to 7 or 11, you win your bet; if the first roll adds up to 2, 3, or 12, you lose your bet. If any other number comes up, it's your "point." If you roll your point again, you win, but if a 7 comes up again before your point is rolled, you lose.

Don't Pass Line   Betting on the "Don't Pass" is just the opposite of betting on the Pass Line. This time, you lose if a 7 or an 11 is thrown on the first roll, and you win if a 2 or a 3 is thrown on the first roll. If the first roll is 12, however, it's a standoff, and nobody wins. If none of these numbers is thrown and you have a point instead, in order to win, a 7 will have to be thrown before the point comes up again. A "Don't Pass" bet also pays even money.

Come   Betting on "Come" is just the same as betting on the Pass Line, but you must bet *after* the first roll or on any following roll. Again, you'll win on 7 or 11 and lose on 2, 3, or 12. Any other number is your point, and you win if your point comes up again before a 7.

Don't Come   This is the opposite of a "Come" bet. Again, you wait until after the first roll to bet. A 7 or an 11 means you lose; a 2 or a 3 means you win; 12 is a standoff, and nobody wins. You win if 7 comes up before the point. (The point, you'll recall, was the first number rolled if it was none of the above.)

Field   This is a bet for one roll only. The "Field" consists of seven numbers: 2, 3, 4, 9, 10, 11, and 12. If any of these numbers is thrown on the next roll, you win even money, except on 2 and 12, which pay two to one.

Big 6 and 8   A "Big 6 and 8" bet pays even money. You win if either a 6 or an 8 is rolled before a 7.

Any 7   An "Any 7" bet pays the winner five to one. If a 7 is thrown on the first roll after you bet, you win.

"Hard Way" Bets   In the middle of a craps table are pictures of several possible dice combinations together with the odds the bank will pay you if you bet on any of those combinations being thrown. For example, if 8 is thrown by having a 4 appear on each die, and you bet on it, the bank will pay eight for one; if 4 is thrown by having a 2 appear on each die, and you bet on it, the bank will pay eight for one;

if 3 is thrown, the bank pays fifteen for one. . . . You win at the odds quoted if the *exact* combination of numbers you bet on comes up. But you lose either if a 7 is rolled or if the number you bet on was rolled any other way than the "Hard Way" shown on the table. In-the-know gamblers tend to avoid "Hard Way" bets as an easy way to lose their money. And note that the odds quoted are *not* 3 to 1, 4 to 1, or 8 to 1; here the key word is *for*—that is, 3 for 1 or 8 for 1.

Any Craps Here you're lucky if the dice "crap out"—if they show 2, 3, or 12 on the first roll after you bet. If this happens, the bank pays eight to one. Any other number is a loser.

Place Bets You can make a "Place Bet" on any of the following numbers: 4, 5, 6, 8, 9, and 10. You're betting that the number you choose will be thrown before a 7 is thrown. If you win, the payoff is as follows: 4 or 10 pays at the rate of nine to five; 5 or 9 pays at the rate of seven to five; 6 or 8 pays at the rate of seven to six. "Place Bets" can be removed at any time before a roll.

SOME PROBABILITIES Because each die has six sides numbered from 1 to 6—and craps is played with a pair of dice—the probability of throwing certain numbers has been studied carefully. Professionals have employed complex mathematical formulas in searching for the answers. And computers have data-processed curves of probability.

Suffice it to say that 7 (a crucial number in craps) will be thrown more frequently than any other number over the long run, for there are six possible combinations that make 7 when you break down the 1 to 6 possibilities on each separate die. As to the total possible number of combinations on the dice, there are 36.

Comparing the 36 possible combinations, numbers—or point combinations—run as follows:

2 and 12 may be thrown in *1 way only.*
3 and 11 may be thrown in *2 ways.*
4 and 10 may be thrown in *3 ways.*
5 and 9 may be thrown in *4 ways.*
6 and 8 may be thrown in *5 ways.*
7 may be thrown in *6 ways.*

So 7 has an advantage over all other combinations, which, over the long run, is in favor of the casino. You can't beat the law of averages. Players, however, often have winning streaks—a proven fact in ESP studies—and that's when the experts advise that it's wise to increase the size of bets. But when a losing streak sets in, stop playing!

KENO

This is one of the oldest games of chance. It's origin is Chinese, and it dates back to a time before Christ, when it operated as a national lottery. Legend has it that funds acquired from the game were used to finance construction of the Great Wall of China.

Keno was first introduced into the United States in the 1800s by Chinese railroad construction workers. Easy to play, and offering a chance to sit down and converse between bets, it is one of the most popular games in town—despite the fact that *the house percentage is greater than any other casino game!*

To play, you must first obtain a keno form, available at the counter in the keno lounge and in most Las Vegas coffee shops. In the latter, you'll usually find blank keno forms and thick black crayons on your table. Fill yours out, and a miniskirted keno runner will come and collect it. After the game is over, she'll return with your winning or losing ticket. If you've won, it's customary to tip something, the amount depending on your winnings.

Looking at your keno ticket, and the keno board, you'll see that it is divided horizontally into two rectangles. The upper half (in China the yin area) contains the numbers 1 through 40, the lower (yang) half contains the numbers 41 through 80. You can win a maximum of $25,000, though that's highly unlikely (the probability is less than a

			PRICE PER WAY		PRICE PER GAME
$50,000.00 LIMIT TO AGGREGATE PLAYERS EACH GAME					
MARK NUMBER OF SPOTS OR WAYS PLAYED			NO. OF GAMES		TOTAL PRICE

WINNING TICKETS MUST BE COLLECTED IMMEDIATELY AFTER EACH KENO GAME IS CALLED.

1	2	3	4	5	6	7	8	9	10
11	12	13	14	15	16	17	18	19	20
21	22	23	24	25	26	27	28	29	30
31	32	33	34	35	36	37	38	39	40

WE PAY ON MACHINE ISSUED TICKETS – TICKETS WITH ERRORS NOT CORRECTED BEFORE START OF GAME WILL BE ACCEPTED AS ISSUED.

41	42	43	44	45	46	47	48	49	50
51	52	53	54	55	56	57	58	59	60
61	62	63	64	65	66	67	68	69	70
71	72	73	74	75	76	77	78	79	80

WE ARE NOT RESPONSIBLE FOR KENO RUNNERS TICKETS NOT VALIDATED BEFORE START OF NEXT GAME.

hundredth of a percent). Mark up to 15 out of the 80 numbers; bets range from about 70¢ on up. A one-number mark is known as a one-spot, a two-number selection is a two-spot, and so on. After you have selected the number of spots you wish to play, write the price of the ticket in the right hand corner where indicated. The more you bet, the more you can win if your numbers come up. Before the game starts, you have to give the completed form to a keno runner—or hand it in at the keno lounge desk—and pay for your bet. You'll get back a duplicate form with the number of the game you're playing on it. Then the game begins. As numbers appear on the keno board, compare them to the numbers you've marked on your ticket. After 20 numbers have appeared on the board, if you've won, turn in your ticket immediately for a payoff—before the next game begins. Otherwise, you will forfeit your winnings, a very frustrating experience to say the least.

On a straight ticket that is marked with one or two spots, all of your numbers must appear on the board for you to win anything. If you mark from three to seven spots, three numbers must appear on the board for you to win anything. If you mark eight to 12 spots, at least five numbers must come up for you to win the minimum amount. And if you mark 13 to 15 spots at least six numbers must come up for a winning ticket. To win the maximum amount ($25,000), which requires that all of your numbers come up, you must select at least eight spots. The more numbers on the board matching the numbers on your ticket, the more you win. If you want to keep playing the same numbers over and over, you can replay a ticket by handing in your duplicate to the keno runner; you don't have to keep rewriting it.

In addition to the straight bets described above, you can split your ticket, betting various amounts on two or more groups of numbers. To do so, circle the groups. The amount you bet is then divided by the number of groups. You could, if you so desired, play as many as 40 two-spots on a single ticket. Another possibility is to play three groups of four numbers each as eight spots (any two of the three groups of four numbers can be considered an eight spot). It does all get a little complex, and combination betting options are almost infinite. Helpful casino personnel in the keno lounge can help you with combination betting.

BLACKJACK

The dealer starts the game by dealing each player two cards. In some casinos they're dealt to the player faceup, or one down and one up, or both down, but the dealer always gets one card up and one card down. Everybody plays against the dealer. The object is to get a total of 21 or as close to it as possible. All face cards count as 10; all other number cards except aces count as their number value. An ace may be counted as 1 or 11, whichever you choose it to be.

Starting at his or her left, the dealer gives additional cards to the players who wish to draw (be "hit") or none to a player who wishes to "stand" or "hold." If your count is nearer to 21 than the dealer's, you win. If it's under the dealer's, you lose. Ties are a standoff and nobody wins. After all the players are satisfied with their counts, the dealer exposes his or her facedown card. If his two cards total 16 or less, the dealer must "hit" (draw an additional card) until reaching 17 or over. If the dealer's total goes over 21, he or she must pay all the players whose hands have not gone "bust." It is important to note here that the blackjack dealer has no choice as to whether he or she should stay or draw. A dealer's decisions are predetermined and known to all the players at the table.

HOW TO PLAY   Here are eight "rules" for blackjack.

1. Place the amount of money that you want to bet on the table.
2. Look at the first two cards the dealer starts you with. If your hand adds up to the total you prefer, place your cards *under your bet money,* indicating that you don't wish any additional cards. If you elect to draw an additional card, you tell the dealer to "hit" you by making a sweeping motion with your cards, or point to your open hand (watch your fellow players).
3. If your count goes over 21, you go "bust" and lose—even if the dealer also goes "bust" afterward. Unless hands are dealt faceup, *you then turn your hand faceup on the table.*
4. If you make 21 in your first two cards (any picture card or 10 with an ace), you've got blackjack. *You expose your winning hand immediately,* and you collect 1½ times your bet—unless the dealer has blackjack, too, in which case it's a standoff and nobody wins.
5. If you find a "pair" in your first two cards (say, two 4s or two 10s) you may "split" the pair into two hands and treat each card as the first card dealt in two separate hands. *Turn the pair face up on the table,* place the original bet on one of these cards, then place an equal amount on the other card. *Split aces are limited to a one-card draw on each.*
6. If your first two cards total 11 or under, you may, if you choose, double your original bet and make a one-card draw. *Turn your hand faceup* and you'll receive one more card facedown.
7. Anytime the dealer deals himself or herself an ace for the "up" card, you may insure your hand against the possibility that the hole card is a face card, which would give him or her an automatic blackjack. To insure, you place an amount equal to one-half of your bet on the "Insurance" line. If the dealer does have a blackjack, you do not lose, even though he or she has your hand beat, and you keep your bet and your insurance money. If the dealer does not have a blackjack, he or she takes your insurance money and play continues in the normal fashion.
8. *Remember!* The dealer *must* stand on 17 or more and *must* hit a hand of 16 or less.

PROFESSIONAL TIPS   Advice of the experts in playing black-jack is as follows.

1. *Do not* ask for an extra card if you have a count of 17, 18, 19, 20, or 21 in your cards, no matter what the dealer has showing in his or her "up" card.
2. *Do not* ask for an extra card when you have 13, 14, 15, 16, or

more . . . *if* the dealer has a 2, 3, 4, 5, or 6 showing in his or her "up" card.

3. *Do* ask for an extra card or more when you have a count of 13 through 16 in your hand . . . if the dealer's "up" card is a 7, 8, 9, 10, or ace.

There's a lot more to blackjack-playing strategy than the above, of course. So consider this merely as the bare bones of the game.

A Final Tip   Avoid insurance bets; they're sucker bait!

POKER

Poker is *the* game of the Old West. There's at least one sequence in every western where the hero faces off against the villain over a poker hand. In Las Vegas poker is a tradition, although it isn't played at every casino.

There are lots of variations on the basic game, but one of the most popular is Hold 'Em. Five cards are dealt faceup in the center of the table and two are dealt to each player. The player takes the best five of seven, and the best hand wins. The house dealer takes care of the shuffling and the dealing and moves a marker around the table to alternate the start of the deal. The house usually has a 5% "take" from each pot. Most casinos include the usual seven-card stud and a few have five-card draw and hi-lo split.

If you don't know how to play poker, don't attempt to learn at a table. Find a casino that teaches it in free gaming lessons.

Pai-gow poker is a variation on poker that has become increasingly popular. The game is played with a traditional deck plus one joker. The joker can be used only as an ace to complete a straight, a flush, or a straight flush. Each player is dealt seven cards to arrange into two hands—a two-card hand and a five-card hand. Rankings are based on basic poker ratings; therefore the highest two-card hand would be two aces, and the highest five-card hand would be a Royal Flush. The five-card hand *must* be higher than the two-card hand (if the two-card hand is a pair of sixes, for example, the five-card hand must include a pair of sevens or better). Any player's hand that is set incorrectly is an automatic lose. The object of the game is for both of the player's hands to rank higher than both of the banker's hands. Should one hand rank exactly the same as the banker's hand, this is a tie, *and the banker wins all tie hands.* If the player wins one hand but loses the other, this is a "push," and no money changes hands. The house dealer or any player may be the banker. The bank is offered to each player, and each player may accept or pass. Winning hands are paid even money, less a 5% commission.

ROULETTE

Roulette is an extremely easy game to play, and it's really very colorful and exciting to watch. The wheel spins, and the little ball bounces around, finally dropping into one of the slots, numbered 1 to 36, plus 0 and 00. You can bet on a single number, a combination of numbers, or red or black, odd or even. If you're lucky, you can win as much as 35 to 1 (see the table). The method of placing

Roulette Chart Key	Odds	Type of Bet
		Straight Bets
A	35 to 1	*Straight-up:* All numbers, plus 0 and 00.
B	2 to 1	*Column Bet:* Pays off on any number in that horizontal column.
C	2 to 1	*First Dozen:* Pays off on any number 1 through 12. Same for second and third dozen.
D	Even money	
		Combination Bets
E	17 to 1	*Split:* Pays off on 11 or 12.
F	11 to 1	Pays off on 28, 29, or 30.
G	8 to 1	*Corner:* Pays off on 17, 18, 20, or 21.
H	6 to 1	Pays off on 0, 00, 1, 2, or 3.
I	5 to 1	Pays off on 22, 23, 24, 25, 26, or 27.

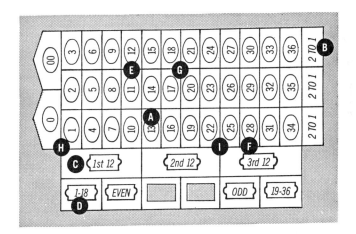

single-number bets, column bets, and others is fairly obvious. The dealer will be happy to show you how to "straddle" two or more numbers and make many other interesting betting combinations. Each player is given different-colored chips so that it's easy to follow the numbers you're on.

A number of typical bets are indicated by means of letters on the adjoining roulette layout. The winning odds for each of these sample bets are listed here. These bets can be made on any corresponding combinations of numbers.

BACCARAT

The ancient game of baccarat—or chemin de fer—is played with eight decks of cards. Firm rules apply, and there is no skill involved other than deciding whether to bet on the bank or the player. Any beginner can play, but check the betting minimum before you sit down. The cards are shuffled by the croupier and then placed in a box that is called the "Shoe."

Players may act as banker or play against the bank at any time. Two cards are dealt from the Shoe and given to the player who has the largest wager against the bank, and two cards are dealt to the croupier acting as banker. If the rule calls for a third card (see rules on chart opposite), the player or banker, or both, must take the third card. In the event of a tie, the hand is dealt over.

The object of the game is to come as close as possible to the number 9. To score the hands, the cards of each hand are totaled and the *last digit* is used. All cards have face value. For example: 10 plus 5 equal 15 (score is 5); 10 plus 4 plus 9 equal 23 (score is 3); 4 plus 3 plus 3 equal 10 (score is 0); and 4 plus 3 plus 2 equal 9 (score is 9). The closest hand to 9 wins.

Each player gets a chance to deal the cards. The Shoe passes to the player on the right each time the bank loses. If the player wishes, he or she may pass the Shoe at any time.

Note: When you bet on the bank and the bank wins, you are charged a 5% commission. This must be paid at the start of a new game or when you leave the table.

BIG SIX

Big Six provides pleasant recreation and involves no study or effort. The wheel has 56 positions on it, 54 of them marked by bills from $1 to $20 denomination. The other two spots are jokers, and each pays 40 to 1 if the wheel stops in that position.

All other stops pay at face value. Those marked with $20 bills pay 20 to 1; the $5 bills pay 5 to 1; and so forth.

SPORTS BOOKS

Most of the larger hotels in Las Vegas have sports book operations— looking much like commodities-futures trading boards. In some, almost as large as theaters, you can comfortably sit and watch ball games, fights, and, at some casinos, horse races on huge TV screens. To add to your enjoyment, there's usually a deli/bar nearby that serves sandwiches, hot dogs, soft drinks, and beer. As a matter of fact, some of the best sandwiches in Las Vegas are served next to the sports books.

Sports books take bets on virtually every sport.

BACCARAT RULES

Player's Hand

Having

0-1-2-3-4-5   Must draw a third card

6-7   *Must stand.*

8-9   Natural. Banker cannot draw.

Banker's Hand

Having	**Draws** When giving Player 3rd card of:	**Does Not Draw** When giving Player 3rd card of:
3	1-2-3-4-5-6-7-9-10	8
4	2-3-4-5-6-7	1-8-9-10
5	4-5-6-7	1-2-3-8-9-10
6	6-7	1-2-3-4-5-8-9-10
7	*Must stand.*	
8-9	Natural. Player cannot draw.	

If the player takes no third card, the banker must stand on 6. No one draws against a natural 8 or 9.

2. THE CASINOS

Each casino has its own personality and special features. A rundown describing each, including exact gaming facilities, follows:

ON OR NEAR THE STRIP

BALLY'S   Bally's festival-themed casino is the most cheerful on the Strip—a large (it's the size of a football field), brightly lit facility with lots of colorful signage, confetti-motif carpeting, and bunches of helium balloons tied to the gaming tables. There's a Most Valuable Player (MVP) club for slot players; members are eligible for room discounts, free meals and show tickets, and invitations to special events, among other perks. A unique feature here is the Festival of Games fun pit, offering a more casual setting with friendlier dealers, special games (like Caribbean stud poker), and lower minimum bets. There are slot tournaments several times a month. Facilities include a keno lounge, a state-of-the-art race and sports book, 50 blackjack tables, 10 craps, 7 roulette, 2 baccarat, 2 minibaccarat, 1 Caribbean stud poker, 1 pai gow, 2 pai-gow poker, 1 big six wheel, and 1,401 slot/video poker machines.

BARBARY COAST   The Barbary Coast has a cheerful 1890s-style casino ornately decorated with $2 million worth of gorgeous stained-glass skylights and signage and immense crystal-dangling globe chandeliers over the gaming tables. It's worth stopping in just to take a look around when you're in the central "four corners" area of the Strip. Nick the Greek gambles here frequently. The casino has a Fun Club for slot players. Participants earn points towards catalog prizes and free hotel rooms and meals. Gaming facilities include a race and sports book, keno, 32 blackjack tables, 4 craps, 2 roulette, 2 minibaccarat, 4 pai-gow, and 700 slot/video poker machines.

CAESARS PALACE   Caesars has two interconnecting deluxe gaming rooms—the high-end **Forum Casino** (with the action under crystal-fringed black domes) and the slightly more casual **Olympic Casino.** A notable facility in the latter is the state-of-the-art Olympiad Race and Sports Book, with huge electronic display boards and giant video screens. The Olympiad pioneered computer-generated wagering data that can be communicated in less than half a second and sophisticated satellite equipment that can pick up virtually any broadcast sporting event in the world. The domed VIP slot section of the Forum Casino (minimum bet is $5, but you can wager up to $1,500 on a single pull!) is a plush, crystal-chandeliered precinct with seating in roomy adjustable chairs; a butler comes by with drinks and hors d'oeuvres. All slot players can accumulate bonus points toward gifts and gratis show tickets, meals, and rooms by joining the Emperors Club. Club membership also lets you in on grand prize drawings, tournaments, and parties. Most upscale of the Caesars gaming room is the intimate European-style casino adjoining the **Palace Court** restaurant. Total facilities in all three casinos comprise 12 craps tables, 64 blackjack, 10 roulette, 6 baccarat, 2 minibaccarat, 3 pai gow, 2 pai-gow poker, 2 big six wheels, over 2,000 slot/video poker machines, and a keno lounge.

CIRCUS CIRCUS   This vast property (it's so large there's a Disney World–style monorail out back to connect buildings) has three full-size casinos that combined comprise one of the largest gaming operations in Nevada (over 100,000 square feet). The main casino is the one entered via the front door off the Strip. In the more laid-back West Casino, all gaming tables are nonsmoking. And there are additional gaming facilities in the Skyrise building. Circus Circus fun books offer coupons for free win-a-car slot pulls. And Circus Bucks progressive slot machines here build from a jackpot base of $500,000, which players can win on a $2 pull. Gaming facilities include a 10,000-square-foot race and sports book with 30 video monitors ranging from 13 to 52 inches, 40-seat and 160-seat keno lounges, 16 poker tables, 88 blackjack, 7 craps, 6 roulette, 2 big six wheels, and 2,650 slot/video poker machines.

THE DESERT INN   This is one of my favorite Las Vegas casinos—a low-key setting typical of the hotel's country club elegance. Large circular brass chandeliers replace the usual neon glitz, and tables are comfortably spaced. The ambience is reminiscent of intimate European gaming houses. There are fewer slot machines

IMPRESSIONS

Stilled forever is the click of the roulette wheel, the rattle of dice, and the swish of cards.
—SHORT-SIGHTED EDITORIAL IN THE *NEVADA STATE JOURNAL*
AFTER GAMBLING WAS OUTLAWED IN 1910

here than at most major casinos, so there's less noise of ringing bells and clinking coins. Most table games have $5 minimums. Facilities include a race and sports book, a poker room, 30 blackjack tables, 6 craps, 1 pai gow, 2 pai-gow poker, 1 minibaccarat, 2 baccarat, 3 roulette wheels, a big six wheel, and 371 slot/video poker machines. A sophisticated casino lounge featuring name artists like Nell Carter and Don Cherry is a plus.

EXCALIBUR   As you might expect, the Excalibur casino is replete with suits of armor, stained-glass panels, knights, dragons, and velvet and satin heraldic banners, with gaming action under vast iron and gold chandeliers fit for a medieval castle fortress. King's Pavilion, an exclusive slot area under an imperial purple and red canopy, is a plush precinct for players who spend $5 to $25 on a single pull (one customer recently hit five jackpots here in four days and went home with $85,000!). And like its sister hotel, Circus Circus, Excalibur offers Circus Bucks—a progressive slot machine that builds from a jackpot base of $500,000 that players can win on a $2 pull. Excalibur's 100,000-plus square feet of gaming facilities also include a race and sports book, a keno lounge, a poker room with 18 tables, 78 blackjack tables, 7 craps, 6 roulette, 2 pai-gow poker, 2 big six wheels, and 2,630 slot/video poker machines.

FLAMINGO HILTON   The Flamingo's cheerful, Caribbean-themed casino is lit by rainbow-hued neon lights. There are $2 slots here offering around-the-world trips as jackpots. And slot players qualify for free meals, shows, and other play-based incentives when they join the Slot Magic program. Gaming facilities include a keno lounge, race and sports book, poker room, 39 blackjack tables, 9 craps, 6 roulette, 2 minibaccarat, 1 pai-gow poker, 1 sic bo, 1 big six wheel, and 1,601 slot/video poker machines.

HACIENDA RESORT   Styled after a Mexican hacienda, this lovely 35,000-square-foot casino has white stucco walls adorned with colorful paintings of flowers, fruit, and tropical birds. Slot players can join Club Viva! to earn points towards free stays, meals, show tickets, gifts, and tournament invitations. The Hacienda hosts many special

IMPRESSIONS

If you aim to leave Las Vegas with a small fortune, go there with a large one.
—ANONYMOUS AMERICAN SAYING

events and blackjack and slot tournaments, and all entry fees go to prize money. Gaming facilities: keno lounge, race and sports book, 19 blackjack tables, 2 craps, 2 roulette, 5 poker, 2 pai-gow poker, 1 red dog, 1 big six wheel, and 1,050 slot/video poker machines.

HARRAH'S Mirroring its exterior, Harrah's casino is Mississippi riverboat–themed, with flocked red wallpaper, turn-of-the-century-style crystal chandeliers, and dealers attired as riverboat gamblers. New Orleans bands stroll through the casino at intervals playing Dixieland music. At 79,000 square feet, Harrah's is one of the larger facilities in town. It is the scene of numerous year-round slot, keno, and blackjack tournaments offering big prizes; it was the first Las Vegas casino to introduce computerized bingo; and it is the only casino offering computerized video bingo and "no intermission" bingo. Slot and table game players can earn bonus points towards complimentary rooms, meals, show tickets, and more, by acquiring a Harrah's Gold Card in the casino. Facilities include an 8,000-square-foot race and sports book, a keno lounge, a poker room, 51 blackjack tables, 7 craps, 7 roulette, 3 minibaccarat, 4 pai-gow poker, 3 red dog, 1 big six wheel, and 1,907 slot/video poker machines.

IMPERIAL PALACE The 70,000-square-foot casino here reflects the hotel's pagoda-roofed Asian exterior with a dragon-motif ceiling and giant wind-chime chandeliers. Visitors can get free Scratch Slotto cards for prizes up to $5,000 in cash (cards and free passes to the auto collection are distributed on the sidewalk out front). And many slot machines offer prizes like cars (a Mercedes for a $1 pull, a Mazda Miata for 25¢) or vacation cruises. The I.P. boasts a 230-seat race and sports book, attractively decorated with oil murals of sporting events. The room is tiered like a grandstand, and every seat has its own color monitor. Other gaming facilities include a keno lounge, 35 blackjack tables, 5 craps, 3 roulette, 1 minibaccarat, 2 pai-gow poker, 1 Caribbean stud, 1 big six wheel, and 2,000 slot/video poker machines.

LAS VEGAS HILTON Massive Austrian crystal chandeliers, hand-cut leaded glass, and imposing Italian marble columns combine to make the Hilton casino one of the city's most elegant. Especially plush are the baccarat room—under a gorgeous crystal chandelier, its walls adorned with beautiful period paintings—and the VIP slot area—a mirrored gazebo where personnel are attired in tuxedos. Both areas offer gracious service to players. The Hilton's SuperBook is, at 30,500 square feet, the world's largest race and sports book facility. Centered on a life-size bronze statue of the legendary thoroughbred, Man o' War, it, too, is a luxurious precinct equipped with the most advanced audio, video, and computer technology available, including 53 TV monitors, some as large as 15 feet across. And a comfortable poker room offers many varieties of the game, including seven-card stud, hold 'em, and Omaha. The Hilton's "Around the World" slots offer a vacation prize worth $15,000 on a $2 pull. By joining the SuperSlot Club, you can amass bonus points towards cash prizes, gifts, and complimentary rooms, meals, and show tickets. And every Saturday night the Hilton features slot tournaments that, for a $15 entry fee, provide an opportunity to win a share of over $1,200 in cash and prizes. In addition to the above, gaming facilities include a keno lounge, 43 blackjack tables, 8 craps, 4 roulette, 4 baccarat, 2 pai-gow, 2 pai-gow poker, 1 big six wheel, and 1,285 slot/video poker machines.

MAXIM This friendly, but very dimly lit, casino, presents plaques to big slot winners. It also has slot machines featuring a real Wurlitzer jukebox and a Harley-Davidson motorcycle as jackpots. Even if you don't win, you can have a free souvenir snapshot of yourself taken on the bike. Gaming facilities include a keno lounge, sports book, 24 blackjack tables (one is multiple action), 3 craps, 2 roulette, 3 poker, 1 pai gow, and 730 slot/video poker machines.

THE MIRAGE Entered via a tropical rain forest, this 95,400-square-foot casino is designed to resemble a Polynesian village with gaming areas under separate roofs to create a more intimate ambience. Facilities include a separate poker room and a plush European-style salon privé for high rollers at baccarat, blackjack, and roulette; an elegant dining room serves catered meals here. Slot players can join the Club Mirage and work towards bonus points for cash rebates, special room rates, complimentary meals and/or show tickets, and other benefits. The elaborate race and sports book offers theater stereo sound and a movie theater-size screen. Other gaming facilities here: a keno lounge, 76 blackjack tables, 12 craps, 12 roulette, 8 baccarat, 2 minibaccarat, 2 pai gow, 4 pai-gow poker, 1 red dog, 2 big six wheels, and over 2,200 slot/video poker machines.

THE RIO This Brazilian carnival–themed resort has an exotic tropical casino with shell-motif carpeting and gaming tables amid a veritable forest of plastic palm trees. Rio Rita—a Carmen Miranda look-alike in a towering fruit-covered hat—presides over the casino from a thatched hut. She greets visitors, congratulates winners, announces contests and promotions, and runs frequent slot, craps, and blackjack tournaments. Daily tournaments take place within the lush foliage and live palms of Jackpot Jungle, its slot and video poker machines equipped with TV monitors that air old movies and in-house information while you play. Rio gaming facilities include a keno lounge, race and sports book, 22 blackjack tables, 4 craps, 2 roulette, 1 baccarat, 1 pai gow, 1 Caribbean stud, and 1,100 slot/video poker machines.

THE RIVIERA The Riviera's 125,000-square-foot casino—one of the largest in the world—is also one of the most attractive on the Strip. A wall of windows lets daylight stream in (most unusual), and gaming tables are under gleaming brass arches lit by recessed pink neon tubing. The casino's Star Club allows slot players to earn bonus

---

IMPRESSIONS

The most exciting thing in craps is to win.
The next most exciting thing is to lose.
—NICK THE GREEK

points towards free meals, rooms, and show tickets. And a "Gambler's Spree" program offers round-trip airfare, deluxe accommodations, all shows, and more to customers who gamble eight hours (at minimum $5 tables or $1 slot machines) over a two-night/three-day stay, 10 hours over a 3-night/4-day stay, or 12 hours over a 4-night/5-day stay. The race and sports book here offers individual monitors at each of its 250 seats, and this may be the only place in town you can play the ancient Chinese game of sic bo (a fast-paced dice game akin to craps). Additional facilities include a large keno parlor, 42 blackjack tables, 5 craps, 3 roulette, 2 baccarat, 3 pai-gow poker, 3 big six wheels, and over 1,200 slot/video poker machines.

THE SAHARA The Sahara has a large, simpatico casino overseen—in keeping with the hotel's desert theme—by statues of turbaned soldiers with scimitars at the ready. Not to worry, though; the dealers are friendly. There's even a host in the keno lounge to welcome guests and explain possible betting combinations. The casino offers a free slot pull, with a chance to win $1,000 and a booby prize if you don't. And weekdays at noon and 2, 4, and 6pm, there's a drawing for a "Shower in Cash"—60 seconds in a glass booth filled with thousands of dollars flying around in a whirlwind (whatever you can capture is yours). The Sahara also hosts frequent slot tournaments and other gaming events. Facilities include a race and sports book, keno lounge, 31 blackjack tables, 4 craps, 3 roulette, 2 baccarat, 7 poker, 1 red-dog poker, 2 pai-gow poker, a big six wheel, 1,004 slot/video poker machines, and 8 pan tables. *Note:* This is the only Strip casino to offer pan, a card game.

THE SANDS This 30,000-square-foot casino features a "Never Ending Slot Tournament"—a daily contest played every 10 minutes, with the top scorer winning either $500 or the chance to play every slot machine in the house free! The Sands also has a Patriot Poker machine that pays jackpots up to $50,000 and a nickel slot area called Red Hot Nickel Nook. The Easy Money Slot Club gives players bonus points toward prizes. Gaming facilities include a keno lounge, race and sports book, 30 blackjack tables, 5 craps, 3 roulette, 1 baccarat, 1 minibaccarat, 2 pai gow, 3 pai-gow poker, 1 big six wheel, and 800 slot/video poker machines.

THE STARDUST The Stardust features 90,000 square feet of lively gaming action, including a 250-seat race and sports book with a sophisticated satellite system and over 50 TV monitors airing sporting events and horse racing results around the clock. Adjacent to it is a sports handicapper's library featuring comprehensive statistical information concerning current sporting events. Stardust Slot Club members win cash rebates, with credit piling up even on 25¢ machines. Free rooms, shows, meals, and invitations to special events, are other possible bonuses. Other gaming facilities: a large, well-lit keno lounge, a poker room with 12 tables, an elegant baccarat lounge with 2 tables, 48 blackjack tables, 6 craps, 5 roulette, 1 minibaccarat, 4 pai-gow poker, 1 big six wheel, and 1,837 slot/video poker machines.

THE TROPICANA The Trop casino is simply gorgeous, with gaming tables under a massive stained-glass archway, art nouveau lighting fixtures, and acres of tropical foliage. It has something totally unique—a year-round swim-up blackjack bar located in the hotel's stunning 5-acre water-park swimming pool. There are also outdoor slot/video poker machines poolside under the palms. Slot and table game players can earn bonus points toward rooms, food, even cash, by obtaining a Winners Club card in the casino. A luxurious high-end slot area has machines that take up to $100 on a single pull. Numerous tournaments take place here. Gaming facilities include a sports book, a keno lounge, poker room, 32 blackjack tables, 6 craps, 4 roulette, 3 baccarat, 1 pai gow, 1 red dog, 1 big six wheel, and 1,248 slot/video poker machines.

WESTWARD HO HOTEL & CASINO This small but very centrally located strip casino hosts many slot tournaments, and slot players who obtain Preferred Customer cards can amass credits towards complimentary rooms, meals, and shows, among other benefits. Gaming facilities include 14 blackjack tables, 1 craps, 1 roulette, 1 big six wheel, and 1,000 slot/video poker machines.

DOWNTOWN

CALIFORNIA HOTEL/CASINO The California caters to a largely Hawaiian clientele, hence dealers in its attractive marble and crystal-chandeliered casino wear colorful aloha shirts. This friendly facility actually furnishes sofas and armchairs in the casino area—an unheard-of luxury in this town. Players can join the Cal Slot Club and amass points toward gifts and cash prizes or participate in daily slot tournaments. Gaming facilities include a keno lounge, sports book, 24 blackjack tables, 6 craps, 2 roulette, 1 minibaccarat, and 1,000 slot/video poker machines.

FOUR QUEENS The Four Queens' casino was recently remodeled, and it's looking very cheerful with all new light-beige slot machines and gaming tables under turn-of-the-century-style globe chandeliers. The facility boasts the world's largest slot machine (over 9 feet high and almost 20 feet long); six people can play it at one time! There's a special club for players 55 and over (Club 55), which provides discounts at the hotel's bars and restaurants and invitations to special slot tournaments, dances, parties, and other events. Its members are automatically enrolled in the Reel Winners Club, a slot club offering players bonus points toward perks and prizes. You can play $1 blackjack and 25¢ craps here. The casino also offers exciting multiple-action blackjack (it's like playing three hands at once with

---

IMPRESSIONS

I am, after all, the best hold 'em player alive. I'm forced to play this tournament, you understand, to demonstrate this fact.
—CASINO OWNER BOB STUPAK ON WHY HE ENTERED BINION'S HORSESHOE WORLD SERIES OF POKER

separate wagers on each). And there are frequent poker, slot, and blackjack tournaments. Gaming facilities include a keno lounge, race and sports book, 28 blackjack tables, 5 craps, 2 roulette, 1 minibaccarat, 6 poker, 2 pai-gow poker, and 1,400 slot/video poker machines.

EL CORTEZ This friendly downtown casino features frequent big-prize drawings (up to $50,000) based on your social security number. It's also popular for low limits (10¢ roulette and 25¢ craps). Gaming facilities include a race and sports book, keno, 15 blackjack tables, 4 craps, 2 roulette, 1 minibaccarat, and 1,500 slot/video poker machines.

GOLDEN NUGGET This luxurious resort has a gorgeous casino reminiscent of the opulent gaming houses of Europe. Tables are under stained-glass panels, and neon glitz is replaced by tivoli lighting. Slot players can earn bonus points towards complimentary rooms, meals, shows, and gifts by joining the 24 Karat Club. Gaming facilities include an attractive and comfortable keno lounge, a race and sports book, 47 blackjack tables ($1 minimum bet), 7 craps, 3 roulette, 3 baccarat, 1 pai gow, 3 pai-gow poker, 1 red dog, 1 big six wheel, and 1,136 slot/video poker machines.

JACKIE GAUGHAN'S PLAZA HOTEL/CASINO The Plaza has a lively and attractive crystal-chandeliered casino whose gaming facilities include a keno lounge, race and sports book, 26 blackjack tables, 4 craps, 4 roulette, 1 baccarat, 10 poker, 2 pai gow, 1 red dog, 16 pan, 1 big six wheel, and 1,520 slot/video poker machines.

LADY LUCK I like to gamble at the Lady Luck casino, a friendly downtown facility where daylight streams in through windowed walls and central areas are designated nonsmoking. The Mad Money Slot Club offers scrip, cash, meals, accommodations, and prizes as incentives. There's also a Most Valuable Player (MVP) Club for table game players. Liberal game rules are a lure to gamblers. Sunday through Wednesday guests can enter "Fun 21" tournaments for $25, and many slot tournaments take place each day (maximum prize $500). You can play "fast action hold 'em" here—a combination of 21, poker, and pai-gow poker. Other gaming facilities include a keno lounge, 20 blackjack tables, 3 craps, 2 roulette, 1 minibaccarat, 1 pai-gow poker, and 800 slot/video poker machines.

SAM BOYD'S FREMONT HOTEL & CASINO This spacious 36,000-square-foot casino offers a relaxed atmosphere and low gambling limits ($1 blackjack, 25¢ roulette). Casino guests can play multiple-action blackjack here, accumulate bonus points redeemable toward cash by joining the Five Star Slot Club, and take part in frequent slot and video poker tournaments. Gaming facilities include two keno lounges, a 120-seat race and sports book, a comfortable poker room (nine tables offering seven-card stud, Texas hold-'em, and Omaha hi-lo split; free poker lessons are offered every morning from 6 to 9am), 23 blackjack tables, 4 craps, 3 roulette, 1 minibaccarat, 1 pai-gow poker, and 1,000 slot/video poker machines.

THE CASINOS • 181

SHOWBOAT   Though it's slightly out of the way, you won't find a more delightful casino than this one. In keeping with the hotel's theme, it evokes the Mississippi riverboat era. Peach and lavender walls are adorned with beautiful oil paintings of gracious Southern plantations, and planters of flowers abound. Especially gorgeous flower murals, and trellised arches laced with flowery vines, embellish the Showboat's vast 24-hour bingo parlor—a facility also noted for high payouts. Slot players can join the Officers Club and accumulate bonus points towards free meals, rooms, gifts, and cash prizes. The casino hosts twice weekly blackjack tournaments, twice monthly craps tournaments, and monthly video poker tournaments. And if you're traveling with kids ages 2 to 7, you can leave them at an in-house babysitting facility free for three hours while you gamble. Older kids might be dropped at the Showboat's 106-lane bowling center. In addition to bingo, gaming facilities include a keno lounge, race and sports book, 20 blackjack tables, 2 craps, 2 roulette, 1 pai gow, and 2,012 slot/video poker machines.

CHAPTER 10

LAS VEGAS SHOPPING

1. THE MALLS
2. HOTEL SHOPPING ARCADES

Unless you're looking for souvenir decks of cards and miniature slot machines, Las Vegas is not exactly a shopping mecca. It does, however, have several noteworthy malls that amply supply the basics. And many hotels also offer comprehensive shopping arcades.

---

1. THE MALLS

BOULEVARD MALL, 3528 S. Maryland Pkwy., between Twain Ave. and Desert Inn Rd. Tel. 735-8268.

The Boulevard's 140 stores and restaurants are arranged in arcade fashion on a single floor occupying 1,131,000 square feet. In terms of size, it's the largest in Nevada, and, when it opened in 1968, it was the first, fully enclosed air-conditioned mall in the state. It's geared to the average consumer, not the carriage trade, with anchors like Sears, J.C. Penney, Woolworth, Broadway Southwest, Dillard's, and Marshalls. There's a wide variety of shops offering moderately priced shoes and clothing for the entire family, books and gifts, jewelry, and home furnishings, plus over a dozen fast food eateries. In short, you can find just about anything you need here. A triplex movie theater is on the premises. Valet parking is complimentary.

Open: Mon–Fri 10am–9pm, Sat 10am–6pm, Sun noon–5pm.

FASHION SHOW MALL, 3200 Las Vegas Blvd. S., at the corner of Spring Mountain Rd., near the Frontier Hotel. Tel. 369-0704.

This luxurious and very centrally located mall—one of the city's largest—opened in 1981 to great hoopla. Designers Adolfo, Geoffrey Beene, Bill Blass, Bob Mackie, and Pauline Trigere were all on hand to display their fashion interpretations of "the Las Vegas look." And Danny Thomas, Doc Severinson, Johnny Carson, Juliet Prowse, Anthony Newley, Wayne Newton, and Tony Bennett put their handprints and signatures into wet cement, inaugurating the mall's Promenade of Stars (today 33 Las Vegas stars are so honored).

The mall comprises 140 shops, restaurants, and services. It is anchored by Neiman-Marcus, Saks Fifth Avenue, Bullock's, May Company, and Dillard's. Other notable tenants: Abercrombie & Fitch, the Disney Store, The Gap, Benetton, Uomo-Uomo Sport, Banana Republic, Victoria's Secret, Cache, Lane Bryant, Louis Vuitton, and Sharper Image. There are several card and book shops, a wide selection of apparel stores for the whole family (including large sizes and petites), 10 jewelers, 16 shoe stores, art galleries, and gift and specialty shops. Eating places range from the very elegant Chin's (details in Chapter 6) to dozens of fast-food outlets. Valet parking is an option, and you can even arrange to have your car hand washed while you shop.

Open: Mon–Fri 10am–9pm, Sat 10am–7pm, Sun noon–6pm.

THE MEADOWS, 4300 Meadows Lane, at the intersection of Valley View Blvd. and U.S. 93/95. Tel. 878-4849.

Another immense mall, the Meadows comprises 144 shops, services, and eateries, anchored by four department stores—the Broadway, Dillard's, Sears, and J.C. Penney. In addition there are 16 shoe stores, a full array of apparel for the entire family, a food court, toys, books, gifts, jewelry, and so on. Fountains and trees enhance the Meadows' ultramodern, high-ceilinged interior. A plus for kids is a replica of a turn-of-the-century carousel in Center Court.

Open: Mon–Fri 10am–9pm, Sat 10am–6pm, Sun noon–5pm.

2. HOTEL SHOPPING ARCADES

Just about every Las Vegas hotel offers some shopping opportunities. The following have the most extensive arcades. *Note:* The Forum Shops at Caesars are in the must-see category.

BALLY'S   Bally's claims one of the largest shopping malls inside any Las Vegas hotel. It has some 40 shops vending pro-team sports apparel, toys, men's and women's shoes and clothing, children's apparel, gourmet chocolates, liquor, jewelry, nuts and dried fruit, movie memorabilia, flowers, Mexican imports, clocks and telephones, luggage and handbags, lingerie and swimwear. In addition, there are several gift shops (brass and copper, blown glass and crystal, handcrafted and personalized gifts), logo items, art galleries (figurines and enameled paintings, American Indian crafts, sculptures, arts of Asia), and a movie-set photo studio. You can dispatch the kids to a video arcade on this level while you shop and take them to Swensen's for ice cream sundaes afterwards.

CAESARS PALACE   Caesars has always had an impressive arcade of shops called the **Appian Way,** centered on an immense white Carrara marble replica of Michelangelo's *David* standing more than 18 feet high. Its shops include the aptly named Galerie Michelangelo (original and limited edition artworks), several jewelers (including a branch of Cartier), a logo merchandise shop, several shops for men's and women's clothing (including Ungaro designer fashions), Gucci, a toy store, a gift shop, and a posh women's shoe shop. All in all, a very respectable grouping of hotel shops. But in the hotel's tradition of constantly surpassing itself, in 1992 it inaugurated the fabulous **Forum Shops**—a 240,000-square-foot Rodeo-Drive-meets-the-Roman-Empire affair complete with a painted Mediterranean sky that evolves from sunrise to sunset every few hours, acres of marble, lofty gold-topped columns, and a goddess of fortune under a central dome. Storefront facades resemble an ancient Roman streetscape, with archways, piazzas, ornate fountains, and a barrel-vaulted ceiling. And at the Festival Fountain seemingly immovable marble statues of Bacchus (slightly in his cups), Apollo, Plutus, and Venus come to life for a 7-minute revel with high-tech laser-light effects; it begins every hour on the hour. Not all of the 70 shops and restaurants are in place at this writing. Prestigious emporiums already include Louis Vuitton, Escada, Gucci, Ann Taylor, and Gianni Versace, among 27 clothing, shoe, and accessory shops. Other residents: a Warner Bros. merchandise outfit, an art gallery featuring the paintings of Tony Curtis (one of several, some dealing in very valuable artworks), Just For Feet (the world's largest athletic shoe store, with an on-premises basketball court where shoppers can test out the footwear), the Museum Company, Brookstone, and Victoria's Secret. And among your dining options are Boogie's Diner of Aspen, Wolfgang Puck's Spago, the Palm, and a branch of New York's famed Carnegie Deli. The complex, entered from the Strip via a moving walkway (the only way out is through the casino), is as much a sightseeing attraction as a shopping mall. Valet parking is available.

CIRCUS CIRCUS   About a dozen on-premises shops offer a wide selection of gifts and sundries, logo items, casual clothing, toys and games, jewelry, liquor, old-fashioned candy/soft ice cream, and, fittingly, clown dolls and puppets. At the Talking Photo Booth, you can have your picture taken in a choice of over 50 Las Vegas backdrop scenes with your own voice message.

EXCALIBUR   The shops of "The Realm," for the most part, reflect the hotel's medieval theme. Ye Olde Candlemaker, for example, vends intricately sculptured candles, Heraldry offers sewn and painted family crests, the Glass Cage features hand-blown items (many of them produced on the premises), and the White Wizard creates clay wizards and other magical characters while you watch. Other shops carry more conventional wares—gifts, candy, jewelry, women's clothing, and logo items. A child pleaser is Kids of the Kingdom, which displays licensed character merchandise from Dis-

---

A LAS VEGAS SPECIALTY STORE

GAMBLER'S BOOKSTORE, 630 S. 11th St., just off Charleston Blvd. Tel. 382-7555 or 800/634-6243.

Here you can buy a book on any system ever devised to beat casino odds. Owner Edna Luckman carries over 4,000 gambling-related titles, including many out-of-print books, computer software, and videotapes. She describes her store as a place where "gamblers, writers, researchers, statisticians, and computer specialists can meet and exchange information." On request, knowledgeable clerks provide on-the-spot expert advice on handicapping the ponies and other aspects of sports betting. The store's motto is "knowledge is protection."

Open: Mon–Sat 9am–5pm.

ney, Looney Tunes, Garfield, and Snoopy, and there's a photography shop where you can have your picture taken in Renaissance costumes. Also check out Fantasie Faire, down a level from the casino, where colorful stalls and gypsy wagons are laden with international gifts and folk art.

FLAMINGO HILTON   The shopping arcade at the Flamingo Hilton contains men's and women's clothing stores, gift shops, and a variety of other emporiums selling high-fashion jewelry, dried fruits and nuts, logo items, children's gifts and novelties, toys and games, and leather goods. A shop called the Wizard's Den carries magic-related items and masks, and Henri's sells ice cream, candies, and homemade fudge.

HARRAH'S   Just outside the hotel, Harrah's offers a 6,000-square-foot New Orleans–style shopping complex called **Jackson Square.** Shops include Maison Rose for women's fashions (some items for men and children, too), Louisiana Limited (an old-fashioned general store for Louisiana gifts), Holiday Jazz (sports items and team memorabilia), Cajun Spice (New Orleans gourmet items), and Unique Southwest (regional gifts). A Dixieland band, a costumed riverboat captain, a caricaturist dressed as a Southern belle, and a fresh-squeezed lemonade stand add a festive note. Inside the hotel are a gift shop, logo shop, and an Ethel M Chocolates outlet.

LAS VEGAS HILTON   The **Hilton Shops** comprise Addi Galleries, representing artists ranging from comedian Red Skelton to Miró and Chagall, an Ethel M Chocolate shop, and other emporiums vending fine crystal, exclusive men's and women's fashions, Italian porcelains and ceramics, logo items, leather handbags and gifts, women's shoes, imported toys and children's clothing, jewelry, and sportswear.

THE RIVIERA   The Riviera has a fairly extensive shopping arcade comprised of art galleries, jewelers, a creative photographer, and shops selling women's shoes and handbags, clothing for the entire family, furs, gifts, logo items, toys, phones and electronic gadgets, and chocolates.

THE SAHARA   The Sahara Shopping Arcade includes a Marshall Rousso's for women's apparel, Sahara's Apparel for Men, and Joey's for children's clothing and toys. Other shops carry luggage and handbags, gems, brass, lingerie/bath accessories, flowers, logo items, jewelry, and gifts. Henry's Candy Store sells ice cream, candy, and homemade fudge. You can have a photograph taken of yourself using antique costumes and sets at Night Hawk. Or have your own shots developed at Resort Photo.

LAS VEGAS NIGHTS

No city in the world offers more excitement after dark than Las Vegas. In addition to casino gambling (see Chapter 9), you have your choice of dozens of shows ranging from lavish production spectaculars to superstar entertainment. There are also comedy clubs, female impersonator shows, mind-boggling magicians, and sexy revues, not to mention free lounge shows.

On my last visit, during a 2-week period, the following big-name entertainers were performing at hotel showrooms: George Carlin, Bob Newhart with Nell Carter, Paul Anka, Neil Sedaka, Randy Travis, the Righteous Brothers, Julio Iglesias, Dionne Warwick with Burt Bacharach, Buddy Hackett, Andrew Dice Clay, Tom Jones, Don Rickles, Wayne Newton, Elaine Boosler, Melissa Manchester, Lou Rawls, the Temptations, Gladys Knight with the Four Tops, Liza Minnelli, and Rich Little. And the Grateful Dead were also in town at the University of Nevada's Silver Bowl.

There were, and are, at least a dozen elaborate production shows in town, including magic/illusion shows, all featuring high-tech lighting and laser effects, sexy showgirls in elaborate feathered and sequined costumes, and great choreography. These shows cost a lot of money to produce, so they have long runs. I've described every show now running in Las Vegas in detail, and though most will still be on when you read this book, some will no doubt have closed. Things change.

Casino lounge shows, which are either free or charge a one-drink minimum also offer first-rate entertainment. Many of the headliners you see on major stages started out as lounge acts. You could have a great time just going from lounge to lounge without spending very much money. My favorite casino lounge is at the Desert Inn. It features top jazz artists like Don Cherry.

Admission to shows runs a wide gamut, from about $12.50 for *An Evening at La Cage* (a female impersonator show at the Riviera) to over $70 for top headliners or Siegfried & Roy. Prices may include two drinks or dinner.

To find out who will be performing during your stay, you can call the various hotels featuring headliner entertainment, using toll-free numbers. Or call the Las Vegas Convention and Visitors Authority (tel. 702/733-2336) and ask them to send you a free copy of *Showguide*.

Every hotel entertainment option is described below, with information as to ticket prices, what is included in the price (drinks, dinner, taxes, and/or gratuities), showroom policies (as to assigned or maitre d' seating and smoking), and how to make reservations. Where possible, reserve in advance, especially on weekends and holidays. If the showroom has maitre d' seating (as opposed to assigned seats), you may want to tip the maitre d' to upgrade your seat. A tip of $15 to $20 per couple will usually do the trick at a major show, less in a small showroom. An alternative to tipping the maitre d' is to wait until the captain shows you to your seat. Perhaps it will be adequate, in which case you've saved some money. If not, you can offer the captain a tip for a better seat. If you do plan to tip, have the money ready; maitre d's and captains tend to get annoyed if you fumble around for it. They have other people to seat. You can also tip with casino chips (from the hotel casino where the show is taking place only) in lieu of cash. Whatever you tip, the proper etiquette is to do it rather subtly—a kind of palm-to-palm action. There's really no reason for this, since everyone knows what's going on, but being blatant is bad form. Arrive early at maitre d' shows to get the best choice of seats.

If you buy tickets for an assigned-seat show in person, you can look over a seating chart. Avoid sitting right up by the stage if possible, especially for big production shows. Dance numbers are better viewed from the middle of the theater. With headliners, you might like to sit up close. Women in the first row at Wayne Newton's shows often get kisses.

Note: All of these caveats and instructions aside, most casino-hotel showrooms offer good visibility from just about every seat in the house.

Not to be missed: the incomparable *Siegfried & Roy* at the Mirage—far and away the best show in town. It and other highly recommended production shows are starred in listings below.

1. ENTERTAINMENT AT HOTELS: ON OR NEAR THE STRIP

ALEXIS PARK RESORT, 375 E. Harmon Ave. Tel. 796-3300.

The very upscale Alexis Park offers live entertainment in its beautiful **Pisces Lounge**—a candlelit room under a 30-foot domed ceiling crossed with rough-hewn beams. Balconied tiers are hung with greenery, and a glass-covered fish pond reflects the Piscean theme. When the weather warrants, it's lovely to sit at umbrella tables on a terra-cotta-tile patio overlooking the pool. Mellow jazz is featured Tuesday through Sunday nights from 8pm till about midnight. Pasta dishes and desserts are available, along with liqueur-spiked coffees. No cover or minimum.

Alexis Park also hosts poolside **Sunsplash** parties during the summer from 3 to 10pm, with live music provided by a steel drum band through 7pm and a deejay playing music for dancing the rest of the evening. An admission price of $12 per person includes a hearty buffet meal—barbecued steak, chicken, and ribs, salads, desserts, and more. Bring your bathing suit.

BALLY'S, 3645 Las Vegas Blvd. S. Tel. 739-4567 or toll free 800/237-7469.

Bally's offers a wide spectrum of entertainments in two full-sized showrooms, a major concert hall, and a cabaret.

The 1,100-seat Ziegfeld Theatre—with its vast stage, excellent design (not a bad seat in the house), and state-of-the-art technical equipment—presents a classic Las Vegas spectacular called *Jubilee*. It features dazzling sets and lighting effects and a magnificently costumed cast (many outfits were designed by Bob Mackie) of over 100 singers and dancers. There are beautiful topless showgirls in sequins and feathers and hunky guys in studded-leather thongs. The show ranges from nostalgia numbers—honoring Maurice Chevalier, Bing Crosby, Eddie Cantor, and other stars of yesteryear—to lavish production extravaganzas themed around Samson and Delilah (culminating in the fiery destruction of the temple), the sinking of the *Titanic* (involving 5,000 gallons of water cascading through the set), and a World War I air battle. Interspersed with these are an excellent comedy sketch featuring a very deft pickpocket, Argentinean gauchos (almost every Strip spectacular has bolo-twirling gauchos, but these are the best), a thrilling sharpshooter act, and salutes to songwriting greats like Cole Porter and George Gershwin. The grand finale is "The Great Ziegfeld Walk"—a parade of showgirls that was a hallmark of the Ziegfeld Follies.

Showroom Policies: Nonsmoking with preassigned seating.

Price: $36 (tax and gratuity included, drinks extra).

Show Times: Nightly except Wednesday at 7:30 and 11pm.

Reservations: You can reserve by phone up to three weeks in advance.

Superstar headliners play the 1,408-seat **Celebrity Room.** Dean Martin inaugurated the facility and still plays here. Other frequent performers include Rodney Dangerfield, Tom Jones, Barbara Mandrell, the Righteous Brothers, Randy Travis, the Oak Ridge Boys, Engelbert Humperdinck, Harry Connick, Jr., George Carlin, and Andrew Dice Clay.

Showroom policies: Nonsmoking with preassigned seating.

Price: $25–$45, depending on the performer (tax and gratuity included, drinks extra).

Show Times: There are one or two shows a night at varying times (this also depends on the performer).

Reservations: You can reserve up to three weeks in advance.

Bally's additionally houses a major performance facility—the 5,000-seat **Goldwyn Events Center**—which presents major concerts about once a month. Among those who've recently played this stage are Don Henley, the Moody Blues, Michael Bolton, the Doobie Brothers, Huey Lewis & the News, James Brown, and Dire Straits—even the very un-Vegasy Bob Dylan. Sometimes this facility is also used for boxing matches.

Showroom Policies: Nonsmoking with preassigned seating.

Price: $22–$34, depending on the performer (tax and gratuity included, drinks extra). Boxing matches $15–$45.

Show Times: There are one or two shows a night at varying times (this also depends on the performer).

Reservations: You can reserve by phone up to three weeks in advance. For boxing tickets call 739-4111.

Catch a Rising Star (tel. 739-4397) is a comedy club located on the hotel's shopping arcade level. Seating up front at long banquet tables puts you close to the stage, but I much prefer the seating further back on plushly upholstered couches. It's infinitely more comfortable. There's live music while you're waiting for the show to begin. Three comics perform during each show. These are the people you've seen on the "Tonight Show" who play the national comedy club circuit.

Showroom Policies: Nonsmoking with maitre d' seating.

Price: $12.50 (tax and gratuity included, drinks extra).

Show Times: 8 and 10:30pm nightly.

Reservations: Tickets can be purchased at any time at the Catch a Rising Star box office next to the theater.

Finally, there's the **Celebrity Lounge** in the casino, featuring small combos and singers daily from 3pm–1:30am. No cover, one-drink minimum.

CAESARS PALACE, 3570 Las Vegas Blvd. S. Tel. 731-7333 or toll free 800/445-4544.

You can make quite a night of it—or two or three—at Caesars. This is one hotel that doesn't stint on entertainment. In fact, just walking around the premises is quite a thrill.

From its opening in 1966, Caesars' 1,200-seat Circus Maximus Showroom has presented superstar entertainment—everyone from Judy Garland to Sinatra. Many current headliners started out here as opening acts for established performers, among them Richard Pryor for singer Bobbie Gentry, Jay Leno for Tom Jones, and the Pointer Sisters for Paul Anka. In addition to the hundreds of headliners who have sparkled in the spotlight here, Caesars' entertainment history includes many long-running theatrical productions. Theodore Bikel starred in a long run of *Fiddler On the Roof,* and Tony Randall performed *The Odd Couple* for the first time in the Caesars Palace production, launching a hit run on Broadway and a top-rated television show.

These days the format is headliners only, and the current lineup of luminaries includes Jay Leno, Olivia Newton-John, Julio Iglesias, David Copperfield, Reba McEntyre, Burt Bacharach and Dionne Warwick, and Johnny Mathis. The luxurious showroom keeps to the Roman theme. Illuminated shields along the wall are replicas of those used by the legions of Caesar, and plush royal-purple booths are patterned after Roman chariots (these can be reserved if you're willing to pay extra for tickets).

Showroom Policies: Nonsmoking with preassigned seating.

Price: $40–$66, depending on the performer (including tax, gratuity extra, drinks optional). Booth seating about $6 more.

Show Times: One or two shows nightly; times depend on performer.

Reservations: You can reserve up to a month in advance via credit card.

I saw my first Omnimax movie at Caesars when the hotel pioneered this exciting entertainment in the 1970s, and though I've seen dozens of them since the thrill has never abated. If you're familiar with Omnimax movies, you probably agree. If you've never seen one, you're in for a treat. The **Omnimax Theatre** here is housed in a geodesic dome—a space-age environment with 368 seats that recline 27 degrees, affording a panoramic view of the arced 57-foot screen. The movies, projected via 70mm film (which is 10 times the frame size of ordinary 35mm film), offer an awesome visual display enhanced by a sophisticated "sensaround" sound system (98 speakers engulf the audience). Viewers might soar high above the Rocky Mountains, plummet down steep waterfalls, ride the rapids, travel into outer space, or perch at the rim of an erupting volcano. Shows change frequently, but whatever you see will be stupendous.

Box Office Information: Open daily 10am–11pm. Call 731-7901 or 800/634-6698 for information.

Price: Adults $4.50; seniors, children 4–12, military personnel, and hotel guests $3.

Show Times: Shows on the hour between 2 and 10pm Sun–Thurs, additional showtimes at 1 and 11pm Fri–Sat.

Reservations: Tickets can be purchased at box office on day of performance only.

Live bands play Top 40 dance tunes aboard **Cleopatra's Barge,** a replica of the majestic ships that sailed the Nile in ancient Egypt. This waterborne dance club is also afloat on "the Nile," complete with oars, ostrich-feather fans, statues of ancient pharoahs, furled sails, and a canopied royal box. You board via gangplanks, and hydraulic mechanisms rock the barge gently. There's seating on the main barge, aboard two adjacent lesser craft, and on the dock. Nubian-inspired waitresses in diaphanous togas bring drinks. In the early days of this facility, Caesars found it necessary to construct a dockside fence to keep awestruck sightseers from falling into the river. There's no cover; a two-drink minimum is required on Friday to Saturday nights. Open Wednesday to Saturday 10pm to 4am.

In addition to the above, two casino facilities—the **Olympic Lounge** and the **La Piazza Lounge** offer live entertainment nightly. And there's an ultraelegant piano bar lounge adjacent to the **Palace Court** restaurant—one of my favorite Las Vegas nightspots. No entry or drink minimum at any of these facilities.

THE CARRIAGE HOUSE, 105 E. Harmon Ave. Tel. 739-8000.

Kiefer's, the hotel's rooftop restaurant (see Chapter 6 for details), has a plushly furnished adjoining piano bar/lounge with a dance floor. Windowed walls offer great views of the Las Vegas neon skyline, making this a romantic setting for cocktails and hors d'oeuvres. There's piano music Tuesday to Saturday from 8pm to midnight. No cover or minimum.

THE DESERT INN, 3145 Las Vegas Blvd S. Tel. 733-4444
or 800/634-6906.

The Desert Inn has a long history of superstar entertainment. Frank Sinatra's Las Vegas debut was in the hotel's Painted Desert

Room in 1951, and other early performers included Maurice Chevalier, Noel Coward, Buster Keaton, and Marlene Dietrich. Jimmy
Durante once broke the piano board on a new spinet and yelled into
the audience, "Mr. Hughes, it was broke when I got it!" And on one
memorable night the entire Rat Pack (Dean Martin, Frank Sinatra,
Joey Bishop, Sammy Davis Jr., and Peter Lawford) invaded the stage
when Eddie Fisher was performing! Today this historic showroom is
renamed the **Crystal Room,** and Frank Sinatra still heads its galaxy
of stars. Other major headliners include Paul Anka, Liza Minnelli,
Dean Martin, Steve Lawrence & Eydie Gorme, Barry Manilow,
Willie Nelson, Gladys Knight, Bob Newhart, and Ray Charles.

Showroom Policies: Nonsmoking with maitre d' seating.

Price: $40–$75, depending on the performer (including two
drinks; tax and gratuity extra).

Show Times: 8 and 11pm Tues–Sun.

Reservations: Nonguests can reserve two days in advance,
hotel guests can book shows when making room reservations.

The D.I.'s **Star Lite Theatre** is the most sophisticated casino
lounge in town. It features name performers like Don Cherry, Laura
Taylor, Billy Stritch, Lynn Anderson, the Fifth Dimension, Buddy
Greco, Nell Carter, and the McGuire Sisters, along with talented
newcomers. Its a romantic setting for cocktails and dancing. No
cover; occasionally there's a drink minimum. Open for entertainment
8pm to 2am.

EXCALIBUR, 3850 Las Vegas Blvd. S. Tel. 597-7600.

Excalibur's primary entertainment offering is in keeping with its
medieval theme. *King Arthur's Tournament* is a colorful tale of
gallant knights and fair ladies—of romance, magic, medieval games,
and pageantry, enlivened by pyrotechnics, lasers, fiber optics, and
fancy lighting effects. Bursts of fireworks herald the presence of
Merlin the magician in his star-spangled blue robe, and lasers add
flash and drama to sword fights and jousting contests. The story
revolves around the battle between the evil black knight and the
heroic white knight for the princess's hand in marriage. Each section
of the arena is given a knight to cheer, and the audience is encouraged
to hoot, holler, and pound on the tables (kids adore it). Knightly
battles are complemented by lively dances, equestrian acrobatics,
tumblers, jugglers, and stunt riders. And the show culminates, of
course, in the victory of the white knight and his marriage to King
Arthur's fair daughter in a magnificent court wedding. Dinner, served
during the show by "serfs" and "wenches," is a robust affair eaten in
lusty medieval style without utensils. It includes a pot of creamy
chicken soup, cornish game hen, stuffed baked potato, vegetable,
biscuits, apple tart, and beverage.

Showroom Policies: Nonsmoking with assigned seating.

IMPRESSIONS

*If I stand still while I'm singing, I'm a dead man. I might as well
go back to driving a truck.*
—LEGENDARY LAS VEGAS HEADLINER ELVIS PRESLEY

Price: $24.95 (including dinner, beverage, tax, and gratuity).
Show Times: 6 and 8:30pm "knightly."
Reservations: You can reserve up to six days in advance by phone via credit card.

Excalibur also presents *The Wonderful World of Horses,* starring the world-famous Lipizzaner stallions. These regal white horses were, for hundreds of years, the private preserve of the Austrian nobility and military aristocracy. Developed in Moorish Spain from three superior equine breeds (Spanish Andalusian, Arabian, and the swift and sturdy Karst of the Adriatic coast), they were trained in the elegant and graceful movements of dressage and "haute école" and shown in Vienna's magnificent riding halls. The Excalibur show is in that centuries-old tradition. Riders in the red and white military uniforms of imperial Austria present their stallions in a dignified procession set to classical music and put them through a variety of complex movements—leaps, kicks, battlefield maneuvers, and historic equestrian arts, with a little bit of comic relief thrown in (a drunken horse and rider) for good measure. Movements include the "pesade" (the horse rises on its hind legs and maintains its body at a 45-degree angle for several seconds), the "courbette" (a stallion in the pesade position leaps forward several times), and the "capriole" (the horse leaps simultaneously with all four legs and at the height of the leap kicks out with its hind legs).

Showroom Policies: Nonsmoking; seating, on a first-come, first-serve basis, begins half an hour prior to the show.
Price: $5.95.
Show Times: Noon and 2pm, daily except Fri.
Reservations: Tickets can be purchased up to three days in advance at Excalibur ticket booths.

The medievally decorated **Minstrel's Theatre Lounge** offers live 20th-century bands nightly till about midnight weekdays, 3:40am Friday to Saturday. No cover or minimum. See the hotel listing in Chapter 5 for other Excalibur entertainment options.

FLAMINGO HILTON, 3555 Las Vegas Blvd. S. Tel. 733-3333.

For 10 years a stage spectacular called *City Lites* has been playing to sell-out audiences in the 900-seat Flamingo Showroom. A traditional Las Vegas extravaganza, it has gorgeous bare-breasted showgirls in elaborate spangled and feathered costumes, stunning scenery, and lively dance numbers. Highlights are a novelty act by the Garza Brothers—strongmen who, moving in slow motion, pose as ancient Greek statues in a mesmerizing display of grace and strength; an enchanting Japanese fantasy ice ballet sequence with dancers in butterfly costumes; and magician Joseph Gabriel, who uses beautiful exotic birds in his act. Other production numbers include a tribute to country music, a fabulous ice ballet to "Over the Rainbow" performed by world-champion skaters Ron and Mandy Green, and a tap dance ensemble to "42nd Street."
Showroom Policies: Nonsmoking with maitre d' seating.
Price: Dinner show based on entrée price $28.50–$36.95 (tax and gratuity extra), cocktail show $20.95 (including two drinks; tax and gratuity extra).

Show Times: Dinner show 7:45pm, cocktail show 11pm.

Reservations: You can reserve up to a month in advance.

Bugsy's Celebrity Theatre, a casino lounge, is in the works at this writing. It will offer a revue called *American Superstars*. Details next edition.

IMPERIAL PALACE, 3535 Las Vegas Blvd. S. Tel. 794-3261 or 800/634-6441.

An extravaganza called *Legends in Concert* has been playing at the 900-seat Imperial Theatre since May 1983. It has appeared on Broadway and, in 1991, it toured the Russian cities of Moscow and St. Petersburg. Performers impersonate superstar entertainers with actual singing (no lip-synching), paying tribute to Bobby Darin, Roy Orbison, Marilyn Monroe, the Blues Brothers, Buddy Holly, Neil Diamond, Paul McCartney, Cher, Madonna, Tom Jones, Elton John, Dolly Parton, and Barbra Streisand, among others. Highlights include an impression of Liberace (complete with candelabra and rhinestone-studded fur cape) and Elvis impersonator James Lowrey, who has had himself surgically altered to look more like his idol. The show utilizes dazzling high-tech lighting and laser effects, and singers are backed by a live onstage orchestra. Photographic blow ups of the stars being imitated flank the stage.

Showroom Policies: Nonsmoking, maitre d' seating.

Price: $17.95 (including two drinks or one Polynesian cocktail such as a mai tai or zombie, tax and gratuity extra).

Show Times: Mon–Sat 7:30 and 10:30pm.

Reservations: You can make reservations by phone up to a month in advance.

HACIENDA RESORT, 3950 Las Vegas Blvd. S. Tel. 702/739-8911.

Magician extraordinaire Lance Burton was a player in the Tropicana's *Folies Bergère* for nine years before creating his own show—*Lance Burton: A Magical Journey*—for the Hacienda's Fiesta Theatre in 1991. Lance is a charismatic performer (he looks a little like Elvis) and a first-rate magician who levitates birds and sexy showgirls, has himself executed onstage, makes women appear and disappear, flies into the air, and amusingly spoofs Strip superstar illusionists Siegfried & Roy. The show keeps a lively pace with dance numbers, sword fights, a hilarious comic juggler, and Lance's really expert showmanship. However, even the early show is a little gratuitously sexy, so you might think twice about taking the kids.

Showroom Policies: Nonsmoking with maitre d' seating.

Price: $19.95 (drinks, tax, and gratuity extra).

Show Times: 8 and 11pm Wed–Mon.

Reservations: Tickets can be reserved up to two weeks in advance by phone.

The **Bolero Lounge** in the casino offers live music (oldies and mellow rock bands) nightly from 9pm–3am. No cover or minimum.

HARRAH'S LAS VEGAS, 3475 Las Vegas Blvd. S. Tel. 597-5970 or 800-634-6787.

Harrah's fast-paced and very entertaining magical extravaganza,

Spellbound, A Concert of Illusion, is enlivened by a pulsating rock music score, exciting dance numbers, and futuristic laser and lighting effects. Talented female magician Sherry Lukas runs swords through a box in which her *male* assistant is encased (a first), turns playing cards into doves and doves into miniature poodles, and escapes from a padlocked booth à la Houdini. A tropical dance number, complete with drums, smoke, and flaming torchiers heralds illusionists Kole and Jenny. Kole levitates Jenny and glides her levitated body through a ring of fire, and he not only puts her in a box and runs swords into it, he sets the box on fire. Mexican illusionists Joaquin and Lilia, whose balletlike stagecraft combines pyrotechnics, high-tech laser effects, and folkloric elements, create fascinating illusions using masks, including a sequence based on the *Phantom of the Opera.* The show also features a comedian and over half a dozen jungle cats.

Showroom Policies: Nonsmoking with preassigned seating.

Price: $19.95 (including one drink; tax and gratuity extra).

Show Times: 7:30 and 10pm Mon–Sat.

Reservations: You can charge tickets up to 30 days in advance via credit card by calling the above numbers.

In addition to the above, the **Court of Two Gators,** a New Orleans–themed courtyard-style bar lounge off the casino, features live bands for dancing Tuesday to Sunday from 8pm to 2am. The music ranges from mellow jazz to oldies. Monday night football games are aired in season; the rest of the year Monday is karaoke night. No cover or minimum.

LAS VEGAS HILTON, 3000 Paradise Rd. Tel. 732-5755 or 800/222-5361.

The Hilton bills itself as "America's Show Business Address." Its elegant 1,475-seat showroom, one of the largest and most comfortable in town, features superstar entertainment. Barbra Streisand kicked things off in 1969, and Elvis Presley made his Las Vegas performance home here for 10 years. Among the hundreds of major headliners who have played the Hilton stage over the decades are Milton Berle, Debbie Reynolds, Eddy Arnold, Roseanne Barr, Red Buttons, Diahann Carroll, Ray Charles, Neil Sedaka, Perry Como, Bobby Darin, the Everly Brothers, and Nancy Wilson—almost every big name in show biz really. The Hilton's current galaxy of stars includes the ever-popular "Mr. Las Vegas" Wayne Newton, Don Williams, Bill Cosby, the Temptations, Diana Ross, Crystal Gayle, and George Strait.

Showroom Policies: Nonsmoking with preassigned seating.

Price: $39.95–$49.95 (including one drink; tax and gratuity extra); booths can be reserved at no extra charge on a first-come, first-served basis.

Show Times: Varies with performers, always dark Mon.

Reservations: You can make reservations by phone up to three days in advance.

The Hilton also boasts the 9,900-seat **Hilton Center,** which hosts big-name concerts, world-championship fights, and other major events. Eddie Murphy sold out this immense space during his first Las Vegas appearance here in 1986, and, in 1989, Phil Donahue did his

IMPRESSIONS

I've built my own world here. Wayne's world.
—LAS VEGAS SUPERSTAR WAYNE NEWTON TALKING ABOUT HIS
52-ACRE ESTATE, CASA DE SHENANDOAH, FIVE MILES OUT OF TOWN

---

show live from the Center for a week. Information is available through the above-listed phone numbers.

When sports action is over at the **SuperBook** every night, contemporary soft rock videos are aired on the largest of its monitors, and the room takes on a nightclub atmosphere. No cover or minimum. Drinks and food are available.

And the plush **Hilton Casino Lounge** features live music for dancing nightly through 3am. From 4 to 8pm a three-piece band plays mellow jazz, from 8pm on a band plays Top 40 and country tunes. No cover, two-drink minimum.

MAXIM, 160 E. Flamingo Rd. Tel. 731-4423 or 800/634-6987.

The Maxim **Comedy Cabaret** is a variety show presented in a 218-seat nightclub with seating at small round tables. The emcee is strictly Borscht Belt, but the show offers an entertaining mix of sexy dancers, comedy (impressions of Jack Nicholson, Tony Bennett, Sly Stallone, Peter Falk, and many others), a ventriloquist with a Mexican parrot dummy, and song. The show isn't topless, but lead vocalist Kelly Conelly wears a see-through dress to sing "God Is Watching Us"—somehow an unsettling thought at a Las Vegas show.

Showroom Policies: Smoking permitted, maitre d' seating.

Price: $14.25 (including tax; drinks and gratuity extra).

Show Times: 7 and 9pm Mon–Fri, 7, 9, and 11pm Sat.

Reservations: You can reserve up to a week in advance by phone.

Monday to Friday at 11pm and Sun at 8pm local dealers, pit bosses, and show people put on a free country and western show in the Maxim's showroom. Drinks are available.

THE MIRAGE, 3400 Las Vegas Blvd. S. Tel. 792-7777 or 800/627-6667.

The most spectacular hotel on the Strip also has the ultimate entertainment package featuring illusionists par excellence **Siegfried & Roy.** Not to mince praise, I'd as soon go to India and not visit the Taj Mahal as miss S&R in Las Vegas. For over two decades, the Las Vegas show starring this dynamic duo has been the top show in town, playing to sellout audiences twice a night. Leave it to Steve Wynn to give them carte blanche (aka $25 million) to build the 1,500-seat Theatre Mirage to their own specifications. Producer Ken Feld contributed another $30 million to the new spectacle—making it the most expensive theatrical attraction ever staged. Singer Michael Jackson wrote and produced a song just for the show! The luxurious and very comfortable theater—designed so that no seat is more than 100 feet from the edge of the stage—features the world's most advanced computerized lighting and audio system. And the cast includes a company of 60 dancers and two dozen wild animals. Among the latter are the rare royal white tigers that have become an S&R trademark; they freely roam the stage during the show. These sorcerers supreme make elephants disappear, transform beautiful women into tigers, ride horses sideways and backwards, impale themselves on swords, are captured by aliens, levitate, set the stage on fire, leap through flaming hoops, and shoot each other out of cannons. Enchanting dreamlike dance numbers feature demons, gossamer-winged fairies, and armies of human and mechanized soldiers in gold and silver armor battling a fire-breathing dragon. Laser and lighting effects, costumes, scenery, and choreography are unparalleled. Don't miss this awe-inspiring world of wonders.

Note: Siegfried & Roy perform 44 weeks a year. When they're out of town the Theatre Mirage presents headliners such as Dolly Parton, Cher, Kenny Rogers, and the Highwaymen (Willie Nelson, Waylon Jennings, Johnny Cash, and Kris Kristofferson).

Showroom Policies: Nonsmoking with preassigned seating.

Price: $73 (including two drinks, tax, and gratuity); headliners $50–$75.

Show Times: Siegfried & Roy appear three weeks out of each month. Performances are at 7:30 and 11pm Thurs–Tues. Show times for headliner shows vary with the performer.

Reservations: Tickets can be purchased on day of performance only. Box office opens at 8am. Arrive early.

The internationally acclaimed *Cirque de Soleil,* a second spectacular Mirage offering, is scheduled to move to Steve Wynn's new Treasure Island Hotel when it opens shortly after we go to press. So if—as you're reading this—Treasure Island is open, the show is now there. Performances at the Mirage take place in a huge outdoor 1,500-seat tent. The *Cirque* combines traditional acrobatics with theatrical elements and modern dance to tell a touching story of a man trying to recapture his youth at the circus. It's charming, thrilling, and totally enchanting.

Showroom Policies: Nonsmoking with preassigned seating.

Price: $35 plus tax, drinks and food available at concessions.

Show Times: 7:30 and 10:30pm Tues–Sun.

Reservations: Tickets can be ordered by phone up to a month in advance.

The **Lagoon Saloon** in the tropical rain forest atrium offers live entertainment—reggae, light jazz, Top 40, and Cole Porter classics—for dancing till 2am Sunday to Wednesday, 3am Thursday to Saturday. Seating—in parrot-motif chairs at umbrella tables—is under an arbor of bougainvillea amid waterfalls and lagoons, and the bar top is a glass-covered beach strewn with seashells. Tropical drinks are a specialty. There's no admission; a two-drink minimum is in effect Friday to Saturday only.

In addition, a pianist plays show tunes and classic melodies nightly in the **Baccarat Bar,** adjacent to the baccarat pit off the casino. No cover or minimum. Jacket and tie are required for men.

RIO SUITE HOTEL & CASINO, 3770 W. Flamingo Rd. Tel. 252-7776 or 800/634-6787.

IMPRESSIONS

By creating a series of enchanted moments, we hope our audience will recall the time in their lives when they felt that anything was possible.
—SIEGFRIED & ROY

Shortly after press time, the Rio opened a new show called **Brazilia** in its Copacabana Showroom. Exotic, upbeat, and highly stylized, it stars a Carmen Miranda–like Rio Rita in elaborate ever-changing costumes singing (in English and Portuguese) everything from "Going Bananas" to "Tico-Tico." She also hosts a game show called Rio Fever in which the audience participates and wins prizes. Her costar, Clint Carvalho, adds comic repartee and hosts an innovative exotic bird show. He levitates a hyacinth macaw, is himself levitated by birds, dances with a cockatoo named Peaches, introduces an ostrichlike Australian emu, and sings "Why Do Fools Fall in Love" with a parrot. A talented dance company performs jazz and Latin-influenced numbers, and the music includes tangos, Latin drum solos, and many enchantingly pretty songs. During a marimba/calypso sequence, audience members are invited on stage to do the limbo. The show opens with a dynamic number (enhanced by melodic bird sounds) featuring dancers in feathered headpieces and masks. It culminates in a spectacular carnivale finale, after which the audience congas out of the showroom and into the casino with the cast. High-tech lighting effects add panache.

Showroom Policies: Smoking permitted, maitre d' seating.

Price: $14.95 (including two drinks; tax and gratuity extra).

Show Times: 8 and 10pm Sun and Tues–Thurs, with an additional show at midnight Fri–Sat.

Reservations: You can reserve up to a month in advance; call the above toll-free number to charge tickets.

The very simpatico **Ipanema Bar,** tropically themed with lush plantings and bamboo furnishings, features live music—reggae and Brazilian sounds) through 1am Wednesday to Sunday. Cocktail waitresses are in sexy Ipanema girl costumes, and tropical drinks (such as the "Copa Banana"—banana liqueur, blackberry brandy, dark rum, and grenadine—) are featured. No cover or minimum.

And every Tuesday night throughout the summer, the Rio hosts a festive poolside **"beach party"** with live bands, volleyball games, limbo contests, and a massive outdoor buffet. The shell-shaped swimming pool here is actually surrounded by sandy beach. The price is $6.25 per person.

RIVIERA HOTEL & CASINO, 2901 Las Vegas Blvd. S. Tel. 734-9301 or 800/634-6753.

The Riviera presents four big shows nightly, making it the Strip leader in entertainment offerings. Most lavish is the award-winning *Splash*—a lively revue that has been playing to sell-out audiences in the Versailles Theatre since 1985. As the name implies, the show is an aquacade extravaganza with an onstage

20,000-gallon tank surrounded by dancing fountains and waterfalls. A uniquely thrilling number features three stunt motorcyclists racing inside a 13½-foot sphere. There are gorgeous showgirls, mermaids, seahorses, and starfish, as well as divers, water ballet, comedy, magic, and acrobatic skits, all of which lead up to a spectacular finale—a salute to Hollywood and Broadway hit musicals. The show is enhanced by state-of-the-art lighting and laser technology.

Showroom Policies: Nonsmoking with maitre d' seating.

Price: $27.50 for the early show, $24.50 for the late show, with a $3 surcharge Sat and holidays (including two drinks; tax and gratuity extra).

Show Times: 8 and 11pm nightly. Headliner show times vary with the performer.

Reservations: You can reserve by phone up to a month in advance.

An Evening at La Cage is based on the premise that "boys will be girls," with transvestite performers doing lip-synch impersonations of Diana Ross, Tina Turner, Aretha Franklin, Patti LaBelle, Peggy Lee, Cher, Shirley MacLaine, Roseanne Barr, Carol Channing, Bette Midler, Dionne Warwick, and Liza Minnelli. Frank Marino is "mistress of ceremonies" in the persona of comedienne Joan Rivers. And a performer in half-drag sings "Unforgettable" as both Nat and Natalie Cole. The show has lots of hilarious spicy schtick, and a very overweight Tammy Wynette does a comic version of "Help Me Make It Through the Night." There's also a first-rate Michael Jackson impersonator in the show, though having a female impersonator portray a male performer brings new meaning to the concept of androgyny. The show is presented in a small theater on the third floor Mardi Gras Plaza.

Showroom Policies: Nonsmoking with maitre d' seating.

Price: $12.50 (including two drinks; tax and gratuity extra), $14.50 with dinner. Sat and holidays add a $3 surcharge.

Show Times: 7, 9, and 11 pm nightly except Tues.

Reservations: Tickets can be purchased at the box office only, in advance if you wish.

Crazy Girls—Fantasie de Paris, presented in another intimate Mardi Gras Plaza theater, is probably the raciest revue on the Strip. It features sexy showgirls with perfect bodies in erotic song and dance numbers enhanced by innovative lighting effects. Think of *Penthouse* poses come to life.

Showroom Policies: Nonsmoking with maitre d' seating.

Price: $12.50 (including two drinks; tax and gratuity extra), $14.50 with dinner. Sat and holidays add a $3 surcharge.

Show Times: 7:30, 9, and 10:30pm nightly.

Reservations: Tickets can be purchased at the box office only, in advance if you wish.

If you have cable TV, you've very likely seen Budd Friedman's *An Evening at the Improv*—one of the country's best-known comedy club showcases. Shows feature the rising stars of comedy you see on the "Tonight Show" and Letterman, some of whom will no doubt go on to greater fame. Improv alumni include Whoopi Goldberg, Steve Martin, and Robin Williams, to name just a few. Shows are presented on the second floor of the Mardi Gras Plaza. Four comics perform each night.

Showroom Policies: Nonsmoking with maitre d' seating.

Price: $12.50 (including two drinks; tax and gratuity extra), $14.50 with dinner. Sat and holidays add a $3 surcharge.

Show Times: 8, 10, and 11:30pm nightly.

Reservations: Tickets can be purchased at the box office only, in advance if you wish.

In addition, the Riviera offers occasional **headliner entertainment** featuring Pia Zadora (her husband, Meshulam Riklis, owns the hotel) and costarring George Burns, who at age 96 signed a 5-year contract here! And the elegant **Bistro Lounge** in the casino offers live entertainment through 3am nightly—Top 40 groups, jazz, and country. No cover, two-drink minimum.

SAHARA HOTEL & CASINO, 2535 Las Vegas Blvd. S. Tel. 737-2878.

The Sahara's Congo Theater has traditionally presented headliner entertainment; however, in recent years it's changed its format to long-running shows. The current offering is *Melinda, First Lady of Magic and her Follies Revue.* Melinda is a beautiful blond whose exuberant, high-energy show combines first-rate sleight of hand and illusion with comedy, dance numbers, and variety acts. She produces birds and lions out of thin air, disappears from a locked box, pulls a tiger out of a burning cauldron, levitates, and does something amazing with a white horse. The show also features juggler Anthony Gatto, holder of nine world records (he keeps seven fiery torches going, among other feats). And the all-black King Charles Unicycling Troupe offers a breathtaking display of athletic agility and group coordination, jumping rope (even double Dutch) and playing basketball while mounted on unicycles (picture the Harlem Globetrotters on wheels).

Showroom Policies: Nonsmoking, maitre d' seating.

Price: $17.95 (tax, drinks, and gratuity extra).

Show Times: Tues–Sat 8 and 10:30pm, Sun 8pm.

Reservations: Tickets can be obtained at the box office only.

The *Pacific Rim Island Magic Dinner Show* is a great choice for families. It stars a troupe of exotic beauties—variously attired in grass skirts, sarongs, and lavish costumes—performing songs and dances of the islands. They alternate with muscle-bound island men enacting Samoan and Maori war dances. There's an entertaining comic narrative throughout the show, and the fire dance finale is truly spectacular. This is a dinner show presented in an attractive island-themed nightclub with thatched roofing, Gauguin-like murals, fountained pools, and Polynesian sculpture. The price of admission includes dinner—choice of entrée (stir-fry noodles with beef and chicken, shrimp tempura, baby back ribs, curried chicken, or New York steak) and an extensive salad bar laden with salads, seafood (mounds of shrimp, crab legs, and oysters), fruit, and desserts.

Price: $17.95.

Show Times: Dark Wed, other nights seatings at 5:30 and 8pm.

Reservations: Suggested.

The Sahara's **Casbah Lounge** (in the casino) presents a sexy sizzler called *Seduction*—a fast-paced revue with elaborately costumed "dirty dancing" showgirls and showguys. Comic relief is provided by an emcee's narrative and a ventriloquist. There are two shows nightly Tuesday to Friday at 7 and 9:30pm; three shows Saturday at 7, 9, and 10:30pm, and Monday at 7, 9, and 11pm. Dark Sunday. No admission, two-drink minimum. If you don't mind standing, you can watch the show from the casino.

SANDS HOTEL CASINO, 3355 Las Vegas Blvd. S. Tel. 733-5453 or 800/444-4678.

The famed Copa Room (in its early days the venue for "Rat Packers" Frank Sinatra, Sammy Davis, Jr., Dean Martin, and Joey Bishop) is currently presenting *Bare Essence,* billed as a "sensual adult cabaret." The show will open shortly after press time. According to hotel sources, it features exotic dancing, high-energy rock music, magic, juggling, comedy, and plenty of exposed flesh in scenes set in New York's Times Square and an Asian bath. Max Clever, a comic illusionist and fire eater does a sleight-of-hand routine featuring his cockatoo, Spike.

Showroom Policies: Smoking permitted, maitre d' seating.
Price: $19.95 (tax, drinks, and gratuity extra).
Show Times: 8 and 10:30pm nightly except Thurs.
Reservations: You can reserve in advance by phone.

The Copa also presents a very popular afternoon show called *Viva Las Vegas,* combining comedy, singing, dancing, and magic. The acts change from time to time, but keep pretty much the same mix, and, of course, there are always leggy showgirls in fabulous costumes.

Showroom Policies: Smoking permitted, maitre d' seating.
Price: $10 (tax and one drink included, gratuity extra).
Show Times: Mon–Fri 12:30 and 2:30pm.
Reservations: You can reserve in advance by phone.

And nightly entertainment is featured in the **Winners Circle Lounge.** Changing musical groups offer country, rock, Broadway hits, oldies, or Top 40 tunes. No cover or minimum.

STARDUST RESORT & CASINO, 3000 Las Vegas Blvd. S. Tel. 732-6111 or 800/824-6033.

The Stardust Theatre has traditionally offered top-flight entertainment, and its current show is one of the very best in town. *Enter the Night* is a high-tech, sophisticated version of the classic Las Vegas spectacular—a multimedia production extraordinaire with awe-inspiring laser and lighting effects, stunning sets and costumes, gorgeous showgirls, enchanting dance numbers, and great music that runs the gamut from original songs to Fats Waller tunes. It features the renowned Russian aerialist Vladimir, world champion ice skaters, and Argentinean gaucho dancers, among other superb acts, including an incredibly choreographed number in which six performers dance with laser lights. This show never flags, but moves from height to height, concluding with a massive finale.

Showroom Policies: Nonsmoking with preassigned seating.
Price: $24.90 (including two drinks, tax, and gratuity).
Show Times: 8 and 11pm Wed–Sat, 9pm Sun–Mon.

Reservations: You can reserve up to a month in advance by phone.

The **Starlite Lounge** in the casino offers contemporary live music (small bands and singers) daily from 4pm to 2am. Other times this comfortable cocktail lounge airs sporting events on multiscreen TV. No cover or minimum.

TROPICANA RESORT & CASINO, 3801 Las Vegas Blvd. S. Tel. 739-2411 or 800/468-9494.

The Trop's famous *Folies Bergère* is the longest-running production show in town. It's the quintessential Las Vegas extravaganza with a French accent—an enchanting mix of innovative scenery, lively music, bare-breasted showgirls in lavish feathered/rhinestoned/ sequined costumes, and fast-paced choreography. Scene I is set in a turn-of-the-century Parisian music hall. Scene II salutes American music—gospel, blues, movie melodies, the big band and swing eras—culminating in a medley of oldies from the fifties through the eighties. A highlight is a kaleidoscope dance number (they do it with mirrors). And Scene III once more celebrates the belle époque, leading up to a colorful cancan finale. Acts are punctuated by acrobatic numbers, the "fastest juggler on earth," and comedy routines. *Note:* If you'd like to take a backstage tour of the Folies set, tours are scheduled Tuesday to Saturday at 12:30, 1:30, and 2:30pm. Tickets cost $3.50; call the above phone number for details.

Showroom Policies: Nonsmoking with maitre d' seating.

Price: $18.95–$22.95 (including two drinks; tax and gratuity extra). You can opt for dinner at the 8pm show (admission is based on your entrée price ($26.95–$32.95; tax and gratuity extra).

Show Times: 8 and 11pm Fri–Wed.

Reservations: You can charge tickets in advance via credit card by calling the above number.

A second Tropicana entertainment option is the **Comedy Stop** (tel. 739-2714), featuring three nationally known comedy headliners nightly.

Showroom Policies: Smoking permitted with maitre d' seating.

Price: $12.95 (including two drinks; tax and gratuity extra).

Show Times: 8 and 10:30pm nightly.

Reservations: You can charge tickets in advance via credit card by calling the above number.

The **Tropics Lounge** features karaoke every Tuesday from 8pm to 1am. No cover or minimum.

The **Atrium Lounge** in the casino offers a mix of live music nightly from 9pm to 1:30am. No cover or minimum.

There are **laser light shows** every summer night in the water park behind the hotel.

CIRCUS CIRCUS HOTEL/CASINO, 2880 Las Vegas Blvd. S. Tel. 734-0410.

The show at Circus Circus is free, and it goes on from 11am to midnight daily. The world's largest permanent circus—featuring trapeze artists, magicians, unicyclists, acrobats, high-wire acts, performing dogs, clowns, jugglers, and stunt cyclists—takes place on the midway level.

2. ENTERTAINMENT AT HOTELS: DOWNTOWN

FOUR QUEENS, 202 E. Fremont St. Tel. 385-4011.

The **French Quarter Lounge** of this delightful downtown hotel has a notable casino lounge format. Nightly except Monday it presents well-known oldies groups and performers such as the Platters, Della Reese, Rita Coolidge, Frank Sinatra, Jr., Al Hirt, the Drifters, Little Anthony, Buffalo Springfield, and the Kingston Trio. Performances are at 8 and 10pm. Monday night shows feature jazz artists such as Joe Williams, Billy Eckstine, Charlie Byrd, Mose Allison, and Papa John Creach. Performances are at 7:30, 9:30, and 11:30pm. No cover, two-drink minimum.

GOLDEN NUGGET, 129 E. Fremont St. Tel. 386-8100 or 800/634-3403.

The Nugget books big-name entertainers into its **Cabaret Showroom.** The hotel's current roster of headliners includes Don Rickles, Tony Orlando & Dawn, Melissa Manchester, Neil Sedaka, David Brenner, Bobby Vinton, Tanya Tucker, Yakov Smirnoff, Merle Haggard, the Charlie Daniels Band, the Smothers Brothers, and Lou Rawls.

Showroom Policies: Smoking permitted, maitre d' seating.

Price: $25–$30 (including two drinks; tax and gratuity extra).

Show Times: Vary with the performer; Wednesdays are almost always dark.

Reservations: You can reserve up to a week in advance.

JACKIE GAUGHAN'S PLAZA HOTEL/CASINO, 1 Main St. Tel. 386-2444 or 800/634-6575.

Boylesque, a racy female-impersonator revue currently at the Plaza Theater Showroom, has been playing somewhere in Las Vegas since 1970. It's a totally silly and outrageous evening, with lots of double entendre jokes and even a bit of beefcake (not every performer is impersonating a woman). A talented cast does lip-synching impressions of Dionne Warwick, Madonna, Tina Turner, Whitney Houston, Marilyn Monroe, Dolly Parton, Diana Ross, and others. A group of Argentinean gauchos dancing with bolos adds variety, and witty "hostess" Kenny Kerr keeps up a lively patter that includes ad-lib wisecrack answers to audience questions.

An added attraction here is the **Omaha Lounge** in the casino, which offers live music nightly (Top 40 bands) almost around-the-clock through 4am. No cover or minimum.

Showroom Policies: Smoking permitted, maitre d' seating.

Price: $16.95 (including two drinks; tax and gratuity extra).

Show Times: 8 and 10:30pm Thurs–Tues.

Reservations: You can reserve up to a week in advance by phone.

LADY LUCK CASINO HOTEL, 206 N. Third St. Tel. 477-3000.

Billed as "the sexiest little big top in the world," *Cabaret Circus* offers a mix of comedy, singing, magic, and sexy topless dancing in a circus format, complete with tap dancing "elephants" and a ballet of Andulusian "ponies." The show is internationally themed, featuring "Russian" cossack dancers and "Argentinean" gauchos. The reason everything above is in quotes is that there are no real Russians or Argentineans in the show, and there are no real animals either—it's all a rather charming tongue-in-cheek spoof.

Showroom Policies: Nonsmoking with preassigned seating.

Price: $14.95 (including gratuity; drinks and tax extra); the early show includes a buffet dinner.

Show Times: 7:30 and 10pm Fri–Wed.

Reservations: No phone reservations; you can purchase tickets any time in advance at show desks.

3. HEADLINER STADIUMS

The **Sam Boyd Silver Bowl** at the University of Nevada, Las Vegas (UNLV), Boulder Highway and Russell Road (tel. 739-3900), is a 40,000-seat outdoor stadium. Major headliners such as the Grateful Dead and the Beach Boys occasionally play here. Tickets can be charged to the above number or via Ticket Master (tel. 474-4000).

A more comprehensive concert schedule is offered at UNLV's 18,500-seat **Thomas and Mack Center** (tel. 739-3900). Recent performers here have included Pavarotti, Hammer, Paula Abdul, New Kids on the Block, Metallica, Guns and Roses, Van Halen, and Michael Bolton. Tickets can be charged to the above number or via Ticket Master (tel. 474-4000).

CHAPTER 12

EASY EXCURSIONS FROM LAS VEGAS

1. GOODSPRINGS—A GHOST TOWN

2. HOOVER DAM & LAKE MEAD

3. MOUNT CHARLESTON & LEE CANYON SKI AREA

4. RED ROCK CANYON & BONNIE SPRINGS RANCH

5. VALLEY OF FIRE STATE PARK

Anyone who has seen the cascades of neon along the Strip would agree that the Las Vegas way is to do things on a grand scale. What most visitors to Las Vegas don't realize is that the sense of being amid the extraordinary only shifts gears at the city limits; seeing the stark grandeur of the surrounding desert is an unforgettable experience in its own right. Also within easy reach are some of the country's most imposing natural and manmade wonders, such as the Hoover Dam and Red Rock Canyon; ghost towns, and other places where you can get the flavor of the Old West; and innumerable opportunities for outdoor recreation—from white-water rafting to precipitous downhill skiing to desert hiking—all in a landscape like none other.

The following excursions will take you from 20 to 60 miles out of town. Every one of them offers a memorable travel experience.

1. GOODSPRINGS— A GHOST TOWN

35 miles SW of Las Vegas

GETTING THERE   By Car   Follow Interstate 15 south and turn onto Route 161 west at the Jean-Goodsprings turnoff.

The shadowy phenomenon of ghost towns—once-flourishing areas that were later deserted and abandoned—has always been an intriguing and romantic image. Many of these towns began with one lone traveler who serendipitously stumbled on mineral-rich rocks while out on another pursuit—perhaps tracking game or strayed livestock. He would mark off his area, stuff his pockets and knapsacks with specimens, and rush off to register his claim. Soon adventurers, drifters, and raggedy prospectors would flock to the area, set up meager lodgings, break out picks and shovels, and get to work. If the yield was promising, word would spread quickly, and entrepreneurs would arrive with provisions. A main street would develop around a general merchandise store, followed by other shops

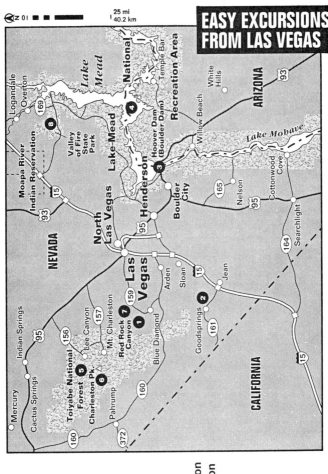

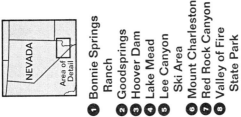

① Bonnie Springs Ranch	⑤ Lee Canyon Ski Area
② Goodsprings	⑥ Mount Charleston
③ Hoover Dam	⑦ Red Rock Canyon
④ Lake Mead	⑧ Valley of Fire State Park

and the inevitable mining-camp saloons, gambling houses, and red-light district. Eventually a real town would evolve.

But then the mines would begin drying up. Little by little, businesses would fold, and the population would dwindle. Vandalism, wind, and fire would ravage the remaining structures, leaving only ghost-inhabited remnants of what had been. And so the town died. Nevada has at least 40 such towns, the closest to Las Vegas being Goodsprings.

Founded in the 1860s, and named for Joseph Good, a prospector, Goodsprings thrived as a silver and lead mining town around the turn of the century. During World War I, the Goodsprings Hotel was advertised in New York newspapers as "the finest in the West," and people from Las Vegas flocked here to shop, gamble, and see shows. The thriving metropolis had a population of 2,000, nine bars, several restaurants, a theater, churches, homes, and businesses. A narrow-gauge railroad carried ore from the surrounding mines to the Union Pacific tracks at nearby Jean. As the biggest town in Nevada, Goodsprings was a regular stop for Barnum & Bailey.

Shortly thereafter, mining days ended and the town began its decline. It has had only one brief brush with fame since. On January 16, 1942, Goodsprings made headlines because it was the closest town to Potosi Mountain where a plane, lost in a storm, crashed with movie star Carole Lombard on board. Her husband Clark Gable stayed briefly at the Goodsprings Hotel while awaiting news of the wreckage. By 1967 Goodsprings' population had shrunk to 62. The hotel had burned to the ground, and one of its last remaining businesses, a general store, was torn down. Today it is an authentic ghost town—an eerie relic of Nevada's boom-and-bust mining era. All that remains of the once-flourishing town is the rotting machinery of mining companies, discarded wrecks of old, abandoned cars—and the still-extant Pioneer Saloon.

WHAT TO SEE & DO

About a half mile before you enter Goodsprings, you'll pass the cemetery. Stop here and poke around a bit. It's a down-at-the-heels sort of place where perpetual care has not been a big thing. A couple of markers are wood, weathered almost to the point of illegibility. Most of the standard headstones are in a segment of the yard that has been fenced off by a low rail. All of these stones belong to the Fayle family, who were prominent Goodsprings citizens in the town's heyday. Surprisingly, there are some recent graves of desert-rat bikers here. In the area near the cemetery, you can search for Native American arrowheads, spearheads, and other artifacts.

The heart of Goodsprings is the **Pioneer Saloon** (tel. 874-9362), which from its dusty, rundown exterior does not look operative. It has, however, been a going concern since 1913. The only complete decorative-metal building left standing anywhere in the United States, the saloon has pressed-tin walls (interior and exterior) and ceiling. If you're nostalgic about old-time western saloons, you'll love the Pioneer. It's heated by a potbelly stove in winter and a swamp cooler in summer. Many of its fixtures and furnishings (even the curtains) are original to the saloon. Owner Don Hedrick tends the century-old cherry and mahogany bar and regales customers with anecdotes about Goodsprings' past. A copy of the 1916 *Goodsprings Gazette* that carries an advertisement for the saloon is displayed on one wall, and while you're looking at the walls note the bullet holes—legacy of a long-ago gunfight over a poker game. In addition to authentic ambience, the Pioneer offers such diverse entertainments as a pool table, dart board, jukebox, and poker machines. Personally, I found it thrilling to play pool in a ghost town. The Pioneer is open daily from 10am to midnight.

These days, Goodsprings may be making a bit of a comeback. Two big casino hotels, the **Gold Strike** and **Nevada Landing,** have gone up close by, and the town even has a semifamous resident: Bill Cash (Johnny's cousin) lives here in a trailer.

2. HOOVER DAM & LAKE MEAD

30 miles SE of Las Vegas

GETTING THERE **By Car** Take U.S. 93 south (93/95 is a continuation of Fremont Street downtown). As you near the dam, you'll see a large parking lot. Park here and take one of the shuttle buses that runs between the lot and the exhibit building about every five minutes. Plans are in the works for a new, more elaborate five-story visitor center to house extensive displays, a 200-seat theater, and on-premises parking; if this is completed when you're reading this book, signage will direct you to it. Arrive early to beat the crowds, and, if possible, avoid weekends and holidays when you could easily be stuck in traffic for lengthy periods.

By Bus **Gray Line** (702/384-1234) offers a full-day tour that includes a half-hour cruise on Lake Mead, a buffet lunch, and a tour of the dam. Price is $31.60 per person. Half-day morning or afternoon excursions are $17.95. And a third tour that includes the Ethel M Chocolate Factory and lunch is $21.50. You can inquire at your hotel sightseeing desk about other bus tours.

This is one of the most popular excursions from Las Vegas, visited by 2,000 to 3,000 people daily. Wear comfortable shoes; the dam tour involves quite a bit of walking. The optimum plan is to tour the dam in the morning, have lunch in Boulder City, take the Lake Mead dinner cruise, and stay a night or two at Lake Mead Lodge (details below) enjoying the area's scenic beauty and recreation facilities. Drive back to Las Vegas through the Valley of Fire. From Lake Mead Lodge take Highway 166 (Lakeshore Scenic Drive) north, make a right and continue north on Highway 167 (North Shore Scenic Drive), turn left on Highway 169, and follow the signs. The Valley of Fire is about 60 magnificently scenic miles from Lake Mead, so purchase gas before your start.

HOOVER DAM

Until Hoover Dam was built, much of the southwestern United States was plagued by two natural problems—parched, sandy terrain that lacked irrigation for most of the year and extensive flooding in spring and early summer when the mighty Colorado River, fed by melting snow from its source in the Rocky Mountains, overflowed its banks and destroyed crops, lives, and property. On the positive side, raging unchecked over eons, the river's turbulent, rushing waters carved the Grand Canyon.

In 1928, prodded by the seven states through which the river runs during the course of its 1,400-mile journey to the Pacific, Congress authorized construction of a dam at Boulder Canyon (later moved to Black Canyon) under the auspices of the Bureau of Reclamation, U.S. Department of the Interior—the agency that still operates it today. The Senate's declaration of intention was that "A mighty river, now a source of destruction, is to be curbed and put to work in the interests of society." Construction began in 1931. Because of its vast scope, and the unprecedented problems posed in its realization, the project generated significant advances in many areas of machinery production, engineering, and construction. An army of over 5,200 laborers was assembled, and work went on 24 hours a day. Completed in 1936, two years ahead of schedule, the dam stopped the annual floods and conserved water for irrigation, industrial, and domestic use. Equally important, it became one of the world's major electrical generating plants, providing low-cost, pollution-free hydroelectric power to a score of surrounding communities. Hoover Dam's $175-million cost has been repaid with interest by the sale of inexpensive power to a number of California cities and the states of Arizona and Nevada. The dam is a government project that paid for itself, a feat almost as awe inspiring as its engineering.

The dam itself is a massive horseshoe-shaped wall, 660 feet thick at the bottom and tapering to 45 feet where the road crosses it at the top. The highest concrete dam in the Western Hemisphere, it towers 726.4 feet above bedrock (about the height of a 60-story skyscraper) and acts as a plug between the canyon walls to hold back the millions of gallons of water in Lake Mead—the reservoir created by its construction. Four concrete intake towers on the lake side drop the water down about 600 feet to drive turbines and create power, after which the water spills out into the river and continues south. All the architecture is on a grand scale, with beautiful art deco elements unusual in an engineering project. Note, for instance, the monumental 30-foot bronze sculpture, *Winged Figures of the Republic,* flanking a 142-foot flagpole at the Nevada entrance. According to its creator, Oskar Hansen, the sculpture symbolizes "the immutable calm of intellectual resolution, and the enormous power of trained physical strength, equally enthroned in placid triumph of scientific achievement."

The dam has become a major sightseeing attraction along with Lake Mead—America's largest man-made reservoir and a major Nevada recreation area.

Seven miles southwest of the dam on U.S. 93, you'll pass through **Boulder City,** which was built to house managerial and construction workers. Sweltering summer heat (many days of 125° weather) ruled out a campsite by the dam, whereas the higher elevation of Boulder City offered lower temperatures. The city rose up in a single year, turning a desert waste into a community of 6,000 with tree-shaded lawns, homes, churches, parks, restaurants, hotels, and schools. By 1934, with a population of over 6,000, it was Nevada's

IMPRESSIONS

Everybody knows Las Vegas is the best town by a dam site.
—MASTHEAD SLOGAN OF THE *LAS VEGAS REVIEW JOURNAL*

third-largest town. Today, the town continues to thrive with a population of 11,500. You might plan on lunch in this pleasant little town (details below).

About 300 yards past Boulder City, at the top of a slight incline, Lake Mead comes into view. Unless signage directs you otherwise, park your car when you come to the large Nevada lot and take a shuttle bus to the exhibit building. After your tour, return to the exhibit building to see photographs of the dam in construction and hear a 10-minute taped lecture about the Colorado River. In an adjacent blue dome, you can see a fascinating free movie about the construction of the dam and the rise of Boulder City. Footage from the construction period will give you a good feel for the hazardous work involved and the impressive scope of the achievement. There's also a cafeteria and a gift/book shop on the premises.

Some Hoover Dam miscellanea:

The amount of concrete used in the construction of the dam could pave a standard highway from San Francisco to New York.

The minimum wage paid on the project was $4 a day.

Ninety-six men died building, excavating, blasting, and scaling mountains during construction, and on-the-job injuries totaled about 1,500 a month.

In summer, the canyon rocks are so hot you could literally fry an egg on them.

Lake Mead contains enough water to cover the entire state of New York to a 1-foot depth.

The dam was originally called Boulder Dam for its first-designated canyon site, renamed Hoover Dam in 1930 to honor Herbert Hoover's years of work making the project a reality, and unofficially renamed Boulder Dam by FDR who did not wish to honor Hoover; it finally regained the name Hoover Dam under Truman, who, in 1947, asked the 80th Congress to find out just what the "dam" name really was. Both names are still in popular usage.

THE TOUR Thirty-five-minute tours of the dam depart every few minutes from the exhibit building daily except Christmas. Hours are 9am to 4:15pm Labor Day to Memorial Day, 8am to 6:45pm the rest of the year. Admission is $2 for adults, $1 for seniors, and free for children 15 and under.

The tour begins with a taped narrative during a 528-foot elevator descent deep into the dam's interior to one of the many galleries used for maintenance and inspection. There are over two miles of these galleries inside the dam at various levels. From the gallery, you'll proceed into the power plant, downstream through the thickness of the dam. Note, en route, the terrazzo floors that are inlaid with basketry and pottery designs of southwestern Native American tribes. The power plant consists of two similar wings, each 650 feet long, on either side of the river. From the visitor's balcony of the Nevada wing, you'll see eight huge hydroelectric generators (nine from the Arizona wing). These generators are driven by individual turbines located 40 feet below the floor. Water is delivered from the reservoir to the turbines (through canyon walls) via massive 30-foot-diameter pipes called penstocks. You'll learn about the manufacture of these generating units, each of which produces sufficient electrical energy to supply the domestic needs of a city of 65,000 people. Units lighted at the top are in operation. After visiting the generating room below, you'll see a tunnel through the 600-foot canyon wall that provides access to vehicles entering the power plant area. However, heavy equipment is lowered by a cableway that has a capacity of 150 tons! Looking up, you can see the control room for the cable operation. During construction, entire railroad cars loaded with materials were lowered into the canyon via this cableway. The drumlike tanks on the deck above are electrical transformers. Moving on to the Arizona wing, your guide (with the aid of a diagram) will explain construction procedures of the four tunnels that were drilled and blasted through solid rock and used to divert the river around the damsite. These diversion tunnels averaged 4,000 feet in length and 56 feet in diameter. When construction work advanced beyond the point where it was no longer necessary to divert water around the damsite, the tunnels were permanently sealed off. You'll also learn about the four intake towers which control the supply of water drawn from Lake Mead for the power plant turbines, and the spillways which, one on each side of the lake, control its maximum depth and ensure that no flood will ever overflow the dam. Finally, visitors stand in one of the diversion tunnels and view one of the largest steel water pipes ever made (its interior could accommodate two lanes of automobile traffic).

LAKE MEAD NATIONAL RECREATION AREA

Under the auspices of the National Park Service, the 1.5-million-acre Lake Mead National Recreation Area was first formed in 1936 around Lake Mead (the reservoir lake created in the construction of Hoover Dam) and later Lake Mohave to the south (created in the construction of Davis Dam). Before the lakes' creation, this desert region was brutally hot, dry, and rugged—unfit for human habitation. Today it is one of the nation's most popular playgrounds, attracting about 9 million visitors annually. The two lakes comprise 290.7 square miles. At an elevation of 1,221.4 feet, Lake Mead itself extends some 110 miles upstream toward the Grand Canyon. Its 550-mile shoreline, backed by spectacular cliff and canyon scenery, creates the perfect setting for a wide variety of water sports and desert hiking. In addition to these natural attractions, visitors can gamble at the nearby **Gold Strike Inn** casino on U.S. Highway 93 in Boulder City, three miles west of Hoover Dam (tel. 293-5000 or 800/245-6380).

INFORMATION The **Alan Bible Visitor Center,** four miles northeast of Boulder City on U.S. 93 at Nevada Highway 166 (tel. 293-8906), can provide information on all area activities and services. You can pick up trail maps and brochures here, view informative films, and find out about scenic drives, accommodations, ranger-guided hikes, naturalist programs and lectures, bird watching, canoeing, camping, lakeside RV parks, and picnic facilities. The center also sells books and videotapes about the area. It's open daily 8:30am to 4:30pm. For information on accommodations, boat rentals, and fishing also call **Seven Crown Resorts** at 800/752-9669.

ACTIVITIES   Hiking   The optimum season for hiking is November through March (too hot the rest of the year). Some ranger-guided hikes are offered via the Alan Bible Visitor Center, which also stocks detailed trail maps. Three trails—a ¾-, 5- and 6-mile loops, originate at the Visitor Center. The 5-mile trail goes past remains of the railroad built for the dam project. Be sure to take all necessary desert-hiking precautions (see details above in Chapter 7).

Camping   Lake Mead's shoreline is dotted with campsites, many of them equipped with running water, picnic tables, and grills. Available on a first-come, first-served basis, they are administered by the **National Park Service** (tel. 293-8906). There's a charge of $6 per night at each campsite.

Boating and Fishing   A store at **Lake Mead Resort & Marina,** under the auspices of Seven Crown Resorts (tel. 293-3484 or toll free 800/752-9669), rents fishing boats, ski boats, patio boats, even fully equipped houseboats. It also carries marine supplies, sporting goods, waterskiing gear, scuba and fishing equipment, and bait and tackle. You can get a fishing license here ($45 a year, $30.50 for 10 days, $17.50 for three days, $8.50 for children 12 to 15.). The staff is knowledgeable and can apprise you of hot fishing spots. Largemouth bass, striped bass, channel catfish, crappie, and bluegill are found in Lake Mead, rainbow and cutthroat trout in Lake Mohave.

Scuba Diving   October to April, there's good visibility, lessened in summer months when algae flourishes. A list of good dive locations, and nearby dive shops, is available at Alan Bible Visitor Center.

Rafting   Rafting trips on the Colorado River are offered February 1 through November 30 by **Black Canyon, Inc.,** 1297 Nevada Hwy. in Boulder City (tel. 293-3776). Twelve-mile trips begin at the base of Hoover Dam. You'll see canyon waterfalls and wildlife (bighorn sheep, wild burros, chuckwalla lizards, mallards, grebe, and the occasional golden eagle), traverse gentle rapids and penetrate quiet coves, ending up at Willow Beach for lunch at a riverside restaurant. There are stunning rock formations en route, and the area is rich in history—southern Paiute rock shelters, 19th-century steamboat barge hooks embedded into the canyons, and 1920s river-gauging stations and cableways. Guides are very knowledgeable about local lore. Prices (including lunch): $59.95 for adults, $35 for children ages 5 to 12, under 5 free. Bus transportation back to Las Vegas is available. Even if you don't go rafting, stop by Black Canyon Inc.'s Boulder City headquarters to see exhibits about the area and a film on Hoover Dam. Their office also functions as an information center for a wide array of area activities.

Canoeing   The Alan Bible Visitor Center can provide a list of outfitters who rent canoes for trips on the Colorado River. There's one catch, however: A free canoeing permit is required in advance from the Bureau of Reclamation. Call 702/293-8356 Monday through Thursday to apply.

Lake Cruises   A delightful way to enjoy Lake Mead is on a cruise aboard the *Desert Princess* (tel. 293-6180), a Mississippi-style paddle wheeler. Cruises depart year-round from the Lake Mead Resort Marina (near the lodge). It's a relaxing, very scenic trip (enjoyed from an open promenade deck or one of two fully enclosed, climate-controlled decks) through Black Canyon and past colorful rock formations known as the "Arizona Paint Pots" en route to Hoover Dam, which is lit at night. Options include buffet breakfast cruises ($16.50 adults, $8 children under 12), narrated midday cruises (light lunch fare available, $12 adults, $5 children), cocktail/dinner cruises (mid-March through mid-November only; $23.50 adults, $10.50 children or $12 adults, $5 children without dinner), and sunset dinner/dance cruises with live music ($32.50 adults, children not allowed). Dinner cruises include a meal of salad, hot garlic bread, entrée (New York steak or baked Alaskan halibut), fresh vegetable, rice pilaf or baked potato, dessert, and tea or coffee; it's served in a pleasant, windowed air-conditioned dining room. There's a full bar on board. Call for departure times.

WHERE TO STAY

LAKE MEAD LODGE, 322 Lakeshore Rd., Boulder City, NV 89005. Tel. 702/293-2074 or toll free 800/752-9669. 45 rms. A/C TV

$ Rates: Mid-Mar–early Oct $50–$65 single or double, the rest of the year $30–$45. Extra person $6. Children under 5 stay free in parents' room. MC, V.

If you aren't properly outfitted for camping at Lake Mead (see above), it's heavenly to spend a few nights relaxing at this tranquil lakeside resort, enjoying the area's numerous recreational activities and, perhaps, a leisurely dinner cruise. It's an easy drive from Hoover Dam. The rooms, housed in terra-cotta roofed cream-brick buildings, are comfortable and attractive with wood-paneled ceilings and walls of white-painted brick or rough-hewn pine. All offer full baths, color cable TVs, and clock radios and have patios overlooking the lake. A lovely pool/sun deck glitters in its lakeside setting, surrounded by mountains and beautifully landscaped grounds planted with pines and palm trees, cypresses, and flowering oleander bushes. Weathered-wood roped dock posts add a nautical look to the resort. You might relax with a good book in one of the gazebos on the property. About a block away is the marina, where you can while away a few hours over cocktails on a lakeside patio. The marina is headquarters for boating, fishing, Lake Mead cruises, and water sports and it also houses a large gift shop. And Boulder Beach, also an easy walk from the lodge, has waterfront picnic tables and barbecue grills.

Dining/Entertainment: There's a nautically themed restaurant at the marina, its rough-hewn pine interior embellished with harpoons, figureheads, ship lanterns, ropes, pulleys, and steering wheels—even a mannequin of an old salt at the entrance. Open from 7am to 9pm Sunday to Thursday, till 10pm Friday to Saturday, it serves hearty breakfasts; sandwiches, salads, and burgers at lunch; and steak-and-seafood dinners, all at moderate prices. There's live music Friday and Saturday nights.

WHERE TO DINE

CASA FLORES, 930 Nevada Hwy., at Fir St. Tel. 294-1937.

    Cuisine: MEXICAN. **Reservations:** Recommended.

$ Prices: Lunch specials $3.95, lunch and dinner entrées $4.95–$10.25. AE, MC, V.

    Open: Wed–Thurs and Sun–Mon 11am–10pm, Fri–Sat 11am–11pm.

If you'd like to see Boulder City, the town created to house Hoover Dam workers, plan to lunch here after your tour. Casa Flores is a festive family-owned Mexican eatery with red and burgundy leather booths and chairs and soft lighting emanating from candles and wrought-iron chandeliers with amber glass fixtures. Big baskets of cloth flowers add a cheerful note, and stucco archways enhance the south-of-the-border ambience.

    A good choice is a combo plate of beef and chicken fajitas, served with rice and beans, a stack of flour tortillas, and grilled peppers, tomatoes, and onions. There are also many taco/tamale/burrito/enchilada combinations. Or you might opt for a tostada salad of refried beans, melted Monterey Jack, lettuce, tomatoes, guacamole, and sour cream on a crisp hot corn tortilla. A pitcher of sangría with your meal is recommended.

3. MOUNT CHARLESTON & LEE CANYON SKI AREA

Mount Charleston 40 miles NW of Las Vegas;
Lee Canyon 47 miles NW of Las Vegas

GETTING THERE **By Car** Take I-15 north and stay in the Reno Lane to U.S. 95 north. Make a left on Highway 157.

By Bus There is no bus transport to Mount Charleston. In ski season you can catch a bus in Las Vegas to the Lee Canyon Ski Area from several major Strip hotels. Round-trip fare is $15. For details call 702/646-0008.

In summertime, the mountains that encircle Toiyabe National Forest are as much as 30° to 40° cooler than the sweltering desert city. These mountains, once an island in an ancient sea, are today a cool oasis in the desert. The highest peak towers 11,918 feet above sea level. It's a beautiful drive. Highway 157 winds up for about 16 miles through gorgeous canyon scenery, and, as you ascend, desert vegetation—cactus, yucca, creosite bush, and Joshua trees—gives way to stands of juniper and bristlecone pine, and at further elevations dense ponderosa forests and aspen firs. The highway eventually dead ends, and a dirt road leads to the lovely **Mount Charleston Restaurant & Lounge.** You can plan a day around lunch here, with activities like hiking, camping, canoeing, biking, bird watching, and horseback riding. In winter, there are sleigh rides and snowmobiles, and you can ski at nearby **Lee Canyon.** In summer, there are hayrides, scenic chair-lift rides in the ski area, barbecues, and a music festival.

It's a twilight-zone feeling to come from hot and air-conditioned Las Vegas to this sometimes snowy region where you can sit before a blazing fire sipping a hot buttered rum. Both the Mount Charleston Restaurant & Lounge and the Mount Charleston Hotel serve as information centers for area activities. In addition to the below-listed attractions, see "Sports and Recreation" in Chapter 7.

Under the auspices of the Mount Charleston Restaurant & Lounge are the **Mt. Charleston Riding Stables** (tel. 702/872-7009, 386-6899 from Las Vegas), offering marvelously scenic trail rides to the edge of the wilderness. There are as many as 20 rides a day departing from stables on Kyle Canyon Road. Weekday rates are $18 per hour, $32 for two hours, $44 for three hours; weekends and holidays rates are $22 per hour, $35 for two hours, and $45 for three hours. The stables also offer horse-drawn sleigh rides Thanksgiving Day through March ($6 for adults, $3 for children 10 and under) and hayrides Memorial Day through Labor Day ($3 per person).

There are numerous **hiking trails,** ranging from short panoramic walks to waterfalls near the restaurant/lounge to more difficult hikes further afield. A popular 5-mile trail beginning at Lee Canyon Highway takes you through a canyon of aspen and into forested areas of ponderosa, white fir, and bristlecone pine. There are picnic areas and campsites along some trails. For information on camping and hiking trails contact the U.S. Forest Service, 550 E. Charleston Blvd., Las Vegas, NV 89104 (tel. 702/388-6255). For camping information and reservations you can also call 800/283-2267. Both the Mount Charleston Restaurant & Lounge and the Mount Charleston Hotel can provide trail maps.

Lee Canyon Ski Area, at the end of State Highway 156 (tel. 702/646-0008), has a base elevation of 8,510 feet that, along with an extensive snow-making system, provides an almost ideal climate and snow cover for skiing Thanksgiving Day through Easter Day. Facilities include a lodge, a complete ski school, extensive ski-rental shop, a coffee shop, and a lounge with blazing fireplace and sun deck. Three double chair lifts carry skiers over 40 acres of well-maintained slopes. In summer, Lee Canyon is the scene of a country/bluegrass music festival.

WHERE TO STAY

THE MOUNT CHARLESTON HOTEL, 2 Kyle Canyon Rd. (on Hwy. 157). Tel. 702/872-5500. 60 rms, 3 suites. A/C TV TEL

$ Rates: Single or double weekdays $49–$59, weekends $64–$74, $150 suite. Extra person $5. Children under 12 stay free in parents' room. AE, CB, DC, DISC, MC, V.

Nestled in the mountains, this three-story property offers lodgings in a rustic log and stone building. Its lobby, with massive stone fireplaces, mounted deer heads, and a lofty beamed pine ceiling, evokes a ski lodge. Rooms aren't fancy, but they're attractively decorated in earth tones and forest green with half-canopies over the beds. Cathedral ceilings and balconies make third-floor rooms especially desirable. And nicest of all are suites with convertible sofas in the living rooms, larger balconies, and wood-burning stone fireplaces. Facilities include a Jacuzzi and sauna in a windowed room, a small video game arcade, and a gift shop. Room service is available from 8am to 9pm.

Dining/Entertainment: The hotel's hexagonal **Canyon Dining Room** has a lot of rustic charm. Decorated in forest green and peach, it has two working fireplaces, windows all around overlooking beautiful mountain scenery, and heavy wrought-iron chandeliers suspended from a cathedral pine ceiling. At night it's romantically candlelit. All meals are available here including full and continental breakfasts. Lunch fare includes moderately priced burgers, sandwiches, fajitas, pizzas, and salads (everything's under $9). And dinner entrées ($8.95–$19.95) offer a choice of lighter fare (pizzas and pasta dishes) along with a steak-and-seafood menu. Like the restaurant, the simpatico adjoining lounge—scene of live music Friday and Saturday nights—has a full window wall and a working fireplace.

WHERE TO DINE

THE MOUNT CHARLESTON RESTAURANT & LOUNGE, end of Hwy. 157. Tel. 702/386-6899 or toll free 800/955-1314.

Cuisine: AMERICAN/CONTINENTAL. **Reservations:** Recommended.

$ Prices: Breakfast entrées $4.50–$9.75; lunch entrées $5–$9.25; dinner appetizers $3–$7.75, entrées $15–$26. AE, CB, DC, DISC, MC, V.

Open: 8am–10pm Sun–Thurs, until 11pm Fri–Sat; the bar/lounge is open 24 hours.

This rustic mountain chalet centers on a vast hooded fireplace stacked high with enormous ponderosa pine and cedar logs. Wagon-wheel chandeliers are suspended from a lofty beamed ceiling, and large windows provide magnificent vistas. Mid-May to the end of October, you can sit at umbrella tables on a patio nestled in the wooded mountains, and you'd be hard pressed to find a more exquisitely peaceful setting. The lounge isn't fancy; it's a casual, kick-back kind of place. At night, however, it is romantically candlelit and there's dancing (a duo plays mellow rock and country music nightly October to June, weekends and holidays the rest of the year). At lunch weekends and holidays a Bavarian oompah-pah band called the Dummkopfs entertains.

The restaurant serves all meals, beginning with hearty country breakfasts (available through 5pm) such as eggs with wild-game sausages, hash browns, homemade biscuits, and gravy. At lunch there are sandwiches, salads, and full entrées ranging from broiled salmon steak with rice pilaf and vegetable to broiled pork chops served with applesauce, vegetable, and fries. And dinner entrées include wild-game specialties such as stuffed roast quail with sweet berry sauce and roast partridge with pear and pine nut dressing in a cinnamon frangelica sauce. Other choices include steaks and seafood. Everything is fresh and cooked on the premises, including homemade breads and desserts. At night the bar here is very popular. Come by after dinner for the music and a hot buttered rum or Mount Charleston coffee—a Jamaican blend spiked with brandy and Drambuie, topped with homemade vanilla ice cream and a dollop of real whipped cream.

Note: At this writing the owners are planning a bed-and-breakfast operation consisting of 24 mountain cabins with working fireplaces, private decks, sitting rooms, Jacuzzi tubs, and steam baths. These may be open by the time you read this. Projected rates, including a full breakfast, are $125–$150 per night.

4. RED ROCK CANYON & BONNIE SPRINGS RANCH

Red Rock Canyon 19 miles W of Las Vegas;
Bonnie Springs Ranch 24 miles W of Las Vegas

GETTING THERE   By Car   Drive west on Charleston Boulevard which becomes State Highway 159. Look for the Visitor Center on your right.

By Bus   Numerous sightseeing companies, including **Gray Line** (384-1234), run bus tours to Red Rock Canyon. Inquire at your hotel tour desk.

By Bike   Not very far out of town (at Rainbow Boulevard), Charleston Boulevard is flanked by a bike path which continues for about 11 miles to the Visitor Center/Scenic Loop Drive, and since it's quite scenic, it's a popular biking route. The bike path is hilly but not difficult if you're in reasonable shape. However, exploring Red Rock Canyon by bike should only be attempted by exceptionally fit and experienced bikers. For bike-rental information see Chapter 7.

RED ROCK CANYON NATIONAL CONSERVATION AREA

Less than 20 miles from Las Vegas, Red Rock Canyon is worlds away experientially—a magnificent unspoiled vista which, in its timeless beauty, is the perfect balm for your casino-jaded soul. You can simply drive the panoramic **13-mile Scenic Loop** (open daily 7am to dusk), or explore in depth. There are many interesting sights and trailheads along the loop itself. The wider National Conservation Area offers hiking trails and internationally acclaimed rock-climbing opportunities (especially notable is the 7,068-foot Mt. Wilson, the highest sandstone peak among the bluffs). There are **picnic areas** along the loop and also in nearby Spring Mountain Ranch State Park five miles south. Since Bonnie Springs Ranch is just a few miles away, it makes a great base for exploring Red Rock Canyon.

The geologic history of these ancient stones goes back some 600 million years. Over eons, the forces of nature have formed Red Rock's sandstone monoliths into arches, natural bridges, and massive sculptures painted in a stunning palate of gray-white limestone and dolomite, black mineral deposits, and oxidized minerals in earth-toned sienna hues ranging from pink to crimson and burgundy. Orange and green lichens add further contrast, as do spring-fed areas of lush foliage. And formations like Calico Hill are brilliantly white where groundwaters have leached out oxidized iron. Cliffs cut by deep canyons tower 2,000 feet above the valley floor.

During most of its history, Red Rock Canyon was under a warm shallow sea. Massive fault action and volcanic eruptions caused this seabed to begin rising some 225 million years ago. As the waters receded, sea creatures died and the calcium in their bodies combined with sea minerals to form limestone cliffs studded with ancient fossils. Some 45 million years later, the region was buried beneath thousands of feet of windblown sand. The landscape was as arid as the Sahara. As time progressed, iron oxide and calcium carbonate infiltrated the sand, consolidating it into cross-bedded rock. Shallow streams began carving the Red Rock landscape, and logs that washed down from ancient highland forests fossilized, their molecules gradually replaced by quartz and other minerals. These petrified stone logs, which the Paiute Indians believed were weapons of the wolf god, Shinarav, can be viewed in the Chinle Formation at the base of the Red Rock Cliffs. About 100 million years ago, massive fault action began dramatically shifting the rock landscape here, forming spectacular limestone and sandstone cliffs and rugged canyons punctuated by waterfalls, shallow streams, and serene oasis pools. Especially notable is the Keystone Thrust Fault, dating to about 65 million years ago when two of the earth's crustal plates collided, forcing older limestone and dolomite plates from the ancient seas over younger red and white sandstones. Over the years, water and wind have been ever-creative sculptors, continuing to redefine this strikingly beautiful landscape.

Red Rock's valley is home to over 45 species of mammals, about 100 species of birds, 30 reptiles and amphibians, and an abundance of plant life. Ascending the slopes from the valley, you'll see cactus and creosote bushes, aromatic purple sage, yellow-flowering blackbrush, yucca and Joshua trees, and, at higher elevations, clusters of forest-green piñon, juniper, and ponderosa pines. In spring, the desert blooms with fiery red globe mallow, magenta monkeyflowers, pink-blossomed redbud trees, pristine white forget-me-nots, golden desert marigolds, and lavender phacelia. Among the animal denizens of the canyon are bighorn sheep, antelope ground squirrels, mule deer, kangaroo rats, lizards, California jackrabbits and desert cotton-tails, gray and kit foxes, tortoises, coyotes, bobcats, rattlesnakes, reclusive gila monsters, even mountain lions. Burros and wild horses are not indigenous, but are the descendants of animals that were set free by, or escaped from, miners in the 1800s. And commonly observed birds include eagles and hawks, roadrunners, turkey vultures, loggerhead shrike, cactus wrens, quail, mourning doves, broad-tailed hummingbirds, woodpeckers, horned larks, western bluebirds, American robins, northern mockingbirds, yellow warblers, sage sparrows, and peregrine falcons.

Archaeological studies of Red Rock—which turned up pottery fragments, remains of limestone roasting pits, stone tools, pictographs (rock drawings) and petroglyphs (rock etchings) along with other ancient artifacts—show that humans have been in this region since about 3000 B.C. (some experts say as far back as 10,000 B.C.). You can still see remains of early inhabitants on hiking expeditions in the park. The Anasazi (also known as the "Basketmaker" people and "the Ancient Ones") lived here from the first century A.D. Originally hunter-gatherers, they learned to farm maize, squash, and beans and began forming communities. From pit houses, they progressed to elaborate structures of up to 100 rooms and became known as the Pueblo Indians. They departed from the area (no one knows why) about 1150 A.D., and the Paiutes—who were still essentially hunter-gather nomads—became the dominant group. Until the mid-1800s, the Paiutes lived here in perfect harmony with nature—a harmony destroyed when white settlers arrived and began felling the pine forests for timber, introducing grazing livestock that destroyed food and medicinal plant sources, and decimating the Native American population with European diseases to which they had no immunity. By the 1880s, the Paiutes were forced onto reservations, their culture and way of life in shambles.

In the latter part of the 19th century, Red Rock was a mining site and later a sandstone quarry that provided materials for many buildings in Los Angeles, San Francisco, and early Las Vegas. By the end of World War II, as Las Vegas developed, many people became aware of the importance of preserving the canyon. In 1967 the Secretary of the Interior designated 62,000 acres as Red Rock Canyon Recreation Lands under the auspices of the Bureau of Land Management, and later legislation banned all development except hiking trails and limited recreational facilities. In 1990 Red Rock Canyon became a National Conservation Area, further elevating its protected status.

Today Red Rock Canyon affords visitors the opportunity to experience nature's grandeur and serenity—to leave the stresses of daily life behind and get in touch with greater realities.

INFORMATION Just off Highway 159, you'll see the **Red Rock Canyon Visitor Center** (tel. 702/363-1921). It's open daily 9am to 4pm. Exhibits, enhanced by an audio tour, tell the history of the canyon and explore its plant and animal life. You'll also see a fascinating video here about Nevada's thousands of wild horses and burros that have been protected by an Act of Congress since 1971. At the Center, you can obtain trail maps, brochures, permits for hiking and backpacking, and other information about the canyon. Call ahead to find out about ranger-guided tours as well as informative guided hikes offered by groups like the Sierra Club and the Audubon Society. Hiking trails range from a 0.7-mile loop stroll to a waterfall at Lost Creek (a spring that flows year-round) to much longer and more strenuous treks involving rock scrambling. A popular 5-mile round-trip hike leads to Pine Creek Canyon and the creekside ruins of a historic homesite surrounded by ponderosa pine trees. On trails along Calico Hills and the escarpment, look for "Indian marbles," a local name for small rounded sandstone rocks that have eroded off larger sandstone formations. And, if you're traveling with children, ask about the special Children's Discovery Trail (a related workbook is available for $1). Books and videotapes are on sale here, including a guidebook identifying over 100 top-rated climbing sites. After you tour the canyon, drive over to Bonnie Springs Ranch (details below) for lunch or dinner. See Chapter 7 for further details on biking and climbing.

BONNIE SPRINGS RANCH/OLD NEVADA

About 5 miles past Red Rock Canyon on Highway 159, nestled in the mountains, is Bonnie Springs Ranch/Old Nevada (tel. 702/875-4191), a kind of Wild West theme park with beautiful accommodations and a charmingly rustic restaurant. Owners Al and Bonnie Levinson bought the property—a former stopover for wagon trains heading to California on the Old Spanish Trail—in 1952. They started out with a restaurant, and as their clientele grew added some buildings which evolved into a motel and the 19th-century replica town of Old Nevada.

If you're traveling with kids, a day or overnight trip to Bonnie Springs is a must, but there's much here for adults, too. It could even be a romantic getaway, offering horseback riding, gorgeous mountain vistas, proximity to Red Rock Canyon, and temperatures 15 degrees cooler than the Strip. For those without transportation there are **shuttle buses** to and from Las Vegas. Call the above number for details.

Old Nevada attractions are detailed below. However, even if you just come out here for lunch, you can enjoy several features free of charge. A **small zoo** on the premises is home to dozens of animals—burros, mouflon sheep, buffalo, steer, racoons, ferrets, ducks, red squirrels, coyotes, coatis, red and blue fox (the latter donated by singer Wayne Newton), porcupines, wolves, bobcats, guinea pigs, and rabbits. There are always baby animals, and llamas, potbelly pigs, deer, and miniature goats roam free and can be petted and fed.

There's also an **aviary** housing peacocks (including a rare white peacock), Polish chickens, peachface and blackmask lovebirds, finches, parakeets, ravens, ducks, pheasants, and geese.

Riding stables offer guided trail rides into the mountain area on a continuous basis throughout the day (from 9am to 3:30pm spring through fall, until 5:45pm in summer). Children must be at least six to participate. Cost is $15 per hour.

And scenic 20-minute **stagecoach rides** cost $5 for adults, $3 for children under 12.

WHAT TO SEE & DO IN OLD NEVADA

Old Nevada (tel. 702/875-4191) is a microcosm of a mid-1800s western Nevada town, its main street lined with weathered-wood buildings fronted by covered verandas. It has a rustic turn-of-the-century **saloon** complete with red flocked wallpaper and wagon-wheel chandeliers overhead. Country music is played in the saloon during the day, except when stage **melodramas** take place (on the hour and half hour between 11:30am and 5pm). In response to cue cards held up by the players, the audience boos and hisses the moustache-twirling villain, sobs in sympathy with the distressed heroine, laughs, cheers, and applauds. It's quite silly, but lots of fun; kids adore it. Drinks and snacks can be purchased at the bar.

Following each melodrama a **western drama** takes place outside the saloon, involving a bank robbery, a shootout, and the trial of the bad guy. A judge, prosecuting attorney, and defense attorney are chosen from the audience, the remainder of whom act as jury. The action always culminates in a hanging. We're not talking Neil Simon or anything, but the dialogue is quite funny.

Throughout the area, cowboys continually interact with visiting kids. Twice a day a posse is formed, and all children are deputized. They get to participate in shootouts, chase bad guys, and help take them to jail. There are also ongoing **stunt shootouts** in this wild frontier town in which a sheriff shoots a varmint off the roof of a building. Some very unsavory characters languish in the town jail. And a **medicine man** touts worm syrups and liver cures.

A **wax museum** contains tableaux with replicas of: John C. Frémont and Kit Carson (who actually stopped at this site in the 1840s), an animated Abraham Lincoln reading the proclamation that made Nevada a state, early trailblazers and mountain men, Brigham Young, 19th-century Paiute chief Old Winnemucca, and early Nevada madam Julia Bulette, among others. A 9-minute film on Nevada history is shown in the wax museum throughout the day.

In the **Old Nevada Photograph Shoppe** you can have a tintype picture taken in 1890s Wild West costume with a 120-year-old camera. Movies (one about nearby Red Rock Canyon, one a silent film) are shown in the **Old Movie House** throughout the day from 10:30am to 5pm. You can test your skills in a **shooting gallery,** peek into an old-fashioned **dentist/barbershop** (and surprise a man in his bath), see a **Bootleg Hill still,** watch **weaving** demonstrations, and tour the remains of the **old Comstock lode silver mine.** The **Trading Post,** a museum and gift shop, displays a variety of 19th-century items (a switchboard, a craps table and slot machine, cash registers, radios, victrolas, typewriters, a printing press, shotguns, and the remains of a New Mexico drugstore with many old-fashioned remedies). Other Old Nevada shops sell hand-blown glass, old-fashioned candy, Native American items (rugs, moccasins, silver and turquoise jewelry, baskets), and western wear and gear. Eateries in Old Nevada are discussed below. There's plenty of parking, and a free shuttle train takes visitors from the parking lot to the entrance.

Admission to Old Nevada is $6.50 for adults, $5.50 for seniors 62 and over, $4 for children ages 5 to 11, and free for children under 5.

The park is open daily from 10:30am to 5pm November through April, and until 6pm during the rest of the year.

WHERE TO STAY & DINE

BONNIE SPRINGS MOTEL, Hwy. 159. Tel. 702/875-4400. 50 rms, including 13 suites and 5 fantasy rms. A/C TV (suites only) TEL

$ Rates: Standard rooms (based on four-person occupancy) $55–$65 Sun–Thurs, $65–$75 Fri–Sat; fantasy suites $110 Sun–Thurs, $125 Fri–Sat; family suites $85 Sun–Thurs, $95 Fri–Sat. An optional breakfast trail ride for motel guests is $15 per person; it departs at 9am every morning. Staying at the motel also entitles you to discounted tickets for Old Nevada. AE, MC, V.

The motel, housed in two-story weathered-wood buildings, is, like Old Nevada, evocative of a 19th-century western town. Even standard rooms offer scenic mountain views and are delightfully decorated with pine-plank-motif carpets, floral-print calico drapes and bedspreads, and handcrafted pine furnishings. Some rooms have working fireplaces, and all feature inviting individual touches—perhaps an antique oak mirror stand with a ceramic bowl and jug, Indian rugs, a Mexican serape artfully draped on a branch, lamps with ruffled calico shades, or Victorian-style lighting fixture/fans overhead. Bonnie Levinson is the talented decorator. All rooms have full baths, in-room coffee makers, and patios overlooking the mountains. There are beautiful family suites with fully equipped kitchens, bedrooms, living rooms (with convertible sofas), and dressing areas; these are equipped with two phones and two TVs. Fantasy rooms are romantic settings with sumptuous Jacuzzi tubs and mirrors over the bed. They're tasteful, not tacky. For instance, a Gay '90s room, decorated in mauve tones, is furnished with velvet-upholstered period chairs. It has a quaint bathtub on brass feet (in addition to an oversized faux-marble Jacuzzi), a lovely porcelain sink with hand-painted floral motifs, and a pink and black lace canopy over the bed. Other fantasy rooms are Chinese, Native American, Old West, and Spanish themed. All fantasy rooms and suites contain large fold-up tables that can be used for patio dining.

Dining: The **Bonnie Springs Ranch Restaurant** is cozily rustic, with rough-hewn pine walls, a beamed ceiling, and glossy cedar-slab tables. A wall of calico-curtained windows overlooks a serene pond with ducks and swans, and an aluminum-hooded wood-burning fireplace is ablaze in winter. Menus, printed on whiskey bottles, offer hearty breakfasts such as a chili-and-cheese omelet with ranch potatoes and homemade biscuits or thick slabs of Texas toast. Sandwiches, salads, burgers, and barbecued beef are featured at lunch ($2.50–$5.75). And dinner entrées ($11.25–$15.25) include barbecued chicken and pork ribs, steaks, and seafood.

In Old Nevada

The **Miner's Restaurant,** another rustic western setting, is right in town and has unfinished pine-plank floors, a beamed ceiling, and red-and-white-checkered tablecloths and ruffled curtains. An old player piano provides honky-tonk music. Inexpensive snack fare (sandwiches, burgers, pizza, hot dogs) is served, along with home-made ice cream and fresh-baked desserts. There are tables out on the porch. You can also get beer and soft drinks in a similarly old-fashioned **Beer Parlor** in Old Nevada. Both are open daily 10:30am–6pm. No credit cards.

5. VALLEY OF FIRE STATE PARK

60 miles NE of Las Vegas

GETTING THERE By Car The quickest way is to take I-15 north to Exit 75 (Valley of Fire turnoff). However, the more scenic route is to take I-15 north, then travel Lake Mead Boulevard east to North Shore Road (Highway 167), and proceed north to the Valley of Fire exit. The first route takes about an hour, the second 1½ hours.

By Bus Numerous sightseeing companies, including **Gray Line** (384-1234), run bus tours to Valley of Fire. Inquire at your hotel tour desk.

Most people visualize the desert as a vast expanse of undulating sands punctuated by the occasional cactus or palm-fringed oasis. The desert of America's Southwest bears little relation to this Lawrence of Arabia image. Stretching for hundreds of miles around Las Vegas in every direction is a seemingly lifeless tundra of vivid reddish earth, shaped by time, climate, and subterranean upheavals into majestic canyons, cliffs, and ridges.

The 39,000-acre Valley of Fire State Park, typifying the mountainous red Mojave Desert, derives its name from the brilliant sandstone formations that were created 150 million years ago by a great shifting of sand and continue to be shaped by the geologic processes of wind and water erosion.

Though it's hard to imagine in the sweltering Nevada heat, for billions of years these rocks were under hundreds of feet of ocean. This ocean floor began to rise some 200 million years ago and the waters became more shallow. Eventually the sea made a complete retreat, leaving a muddy terrain traversed by ever-diminishing streams. A great sandy desert covered much of the southwestern part of the American continent until about 140 million years ago. Over eons, winds, massive fault action, and water erosion sculpted fantastic formations of sand- and limestone. Oxidation of iron in the sands and mud—and the effect of groundwater leaching the oxidized iron—turned the rocks the many hues of red, pink, russet, lavender, and white extant today. Logs of ancient forests washed down from far away highlands and became petrified fossils which can be seen along two interpretive trails.

Human beings occupied the region—a wetter and cooler one—as far back as 4,000 years ago. They didn't live in the Valley of Fire, but during the Gypsum period (2000 B.C. to 300 B.C.), men hunted bighorn sheep (a source of food, clothing, blankets, and hut coverings) here with a notched stick called an atlatl that is depicted in the park's petroglyphs. Women and children caught rabbits, tortoises, and other small game. In the next phase, from 300 B.C. to 700 A.D., the climate became warmer and drier. Bows and arrows replaced the atlatl and the hunters and gatherers discovered farming. The Anasazi people began cultivating corn, squash, and beans and communities began replacing small nomadic family groups. These ancient people wove water-tight baskets, mats, hunting nets, and clothing. Around 300 A.D. they learned how to make sun-dried ceramic pottery. Other tribes, most notably the Paiutes, migrated to the area. By 1150 A.D., they were the dominant group. Unlike the Anasazis, they were still nomadic and used the Valley of Fire region seasonally. These were the inhabitants white settlers found when they entered the area in the early- to mid-1800s. The newcomers diverted river and spring waters to irrigate their farmlands, destroying the nature-based Paiute way of life. About 300 descendants of those Paiute tribespeople still live on the Moapa Indian Reservation (about 20 miles northwest) that was established along the Muddy River in 1872.

Some of the most notable formations in the park have been named for the shapes they vaguely resemble or evoke—a duck, an elephant, seven sisters, domes, beehives, and so on. Mouse's Tank is a natural basin that collects rainwater, so named for a fugitive Paiute called Mouse who hid there in the late 1890s. And Native American petroglyphs etched into the rock walls and boulders—some dating as far back as 3,000 years ago—can be observed on self-guided trails. Petroglyphs at Atlatl Rock and Petroglyph Canyon are both easily accessible. Always awe-inspiring, the park is especially beautiful in early spring when the desert blooms with wildflowers—mallow, desert marigold, and indigo bush—in dramatic contrast to the predominant earth tones. Other desert life forms include bighorn sheep, ground squirrels, bats, kit foxes, jackrabbits, gila monsters, rattlesnakes, and lizards. And numerous birds—cactus and rock wrens, ravens, finches, and sage sparrows, as well as migrant species—are best observed in the early morning or late afternoon. In summer, when temperatures are usually over 100°, you may have to settle for driving through the park in an air-conditioned car.

INFORMATION   The Valley of Fire can be visited in conjunction with Lake Mead. My preference is to visit Hoover Dam/Lake Mead one day, stay overnight at Lake Mead Lodge (details above), and spend a full day at Valley of Fire on the way back to Las Vegas. From Hoover Dam take Highway 167 (North Shore Road) north to Highway 169 west, a spectacularly scenic drive. There are no food concessions or gas stations in the park; however, you can obtain meals or gas on Highway 167 or in nearby **Overton** (15 miles northeast on Highway 169). Overton is a fertile valley town replete with trees, agricultural crops, horses, and herds of cattle—quite a change in scenery.

At the southern edge of town is the **Lost City Museum,** 721 S. Hwy. 169 (tel. 397-2193), commemorating an ancient Anasazi village that was discovered in the region in 1924. Its population reached one of the highest levels of Native American culture in the United States. Artifacts dating back 12,000 years are on display, as are clay jars, dried corn and beans, arrowheads, seashell necklaces, and straw baskets of the ancient Pueblo culture that inhabited this region between 300 A.D. and 1150. Other exhibits document the Mormon farmers who settled the valley in the 1860s. A large collection of local rocks—petrified wood, fern fossils, iron pyrites, green copper, and red iron oxide—along with manganese blown bottles turned purple by the ultraviolet rays of the sun are also displayed here. The museum is surrounded by reconstructed wattle and daub pueblos. Admission is $1 for those 18 and over; the museum is open daily from 8:30am to 4:30pm.

Information headquarters for Valley of Fire is the **Visitor Center** on Highway 169, six miles west of North Shore Road (tel. 702/397-2088). It's open seven days a week from 8:30am to 4:30pm. Exhibits on the premises explain the origin and geologic history of the park's colorful sandstone formations, describe the ancient peoples who carved their rock art on canyon walls, and identify the plants and wildlife you're likely to see. Postcards, books, slides, and films are on sale here, and you can pick up hiking maps and brochures. There are ranger-guided programs in the park, usually on Saturdays. Other times, rangers can answer your park-related questions.

Hiking trails, shaded picnic sites, and two campgrounds are available in the park. Most sites are equipped with tables, grills, water, and rest rooms. A fee ($4 per might per vehicle) is charged for use of the campground.

INDEX

GENERAL INFORMATION

SIGHTS & ATTRACTIONS

LAS VEGAS

EXCURSION AREAS

Note: An asterisk (*) after an attraction name indicates that it is an author's favorite.

ACCOMMODATIONS

LAS VEGAS

EXCURSION AREAS

Key to abbreviations: *Ch* = Casino-hotel; *Cg* = Campground; *B* = Budget; *E* = Expensive; *Hs* = Hostel; *M* = Moderate; *VE* = Very expensive; *\$* = Super-value choice; *** = Author's favorite.

RESTAURANTS

LAS VEGAS

BY LOCATION

BY CUISINE

Key to abbreviations: *B* = Budget; *E* = Expensive; *M* = Moderate; *VE* = Very expensive; $ = Super-value choice; * = Author's favorite.

EXCURSION AREAS

Now Save Money on All Your Travels by Joining
FROMMER'S ® TRAVEL BOOK CLUB
The World's Best Travel Guides at Membership Prices

FROMMER'S TRAVEL BOOK CLUB is your ticket to successful travel! Open up a world of travel information and simplify your travel planning when you join ranks with thousands of value-conscious travelers who are members of the FROMMER'S TRAVEL BOOK CLUB. Join today and you'll be entitled to all the privileges that come from belonging to the club that offers you travel guides for less to more than 100 destinations worldwide. Annual membership is only $25 (U.S.) or $35 (Canada and all foreign).

The Advantages of Membership

1. Your choice of three free FROMMER'S TRAVEL GUIDES. You can pick two from our FROMMER'S COUNTRY and REGIONAL GUIDES (listed under Comprehensive, $-A-Day, and Family) and one from our FROMMER'S CITY GUIDES (listed under City and City $-A-Day).
2. Your own subscription to **TRIPS & TRAVEL** quarterly newsletter.
3. You're entitled to a **30% discount** on your order of any additional books offered by FROMMER'S TRAVEL BOOK CLUB.
4. You're offered (at a small additional fee) our **Domestic Trip Routing Kits.**

Our quarterly newsletter **TRIPS & TRAVEL** offers practical information on the best buys in travel, the "hottest" vacation spots, the latest travel trends, world-class events and much, much more.

Our **Domestic Trip Routing Kits** are available for any North American destination. We'll send you a detailed map highlighting the best route to take to your destination—you can request direct or scenic routes.

Here's all you have to do to join:
Send in your membership fee of $25 ($35 Canada and foreign) with your name and address on the form below along with your selections as part of your membership package to FROMMER'S TRAVEL BOOK CLUB, P.O. Box 473, Mt. Morris, IL 61054-0473. Remember to check off 2 FROMMER'S COUNTRY and REGIONAL GUIDES and 1 FROMMER'S CITY GUIDE on the pages following.

If you would like to order additional books, please select the books you would like and send a check for the total amount (please add sales tax in the states noted below), plus $2 per book for shipping and handling ($3 per book for all foreign orders) to:

FROMMER'S TRAVEL BOOK CLUB
P.O. Box 473
Mt. Morris, IL 61054-0473
1-815-734-1104

[ ] YES. I want to take advantage of this opportunity to join FROMMER'S TRAVEL BOOK CLUB.
[ ] My check is enclosed. Dollar amount enclosed_____*
       (all payments in U.S. funds only)

Name_____

Address_____

City_____ State_____ Zip_____

To ensure that all orders are processed efficiently, please apply sales tax in the following areas: CA, CT, FL, IL, NJ, NY, TN, WA, and CANADA.

*With membership, shipping and handling will be paid by FROMMER'S TRAVEL BOOK CLUB for the three free books you select as part of your membership. Please add $2 per book for shipping and handling for any additional books purchased ($3 per book for all foreign orders).

Allow 4-6 weeks for delivery. Prices of books, membership fee, and publication dates are subject to change without notice.

FROMMER'S TOURING GUIDES
(Color-illustrated guides that include walking tours, cultural and historic sights, and practical information)

	Retail Price	Code		Retail Price	Code
☐ Amsterdam	$11.00	T001	☐ New York	$11.00	T008
☐ Barcelona	$14.00	T015	☐ Rome	$11.00	T010
☐ Brazil	$11.00	T003	☐ Scotland	$10.00	T011
☐ Florence	$ 9.00	T005	☐ Sicily	$15.00	T017
☐ Hong Kong/Singapore/ Macau	$11.00	T006	☐ Thailand	$13.00	T012
			☐ Tokyo	$15.00	T016
☐ Kenya	$14.00	T018	☐ Venice	$ 9.00	T014
☐ London	$13.00	T007			

FROMMER'S FAMILY GUIDES

	Retail Price	Code		Retail Price	Code
☐ California with Kids	$17.00	F001	☐ San Francisco with Kids	$17.00	F004
☐ Los Angeles with Kids	$17.00	F002			
☐ New York City with Kids	$18.00	F003	☐ Washington, D.C. with Kids	$17.00	F005

FROMMER'S CITY GUIDES
(Pocket-size guides to sightseeing and tourist accommodations and facilities in all price ranges)

	Retail Price	Code		Retail Price	Code
☐ Amsterdam 1993–94	$13.00	S110	☐ Minneapolis/St. Paul, 3rd Edition	$13.00	S119
☐ Athens, 9th Edition	$13.00	S114			
☐ Atlanta 1993–94	$13.00	S112	☐ Montréal/Québec City 1993–94	$13.00	S125
☐ Atlantic City/Cape May 1991–92	$ 9.00	S004	☐ New Orleans 1993–94	$13.00	S103
☐ Bangkok 1992–93	$13.00	S005	☐ New York 1993	$13.00	S120
☐ Barcelona/Majorca/ Minorca/Ibiza 1993–94	$13.00	S115	☐ Orlando 1993	$13.00	S101
			☐ Paris 1993–94	$13.00	S109
☐ Berlin 1993–94	$13.00	S116	☐ Philadelphia 1993–94	$13.00	S113
☐ Boston 1993–94	$13.00	S117	☐ Rio 1991–92	$ 9.00	S029
☐ Cancún/Cozumel/ Yucatán 1991–92	$ 9.00	S010	☐ Rome 1993–94	$13.00	S111
			☐ Salt Lake City 1991–92	$ 9.00	S031
☐ Chicago 1993–94	$13.00	S122	☐ San Diego 1993–94	$13.00	S107
☐ Denver/Boulder/ Colorado Springs 1990–91	$ 8.00	S012	☐ San Francisco 1993	$13.00	S104
			☐ Santa Fe/Taos/ Albuquerque 1993–94	$13.00	S108
☐ Dublin 1993–94	$13.00	S128	☐ Seattle/Portland 1992–93	$12.00	S035
☐ Hawaii 1992	$12.00	S014			
☐ Hong Kong 1992–93	$12.00	S015	☐ St. Louis/Kansas City 1993–94	$13.00	S127
☐ Honolulu/Oahu 1993	$13.00	S106			
☐ Las Vegas 1993–94	$13.00	S121	☐ Sydney 1993–94	$13.00	S129
☐ Lisbon/Madrid/Costa del Sol 1991–92	$ 9.00	S017	☐ Tampa/St. Petersburg 1993–94	$13.00	S105
☐ London 1993	$13.00	S100	☐ Tokyo 1992–93	$13.00	S039
☐ Los Angeles 1993–94	$13.00	S123	☐ Toronto 1993–94	$13.00	S126
☐ Madrid/Costa del Sol 1993–94	$13.00	S124	☐ Vancouver/Victoria 1990–91	$ 8.00	S041
☐ Mexico City/Acapulco 1991–92	$ 9.00	S020	☐ Washington, D.C. 1993	$13.00	S102
☐ Miami 1993–94	$13.00	S118			

Other Titles Available at Membership Prices

SPECIAL EDITIONS

	Retail Price	Code		Retail Price	Code
☐ Bed & Breakfast North America	$15.00	P002	☐ Where to Stay U.S.A.	$14.00	P015
☐ Caribbean Hideaways	$16.00	P005			
☐ Marilyn Wood's Wonderful Weekends (within a 250-mile radius of NYC)	$12.00	P017			

GAULT MILLAU'S "BEST OF" GUIDES
(The only guides that distinguish the truly superlative from the merely overrated)

	Retail Price	Code		Retail Price	Code
☐ Chicago	$16.00	C002	☐ New England	$16.00	G010
☐ Florida	$17.00	G003	☐ New Orleans	$17.00	G011
☐ France	$17.00	G004	☐ New York	$17.00	G012
☐ Germany	$18.00	G018	☐ Paris	$17.00	G013
☐ Hawaii	$17.00	G006	☐ San Francisco	$17.00	G014
☐ Hong Kong	$17.00	G007	☐ Thailand	$18.00	G019
☐ London	$17.00	G009	☐ Toronto	$17.00	G020
☐ Los Angeles	$17.00	G005	☐ Washington, D.C.	$17.00	G017

THE REAL GUIDES
(Opinionated, politically aware guides for youthful budget-minded travelers)

	Retail Price	Code		Retail Price	Code
☐ Able to Travel	$20.00	R112	☐ Kenya	$12.95	R015
☐ Amsterdam	$13.00	R100	☐ Mexico	$11.95	R016
☐ Barcelona	$13.00	R101	☐ Morocco	$14.00	R017
☐ Belgium/Holland/ Luxembourg	$16.00	R031	☐ Nepal	$14.00	R018
			☐ New York	$13.00	R019
☐ Berlin	$11.95	R002	☐ Paris	$13.00	R020
☐ Brazil	$13.95	R003	☐ Peru	$12.95	R021
☐ California & the West Coast	$17.00	R121	☐ Poland	$13.95	R022
			☐ Portugal	$15.00	R023
☐ Canada	$15.00	R103	☐ Prague	$15.00	R113
☐ Czechoslovakia	$14.00	R005	☐ San Francisco & the Bay Area	$11.95	R024
☐ Egypt	$19.00	R105			
☐ Europe	$18.00	R122	☐ Scandinavia	$14.95	R025
☐ Florida	$14.00	R006	☐ Spain	$16.00	R026
☐ France	$18.00	R106	☐ Thailand	$17.00	R119
☐ Germany	$18.00	R107	☐ Tunisia	$17.00	R115
☐ Greece	$18.00	R108	☐ Turkey	$13.95	R027
☐ Guatemala/Belize	$14.00	R010	☐ U.S.A.	$18.00	R117
☐ Hong Kong/Macau	$11.95	R011	☐ Venice	$11.95	R028
☐ Hungary	$14.00	R118	☐ Women Travel	$12.95	R029
☐ Ireland	$17.00	R120	☐ Yugoslavia	$12.95	R030
☐ Italy	$13.95	R014			